NEPAL
Culture Shift!
Reinventing Culture in the
Himalayan Kingdom

NEPAL
Culture Shift!
Reinventing Culture in the Himalayan Kingdom

Madhu Raman Acharya

ADROIT PUBLISHERS
DELHI-110 053

Published by
ADROIT PUBLISHERS
C-8/2, Yamuna Vihar, Delhi-110 053
Phones : 3266030, 3242552

Branch Office
AKHIL BOOK DISTRIBUTORS
4675/21, Ganpati Bhawan, Ansari Road,
Darya Ganj, New Delhi-110 002
e-mail: akhilbooks@yahoo.com
Phones : 3266030, 3242552

ISBN : 81-87392-26-6

Layout by
Sudhir Kumar Vatsa

Laser Typeset by
Nidhi Laser Point, Shahdara, Delhi.
e-mail: nidhi_vatsa@hotmail.com
Phone : 2825424

Printed in India by
Nice Printing Press, Delhi

The Views expressed in this book are either of those who are quoted
as might appear or are the author's personal views and they
do not reflect the views of the office held by the author
during, before or after the publication.

Foreword

There is a growing academic interest in the dynamism in the culture of the Nepalese people, especially in the rise of ethnicity and nationalism among the ethnic minorities. Some concerns are also expressed in the political speeches, tea-stall talks, in the living room discussions and in newspaper write-ups about the ongoing deterioration in the Nepalese culture. But a comprehensive and detailed account on the dynamics of the contemporary Nepalese culture is not available.

Many books have been written on festivals, religion, and the culture of people of Nepal. Western and Nepalese authors have discussed "unity in diversity", described temples and shrines of worships, explored myths, beliefs and faiths of the people and their relationship with the nature, animals and the gods and goddesses. Empirical studies on the Nepalese people, their customs, culture and religion, were made by some missionaries and British civil servants, who visited Kathmandu between early 18th century and early 19th century. They *did* contribute to the study of contemporary lives and culture of the people of Nepal. But many such accounts on the Nepalese culture only glorify the culture of the bygone era and do not reflect any dynamism in the Nepalese culture. Even the relatively recent anthropological and sociological studies have become too much obsessed with the glorious past of the Nepalese culture, especially of some ethnic groups and of the rural villages. Such studies also ignore the shift in the culture of the modern and urban Nepalese people, who are undergoing startling social and cultural transformations.

There have been efforts to study culture changes in some communities. Researches have been focusing on convulsions of change in communities, castes, regions and religions. These references on culture changes at micro level focused on certain ethnic, linguistic and cultural groups and of people in some regions have been unable to depict the comprehensive, real and dynamic picture of Nepal's changing culture.

The conventional studies on the Nepalese culture, in its totality, ignore the elements of dynamism and often adopt a narrow definition of culture limited to such things as religion, festivals, temples and ethnography of various groups of people. They do not encompass such aspects as distortions in the cultural practices, degrading family values, deteriorating moral fiber, crumbling heritage sties, disappearing interests in festivals, rituals and customs, increasing neglect of institutions and traditions of the past and passion towards self-centered materialistic and hedonistic pursuit and consumer culture.

There is some interest in the changing cultural identity and revivalism of the ethnic minorities in what is called as *"janjati yug"*, the epoch of the ethnic minorities, especially after the establishment of democracy in Nepal. A whole new corpus of "new-age" cultural studies is emerging. Many works are being attracted on areas of nationalism, ethnicity, identity of the ethnic minorities. Gellner *et al* (1997), for example, have analyzed the politics of culture in contemporary Nepal with reference to nationalism and ethnicity of various communities.

But these micro studies on the cultural change and identity, which are focused on traditional dynamism in the Nepalese culture (Hinduization, Sanskritization and Nepalization) and the struggle between the state and the ethnic minorities. They ignore the changes brought about by the influences of modernization, Westernization and globalization. The conventional study of culture in Nepal has not been able to broaden the conventional view of culture, that of pigeon-holing Nepalese society into structured fragments, each dealt with separately without taking into account the dynamism in the emerging realities. The cultural dilemma between revitalization of traditional culture and assimilation to the process of modernization has not been studied even by the corpus of literature on ethnic minorities.

There is some reference in recent studies on impact of globalization in Nepal (Dahal, 1997). But there is not enough work on Nepalese people's changing attitudes, values, norms and lifestyles. Studies on changes in the Nepalese people's changing worries, motivation, dreams and aspirations are very sketchy. Works on the traumas and shocks experienced by the people in Nepal due to an accelerating cultural disorientation and degeneration in their own society is virtually lacking.

In this book, I would like to subscribe to a dynamic and broadened definition of culture encompassing such concepts as education psychology, political ideology, lifestyles, interpersonal relations, status of women in the society, and the changing attitude of the youth in the interpretation of the Nepalese culture. Here, an attempt has been made education psychology, political ideology, lifestyles, interpersonal relations, status of women in the society, and the changing attitude of the youth in the interpretation of the Nepalese culture. Here, an attempt has been made to analyze the contemporary changes in the culture of the people of Nepal at the beginning of the 21st century. It is author's thesis that people of Nepal are witnessing a slow but steady shift in their culture due to the influences of the elements of traditional dynamism (*Sanskritization, Nepalization, Indianization*) as well as the modern influences (modernization, Westernization and globalization). It is the author's view that the Nepalese culture is gradually loosing its traditional landmarks and reference points. Therefore, the contemporary Nepalese culture can and should be interpreted in a relative and dynamic context of change being experienced by the people of Nepal.

Though it may sound like projecting several mistakes of one's own culture, a systematic understanding of the dynamism of culture in the country is necessary to project any reasonably credible course towards preserving the cultural heritage and values, which are the building blocks of the nation and its people's identity. It cannot be predicted that the influences brought about by the recent changes such as globalization will totally disrupt or replace the originality of the Nepalese culture. But if the Nepalese people are to articulate and accommodate the changes, they will have to learn to adjust with the various new elements entering into their culture, consciously or unconsciously. That can only be achieved with a careful analysis and interpretation. I also propose that it is possible to modernize while retaining the Nepalese culture in its meaning, just as the Japanese have modernized themselves without loosing much of their cultural identity.

I propose to argue that both the traditional and *avante garde* notions of culture in Nepal are changing. It is not only the high culture of the urban elite, which is changing, even the peripheral and marginal "folk culture" is being transformed.

In order to build the logic put forward in this book, I have tried to assimilate and coordinate information from various sources to interpret some empirical observations. Inferences are drawn from television shows, advertisements, newspaper articles, books on various disciplines, talks with people of different walks of life, overheard conversations, observations of shopping places, restaurants, and pilgrimage centers, review of literature and theoretical study on the subject. Though some anecdotes from real life experiences have been taken as examples, most of the analyses in this book are subjective and descriptive accounts, which may be known already to most people by way of common sense and everyday observation. Some of the inferences may well be reversed by scrupulous research, which there is a tremendous potential of. The author is conscious of the possibility of controversies that some of the issues covered in this book can raise. Apology has therefore been extended beforehand to all those, whose ideas, values, beliefs and attitudes do not conform to the comments of the author.

As the author has gathered inputs from the informal debate in general conversations, many respondents may not necessarily identify themselves in the narratives that may appear here. Further, names of some peoples, institutions and places have been sometimes omitted or changed in order to give anonymity. Still, several persons may recognize themselves wherever referrals are made in this book. None of the references made are meant to demean or demoralize their personal values, but they appear just to give an expression as to what is the contemporary mind and mood of the Nepalese people regarding a particular matter of interest.

Limitations in this study include the inability to get more accurate information on values of people regarding their private lives mainly because these subjects are relatively less covered in the contemporary discussions, writings and literature. Detailed account of the culture shift being witnessed by several communities has not been encompassed under this study. The references are only indicative of the trends, not the scrupulous details. Many inferences tend to be focused on the people residing in the urban areas or main population centers, and on "urban middle class" and an emerging "neo-rich class". Some of interpretations may not be applicable to the serene and rustic life of the poverty-stricken and isolated people of the rural areas of Nepal, where culture change has not yet been highly visible.

MADHU RAMAN ACHARYA
April 14, 2001
Baisakh 1, 2058 BS

Contents

The Making of a Culture

Though it is difficult to historicize Nepal's culture, it is certain that culture change is not new to Nepal. There have been recurring cultural onslaughts in Nepal's history. Dynastic changes, arrivals of religious persons and pilgrims, immigration of various groups of people fleeing the cultural offensive in the southern plains, wars and annexations, and fragmentation and union of what is now Nepal were events of greater magnitude which influenced the culture of the contemporary times. During the process, the Nepalese people witnessed changes in the seats of civilization, in the practices of religion[1], and in cultural and ethnic compositions. Several religious and philosophical ideas, cults and rituals mushroomed and mingled in this tiny country. Pilgrims, traders, scholars and adventurers crossed the barriers bringing different influences. Immigrants, invaders and visitors made into Nepal during wartime and in times of peace. Nepalese people also witnessed invasions, pillage and destruction of their culture. People were persuaded, and sometimes coerced with changes. During the history, Nepalese people have seen moments of triumphs and tragedies, successes and shames, and glory and grief, which had impacts in the shaping of the Nepalese culture.

Several dynasties ruled Nepal in different epochs of history. Each time one dynasty succeeded another, there were transitions and onslaughts to the culture. Many ruling dynasties, who had come from the Gangetic plains, had brought cultural and religious practices to the people of Nepal. For example, *Shakyas* introduced *Mahayana Buddhism*. The Lichhavis from Vaishali in India, introduced and patronized the *Vaisnaviite Hindu* culture. *Guptas* introduced the *Varna* or caste system.

---

[1] For example, Kathmandu's local deity Bunga Deo was changed to Lord Matsyendranath by the Hindus and to Lord Avalokiteswor by the Buddhists (Rana, 1995, p. 31). Similarly, Kiranteswor, the ancient deity of the Kirants in the valley, is said to have been transformed into the present day Pashupatinath by the Lichhavis.

Although the philosophies and dogmas of Hinduism and Buddhism were blended and harmonized avoiding conflicts and clashes in this country, religious crusades and rampages were not uncommon in Nepal's history. Each of these were shocking to the people of Nepal in the sense that they destroyed religious shrines, burnt holy texts, introduced new languages and new form of religious thoughts, and imposed the alien culture to the people of Nepal. Though Nepal, unlike other regions of South Asia, has never been a theater of contending civilizations (Malla, 1989), Nepalese society has witnessed the trauma of the loss of one civilization after another. But the Nepalese people had survived and maintained their cultural identity. Despite repeated cultural upheavals, the Nepalese people had retained the originality of their culture. During the history, Nepalese society had been successful in synthesizing various religious and cultural strands. The dominant Caucasoid and Mongoloid strands with their religious and cultural practices had assimilated in a unique blend of Hinduism and Buddhism. "Assimilation has been the dominant process underlying the historical and cultural aspects of continuity and change in Nepal" (Shah in Malla, 1989). Nepalese culture has accommodated changes imposed upon by the external influences like the arrival of various religious personages, invasion of ruling tribes from the southern plains, arrivals of pilgrims, travelers and traders, wars fought for unity and national integrity, and changes in the dynasties of rulers.

DYNAMICS OF THE EARLY YEARS

Though there is no documentary evidence of culture change during the millennia before the Christ, the ferment of culture shift centered around the rise of two of the most important civilizations in Nepal's history. There was a republican Shakya state in and around Kapilvastu, which gave Nepal Siddhartha Gautam "Buddha", the founder of Buddhism, five centuries before the birth of Christ. The Shakya State had expanded and risen to a highly civilized society. The architectural remains of Lumbini, the birthplace of Buddha, and other adjoining areas such as *Taulihawa, Sagarhawa, Nigalihawa* and *Gotihawa* reveal that there was a great civilization between 800 and 300 BC. Among its lasting influences was the making of Buddhism as one of great religions of the world, though much of that had to be reinvented and brought back to Nepal in the ferment that would follow in the history of Nepal.

It was the arrival of Emperor Ashok of India to Nepal in the 3rd century BC, which brought back life to Buddhism in Nepal. Emperor Ashok not only visited Lumbini and erected the famous Ashok pillar at Lumbini to commemorate the birthplace of Gautam Buddha, he also helped construct the famous four Ashok Stupas in Patan, which are among the earliest Buddhist structures in Kathmandu Valley. His daughter Charumati, who came on pilgrimage with him, married a Nepali prince, settled at Devpattan in Kathmandu, and erected the famous Charumati Vihar, which still stands as a masterpiece of stupa architecture. Siddhartha Gautam "Buddha", the founder of Buddhism himself is said to have visited the Kathmandu Valley during the reign of the seventh Kirant King Jitedasti.

Yet another civilization had evolved around modern Janakpur, which was flourishing as Mithila until the 5th century BC. It is this civilization which gave birth to famous personalities like Maharshi Janak and his famous daughter Sita, who was married to Lord Rama, the central character in revered Hindu epic *Ramayana*. Mithila culture would later play a very influential role in the making of culture of *Nepal Mandala*, the present day Kathmandu valley. Though the present Janaki Mandir, temple of Sita in Janakpurdham, was built only in 1901, as a tribute to the ancient civilization by Rani Vrishvana Kumari of Tikamgadh state in India, Mithila civilization has played a significant role in the making of the Nepalese culture.

Kathmandu Valley, which was the "melting pot" of civilizations and culture, was visited by various personages even before it started human habitation. If the chronicles, the major sources of Nepalese history, are to be believed, six "human Buddhas" (*Bipaswi, Shikhi, Bishwabhu, Krakuchanda, Kanakmuni* and *Kashyapa*) had visited Nepal much before the birth (567 BC) of Siddhartha Gautam, the founder of Buddhism. While *Bipashwi Buddha* is believed to have arrived in *Satya Yuga*, the epoch of the truth, and to have constructed the great stupa of Swayambhunath, *Shikhi, Kanakmuni* and *Kashyapa* are said to have come in *Dwapar Yuga* and the rest in the *Treta Yuga*. It is also believed that various saints (*sadhus* and *rishis*) had taken long meditation in the sacred soil and quiet forests and mountains of Nepal in the ancient period. Kathmandu Valley, which was then in the form of a lake called Naghrad is supposed to have been drained out by Manjushree cutting a gorge at present day Chovar. There are also legends suggesting that a pilgrim named Dharmakar, from Mahachin (China) came with Maha

Manjushree, and was made the king of Nepal. Later, legends say, Dharmapala, a prince who came from India with Krakuchhanda Buddha, was enthroned in Nepal. History also tells us that Raja Prachanda Dev, King of Gaundha, now in Bengal, had visited Nepal and settled here as a popular preacher named Shantikar, who built the famous *Shantipur* in Swayambhu (Amatya, 1991, p. 194).

Though chronicles written after the 14th century have listed two dynasties (*Gopala* and *Mahishpala*)[2] before the Kirant rule in Nepal Mandala, now Kathmandu Valley, the historical evidence of their rule and their cultural influence is very sketchy. It is said that the Kirant civilization existed around the present day Kathmandu Valley for nearly two millennia before the arrival of Lichhavis around the last quarter of the 4th century AD. Some describe the Kirant Period to have lasted between 625 C and 100 AD (Regmi, 1999). Until the arrival of Lichhavis from Vaishali in India, Kirants, who were skilled in the martial arts and archery, and who lived in a close harmony with the nature, had a very coherent civilization without any outside influence. Though there is no documentary evidence, it seems like the Kirants offered a strong resistance against the Lichhavis. The Hindu treatise of Rigveda, one of the famous four Vedas, refers to a battle between the Kirants and the Aryans and that the latter were defeated at Allahabad, now in India. When the Lichhavis pushed them outside the Nepal Valley, Kirants started to rebuild their culture and society in areas eastern Nepal, which is still known as Kirant Pradesh.

The Lichhavis, who entered Nepal in around 250 AD, ruled Nepal Mandala for nearly five centuries (c. 370-874 AD). Lichhavi period is described as the golden age of Nepalese history. Chinese pilgrim Huen-Tsang (634 AD), in his travelogue, described the majestic palaces, magnificent temples, and religious traditions of the period. Another Chinese traveler Wang Hiuen Tse (646 AD) pointed a "highly cultured Lichhavi state with opulent multi-tiered palaces, sculpture and paintings and wood-carved temples with intricate metalwork and murals" (Rana and Dhungel, 1998, p. 16). Kings used to take pride in erecting wells, waterspouts and public rest houses. Palaces, temples and shrines were

---

[2] According to the chronicles, the cattle herdsmen known as Gopala ruled from around 900 BC to 700 BC. Mahishapala, or the buffalo herdsmen, ruled between 700 BC and 625 BC (Regmi, 1999).

built. Trade expanded across the border to Tibet and India. People lived in peace, harmony and prosperity.

Although they contributed to enrich the culture, the Lichhavis introduced the first wave of Hinduization and Indianization in Nepal. They were republican in Vaishali, where they had come from. But in Nepal, the Lichhavis assumed power through monarchy, which allowed them the power to shape the changes in the Nepalese culture. Among their several influences was the introduction of Vaishnavism, the worship of Lord Vishnu, Hindu preserver God, to Nepal. The famous Changu Narayan temple and other four Narayan shrines, built by the Lichhavis, stand as popular Vaishnavite shrines in Kathmandu Valley, even today. But later Lichhavi Kings also started the worship of Lord Shiva and patronized the famous Pashupatinath, the holiest Shaiviite shrine in Nepal. The Lichhavis introduced and institutionalized Hinduism, particularly the Aryan Brahminism in Nepal. They brought several artistic traditions, mainly temple architecture, which would give Nepal a distinct cultural identity in the future. Even today, many of the famous shrines of Nepal date back to the Lichhavi era. One of the most lasting influences of the Lichhavis was the introduction of Sanskrit language, which not only became the language of the religious texts, its later became a source of authority and superiority in the Nepalese society.

The Lichhavis were also very friendly to Buddhism. It has been said that King Vrisha Deva, the grandfather of famous King Manadeva, was a Buddhist and he has been attributed to have built the famous Swayambhunath stupa, albeit without conclusive evidence. King Manadeva, though a devout Hindu, had also patronized Buddhism.

Towards the end of the Lichhavi rule, Nepal witnessed a traumatic culture shock with further Indianization and Hinduization of the Nepalese culture. During his pilgrimage to Nepal, Shankaracharya (788-820 AD), a Hindu ascetic from southern India, brought "immeasurable havoc" to the culture of Nepal ravaging the *Chaityas* and other Buddhist deities (Varya, n.d., p. 93). Buddhist institutions were attacked and the products of their work demolished. Many Buddhist and non-Brahminic literature was destroyed in public "book-burning" ceremonies. His arrival was also disruptive to the traditional worship of Shiva (Bista, 1991, p. 21). He convinced King Shiva Dev to appoint South Indian Brahmins as priests to Pashupatinath with exclusive rights and privileges. These Brahmins continue to dominate the affairs of the temple of Pashupatinath as the priests, even today. He also destroyed much of the cultural heritage of the Lichhavi period in this process":

> "The Shankaracharya initiated revolution succeeded in eventually toppling Lichhavi society, but in the ensuing turmoil an even more alien social regime was imposed. By the beginning of the next millennium, Buddhist institutions were noticeably overshadowed by those of the high caste Hindus and their public rituals, and the Buddhist Vihars (monasteries) were in the decline...No more Buddhist structures were added, though many temples for the different Hindu deities were being built." (Bista, 1991, p. 22).

There were other arrivals as well. Eminent Buddhist scholar Padma Sambhava (717-775 AD), who brought Buddhist teachings to Tibet from Nalanda, site of famous ancient Buddhist university now in Bihar, also lived in Kathmandu and contributed to the development of Buddhism. Guru Rimpoche, as Padma Sambhava is popularly known by followers of Lamaist Buddhism, is said to have meditated in a cave in Haleshi, in eastern hilly district of Khotang in Nepal. There are also evidences of arrivals of other Buddhist monks, saints, Acharyas, and students at different times of the history. Buddhist influences came also from Bengal. Buddhists who fled the Sen rulers of Bengal and Karnatak Kshtriyas of Bihar in the 11th century AD, found refuge in the Kathmandu Valley. Eminent Buddhist teacher Atisha Dipankara from Bengal brought the mystic cult of *Kalachakrayana*, the cult of the time-wheel. The famous Charya songs and dances of Kathmandu valley are also supposedly influenced by the Pala dynasty in Bengal. This period also saw the translation of Buddhist scriptures in the Tibetan, rise of Buddhist paper manuscripts, and introduction of the art of paper-making from China.

A ninth-century mystic called Gorakhnath also brought influences to Nepal. His cult of *Yogamaya* was so mystifying that Gorakhnath would later be adopted as a patron deity of the royal court. King Prithvi Narayan Shah would introduce the "nath" cult in the Kathmandu valley after unification of modern Nepal and suffix the shrines of Pashupati, and Swayambhu with "nath". He would also rename the local deity Bungadeo as Machhendranath.

In the later part of the 9th century, a uniquely Nepalese calendar era called Nepal Sambat was introduced in 879 AD. Nepal Sambat not only marked the end of Lichhavi rule, it also gave the people of Nepal a new identity. Legends say that this era was introduced by a Newari merchant named Sankhadhàr Sakha to commemorate the freeing of the people of Kathmandu Valley from the burden of debt. Though the exact nature of declaration is debatable, Nepal Sambat would later be extensively used in Nepal until the introduction of Bikram Sambat and would also become a political resource to mobilize the Newar ethnicity in Kathmandu Valley. In 1999, the Nepalese government would recognize Sankhadhar Sakha as one of national heroes.

After the Lichhavis, there was an obscure "transition period" in the Nepalese history before the advent of the Mallas. Even the relatively dark period saw the rise of the tantric cult, which created significant cultural practices, myths and traditions. Tantrism, which came as a fusion of Hinduism and Buddhism, flourished during the Malla Period and dominated the religious cults in the Kathmandu Valley, later on. The advent of Tantrism succeeded not only in bringing union between Shaivism and Buddhism, it also helped the flourishing of "esoteric, erotic, psychometric, mystic and ritualistic" practices in Nepal. In the religious fermentation of the 11th century, there was no major or dominant religious cult. But the syncretic trend started by Tantrism would continue to give Nepal a very tolerant society, culturally.

Like Lichhavis, the Mallas were also republicans in Kushinagar and Pawa states, now in India. While the Lichhavis moved into the Kathmandu Valley, the Mallas had moved into the hilly areas of Western Nepal, where they founded separate rule. The Khas Kings of Karnali basin would later split into Baisi and Chaubisi Rajyas, the famous twenty-two and twenty-four state, and would adopt the title Malla. But the first King to adopt Malla title in Nepal Valley was Ari Malla (1200-1236). The advent of Malla rule (c. 1200-1768) in Nepal Valley is marked with a renewed vigor in the culture left by the Lichhavis. Old temples were renovated and their roofs were gilded with gold. Several new shrines were built. The distinctive art of making pagoda temples that came to Nepal with the Lichhavis further developed during the Malla regime, which added many more temples dedicated to Hindu, Buddhist and Tantric gods and goddesses. Kings donated land for *Guthis* to look after the temples and to conduct worships. They patronized art and literature. Kings and court officials composed, patronized and staged dramas. Nepalese art and culture became so famous that Chinese emperor Kublai Khan invited Nepalese artists to build pagoda temples there. Paitatse, the famous White Pagoda of China, still stands as a masterpiece erected by Nepalese artist Araniko, who went to China in 1261 at the invitation of the Chinese emperor. Malla kings built palaces, courtyards, waterspouts, and rest houses. They dug out ponds, performed religious ceremonies, and even feared dreams and acted accordingly.

King Yaksha Malla's division of Nepal Valley into three kingdoms (Kantipur, Patan and Bhadgaon) in 1481, served to further glorify the contemporary Nepalese culture. The "cultural vigor of the Malla kingdoms were enhanced by political division", writes Stiller in his *Nepal: Growth of a Nation* (1993). "Perhaps rivalry between the kings encouraged the great public expenditures that produced magnificent temples we see in these cities today." (Stiller, 1993. P. 10). Enthused by mutual competition and shocked by the devastation of Muslim and Khas invasions, the Malla kings in three kingdoms of Kantipur, Bhadgaon and Patan gave added zeal to the development of culture in Nepal.

But one of the devastating shocks introduced by the Mallas was the caste system. Because of his Maithali origin and persuaded by the advice of the *Maithali Brahmins*[3] from Bihar, King Jayasthiti Malla (1295-1382) introduced the Hindu caste system and divided people into sixty-four occupational castes. Based on the writings in *Manusmriti*, a Hindu religious code of conduct by ancient Hindu philosopher Manu, the caste system became attractive because it helped establish the social stability and preserved the Malla Kingdom (Bista, 1991). The caste system would enter the Gorkha kingdom during the reign (1606-1623) of King Ram Shah and it would be later perpetuated by the rulers even after the unification of Nepal in 1768, making them legal codes only to

---

[3] *Maithali Brahmans* (also called *Tirhutia Brahmins*) entered Nepal in the seventh century at the invitation of King Shiva Singh. Known for their scholarly capabilities, they were given free land and were settled in Kathmandu Valley as respected priests. Among their several influences, their system of *Kunalism*, i.e. "arranging family trees and keeping genealogies pure by preventing unwise alliances through marriage" (Josephson, 1988, p. 18) was extensively used in Nepal in later years.

be outlawed in 1962 with the introduction of the New Civil Code. The caste system later would be a basis of vertical cleavage among the people of Nepal. But the degree of cleavage and degeneration brought by the caste system would be reflected in the Nepalese society until the beginning of the twenty first century.

Yet another cultural influence during the Malla period was the copying of the Muslim art and culture in Nepal. After the Muslim rule entered the northern India as early as the 11th century AD, and as it flourished there "Muslim habits, attire, social system, language art and architecture seeped into Nepal" (Rana, 1995, p. 43). The influence of the Mughal culture, then flourishing in India, was seen in the Malla coinage in Nepal, the dress of Malla kings, some Muslim dome type architecture, and lattice woodwork and design of the wood carvings. The Muslim invasion also forced a large number of Rajputs and Brahmans to leave the plains for settling in the Western Nepal (Varya, ibid. p. 373). Rajputs entered Nepal through Kumaon and Garhwal and settled as Chand Thakuris in the western Nepal (Rana, 19995, p. 53). A number of Rajput rulers and nobles moved into Nepal seeking refuge after their "heroic defense" and later flight from Chitor now in Rajasthan, India (Singh, 1997). The Rajputs had their greatest impact in the region of the Chaubisi and Baisi Rajyas, the famous twenty-four and twenty-two kingdoms ruled by Thakuri kings. There, they gained control through their talent and rank, indispensability in the affairs of princedom, and overthrowing of the rules and making reign of government (Hamilton, 1819). The arrival of the Rajputs caused considerable disturbance in the balance of power and caused more than a ripple in the religious consciousness of the people of the area, where they were able to settle. The period of Rajput was characterized by progressive Sanskritization, a process of voluntary adoption of the customs of the higher caste Hindus by the so-called lower caste non-Hindus, in the areas (Singh, 1997, p. 2).

But more lasting influence of Muslim rule in India to Nepalese culture was the arrival of fresh stream of Hindu migrants, who brought new wave of Hinduization in the Nepalese culture. But a number of Buddhists from Nalanda and Vikramshila, famous Buddhist universities, who fled the Muslim invasion to enter Nepal, also brought several Buddhist manuscripts and contributed in the growth of Buddhism in Nepal. "After the destruction of Taxila and Nalanda due to Hune invasion towards the close of Gupta period, the Buddhist monks came to Nepal in hundreds with invaluable manuscripts, which are still preserved in the monasteries in Central and northern Nepal", writes Upreti (1996, p. 25). While Buddhism was declining in India during the days of Harsha Vardhan (c. 1000 AD), Nepal "gave shelter to Mahayana Buddhism and "developed many of its Tantric norms and exported them to Tibet" (Upreti, ibid., p. 25).

Many of the Buddhists arriving from the southern plains would contribute to the development of institutions of monasteries and Viharas in Nepal. Along with the rise of several cults, their pantheon of deities and schools of art that developed in the Malla Nepal, came the great art and science of metallurgy, which gave the people the capability to express their creativity as well as their close association with the gods and goddesses. And one of the last, but not least, important contribution of the Mallas to the culture of Nepal was their introduction of eroticism in the Nepalese art, sculpture and woodworks. Elaborate erotic art can still be seen many of the Malla temples in the Kathmandu Valley. The Mallas were also influenced by the Maithali culture around Janakpurdham. Kings in Malla period has special affinity with the Maithalis. Maithali language has even found a place in the Malla royal courts.

During the Malla Period, Nepal also saw the arrival of the first Europeans as Christian missionaries. There have been references to arrival of Christian missionaries in Nepal as early as 1628 during the reign of King Shiva Singh of Kantipur. History also suggests that Christian missionaries were allowed to preach in Nepal during the reign of King Pratap Malla of Kantipur, King Shrinibas Malla of Patan, and King Ranjit Malla of Bhadgaon. Father Giuseppe had led a mission to Nepal at the time of King Jaya Prakash Malla (1734-1768), the last king of Kathmandu as a separate kingdom. Altogether some 62 Christian Missionaries, allowed to enter the Kathmandu Valley during the Malla Period, were chased out by King Prithvi Narayan Shah after conquering the Valley in 1768. The Christian Missionaries would be allowed to establish some schools and hospitals later during the Rana Period (1846-1950) only. The fact that King Pratap Malla had inscribed a polyglot inscription at Hanumandhoka with some French and English words tells us that there were contacts with Europeans during the Malla Period as well. But contacts never scored visible impacts upon the culture of the Nepalese people.

The Sens of Bengal and Bihar, who fled the Muslim invasion in India, found place in Nepal in states such as Makawanpur, Bijaypur and Palpa. They would later form their own kingdoms, which would give a strong resistance to the unification efforts of King Prithvi Narayan Shah. Before their disintegration, the Sens also gave a reasonably credible force for a possible unification of Nepal. In the first half of the fifteenth century, the Sen kingdom, originally with the capital at Makawanpur and later at Palpa, emerged as a strong unifying force. Their kingdom extended along the southern slope of Mahabharat Lekh both east and west of Makawanpur. But this kingdom fragmented after King Mukunda Sen divided it into six petty states and degenerated in their importance (Stiller, 1993).

The Karnatak Kshetriyas from Simraungarh also attempted to invade the Kathmandu Valley in the early 14th century (1300-1324 AD) once targeting Bhaktapur, once to worship the famous deities of the valley (Pashupatinath, Swayambhunath and Machhendranath) and once with the intention of capturing the valley. But they were unable to score big impact as their last king Harisimha Deva was dislodged by Ghiasuddin Tughlaq, the Muslim conqueror of Bengal. They would later flee to Dolkha, bring their Taleju deity to Kathmandu, where it would be adopted as a patron deity of the Malla kings. Also known as Tirahuts, the Karnatak Kshetriya with its capital in Simraungadh, produced sculptures of considerable sophistication and contributed to a "new aesthetic stream" to the culture of Kathmandu Valley. The fusion of the Tirhut stream with the Malla lineage by King Rudra Malla of Bhaktapur gives an example of how the cultural and political strands of the south were absorbed into that of Kathmandu Valley. The rule of Karnatak Kshetriyas from had begun in Nepal in 1097 AD, when a Karnatak ruler named Nanya Dev established his rule in some parts of Nepal Terai with Simaraungarh as the capital.

There had also been instances of Muslim invasions in Nepal in general and Kathmandu in particular, during the first half of the 14th century. The Muslim invaders destroyed Hindu and Buddhist temples and sanctuaries. Some invaders even ransacked the shrines of Pashupatinath and Swayambhunath, the holiest Hindu and Buddhist shrines in Kathmandu. Shamshuddin Ilyas of Bengal is said to have destroyed the lingam of Pashupatinath and the stupa of Syawambhunath during is invasion in the Kathmandu Valley. Many Islamic invasions were short-lived and the reconstruction and restoration following the destruction was speedy. The Malla Kings were not inimical to Muslim people, who were allowed to enter and settle in Nepal. Churetas, Nepal's well-known Muslims, claim proudly to have been allowed to live in Kathmandu Valley since the time of King Ratna Malla (1484-1520).

Towards the end of the Malla period, there were famines, which drained the cultural resources and led to cultural deterioration of the Kathmandu Valley. Even the calamities such as the earthquake of 1255 AD took the toll on the culture. It not only killed nearly one third of the valley's people, it also devastated temples and shrines. Recurring earthquakes, later in 1834 and 1934, would destroy much of the cultural heritage of the Malla Nepal except some pagoda temples, which had resistance to the seismic tremors.

When the Malla kingdoms flourished in the Kathmandu Valley, another civilization also prospered and dismantled around Karnali basin, almost simultaneously. Though the Khas had started to penetrate Nepal as early the early 6th century AD, the Khas kingdom flourished towards the 13th century. Like the kings of Kathmandu Valley, the Khas of Karnali basin adopted the title Malla in the 12th century AD. Until the fourteenth century, the *Khasas* were confined in their principality at Dullu, now in Dailekh district, western Nepal. Their center of civilization was centered around Sinja in present day Jumla, and Dullu in Karnali Basin. During their peak, the Khas had reached up to Bodhgaya and Kapilvastu and even raided the Kathmandu Valley and carried back a large number of icons and sculptures. But the Khas kingdom started to degenerate in the 15th century AD as the kingdom was divided into numerous tiny kingdoms, later known as Baisi and Chaubisi Rajyas, after the death of King Prithvi Malla in 1415. Though all of these principalities were annexed to modern Nepal during the process of unification, the hill-top Rajas would remain recognized until the 1960s, when King Mahendra outlawed their regal status and privileges only to let them retain their titles. But in the process, they distinguished themselves as Thakuri, which claimed to have a superior status than even the all-powerful Chhetris. Recruiting Brahmans to help them in the statecraft, and rewarding them with Birta land, they created a landed aristocracy, which took roots in Nepal as a lifestyle of exploitation of the poor peasants by the wealthy landlords.

Some of the Khas kings also attempted to invade the Kathmandu Valley. There are references of Khas invasion in the Kathmandu Valley around 1287 AD. In 1328 AD, Khas King Aditya Malla is said to have raided the Malla kingdom in Kathmandu. The invasion of the Khas kings from the western hilly areas of Nepal took away a lot wealth and cultural artifacts from the Malla kingdom in the Kathmandu Valley.

The Khas, who played a significant role in the making of the history and culture of Nepal, also adopted the mystic "nath cult" and erected temples with "nath" suffixes. The temples of Chandan Nath and Bhairavnath in Jumla stand in testimony to this. Among other things, their Khas language, which would later become the *lingua franca* as Nepali, helped spread the embrace of Hinduization because it gave the diverse tribals and ethnic groups of people in the contemporary Nepal a link language to adopt the religion and culture of the Khas people.

But it was their well-documented eastward trek, which brought a lot of influences to the culture of Nepal. When they started to gradually populate most of eastern Nepal, they influenced the cultural landscape a lot. In the areas inhabited by Magars (Magrant), and the Gurungs in the western hilly districts, local people assimilated to the Khas culture and copied Brahman rituals and the Khas costumes.

Along with the Khas, other Aryans from India have traveled mostly from the west. Evidence suggests that most Brahmins and Chhetris had poured into Nepal from India. Migration of Kumaon Brahmans to the hills of Nepal was one such significant phenomenon. Throughout the history, during invasions and political upheavals in the subcontinent, the displaced people have found refuge in Nepal. Nepal also saw the immigration of the Koch population from Assam into the eastern region in the 16th century. Some came as traders, others as rulers and still others as subjects. Many naturalized. They became "cultural carriers" to this tiny Himalayan kingdom.

The Hindus are said to have started to come to Nepal in the first century of the Christian era (Sharma, 1977). Other waves of Hindus migrated into Nepal between 12th and 14th century and majority of them settled in Jumla area of West Nepal (Sharma, *ibid.*). This wave of migration brought Hindu society and cultural systems over the indigenous peoples' society and culture. Many of the immigrant Hindus, who were given asylum in Nepal in the wake of Muslim invasion in India, would later infuse cultural influences in Nepal in an unprecedented scale.

People, who migrated into the Kathmandu Valley from parts of India, were assimilated into local populations in the course of time. For example, *Yogi, Dhobi, Jha* were assimilated as non-Buddhist Newar castes. Similarly immigrant *Malla, Mishra* and *Joshi* from the southern plains in India became naturalized as Newars in Kathmandu Valley over the long run. Others adopted Newar customs and Buddhism as their religion.

THE ERA OF INTEGRATION

The making of the modern Nepal was very largely work of one man, King Prithvi Narayan Shah (1723-75), who rose from the little state of Gorkha and unified small principalities through twenty-six years of wars, sieges, annexations, blockades and assaults. His conquest of the Kathmandu Valley (1768) was not only a military and political feat. Culturally, this landmark event induced unprecedented changes in the people of Nepal. The ferment of cultural changes introduced after the unification of modern Nepal is still showing its impacts. Though the Gurkhas "did not possess a homogenous and crystalized superculture of the conqueror to impose upon the conquered" (Rana, 1995), they introduced a lot of new cultural elements in their newly founded modern Nepal. The cultural aspiration of the Gorkhas was to spread a unified Nepalese administration and to spread Hinduization it the country.

In Kathmandu Valley, the Gorkhas did not interfere with the culture of the local people, especially of the Newars. In fact, the King not only allowed the Newar customs to continue, he himself adopted some of such customs to win the trust of the subjects of the Valley.

One of King Prithvi Narayan Shah's most famous contributions to the culture of modern Nepal was the recognition of "multi-ethnicity " as a state principle. "The country is not just earned out of my small pains, it is a garden of all castes-garden of four Varna and thirty six *jat* (castes)", the King had said. King Prithvi Narayan's *Char Varna* was equivalent to the four castes (Brahmans, Chhetris, Shudras and Vaisyas), whereas his *chattis jat* referred to the ethnic multiplicity of Nepal as *jat* could imply the non-caste people (Sharma, 1997). This notion of "garden nation" is still cited to explain the harmony within the cultural diversity in the country. The king had recognized Nepal as a multi-ethnic state with all the people having liberty to live and exercise their own religion and culture. *"Aphnu kuldharma nachhodanu"*, (Don't abandon the customs and religion of your respective communities, the King had said. The King himself adopted Newar customs and traditions of the Kathmandu Valley and allowed the cultural diversity to flourish.

King Prithvi Narayan also adopted a policy of closed state to "arrest" the process of penetration by the Southern rulers, especially the British in India. Prithvi Narayan also used "cultural integrity as a means of protecting the hardly puritan values of his hill nobles from the debilitating impact of the late Muslim culture" (Rana and Dhungel, 1998). Prithvi Narayan's one of the lasting influences in the Nepalese culture was the rise of Nepali nationalism, which would keep Nepal united in the ensuing turmoil both within and outside the country in the time to come. It was his vision of nationalism and warrior wisdom that Nepal could remain insulated from the British Empire that would engulf the rest of the subcontinent. But Nepal could not remain untouched. As the Gorkha ambition continued and they annexed one territory after another in the years to come, they came in contact with the British in India. The resulting war (1814-15) with the British left Nepal confined to roughly present boundaries after the signing of the Treaty of Sugauli in 1816. The courageous Gorkha fighters impressed the British so much that they sought to recruit the Gorkha soldiers (later famous as Gurkha) as the mercenaries. In the initial years after the war, Nepal would not allow such recruitment. So the British started encouraging migration of the Gorkhas into the tea-plantation areas of Darjeeling, where they would recruit the Gorkha men in the army and women as labor in the tea farms. While leaving the subcontinent after the independence of India, the British would sign a tripartite treaty with Nepal and India to continue to recruit the Gorkha mercenaries. The Gorkhas would later not only give Nepal a fame as the land of courageous fighters, they would also become the carriers of the "alien culture" and the modern gadgets to the rural villages in Nepal.

The subsequent Nepalese rulers took the British power as a potential threat to their nationality and sovereignty, and they consolidated the fragmented past of Nepal's traditional fiefdoms divided by the creed, culture and regions to resist further British encroachment. The Ranas maintained good relations with the British for this purpose.

Despite all the good intentions such as acceptance of multi-ethnicity and freedom to all customs and traditions of the ethnic groups of people, the cultural heritage started to erode after the unification of modern Nepal. In order to consolidate the Nepali nationalism, the state started to impose the unification of diverse and scattered people into a hierarchical social order. The most powerful symbols of this nationalism were those of Hinduism and the Nepali language (Gurung, 1998). The slow and gradual process of Hinduization, Sanskritization and Nepalization of indigenous people continued over the years. The unification also led to the spread of the influence of the Nath cult of Gorakhnath. This led to suffixing the shrines like Pashupati with "nath". Bungadeo of Patan was named as Machhendranath, the teacher of Gorakhnath. By the time Nepal was unified in the 18th century, a solid foundation of Hindu legal, and administrative institutions were already established due to the influence of the immigrant Hindus. The Gorkha conquest over most parts of Nepal helped strengthen the Hinduization of the Nepalese culture.

The "cultural concomitant of unification was a gradual process of Hinduization" (Gellner, 1997), as the festivals, values and many of the social practices of the Parbatiyas Hindus (Brahmans, Chhetris, Thakuris) were copied by other non-caste people mainly Gurungs, Rais, Magars and Limbus. After the advent of the influence of *Parbatiya* Hindus in the state affairs, religion (Hinduism) became the basis of cultural hierarchy and authority of the state. Many believe that Hinduization was not coerced or forced upon people by the state and that it was left to the individuals or groups themselves to decide to what extent and in what form to take or leave it (Sharma, 1997). Some say it happened more due to element of imitation of the high caste mannerisms by others (Pfaff-Czarencka, 1997). But some disagree to this notion. For example, Gurung (1997) says "the political conquest at the time of the unification (1768) was followed by imposition of Hindu social order on the subjects". "Vertical cleavage and divisions were introduced as social engineering process. Tamangs were divided into *Athara* and *Barha* Jaats, Sunuwars into *Barha* and *Das Thars*, Bhotiya into *Kufag* and *Ringhin*, Tharu into *Pradhans* and *Apradhans*, Chepang into *Pukunthali* and *Kachhare*, and so on" (Bista, quoted in Gurung, 1997).

As the ruling elite adopted Hinduism as the basis of state power and legitimacy of their superiority, the ethnic population, mainly elite, responded with adoption of specific cultural symbols of the High-caste Hindus. The desire to attain the higher status in Hindu hierarchy pushed minorities to endeavor to adopt the Hindu culture. As the ethnic groups came in contact with high-caste Hindus, the ethnic elite began to be affiliated with the immigrants to gain access to the power. At the same time, they also tried to distinguish themselves from the non-elite ethnic population by introducing some kind of hierarchies. In other words, these ethnic elite displayed elements of Hindu culture in order to gain power and to create a distance from the "lower hierarchy" in their own tribe. The process of cultural imitation, known as *Sanskritization*, in which the non-Hindus worshipped Hindu deities, performed Hindu rituals, adopted Brahman priests, visited Hindu pilgrimage sites and accepted Hindu hierarchy, became pervasive as the Nepalese society started to integrate.

As recruits were drawn into the Gorkha army from all parts of the country, it started to provide a great inertia for cultural contacts and interaction between the people of different regions, communities and ethnic groups of people. One of the lasting impact of the rise of house of Gorkha to modern Nepal was the creation of the name Gurkha, who would be known as a warrior and martial race. The Gurkhas would be recruited as mercenaries and would even fight with much of valor and vigor in the World Wars. Their curved Nepali knife, Khukuri, would be famous around the world as symbol of courage and bravery. The Gurkhas serving abroad would bring back a "Lahure culture", a lifestyle of the returned mercenaries, who wished to copy the language, fashion and modern amenities of the places they had served. They would bring some money to buy a lot of luxury in the rural villages, speak a few words of another language, developing a distinct Lahure accent in the Nepali language and import materials unknown to the rural villages of Nepal. This would greatly deface the cultural scenario in the villages. The desire to go to a foreign country bringing back fame and fortune would continue to shape the dreams of the Nepalese hill youths in the time to come. This would later evolve as a major phenomenon of exodus in the villages of Nepal.

The rise of the house of Gorkha as an unifying factor of modern Nepal brought unprecedented changes in Nepal's diverse culture. Though the Gorkha kings adopted a lot of customs and practices of the Newars, especially in Kathmandu Valley, the state sought to introduce the Gorkha culture to the Newars and other ethnic minorities.

Gorkhanization proceeded as Brahman priests were assigned to the military battalions, as ethnic minorities were asked to speak Gorkhali, an earlier version of Nepali, by replacing the Nepal Sambat of the Newars with Vikram Sambat, and by patronizing Sanskrit. After unification, the Gorkha civil servants, mainly High caste Hindus, gained dominance in the power structure of the state to collect revenue, to administer the remote areas, and they migrated to the tribal areas and gradually absorbed the tribal land and gained dominance in their culture. It is said, Gorkha achieved legitimacy and control over the ethnic people by injunction of some as followers (e.g. Magars), accommodation of some with concession (e.g. assigning Kipat land to the Limbus), by labor exploitation (e.g. Tamangs), by vengeance (e.g. Kirtipur Newars), and by imposing harsh-punishment such as *Gorkhelauri* in Khas people in the Karnali basin (Gurung, 1997).

But the unification of Nepal *did* unify the culture of Nepal creating a Gorkhali identity based on the spread of Gorkhali language, later known as Nepali. The kingdom's first Nepali newspaper was named Gorkhapatra and the committee formed to promote Nepali language and literature was known as *Gorkha Bhasha Prakashini Samiti.* The cultural unification based on the language was further stimulated by poet Bhanu Bhakta Acharya, who gave the Nepalese people the treasured treatise of *Ramayana* translated into Nepali verse. Some describe the "emotional unification of Nepal" by Bhanu Bhakta Acharya (1814-1861) through the spread of the Nepali language as the "cultural hegemony" of the Nepalization era (Des Chene, 1996). Bhanu Bhakta's Hindu epic Ramayana's lucid verse would be recited in every household Nepal and his Ramayana in Nepali would become Nepal's best-selling book for the time to come.

Pfaff-Czarnecka (1997) calls it *Empire Model* or *Integration Model.* After the unification of Nepal in 1768, the Shah and Rana rulers wanted to use their political power to create the framework of a hierarchically differentiated Hindu kingdom with diverse caste and ethnic languages incorporated into a framework the caste-hierarchy. The aim was to integrate the diverse populations of the country into a mainstream culture of the newly unified modern state. But this objective could not fulfilled due to the increasing royal court conspiracies, murders, killing episodes and infighting after the death of King Prithvi Narayan Shah. That pushed the cultural activities to the back seat. No major cultural masterpieces were added, and the traditions were allowed to degenerate.

Further detrimental to the culture was the rise of Rana rule in 1846. After coming to power, Jung Bahadur Rana introduced a family autocracy, in which the ruling clique of the Ranas were obsessed with their self-interest, protecting themselves from the ensuing court conspiracies, coups and counter-coups. Despite that, the Rana administration, which lasted for 104 years, also gave Nepal some lasting cultural influences. Their system of division between the ruler and ruled would continue its legacy even in the democratic dispensation of the country. But it was their concept of *Chakari*, which they used to exact obedience and subordination from the subjects, mainly their civil servants, would continue to plague the Nepalese society, mainly the government bureaucracy, in the time to come. No less important was their practice of vexing the public office in favor of personal gains, which seeped into the Nepalese mentality as corruption, which would be gradually accepted socially and would later be institutionalized.

Prime Minister Jung Bahadur Rana, the founder of the Rana rule, also became the first ruler of Nepal to go to Europe (1850). His visit to Europe not only opened Nepal's horizons, it brought several lasting cultural influences as well. After his tour of Europe, Jung Bahadur Rana introduced Muluki Ain (civil code) in 1854 copying the British common law codes. Though he retained much of the local traditions and practices, he codified the Hinduized version of law based on caste-system and hierarchy. It went to the extent that the dichotomy of the thread-wearing (*Tagadhari*) and alcohol-drinking (*Matwali*) people was also legalized in the coded law. The Hindu-based legal codes had, however, allowed the of the customary practices of different *jatis*. After that, the Ranas developed a distinct craze for the Western taste, which corrupted the Nepalese art, architecture, craft and culture. While the Rana administration (1846-1950) was largely indifferent to the culture, they added alien architectural styles like palatial Durbars. The Ranas built elaborate palaces with distinctive Victorian tastes and started to decorate the interiors with European paintings. Prime Minister Bir Shamsher Rana would even erect the famous *Dharahara*, a clock-tower in the heart of Kathmandu, copying the British Big Ben. The British band music was introduced in the army and the Rana officials copied the flamboyant hunting life styles of the British.

The ousting of the Rana regime in the 1950s was the product of an emerging consciousness and the sentiment of nationalism in the wake of the "winds of change" in the contemporary world. Events like end of the World War II and the independence of India had influenced the minds of the Nepalese people. In the ensuing struggle for democracy, which removed the Ranas from power, a new consciousness based on the freedom of the human person, the right to express and organize and the concept of equality of the people made into the minds of the Nepalese people. Along with the concept of Nepali nationalism, what became evident in the struggle for democracy and after was that a formidable alliance could be developed between the people of all castes, creeds, tribes, religions and regions. Such an alliance would later make impact the development of political parties in Nepal, who would draw members from all the sections of people regardless of their caste, creed, ethnicity and region. *Satasalko Kranti*, the famous revolution of 1950, is still remembered as one of the landmark events in making alliances between the Tagadhari and Matwali, between ethnic and caste people, and between the Terai and the Parbatiya. In the democratic dispensation that followed, political leaders, mostly educated and exiled in India during the struggle for democracy, would adopt Gandhi style nationalism and wear Kurta Salwar as sanctitious dress code in Nepal. Their Hindi accented Nepali would be a subject of amusement to the people of Nepal. But it was their dream of egalitarianism, built around Nehruvian socialism and emerging communist ideology as a remake of Marx, Lenin and Mao, that entered Nepal with the various brands of politicians and students, which would register a lasting influence in the country's political landscape.

During the brief period of a decade between the ousting of the Rana regime and introduction of the Panchayat system, the dormant energy of different groups of people, who had been suppressed by the Ranas, found expression in the new democratic dispensation. But the ferment around the creation of a political system overshadowed the liberation of cultural inertia of different groups of people.

The democracy euphoria lasted only for a decade (1950-1960). Then came the infamous Panchayat regime (1962-90), which sought to integrate the diverse cultural strands into a mainstream Nepali culture. It tried to universalize Hinduism as the state religion and Nepali as the national language. During the Panchayat era, nationalism was advocated by the state as a device of social engineering to produce patriots loyal to the state, which implied loyalty to the one-party political system. Despite the desire to integrate various ethnic groups of people into the mainstream culture, the Panchayat machine promoted the diversity in order to exact loyalty to the system from various groups of people. Tribals would dress up in local costumes and dances in local tunes to amuse the visiting monarch in various parts of the country. The King would appoint the tribal leaders as Zonal Commissioners and nominate them as members to the national parliament and appoint some as Ministers. Gurungs, Magars, Rais, and Limbus succeeded in getting into the armies (British, Indian and Nepali) and brought a lot of influence, money and fame in the villages. Thakalis and Sherpas did well in the country's growing tourism industry. Newars, Marwaris and Manangis did splendidly well with business. Madhesiyas got access to jobs in technical fields like agriculture, engineering, survey etc.

Through the declared slogan of "unity in diversity", the Panchayat regime wanted to create a homogenous and horizontally-integrated Nepali society abolishing the caste structure and assimilating the various ethnic minorities into one national culture. That was intended to make one nation, sharing a "common culture". The Panchayat regime adopted a policy of assimilation, which intended to create a homogenous society, which could respond to the need to develop and modernize. The variables used for integration were the Nepali language, Nepali dress, and Hinduism as the state religion. The state remained a guardian of the Hindu religion conducting Sanskrit schools, donating to temples, legally protecting the "sacred cow", and supporting elaborate Hindu rituals. Nepalese culture was induced in the school textbooks. In the government and political offices, the proof of loyalty started to be expressed by Nepali language and Nepali dress. Even Madhesiyas and Newars used to speak Nepali language and wear Nepali dress on national occasions. People started to copy the extremely sycophantic *Durbari* version of Nepali language

(*Hajaur, Baksyos etc.*) both as the proof of loyalty to the system and as exhibition of the status.

The diverse cultures of ethnic minorities and people of the Terai were sought to be integrated into the mainstream Nepali culture of the *Parbatiya* Hindus. Apart from the adoption of Nepali as a state language, a national dress of the Parbatiyas (*Labeda Suruwal*) and mountain bird *Danphe*, and hilly flower *Laligurans*, were declared the national bird and national flower. Nepali national anthem was made to be known to every one. This was supposed to promote a "national integration", in which different ethnic groups of people would be encouraged to adopt the mainstream Nepali culture. This process of Nepalization was augmented by the "stage-managed" migration of the hill people to the Terai, where the hill people brought with them the Nepali language and the hill culture (Gaige, 1975). This, along with the eradication of malaria, not only unleashed an attack against the thick Terai jungles, which were cleared recklessly, it also ushered an onslaught on the culture of the Terai people.

King Mahendra, founder of the Panchayat system, introduced a new version of Nepali nationalism, which was used to suppress the democratic forces. The King himself composed patriotic poems and songs. An academy of art and culture and a cultural undertaking was created to "integrate" the diverse culture. The King also helped creation of *Guthi Sanshtan*, a public undertaking formed after nationalizing the numerous Guthis in 1964. However, it did not show good results, despite of good intentions. It only shunned the initiatives. and blocked the resource mobilization by the traditional social institutions thus unleashing a callous destruction of the cultural heritage. The most important of all social engineering during the Panchayat era of integration was the introduction of the New Civil Code (Naya Muluki Ain) in 1962. This not only replaced the Civil Code introduced by Jung Bahadur Rana, it also abolished the long-standing caste system, at least legally. Despite such an effort to bring an egalitarian society, the culture of servitude inherited from the Rana period continued to creep into the Nepalese society and caste differentiation and hierarchy continued to exist in the attitudinal level, though outlawed in the books of law.

Yet another effort of social engineering during the Panchayat Period was that of the so-called "land reforms" as a state policy, which aimed at eliminating the uneven pattern of cultivable land holdings existing since the period of landed aristocracy of the Rana regime. Introducing ceilings to the landholdings per family[4] and redistributing the surplus land to the landless people, the policy wanted to promote the concept of an egalitarian welfare state. It was with this desire that the Panchayat system had also adopted a slogan of "exploitation-free society", which, in fact, could not be translated into action. The Panchayat pundits also wanted to reverse the trend of urbanization and conducted a social mobilization campaign asking the people to go back to the villages. But this slogan of "Back to the Villages National Campaign" failed to achieve its social objective but it became a tool of political screening of the Panchayat loyalists.

Described as the *Nationalistic Model* (Pfaff-Czarnecka 1997), the policy towards the culture during the Panchayat regime (1962-1990) presented "national unity" as indispensable means for societal communication and new value orientation towards the progress. Rulers claimed national homogeneity under the aegis of the culture traits of those in power, i.e. of the high caste Parbatiya Hindus. With these efforts, the Panchayat era *did* see an expansion of *Parbatiya* Hindu culture, which was not opposed to the visible extent. "Any claim to ethnic identity was reduced to political subversion" (Pfaff-Czarencka, 1997), and such an effort would be discounted as "communal". Any claim to ethnicity was understood as opposition to the Nepali "nationality".

Though homogenization was sought abolishing the caste system, ethnic minorities started to react strongly the "enforced assimilation" towards the end of the Panchayat regime. Some ethnic minorities started to form organizations of their own, despite the fear of being labeled as "*sampradayik*" (communal). An alliance called *Magurali*, an acronym of four major ethnic minorities, the Magar, the Gurung, the Rai and the Limbu, later extended to Seta Magurali, including the Sherpa and the Tamang, would be a strong cultural and political movement after the establishment of democracy. Among the most visible opposition was that of Newars, who continued to demand the recognition of their Newar language and the Newar (Nepal) Sambat by the state. *Nepal Bhasha Manka Khala*, a famous Newar organization

---

[4] One family could only hold up to 25 Bigha of cultivable land in the Terai and 80 Ropanis of the same in the hills. Anything above that was confiscated by the state and distributed to the landless people.

demanding the rights of the Newar language would later become a political force to reckon with, especially during the *Jana Andolan* and in the early years of the democratic dispensation after 1990.

Along with the Panchayat version of cultural assimilation came the rhetoric of modernization, which brought development as a slogan in the people's lives. Since the 1960s, Nepalese people were indoctrinated to the values of economic development, progress, industry, entrepreneurship, and modern education and communication in the propaganda sold by the state's dream machines, including the Planning Commission. In major urban areas, modernization not only started coming in the form hardware like technical know-how and imported goods and services, the software part of it started to come as economic liberalization, and proliferation of the mass media. The perennial flow of goods, people, information, knowledge and images started to be continuously imbibed by the people of Nepal ignoring the unique and diverse culture and traditions. The Nepalese people succumbed to the forces of modernity without noticing its impacts. In the modernization craze that followed, the ancient cities were expanded with modern concrete houses that spread haphazardly. The euphoria of Modernization[5] started to attract a large number of hill youths to Kathmandu in search of jobs and other opportunities. Some would work as *Bhariya*, the load carriers. Others would pull rickshaw and drive taxis. Still others would end up as domestic servants. Many young men and women started to find some employment with the burgeoning carpet and garment industry. A few found places in the civil service, police and military. As they deserted the villages, a strange sense of nervousness started to unleash there. As the access to education started to increase and that to jobs to decrease, many young people would remain unemployed, disillusioned and frustrated. Some would end up joining the violent "people's war" conducted in the name of Maoists.

But the modernization euphoria did not last long. As the state began to loose its legitimacy (e.g. failure to realize the development slogan, inability to sell dreams and hopes set out in the plans), people

---

[5] Des Chene (1996) views modernization as the "third unification" of Nepal, the first two unification being the unification by King Prithvi Narayan Shah through conquest and unification by Bhanu Bhakta Acharya through Nepali language.

started to oppose the ideals adopted by the state. Such ideals as "shared culture", "unity in diversity", "national integration" started to be questioned, especially by the ethnic minorities, who started to become more assertive and vocal. That plus an increasing exposure to the forces of modernization, Westernization, and globalization would herald an era of "culture shift".

THE CULTURE SHIFT ERA

The ferment of cultural frustration and disillusionment of the Panchayat era was best demonstrated in the Jana Andolan, the people's movement to establish democracy in 1990. The Nepalese people of all castes, creeds, religions, and ethnic groups actively participated in the awakening hoping that their pluralistic cultural aspirations would be best articulated in the new democratic framework. In the ensuing dispensation of democracy, Nepalese people were to witness a dramatic departure from the earlier cultural regimes. In a new democratic and pluralistic framework in the national political discourse and in an open and liberal environment for absorbing the cultural influences coming in the shape of globalization, the Nepalese people started to witness the unleashing of a "Culture Shift" era.

As the constitution declared Nepal a multi-ethnic country and it allowed Nepalis to abandon their "subject" status to become "sovereign citizens", the ethnic organizations that had remained underground during the Panchayat era started to become public. All the castes and ethnic groups were allowed to promote their culture, language ad religion with dignity and without any state interference.

Pfaff-Czarencka (1997) calls it the "*Patchwork of Minorities Model*". In the post-*andolan* era, there is the mutual recognition of diversity. Though the ethnic minorities are still at periphery, their demand for recognition for regional, linguistic and ethnic identity is no more seen as a threat to the national unity. But there are difficulties in accommodating differing viewpoints. While the movement for cultural identity is perceived by some as a politicization of the culture, others regard it as true reflection of the sentiments and aspirations of the people. Some others wish to mobilize the ethnic minorities and cultural groups for their political advantages.

In the democratic dispensation, the people have started asking for redefinition of what should be considered the "national culture". They have started to challenge the "homogenization" of the Nepalese society based on high-caste Hindu domination. The new awakening has resulted in the revivalism of the traditional identities.

When people's identity becomes more diffused, the need for cultural identity becomes more intensified. The customs, traditions, lifestyles, norms and values, which seem irrelevant at one time, start to become more important and relevant. And a new era arousal or awakening becomes evident among the people. In Nepal, the ethnic and linguistic activists are trying to form their own organizations such as welfare associations and committees. Broader alliances (e.g. *Janjati Mahasangh*) are also on the making. They are trying to reinvent and promote their own language, script, grammars, dictionaries and even literature. Some are compiling their family lineage. The "interest in one's own culture" is seen taking the shape of a political movement. The "growing interest in one's own culture, the search for origins, new cultural projects, public discussions of culture, cultural comparison, and cultural competition are partly a reaction to earlier neglect, partly tactical maneuvers, and partly a new type of hobby among the intelligentsia" (Pfaff-Czarencka, 1997). In this sense, the Nepalese people are in the process of reinventing their own culture.

Amid such changes, culture change has started to become accelerated due to a host of other factors such as the growth of the Western consumer culture, and the spread of globalization. This has hastened the pace of culture change in the fluid and dynamic state of the Nepalese culture. Influenced by the Western consumer culture, pop music, fashion and glamour world, and Western values like individual freedom, and economic liberalism, Nepalese people are seen falling in a irreversible cultural trap. Plus the increasing globalization culture with wider international exposure to the Nepalese people started to have bearing on the Nepalese culture. Increasing flows of people as tourists, immigrants, missionaries, refugees, and expatriate workers, arrivals of the multi-national corporations, infusion of technology, rapid flows of capital goods and services in the forms of trade, investment and remittances, inundation of images and information through newspapers, magazines, television and films, influx of ideas such as democracy, freedom, welfare and human rights have created unparalleled influences in the Nepalese culture. The Nepalese people have been plunged into an unprecedented social, cultural, political, economic and technological upheaval.

The Nepalese people are finding themselves at a great unease to cope with such changes. People are struggling to adjust to the changes and to some extent to the shape of things to come. Changes in the information technology, shifting demographic patterns, new structures of the government, emergence of interest groups and opinion leaders, proliferation of the media and entertainment industry, the universalization of free-market economy, globalization, along with emerging global lifestyles and "global village", and spread of the consumer culture are bringing about major shifts in the culture of the people of Nepal. People's thinking (ideas), doing (norms and behavior) and having (materials) is changing rapidly.

In other words, the Nepalese people are changing. These changes are highly visible in their culture. Large-scale transformations are being discerned in the culture of the people of Nepal. That is not only the evident in the new preferences in the dress, food, and music and subjects of interests, the change is also evident in values, attitudes, characters, manners, and beliefs. The way of living and way of thinking is becoming different. Nepalese people are experiencing slow but steady changes in their social, psychological and ideological foundations. Cultural diversity, which is the major characteristics of the Nepalese people, is in the brink of disintegrating and the people are being exposed towards a more homogenous culture. People's identity is at stake and is being rebuilt. Festivals that were celebrated jubilantly have been gradually abandoned. People's interests on rituals, and customs is degenerating. People are exhibiting lesser interest in the traditional practices. The cultural heritage handed down over centuries is allowed to crumble due to disrepair, negligence and absence of linkage with the lives of people. Once known for preserving culture at all costs, the Nepalese people are disregarding and abandoning the heritage to crumble.

The traditional social hierarchy is being reshaped and new economic hierarchies are emerging. The traditional pillars of the Nepalese society are weakening. People's work and wealth ethic is being reshaped. Loss of interest in the traditional art, architecture, music, and entertainment is becoming evident. There are attractions towards things from abroad. The exodus of the Nepalese people in search of jobs and education is becoming alarming. New values including the institutionalization and social acceptance of corruption are being shaped. Ancient cultural norms and ethics are disintegrating. As the family as an expanded unit and core of the cultural life is degenerating, the traditional family values are disintegrating. There are trends towards individualism and nuclear families. Distortions in the language, religion, and bureaucratic culture have been reshaping the society.

The cultural bond that had tied the people for thousands of years in the lap of the Himalayas is unfastening. Nepal, known as the nation of diverse cultural heritage, the sanctuary of temples and pagodas, and the land of colorful festivals, is experiencing a gradual decay of its culture. While people are abandoning traditions and customs and neglecting their heritage, a new consciousness of cultural revivalism is also on the making, especially among the ethnic minorities. As people are loosing their traditional reference points, there is a revival of ethnic identity and an upsurge of nationality among various ethnic groups of people. Nepalese people are in the process of reinventing their own culture. They are seeking their traditional reference points and connections. A new era of cultural revivalism is on the making.

The changes are adopted not only in the context of reforming the superstitious practices, but imposed upon by the degradation of moral values and ethical norms, brought by economic compulsions and communication to the external world. Changes in the attitudes, philosophy and values are built on the dilemma of traditional beliefs and modern realities. The gap between tradition and modernity is widening. The old myths and legends are disappearing and new values, attitudes and beliefs are being formed. The long-established social and institutional values are being replaced with new ones (Rana & Dhungel, 1998, p. xii).

Nepalese people are experiencing "culture shock" from within. They are not only witnessing the traumatic experience due to an exposure to an alien culture, but they are also feeling the psychological disorientation due to the loss of their own culture in their own society. The cost is becoming high and the price the people are paying is becoming unbearable. People are experiencing difficulties to adjust to this fast changing scenario. It is becoming increasingly difficult to use traditional cultural landmarks and definitions to define and interpret the changing social, institutional, cultural, political and economic standpoints and landmarks of the Nepalese people. If not taken otherwise, Nepalese people are facing a "cultural-revolution".

Cultural diversity and pluralism, which had infused dynamism and enriched the Nepalese society, is at risk. "The lack of knowledge of many cultural forms, the absence of any articulation of the grievances of yet other culture groups, which may also be numerical minority, have posed serious problems for the prospects of cultural pluralism", say Baral & Baral (in Toffin, 1993).

It is difficult to isolate and identify the changes in detail. But is plausible to discern certain trends of change. The younger generations are experiencing departures from their ancestors despite of the disapproval of the elders. The opposition to change is getting weaker every day. There is an overwhelming evidence of "Culture Shift" in Nepal.

The attitudes, manners, values, and beliefs and cultural, psychological, sociological, and ideological foundations of the people of Nepal is being influenced by the relentless social, cultural, economic, political and economic changes. The degree of dynamism is accelerating a discernible shift in the Nepalese culture. Not only are the departures from *status quo* evident, the traumas of changes are becoming obvious and people are finding themselves in an extremely difficult situation to cope with the changes.

With increasing materialistic, hedonistic, amoral, and atheistic pursuits in their lives, Nepalese people are increasingly allured towards the philosophy of "consume and be merry". The moral fiber is deteriorating and there is an increasing apathy toward the social correctness. As women are coming out of the domestic control and entering the workplace, old discriminations are being challenged. Their awareness and political empowerment have become slogan for social mobilization. People are not only becoming instantaneous and they have adopted new manners of indifference. Religion is also being reshaped as level of commitment to the same is changing. Many traditional occupations have given way to new technological innovations adopted in the country.

While architecture is becoming anarchic with the expansion of the "concrete jungle" forgetting the aesthetic and cultural significance of the past, Nepalese towns are being turned into slums due to indiscriminate expansion. A new type of entertainment industry based on the attraction to the upbeat pop culture is on the rise as people have abandoned the traditional institutions like *Rodhighar*. With the get-rich fast mentality and craze for easy money, corruption has got a social acceptance. New economic realities have generated a competition anxiety. Gaps between the rich and the poor are increasing. While the aged-ones are being abandoned, the youngsters are liberated and out of control of the family domain, but are in utter confusion. The youngsters have become frustrated and falling prey to the "snob values" and "mock culture".

As every thing else changes, so does political culture. While there is an increased awakening and rise of expectations in the new democratic framework, an increasing apathy and disillusionment about the politics in general is also on the making. Dependency syndrome created by foreign aid is inflicting the people's lives and development has become a drama rehearsed in the national stage, without much fruition after decades of efforts.

Some changes are evident. Some others are only in the form of discernible trends, and some can be interpreted in a relative context. There are shifts from extended to nuclear families, from collectivism to individualism, from past to instant orientation, from preservation to consumption, from spiritual to physical achievement, and the like. The psychological emphasis is on the everyday life not on the quality of the long period of time. There are changes in life goals, values and measures of achievement. People are becoming less and less committed towards one's own traditional values, norms and culture. More and more Nepalese people are abandoning the appreciation of their own way of life, culture, religion and the nation and there is high degree of passion for the Western modernity, money, and development. Nepalese culture has shifted more due to borrowing of elements from abroad than from its own innovation.

For centuries, the rules of conduct in the Nepalese society were rigid. Strict sanctions were applied against violations of the norms of the society. In every phase of Nepal's history, though every race or group that came for trade or for conquest left its stamp on Nepal's culture, there has been a continuous renewal of the Nepalese culture. Each time, a new culture was imposed upon the people from outside, the Nepalese people had taken such shifts with much of resistance and disliking.

Unlike the shifts of the past, the changes this time are mostly voluntary and conscious. This time, the Culture Shift is quiet but alarming. This time the changes are of a different nature. People are adapting to the cultural ethos dominated by the Western values and symbols. Nepal is increasingly exposed to the shifts in the culture, which are becoming difficult to sustain.

Boundaries Exposed

Despite moments of contacts with traders, invaders, pilgrims and immigrants, Nepalese people had lived in isolation until the second half of the twentieth century. Isolation was not only confined in the nation state, but it also existed within the different ethnic groups. The presence of physical barriers such as mountains, rivers, and thick malaria-infested jungles had nurtured a cultural diversity among the people inhabiting different regions. Besides, the patronizing of different cultural traditions by the rulers of several principalities had further strengthened the diversity (Baral & Baral, in Toffin, 1993). While the difficult terrain had isolated the diverse ethnic groups from coming into contact with each other, absence of large-scale outside invasion and presence of the Himalayan barrier had kept the Nepalese people in detachment from outside contacts and influences. Thus, Nepal's culture had been "introvert" (Sharma, 1989) and it had become possible to retain the various traditions and a diverse heritage.

In spite of being located between two big civilizations, India in the south and China in the north, Nepal had always retained her own culture without succumbing to the culture of the both and absorbing a lot of influences and assimilating cultural elements into her own culture. From the southern plains, immigrants and rulers came and introduced their culture, which was naturalized in the long run. The Tibetan and the Chinese influence in the highland also accustomed to the Nepalese culture.

The metaphor that "Nepal is a root between two rocks", which is often quoted from the famous *Dibyopadesh*, the divine quotations of King Prithvi Narayan Shah, unifier of modern Nepal, owes to Nepal's unique geographical position sandwiched between two culturally giant neighbors, India and China. The concept had significance and influence not only in the politics, economy and the international affairs of the country, it had its cultural dimensions as well. In order to protect the country's political and economic independence, King Prithvi Narayan Shah had given a prescription of insulation of from any outside influence. This had helped shield the country from the cultural influence of the outside world as well.

During the subsequent encounters with the British, especially during the British-Nepal War (1815-16), Nepal had managed to retain her cultural identity along with the political sovereignty, though Nepal had to squeeze the territorial advances made by several Nepalese war heroes. The conclusion of the Treaty of Sugauli (1816), which defines the present frontiers of Nepal, had a lasting influence in the making of the Nepalese culture, especially in the concept of Nepali nationalism. Even during the Rana rulers, who tried to appease the British in India allowing them to recruit Nepalese people as their mercenaries, the outside influence was kept at minimum. As they preferred isolation, the culture and traditions were preserved by default.

The psychological aspects of Nepal's worldview, based on gigantic neighbors on either side, high degree of cultural intimacy and dependence with India and the need to maintain an independent identity had greatly limited Nepal's external contacts. Further, the psychology of the land-lockedness, the handicap of being a least developed country, coupled with the difficulties of the mountain terrain and Himalayas as the physical and climatic barriers had put Nepal the Nepalese culture confined within the natural boundaries. Though there was porous border with India and the people from both sides could freely move freely into each other's territories, the movements were confined to pilgrimages, some migrations, and some trade.

But these boundaries seem to have been exposed. In the last five decades or so, Nepal has seen influx of tourists, and exodus of Nepalese youth abroad to seek jobs and education. Nepalese products like carpets, ready-made garments and handicraft have reached various parts of the world. Diplomatic relations are established with countries in far corners of the globe. Nepal is an active player in the United Nations and the Non-aligned Movement. Nepalese academicians, professionals, and skilled workers have found places in various parts of the globe. Nepalese peacekeepers and the Gurkha mercenary soldiers have served in various nooks and corners of the world. Various development workers started to come to Nepal in foreign assistance packages. And the expansion of consumer culture and satellite television has given relentless exposure to the Nepalese people. In the process of modernization and development, Nepal has welcomed new ideas and technology to flow into the country. The new wave of parliamentary democracy and liberal open market economy has further widened the erstwhile isolation of the country. Each has widened contacts with other cultures and produced profound influences. A new Nepalese worldview is emerging.

Today, there has been a gradual opening of the country to the tourists and development workers, to foreign trade and investment, and to new modes of transport and communications. All these have started to shape a new Nepalese worldview, which is totally different from the one of isolation and introversion.

Even the contacts among each other have been facilitated by the developments in the transport and communications within the country. The rugged mountain terrain has ceased to deter people move from one place to another. Mountain passes have been discovered, jungles cleared for human settlements, and bridges built across the river barriers. Channels of communication have opened between people of different caste, and ethnic groups. The interaction between people of different historical, political and economic background and tradition has led to a cultural diffusion (Baral & Baral, in Toffin, 1993). Today, the cultural changes are experienced due to migrations, contacts with new people, economic transactions, new technologies, accesses to education, increased communication, and the like.

If tourism opened the country for foreigners, it was the diversification of development cooperation that brought an unlimited exposure to the Nepalese people. Aid offices were opened. Projects were introduced. Foreign aid became omnipresent and accounted up to two-thirds of the kingdom's budget and plan finances. Hordes of expatriate staff including technicians, consultants, volunteers and others started to come to the country. They all brought influences. And Nepalese people were quick to learn from them.

Among the foremost of all influences was the impact upon people's ability to speak another language, mainly English. Though many of the aid workers and expatriates would also learn Nepali, the Nepalese youth started to be fascinated with English language. Even in the rural areas, the people started know little bit of this language. While language was learnt very soon, no later was the attraction to the West became evident. Nepalese Villagers started to develop attractions to the modern amenities, plastic gadgets, and even the dress codes. The most vulnerable to this trap were the Nepalese youngsters who were to assist the development workers. The Nepalese youths started to accumulate the dreams to go to abroad, where all the nice things were supposed to be found. Borrowing of cultural practices and copying of new lifestyles started to become evident in the areas of music to fashion, and food. The copied elements of the culture started to get diffused into the national mainstream.

But the real outward orientation started with Nepal's adoption of liberal economic policies, especially with liberal policy for importing all kinds of consumer goods. This exposed the Nepalese people to an insatiable desire to possess electronic gadgets and consume goods brought from outside the country.

COMING OUT OF ISOLATION

Though Nepal is one of the oldest and ever-independent nations in the world, she is relatively a new appearance in the world affairs. Nepalese people had lived in a kind of self-imposed isolation until the first half of the twentieth century. Apart from the majestic Himalayas including the world's highest mountain Mt. Everest and the brave and courageous "Gurkha" fighters, very little was known about Nepal and the people of this mountain kingdom. Nepalese people had limited contact with people from other countries. There were some contacts and relations with the immediate neighbors and powers present in the region. Maintaining contacts with foreign powers and countries in the region, the rulers of the contemporary Nepal had the plain objective of retaining and exercising the territorial independence and sovereignty of the country. That objective was achieved by a threefold strategy.

The first of these strategies was devised by the unifier of modern Nepal, King Prithvi Narayan Shah. That was the policy of isolation and non-involvement with the big powers. The policy devised by King Prithvi Narayan Shah helped shield the Himalayan kingdom from influence of the outside world, mainly the British in India. Immediately after unification of Nepal from small principalities in 1776, King Prithvi Narayan Shah recognized the unique geo-political situation of Nepal, i.e. the presence of two big powers on either side of the country, India in the south and China in the north. The presence and advances of powerful conquering forces (Moghuls and the British) in the region had left Nepal with no option but to observe a policy of introversion and non-involvement with the both. King Prithvi Narayan knew this fact very well. That is why, the King had described Nepal as a "yam between the two boulders". This geo-strategically vulnerable position of Nepal was the basis of Nepal's isolation in all the spheres. The king very well knew that the British in India was a colonial power never satisfied with their expansionist desires. China in the north was a sleeping giant, which the rulers of Nepal would least want to disturb. While King Prithvi Narayan avoided conflicts with the forces in contemporary India and China by maintaining a defensive foreign policy (*jai katak nagarnu, jhiki kakatk garnu*), Nepal's strategy for survival, independence, and a dignified role in the history was secured by the tactical maneuvering and diplomacy of the rulers of Nepal after him.

Second, the Nepalese rulers of the contemporary times continued to expand the territories of Nepal and resisted any advances and manipulations from the British power in the South. It was in this context that Nepal had fought a war with the British in India in 1814-15. In the resulting Treaty of Sugauli (1816) Nepal lost almost one-third of its territories and was confined to the present boundaries.

Third, a strategy of maintaining friendly relations with the powers in the region (e.g. China and the British in India), was adopted by the Rana rulers. Taking the unpleasant experience of having to fight a war with the British in 1814-15, the contemporary rulers of Nepal after that brief encounter maintained excellent relations with the British power. The Ranas, who ruled Nepal for over a hundred years as a family autocracy, maintained excellent relations with the British power. Though their main motive was to safeguard their personal interest, they also preserved the sovereignty of the country by default. The Ranas sent their troops to assist the British in suppressing the "Sepoy Mutiny" (1857) and in the World Wars. That would not only ensure a separate higher status to the Rana rulers than that offered by the British to India's numerous Maharjas, that policy was also rewarding as Nepal could get back some of the areas lost in the Treaty of Sugauli[1]. Though that type of foreign policy was designed to suit the personal interests of the rulers, it was also able to preserve the country's survival.

---

[1] The Terai district of Banke and Bardiya was returned to Nepal by the British as reward of Nepal's assisting them in the Sepoy Mutiny. This area is still known as "Naya Muluk" (new territories).

Though Nepal had been "beset by a seemingly irresistible array of interested outside parties, eager to assist, advise and manipulate" for nearly two centuries following the unification in 1776 (Rose, 1971), Nepal's contact abroad was very limited until after the revolution in the 1950, which ousted a century-old autocratic regime of the Ranas. Even during the period of Rana rulers, who tried to appease the British in India allowing them to recruit Nepalese people as their mercenaries, the outside influence was kept at minimum.

Considering the geo-political and geo-strategic realties of the period after the unification of Nepal in 1768, the seemingly isolationist stand in the foreign policy until the 1950s, could have been a conscious choice of the contemporary rulers of Nepal. Before embarking into an outward-looking posture in the foreign policy, the isolationist foreign policy was able to preserve Nepal's independence and dignity. Professor Khanal (1996) has said that the posture of isolation adopted during the Rana regime was "tailored to the need of the survival o the country". Isolationism was "a product of the uneasy compromise between the traumatic experience and the harsh international reality of the nineteenth century". As a result, the foreign policy of Nepal had become "forbidden field open only to the close and secret few" and "with secret negotiations, agreements, and treaties, it fostered an atmosphere of secrecy, which in time solidified into a tradition even now hard to shed" (Khanal, 1996).

The first wave of Nepal's wave of exposure to the outside world came with contact of Nepal with the British in India. After a brief war encounter, Nepal embarked into friendly relations with the British in India. The British started to appoint Nepalese mercenaries, who would be alter known as Gurkhas. The Gurkhas not only brought home some money and modern gadgets, they also started bringing the experiences of the outside world to the remote villages of Nepal. In the later years, the youths in the remote villages of Nepal would carry the dream of becoming the Gurkha soldiers and that would interestingly bring a new cultural exposure to Nepal.

But the real outward-orientation in Nepal started after the changes in the 1950s. After the British had left the Indian subcontinent and with the wave of changes in the world, especially after the World War II, a new consciousness aroused in Nepal. In the consequent awakening and the ensuing revolution, Nepalese people overthrew the 104-year Rana family autocracy and established democratic dispensation, which would only last for a brief period of ten years. In the democratic openness and new era of friendly contact between countries around the world, Nepal ventured to establish diplomatic linkages with the countries around the world. Nepal started to become an increasingly active member of the international community and of the United Nations and most of its agencies. Nepal also became a vocal advocate of the Non-aligned Movement, which provided a safe refuge for the nations, which did not want to fall into the orbit of the superpowers.

The advent of democracy in 1950 after the successful overthrowing of the autocratic Rana regime marked the beginning of a new era in Nepal's outward orientation. Nepal's entry into the comity of nations, establishing new diplomatic relations and joining international organizations of nations gave Nepal the fresh opportunities to introduce herself in the international community.

Even during the Panchayat era (1960-1990), which limited the political and democratic rights of the people, Nepal took significant strides in outward-orientation and continued to diversify its relations with other countries. In unique example of pro-active diplomacy pursued by the state during the period, Nepal ventured a "Zone of Peace Proposal", which received support of over 110 countries from around the world.

Further openness and exposure came with the re-establishment of democracy in the 1990s. The new democratic dispensation ushered an era of openness, both internally and externally. In the democratic dispensation, the openness in public debate, the reflection of the sentiments of the people, and the desire to create a prosperous society in a pluralistic framework changed Nepal's outlook. "Re-assertion of commitment to values of freedom, justice, human rights, and above all, human dignity, has brought Nepal into line with the growing number of democratic countries" (Khanal, 1996, pp. 70-71). Today, Nepal has either signed or adopted all the major international conventions on human rights. Nepal has always advocated the cause of peace, justice and self-determination of the people's around the world. Nepalese soldiers have been serving in various peacekeeping missions under the United Nations.

In the economic front, Nepal has gradually opened up the markets, allowing the capital, goods and services from abroad to move freely in the country. The policies of economic liberalization, and privatization, coupled with the adoption of the outward-oriented economic policies and private-sector led open market economy has unleashed new forces of openness in the country.

THE DIFFUSION FROM THE SOUTH

Increasing contacts between the people of India and Nepal is one of the several factors contributing to the expansion of the cultural boundaries of the Nepalese people. Cultural connections between the people of Nepal and India have existed for ages. From times immemorial, the Nepalese people used to go on pilgrimages in India and they used to take pride in the sharing the cultural heritage based on religious and cultural similarities. It is not only the geographical proximity that keeps people of Nepal and India close to each other, a strong cultural sentiment attaches the people of the both countries. Cultural affiliation between people of India and Nepal has been as old as history. There are cultural connections, shared practices and common philosophical background that have tied the people of the two countries in the continuum of time. Many Nepalese people, who came from across the southern border over the passage of history, continue to share the beliefs, cultural and linguistic practices from the South. Many Nepalese such migrated have retained the cultural practices of the places where they come from[2]. Some Hindus, especially Brahmins and Chhetris continue to practice the religious-cultural practices of the places they come from and many continue to go to the famous pilgrimages in India. They perform rituals to pay homage to their ancestor (*Shraddha*) in Gaya, an ancient town on the famous Ganges River, which they consider to be taken holier than the sacred Himalayan rivers of Nepal. While taking baths, many traditional Hindus, especially Brahmins, still take the name of the "holy rivers" in India such as *Ganga, Jamuna, Sindhu, Saraswoti,* and *Kaberi,* instead of the Nepalese sacred rivers such as *Karnali, Bagmati* and *Gandaki.* Despite of difficulty in transport and communication, the Nepalese people would reach to the *Char Dham,* the famous four pilgrimages, and would go to Gaya to perform the ancestral rites and

---

[2] Most Brahmins and Chhetris are supposed to have migrated into Nepal from area between *Ganga* and *Jamuna* rivers in northwestern India (*Kanyakubja*) and are said to be continuing to practice the cultural legacy into Nepal.

to live in Indian holy places to earn religious merit. As the contacts through the porous border became easier than ever before with the improvement of road and air communication between the two countries, the Nepalese culture started succumbing to the influences of the Indian culture. Some blame a "Heritage Hindustan" (Gurung, 1997), the continuing legacy of the immigrant Hindus, especially Khas Aryans, to be the major factor behind the perpetuation of *Indianization* of the Nepalese culture. Those hardly recited words of prologue of religious texts describing Nepal as *Himabatkhand*, the northern extension of *Jambudweep-Bharatbarsha*, and that expression by King Prithvi Narayan Shah that this is pure land of Hindus (*Yo Alsi Hindustan Ho*) are cited as examples of the "heritage" from the south.

One may disagree with these interpretations. But there is no denying that there exists a high degree of passion among the Nepalese people towards the Indian culture. It is especially relevant to the Hindi movies and Indian fashion world, which mesmerizes the Nepalese people as it does with the people of the rest of the subcontinent. These passions are not related to the traditional cultural affinity ad similarities. As the Indian culture is also modernizing, its influence to the Nepalese culture is also changing with the passage of time.

In fact, the passion with the Indian political culture seeped into Nepal with the prominence of the India-educated Nepalese elite in politics and in bureaucracy, especially after the establishment of democracy in 1950s. The politicians, who conducted the fight for democracy remaining in exile in India, took pride in wearing Gandhi style cotton *Kurta-Pyjama*, which would later become the dress code of one of major political parties in Nepal. A whole breed of the Venaras-educated bureaucrats would almost dominate the higher echelon of the Nepalese government bureaucracy till the end of the twentieth century. Though there is some apprehension about the copying of the political culture, especially that of criminalization and communalization in the Indian politics, there is a high level of passion towards things and culture of the southern neighbor. Even the political apprehension has been inspired by the cultural affiliations. J. N. Dixit, one time Foreign Secretary of India in his *South Block Years* (1991-94) has said:

Nepal being a Hindu majority country with much closer cultural linguistic and religious links with India, is legitimately apprehensive about its political independence and separate identity being either eroded or submerged because of elemental forces of geography and socio-cultural factors (Dixit, 1996, p. 87).

During the Panchayat era, this apprehension was expressed to raise the nationalistic sentiments and to insulate the political system from the fighters for democracy, many of whom were struggling from the Indian soil. Today, the cultural allure is continuing is not because of the historical affiliations. It is mostly because of the attraction towards the modern Indian culture, which is also changing rapidly. The increasing *Indianization* of the Nepalese culture is evident by the rising popularity of Indian movies in Kathmandu, and spread of Hindi as a very common regional language, increasing popularity of Indian fashion, food and music in Nepal. India has become fashionable even in the West. Indian food (curry), yoga, Ayurveda spirituality, fashion (*salwar kameez*), Indian pop songs (like *Bhangra*) and Indian movies have captured the taste of the Western populations as well. Nepal cannot be excluded from that embrace.   And that has been reshaping the Nepalese cultural identity.

Even today, people aspire to go to Indian pilgrimage sites, buy Indian religious texts and Indian goods. Increasingly large number of Nepalese people's choices have been guided by Indian movies, fashion, and music. With continuing influence from the south, Nepal's cultural landscape has been changing.

Indianization of the Nepalese culture was also contributed by the Indianization of the economy in Nepal. People from the southern plains, especially *Marwaris*, who possess a great deal of flexibility entrepreneurship and profit earning skills, have become highly successful in Nepal and brought several impacts. Trade and business, brought about by these contacts, has been a major element for bringing changes in the culture of people of Nepal in the form of entrepreneur culture. Besides, the swarms of Indian street vendors of fruits and vegetables and numerous semi-skilled carpenters, masons and other occupations in Kathmandu and other major urban areas, have started to inject the feeling of competition and hard-working mentality for doing business.

Today, the Indianization of the economy has become tantamount to the Indianization of culture. Nepalese markets are flooded with the Indian products. Nepalese people have been using Indian gadgets, goods and services as their cultural symbols not for their easier access, availability and cheaper prices, but also for the cultural values they represent to the Nepalese people. That is why the Nepalese women feverishly buy Indian dresses and the youngsters die for the Indian films and music.

Though rejected and resisted at the academic and political rhetoric level, the Indian influence in the Nepal is increasing at the popular level. That is justified by the unrestricted immigration of people through the unregulated and porous border, the presence, in a large number, of skilled and semi-skilled Indian workers such as masons, carpenters etc. in the Nepalese labor market, streams of Indian vendors in the major urban areas, dominance of Indian merchants and businessmen in the economy, and increasing population of Indian origin, especially in Terai. In a controversial report, Dr. Harka Bahadur Gurung, a noted writer on Nepal, had went to the extent that Indian populace is on the increasing trend and that there should be some restrictions on their entry. Although that report was attacked by many, some degree of apprehension of Indian dominance in the political, economic and demographic level exists among some Nepalese people. But influence at cultural level goes unnoticed and people are allured to the Indian culture with the exposure to the celluloid, print and electronic media and increasing contacts at different levels.

It is sometimes argued that globalization would have eventually gripped the Nepalese culture, even without the engulfing of Indianization. Others say globalization is better than Indianization.[3] But globalization or Westernization does not prevent Indianization. And neither is better, for it erodes the Nepalese culture. In fact, the Indian culture is being Westernized and globalized to some extent. There the Indian culture is also contributing some to the global culture. But sadly, we are at the receiving end. Today, Nepalese youth feverishly watch every single Hindi movie. They are fans of Daler Mehndi's *Bhangra* and keep track of every Indipop song released in Bombay. Listen to the subscribers of the songs in one of

---

[3] In his comments on *Impacts of Globalization in Nepal* by Dahal (1998), Shridahr Khatri speaks on how the Nepalese society would have responded to the Indianization process if there had not been the Western impact? "It is most likely that instead of watching Bruce Wills and Julia Roberts on the celluloid screen, drinking Carlsberg, speaking English and watching BBC or CNN, we would most likely be glorifying Shah Rukh Khan and Madhuri Dixit, speaking Hindi, and managing with Doordarshan"

several FM channels in Kathmandu. Youths today still have the passion towards the Indian movies and songs, especially the latest fashion of non-film music.

Whether one likes or not, Nepalese people carry a guilt of the Indianization of their culture in the back of their mind. One is reminded of the Indian influence when women wear Indian saree as Nepali national dress, where Indian curry is served in Nepali dinners, when Hindi songs are played at parties and when Indian film is music blasted at weddings and other social occasions. In foreign land, wherever they go, the Nepalese are likely to be identified or at least confused as Indians. That darkish color of the skin, that pointed nose (if one is not among privileged few from the Himalayan and highland areas) that black moustache, and the Indianized accent in English would always put the Nepalese in the category close to the Indians. Thus, Indianization of the Nepalese culture becomes burdensome to the Nepalese identity in the world community.

The diffusion of the cultural boundaries was also complimented with the process so-called Nepalese Diaspora[4]. The increasing dispersion of and the struggle for identity of the Nepalese Diaspora has been widening the boundaries of the Nepalese culture. The foremost advances of the Nepalese people beyond the boundaries of the kingdom started in the form of economic migration. In fact, the hill communities of Nepal were highly mobile throughout the history. There is a very strong evidence of the eastward trek of the Khas and the Brahmans, first from India to the Karnali basin, then from the Karnali basin towards the rest of Nepal and more eastwards. The process of Nepalese Diaspora had started when the modern Nepal expanded eastwards conquering[5] the Darjeeling Hills and part of Sikkim (1780). The permanent settlement of Nepalese people outside the Kingdom's modern border started to appear in the eighteenth century and continued until the early 20th centuries (Hutt, 1997, p. 109). Pradhan (1991) has estimated that between 12 and 15% total Kirant population emigrated from the eastern Nepal to Darjeeling between 1840 and 1860, as the *Parbatiya* cultivators

---

[4] The term "Nepalese Diaspora" is used to denote the permanent presence of a Nepali speaking community outside the borders of present-day Nepal (Hutt, 1997).

[5] The territories were held by Nepal until it was surrendered to the British India after the Treaty of Sugauli in 1816.

began encroaching the ancestral lands of the local Rai and Limbu people. The eastward drift of a culture based on the Nepali language, the dominance of Brahmans, and of agricultural practices based on the use of the plough and the cultivation of maize has been attributed to the proliferation of tea farming and intake by British India of Nepalese youths in their army in the Darjeeling hills (Hutt, *ibid.*, p. 109). As these populations moved eastwards, they reached parts Assam, Meghalaya, Bhutan, and up to Burma.

As the Nepalese Diaspora started to diffuse eastwards, the search for identity started to take the shape of the struggle for recognition of the Nepali language in the respective territories. Nepali language with a distinct hill accent became the basis of their identity. It was through the struggle demanding recognition of Nepali language that the ethnic identity of the Nepalese Diaspora culminated into the recognition[6] of Nepali language by the Indian constitution in 1992. With that, the long-standing aspiration and struggle of over 5 million people with Nepali as their mother tongue was partially fulfilled. While the Nepalese Diaspora community continued to seek their identity demanding the recognition of the Nepali language, they promoted and contributed to the development the language and literature significantly. A separate category of Nepali literature called *Prabasi Nepali Sahitya*, the literature contributed by the Nepali-speaking people living outside the Nepalese soil, has been established as a major stream of the Nepalese literature. Today, the quintessential word *"prabasi"* has made an entirely new category of the Nepalese identity living outside the Nepalese territories. Similarly, the contributions to modern Nepali music from the Diaspora community and the contribution to modern education from the Diaspora area have been very significant. Many Darjeeling-educated men and women have been absorbed in various professions, and in the trendy jobs at hotels, tourism industry and in foreign-aided project offices.

Nepali-speaking people outside Nepal, whether born there or living there through generations, were always considered as

---

[6] The movement for recognition of Nepali in the Indian soil had started as demand for adoption (1927) of Nepali as medium of instruction in schools in Darjeeling, where Nepali was adopted as official language in 1971. After a long and arduous struggle, Nepali was included in the 8th Schedule of the Constitution of India on August 20, 1992.

foreigners and immigrants. On account of being grouped with the Nepalese of Nepal, the Indian Nepalis have not only been facing discriminations, they have lost their identity as well[7]. At times, the Nepalis have faced expulsions as well. At least, that was the fate of the Nepalese, who faced the exodus from Assam (1980) and Bhutan (1990-91). Similarly, some 13,000-17,000 Nepalese were expelled from Meghalaya (1980-86) in the course of *Bhumiputra* movement called "sons of the soil". Some 8,000 were expelled from Mizoram in 1967, and 2,000 from Manipur in 1980 (Hutt, 1997, p. 124). Many Nepali-speaking people left Burma in 1964, when Burma introduced its Nationalization Act.

Because of discrimination and exploitation, sense of insecurity, instances of exodus and rivalry with local population, the Nepalese Diaspora have invoked and renewed the bond with the "mother culture" in times of crises. This is aptly proved by the fact that the expelled Diaspora populations have found sanctuary and asylum in Nepal at different times. People expelled from Assam, Meghalaya, and Manipur were granted asylum and sanctuary in Nepal. More recently, some 100,000 Nepali-speaking Bhutanese have been granted asylum in Nepal since 1990, when they left Bhutan as the Bhutanese government tried to impose an uniform culture on its diverse populations. Until the time of this writing, these Bhutanese refugees are languishing in refugee camps in east Nepal as progress on the negotiations between the governments of Nepal and Bhutan for their repatriation has been painfully slow.

There has also been a relatively recent Diaspora of the Nepalis to north Indian cities to seek work, mostly as household help, security guards, and other manual jobs. But this has not yet produced large culturally cohesive communities like those in the older eastern Diaspora (CNAS, 1987, Dixit, 1988). But the ubiquitous presence of Nepalese in the domestic service and security guards has almost generated a new image and identity of the Nepalese working in India. *Bahadur* and *Kanchha* have become household words many urban areas in India. These workers not only bring some money and various gadgets when they come back home, they also bring back the Hindi accent and an exposure to yet another culture and the experience of work in a different place. In rural villages, young men have started to grow up with dreams of going

---

[7] *Mahendra P. Lama, in Himal Khabarpatrika, 2-31 October, 2000.*

abroad in search of jobs. Even the jobs of a *Chowkidar* started to be glorified. And the number of modern gadgets that started to enter the villages with the Nepalese workers in India started to pour the craze for materialistic consumer culture in the rural villages of Nepal. Many started to understand and learn Hindi. And in some cases, the Nepalese language started to absorb a distinct Hindi accent brought about by these workers. All of these factors has contributed to the increasing Indianization of the Nepalese culture, which is simultaneously exposed to other threats such as modernization, Westernization and globalization.

THE ACCELERATOR OF CULTURE SHIFT

If anything has contributed most to the broadening of the Nepalese worldview today, the credit should go also to the developments in information technology, mainly the computer and the Internet. Not only are a large number of Nepalese living abroad have a constant access to the Internet, even home-based individuals and organizations have found it easy and suitable to use the cyberspace. While use of email has become common, many net-savvy organizations and individuals have their own home pages and websites. Today, news from Nepal can be read in Munich and Miami almost in real-time. Thanks to the several news-related sites. Many Nepalese youths living abroad dedicate songs in the FM broadcasts in Kathmandu through the net. There are several email providers and professionals devoted to the development of website and home pages. On surfing through home pages and web sites of various Nepalese Associations based abroad and similar website of offering information on Nepal, one can see there are the emerging "e-patriots", who are located in different corners of the world and seek the cyberspace to flag their diffusing identities.

Today, almost all business organizations and even government offices in Nepal have started to fashionably use emails and web pages to promote their businesses. The business cards of many Nepalese professionals, academicians, and even government officials, today, contain email addresses. More and more Nepalese businessmen, academicians, professionals, and NGO leaders and even government officials have their own emails, their home pages and web sites, and they have a wider access to the computer and the Internet at home and at work. Even teenagers have increasing access to the Internet, online service and an email with increasing interest in the areas of search engines, music sites, games, TV and movie sites, sports sites, and chat rooms. Many have started building their own home pages.

Lately, a large number of private schools in Kathmandu Valley have started to sport computer education. Even the government has pledged to make computers and internet available in all government schools in Kathmandu Valley. Fashionably enough, the members of parliament are also given free access to the Internet for a token period. There is the mushrooming of several computer-training institutes. A look at the advertisements in the local media proves this. Many Nepalese students are going abroad to seek education in computer science and information technology. Their "silicon dream" is perhaps the most common drive for study abroad.

Though most of the Nepalese people are still on the "have not" side of the "digital divide", a relatively good number of people have access to the computers, especially in the urban areas. According to a write up,[8] there were 50,000 personal computers, 10 Internet Service Providers (ISPs), 25,000 Internet accounts and 100,000 Internet users in Nepal in 2000. Though the use of computers is restricted to the urban rich or middle-class English-savvy people, the Nepalese entrepreneurs are committed to secure Nepal's place in the global IT Map. While, the private sector is emerging in IT, even the government is focusing to developing IT as a potential business sector.

The Internet started becoming common in Nepal since 1995. In fact, the non-resident Nepalese had been extensively using the "e-zines" and the mailing lists, even before the Internet came to Nepal. For example, the Nepal Digest, the first e-zine was established in 1992. Thanks to these channels and "white pages", which have helped the Nepalese people around the globe to have a relatively better network. One such Nepali White Page aims to "provide the Cyber Nepalese community and friends around the world with a reference that would possibly re-unite friends, create new friendship and make us feel closer to home Nepal". Networks like these have connected a large number of Nepalese people, both home and abroad, through the cyberspace.

Today, the Nepalese living abroad can access to the news in Nepal almost in real time. Thanks to the Nepalnews service developed

---

[8] *The Spotlight*, Information Technology, The Incoming Boom, January 26-February 1,2001.

by a leading Internet service provider. Youngster dedicate Nepali songs aired on the FM channels from around the world sending emails. In fact, the new channels of communication, especially the email, has revolutionized the pattern of communication between Nepalese people living around the world. To the Nepalese living around different parts of the globe, the world has really become a "global village".

The access to the cyberspace has reshaped the Nepalese worldview significantly. This has not only widened the *"Nepal Khaldo"* mentality, which meant that the Nepalese at times least cared about what went outside the Kathmandu Valley. Today, professionals and academicians and business leaders are finding the world as a common space.

But there are bad side effects of the access to the cyber space. It is not the pornography and fear of being addict to the Internet, which are alarming among the Nepalese youth. But the access to the cyberspace has also put the Nepalese youth at a risk of being alienated from their own culture.

"The Internet isn't changing Nepal like it is changing America", says Peter Rojas, "it is only accelerating a cultural shift that began years earlier when Nepali teens first discovered Western style pop culture".[9] There is no denying. While the Internet is bringing unprecedented opportunities for the exposure of the people of Nepal to the outside world, it is also posing a threat of erosion of the traditional fabric of society with an unprecedented exposure to the Western culture.

THE OPENING OF SHANGRI-LA

Hardly known to the outside world five decades ago, Nepal today is one of the world's most famous tourist destinations. Apart from being the world's only Hindu kingdom, the birth place of Lord Buddha, and the land of the Living Goddess, Nepal is also know as the land of the Himalayas including the Mt. Everest, the highest mountain of the world and for the diverse cultural heritage. As a land of diversity, a destination with difference, Nepal is a famous tourist's Shangri-La.

Tourists started to come to Nepal since it was opened to foreign travelers in the 1950s. Today, tourism is a burgeoning industry in

---

[9] Peter Rojas, Lost Kingdom, at http://www.thealarmclock.com/

Nepal. Nepal has created reasonably good services and infrastructure in the sector. Nearly half a million foreigners visit Nepal, every year. And tourism has become a major earner of country's foreign exchange and a source of employment of several Nepalese people. But the kind of exposure tourism has brought to Nepal is not without cultural implications. Today, it is said that tourism in Nepal is not exactly compatible with the preservation of local culture. After the tourists started pouring into Nepal in large numbers, the capacity of Nepal's cultural heritage and environment almost has reached a threshold. Plus the influences in the lifestyles and culture have started to be noticed.

Today, tourism has become a major harbinger of cultural change in several communities in Nepal, especially at the youth levels. Influence of tourism has been noticed even in the remote villages, where people come into contact with the foreign travelers, trekkers, and mountaineers. For example, Fuhrer-Hiamendorf (1984) had discerned "a radical reordering" of the socio-economic relations and statuses brought about by tourism among the Sherpa youth in the Khumbu region. Many had abandoned their traditional occupation and adopted new professions as guides, small hotel owners, porters, and travel assistants. In doing so, they had started to dissociate themselves from their traditions and culture[10]. Similar influences can be see among Thakalis in Mustang area. The Thakalis in the area have specialized in service industry such as lodges, local restaurants and bars catering to the tourists.

While tourism has put substantial demands on heritage conservation, it has altered the already fragile and vulnerable state of the national heritage. For instance, a government report (IUCN/HMGN, 1992) admits that the folk music, folk dance and *Thangka* paintings have been severely compromised in an effort to service the tourist market. Their "links with religion have been broken and the original purpose and meaning have been lost." The urge to

---

[10] Though some studies have indicated that the maintenance of religious practices, traditional cultural knowledge, and ethics have eroded with the advance of tourism among the Sherpas in Khumbu area (Fuhrer-Hiamendorf, 1989), others show that Sherpas have maintained their culture and identity. Religious observation has actually increased among Sherpas with the growth of tourism and the Sherpa identity has intensified (e.g. Fisher, 1990) and that Sherpas are actively engaged in reconstructing and reconsolidating their culture.

commercialize the traditional art and craft for catering to the need of the tourists brings the threat of their distortion and change from their originality. The metal and woodcraft products, produced indiscriminately and sold to the tourists purporting to be original pieces of artwork, defy the artistic dignity of the Nepalese craft. The preservation of the cultural heritage has become deceptive, as the task of achieving the commercial success without infringing the originality of the local craft has started to become difficult. When the craft vendors in various tourist sites sell artifacts of cultural importance, they may be promoting the diversity of the cultural heritage. But they put an indirect pressure on the traditional usage of them by raising the prices. They not only threaten the survival of the cultural integrity of the objects. At the same time, the traditional dexterity, quality and aesthetics in the art form is compromised in order to satiate the commercial and competitive demand of the craft among the tourists. As cultural rules are bent in order to achieve economic benefits, the ownership and control of the intellectual and cultural property of the people also become jeopardized.

When the heritage sites become tourist attractions, a few polluting effects will be obviously there. There will be a crowding of vehicles, logistic delivery systems, and hawkers around the sites. But the real threat comes when tourism might start interfering on the real purpose of the sites, such as regular worships in the temples. This can detach the cultural significance of a heritage area and lead to the decline of the importance of the live heritage.

The interaction between the tourists and the local people has been generating more lasting impacts on the Nepalese culture. That is fostering a new kind of acculturation, the diffusion of ideas, innovations, and new technologies that could prompt new lifestyles and aspirations, say Karan and Ishii (1996). While tourism provides additional employment, new careers and seasonal work opportunities, it also makes available a disposable income among the local populations. That has changed the affordability of people to buy consumer goods and copy the new lifestyles. When the local people absorb the otherwise "culturally inappropriate" dresses, food, etiquette and norms of the tourists, the cultural identity itself becomes highly vulnerable. These trends have started to become visible in Nepal.

THE NEPALESE GLOBAL VILLAGE

According to a report[11], some 660,000 Nepalese were working in various countries of the world.[12] That included 15,000 Nepalese in the Western countries, 40,000 in the Gulf countries, 42,000 in the Eastern countries, and 250,000 in India. And they were sending home some 6.90 billion rupees annually as remittances of their income abroad. These figures may sound small compared to the total population (22.5 million) of Nepal. But in terms of percentage of the economically active population, the population of the Nepalese workers abroad stands at 10%.

A cursory look on the advertisements in the local newspapers in Kathmandu shows that a large number of Nepalese people are being wanted abroad for education, jobs, business, and other opportunities. Most common of them are the advertisements related to recruitment of workers in the Gulf countries. Many others are study-abroad messages put by numerous colleges and universities around the globe. There is an emerging phenomenon that is alluring the Nepalese youth abroad in search of education and job opportunities. Caught by the moneymaking spree, and enchanted by the dream of *"bidesh"*, the utopian foreign land, many young people are swarming abroad in search of better opportunities. They are aspiring to do so and are putting a lot of energy and resources for the same.

This has taken the shape of a "silent exodus". There are three distinct categories of people who are in a process this exodus. First, a large number of Nepalese youths go to the Gulf and Southeast Asian countries to get employment in low-skilled manual and hardship jobs in very difficult circumstances. Second, a substantially large number of Nepalese people go to India to work as the *Durban, Chowkidar, Bahadur* or household help. Some Nepalese women are trafficked to the infamous sex trade in Bombay and other Indian cities. Third, there are a large number of professionals, and students pursuing higher studies, who espouse an eventual dream to go abroad and even settle there.

---

[11] Report of the British foreign development cooperation agency DFID quoted in *Kantipur*, October 9, 1999)

[12] This figure is comparable to the total number of Nepalese working abroad in 1991, when there were 402,997 Nepalese working abroad (HMGN, 1991 Census).

This exodus has become a distinctive cultural phenomenon, which justifies that the Nepalese people are deserting their homeland and opting to go abroad to sell their brains and muscles.

Those who can make to the foreign countries and somehow make a living there are considered lucky enough. But these young Nepalese people end up doing all the odd and difficult jobs, which they would not think of doing back home. Many enter as students and end up doing these little errands to make living, instead of continuing their academic career, which they often have to abandon. For a few dollars, they deliver newspapers to houses by 6.00 a.m., fill gasoline at gas stations until 11 p.m., and many clean dishes in restaurants until midnight and drive taxis the whole night. The Nepalese youth in the United States categorize these jobs as OCDC (Onion Cutting, Dish Washing). In the Gulf countries, some of the Nepalese work as camel jockeys, shepherds, and household jobs under harshest climate and repressive working conditions. Others work with very unfriendly and unfamiliar machines unknown to them. Some of the jobs are so dangerous that some of the Nepalese workers also face the threat of loosing limbs and life. In Korea, they call it 3Ds- dirty, dangerous and difficult jobs. It goes to the extent that these Nepalese workers experience the revival of slavery.[13] Some Nepalese youths say "if you could struggle this much you would definitely be better off back home".

That does not distract other Nepalese from going abroad. Despite such difficulties, the glory of living abroad is seen a big success back home. And the fellow compatriots seek to emulate them. The interesting aspect of this exodus is that not all of these Nepalese workers and youngsters go abroad because of poverty of lack of economic opportunities to sustain their lives back home. In fact, only such Nepalese, who can mobilize some economic resources, such as by selling their landed property or borrowing from local usurers, can make their way to foreign countries. Many of them are just caught in the myth of a foreign land, in the craze for consumerism, and in the lure for making money at all costs.

The Nepalese youths started going abroad to serve as the mercenaries of the British and India army as the famous Gurkhas. They not only introduced the valor and courage of the Nepalese youth to the world, they also brought back cultural influences. One

---

[13] C. K. Lal in an essay in *Himal* 2-31, October 2000.

such influence is the rise of the dream of most of the rural hill youths to go abroad to make better earning as well as to get acquainted to the rest of the world. In fact, the Gurkhas have contributed to the emergence of a distinct *Lahure Culture*[14], the distinctive life styles of the ex-servicemen who had served in the British or Indian army. During the spell of going abroad as foreign mercenaries, the Nepalese youth in the rural villages developed a distinctive language accent, they brought several plastic gadgets, and infused a lot of money and spending spree in the rural villages. Apart from the disposable income to spend for consumer items, the *Gurkha*s also brought fame, legends and stories of their heroic deeds, which allured the youngsters in the jobs abroad. Before the tripartite treaty among Nepal, India and Britain was concluded in order to hire Nepalese mercenaries in the two countries abroad, virtually no people had the attraction of going abroad in another country. Today, almost everybody aspires for the same.

Today the mania of going abroad has captured the mood of the young people, both in the rural hills and in the urban areas. Many Nepalese youth dream, aspire, and try to go abroad in order to make money and bring back fame and experience. Though some political groups reject "selling one's blood and muscle to another country," Nepalese youths are prepared and even actively seek to go abroad as foreign mercenaries. The first choice would be to be recruited as "Gurkha" soldier. But recruitment is decreasing it is not that easy to get selected. Apart from certain physical attributes, you have to be from certain ethnic group or from certain area to get preference. The second choice becomes the Indian army. Now the trend is that there is more attraction for manual and intellectual jobs other than the military and the police. Young men, especially from the rural hills go to the Indian cities and end up in doing jobs like *"chowkidars"*, the security guards. This *bahadur* or *kanchha* has become a quintessential symbol of honesty, bravery, loyalty and ignorance. Despite perennial salutes and solemn smiles, they get paid very little, albeit enough to survive.

---

[14] As one of the early recruits of the Gorkha soldiers were sent to Lahore in Pakistan, the term *Lahure* has become a popular vocabulary applicable for all the people who go abroad in search of jobs, mainly in military, police and security-related ones. Now this term is used generically to all returnees home after making money from foreign employment.

Others go to the countries in the Gulf. Despite the ubiquitous cheating by the agents, maltreatment and underpayment by the employers, and harsh and repressive working conditions, the Nepalese youths continue to swarm abroad in search of low key jobs in these countries. Many even sell their landed property and other borrow from usurers to get these jobs, for one has to pay handsome amount to get selected. The desire to go abroad is so pronounced and obsessive that many youths do not even hesitate to enter such countries without proper documents and legal permits for employment. Many get stranded. Stories of Nepalese youths stranded in different countries have become quite common.

This lure is continuing among most young people, who are trying to go to foreign countries to serve as unskilled workers. Many people from the rural areas are being flown to different parts of the world to work as physical laborers. One can see long queues of Nepalese youths in front of the passport offices, in front of foreign embassies to get visas and in the foreign employment agencies to get foreign working permit or access to an employer abroad.

Attraction to go abroad in order to make money and better living is changing the youth mentality in the urban areas as well. Going to such places, the Nepalese people no only aspire for money, they also see success, admiration and better knowledge of the outer world in these opportunities. In today's Nepalese society, going to a foreign country is in itself regarded as an accomplishment. Add to that the attraction of bringing back dollars and praise and status achieved in the society. Thus the swarm of the youths may not only be limited to the lack of opportunities in Nepal. They are also caught with the dream of a "quick and easy money" that has found place in the Nepalese society with the rise in the practices of corruption.

Despite the fact that the Nepalese human resource development policy hardly recognizes the benefit and importance of sending workers abroad to solve the unemployment and disillusionment and to bring back money, large number of Nepalese people have made their way to jobs abroad and many have even settled abroad.

It is not only jobs. Even the students aspire to go abroad to pursue their academic career. A large number of Nepalese people are sending their children abroad for seeking better education at foreign schools and universities. In fact, it has become a kind of status symbol in Kathmandu to have one of one's children living abroad for education. If you do not have one of your children abroad, you are nobody in Kathmandu. Before a decade ago or so, the Nepalese parents used to send their children for better education to Darjeeling, Massourie, Banglore, Nainital, Dehradun and many other places in India. In his book *Dimensions of Development* (1989), Dr. Harka Gurung observed that most of the prominent personalities then featuring in *Who Is Who* in Nepal had their higher education in India, mainly from the city of Venaras. Even today, these returnees form Venaras occupy very significant political and administrative positions in Nepal.

Today, many students are going to as far as the Philippines, Russia, United States of America, Australia and Canada to pursue higher studies and even for moderate schooling. Today I-20, the US student visa form, have become the status symbols to many young Nepalese students trying to go abroad in search of education. This exodus is exacting a handsome amount of foreign exchange from the nation and creating a lot of frustrations in the youngsters. Many try to score a job for living abroad. Some return only to be frustrated. On return from abroad, they often experience "culture shocks" in their own country since they find most things back home stagnant and not working up to their expectation.

The Nepalese people who have studied abroad are increasingly finding it difficult to get a job in Nepal. Except for some people who are able to exert political influences to get appointments in lucrative jobs, hardly any young people educated abroad are gaining access in the Nepalese job market, including that of the government bureaucracy. Yet another barrier to such an access is that people who have studied abroad have ambitious demands in the sense that they ask for much more prestigious job than those who have equivalent academic degrees from within the country. The frustrations thus generated have been affecting the Nepalese youth quite a lot. Unable to cope with frustrations, many of them settle abroad giving up the idea of coming back.

Some manage to return and get into the government jobs and business. When the return from abroad, they tend to propagate that everything from the West is better and back home is worse. The idealism inherited from "there" (*uta*) becomes so much obsessive that people tend to be rigid in making small-step changes and want to impose the things from the abroad in entirety, only to be frustrated by the "system" back home which does not respond easily to such changes. The slow response to the sweeping changes worldwide frustrates them perpetually.

These West-trained "smart species" bring back a superiority complex, and become grossly unable to match to the real world necessities thus resorting to academics, where they can contribute to flood with jargons and rhetoric in articulate English speeches and writings made here and there. They become part of what they claim to be the intellectuals. Being invited to seminars, speaking on any trivial subject over the television, writing flimsy arguments in the local tabloids, and trying to manipulate people in power to get some perky assignments becomes their regular activities. If unable to make into the power plugs, they criticize the politicians for not being able to recognize the talents and genius bestowed upon them by the education they have earned abroad.

Most Nepalese, like the contemporary emigrants, leave their home in search of material improvement, money, and professional and academic pursuit, which they cannot get in their own country. Despite the intention to return after a few years, with a little more money and some experience, new linkages like careers, spouses, children's schooling, and the like becomes quite indulging and they cannot come back. They settle down half-heatedly making compromises, only to realize later that they have disconnected the linkages to comeback. Despite the guilt of abandonment of their own culture and reminded by the color of the skin and second-class citizen treatment in many things, some perpetuate the fondness of the modern lifestyles and never get tired criticizing their own country. Mismanagement, inefficient politicians and bureaucrats, widespread poverty, degrading environment, lack of civic sense, and too many social obligations back home become things to blame in a manner "grapes are sour".

Though many have sincere concerns of the fate of the affairs back home, the dominant thought is that everything back home is worse. Things abroad are appreciated and back home deplored. Even the thought of return back home reminds harassment at customs, filthy public toilets, lack of hygienic food, crowding in the public transports etc. rather than the attachment to the cultural values and the "scent of the soil". The glory of the attachment to the ancient culture and tradition are compromised to the green cards and a few hundred dollars. The linkage to the past is gradually forgotten and abandoned by the successive generations, which are born and grown up abroad.

Unlike other communities abroad, for example Indians, who still continue to maintain cultural contacts and legacy, the Nepalese living abroad tend to be merged into the mainstreams, hardly recognizable as separate cultural identify. First, there are not that many Nepalese living in any one particular area to be a recognizable Nepalese community. Second, the Nepalese living abroad tend to quickly assimilate the local culture abandoning their cultural identity. In fact, there are some extreme cases, in which the Nepalese living abroad take pride to demonstrate how fast they have changed themselves and adapted to a new lifestyle.

Not all agree that people living abroad have diffused their culture and assimilated to the local culture. Bishnu Poudel, a Nepali American citizen living in the United States believes that Nepalese people in the U.S. live in their own microcosms and that they have retained not only Nepali culture, but they have kept alive the culture of the region or community they have come from. He thinks in a country like the United States, "you can continue to be proud of being any nationality and enjoy your cultural freedom better than anywhere else". Some may have reasons to disagree.

Despite the problems of adjustment with racism, alienation, second class citizenship, identity crisis, nostalgic feelings of the past, and sense of rejection, people continue to struggle for life abroad abandoning their traditions and cultural ethos. The conflict over languages spoken at home, the tension of having to mange so many things under intense pressure of time, the question of which passport to keep and which one to relinquish, the fear of discrimination and threat of expulsion continue to haunt them permanently.

On top of that, in all odds, one is likely to be counted and taken as an Indian. That "wheatish" color of the skin, those black hairs and typical moustaches and South Asian accent in the language will never leave room for a separate Nepalese identity abroad, no matter how long and how well one has lived abroad.

Until some decades earlier, the term Nepal was used to denote the Kathmandu valley. Many residents of the valley were even jokingly ridiculed for not being aware of the existence of the world outside it. Today, an increasingly large number of Nepalese have reached various parts of the world in search of job, better education and other economic opportunities. Nepalese have studied abroad, made into various jobs and professions, and many have settled there. The Nepalese worldview is not confined around the *Nepal*

Khaldo. Instead, the Nepalese are finding themselves in the "global village" where outside influence and contacts are increasingly becoming a very common activity. Their exposure is increasing and the Nepalese global village is expanding. At the same time, Nepalese culture is changing assimilating the elements of the global village.

Economically, the Nepalese settled abroad may have made their living easier. But culturally, they are finding themselves in an extremely awkward situation. Loss of the identity and absence of cultural affiliation has been haunting their lives. It has been difficult for the Nepalese people brought up abroad to reconcile their ideas, values and culture with that of their compatriots. Among the Nepalese people settling abroad, especially the generation born outside and grown up there, the loyalty to the cultural legacy has been weakening. Nepalese people living around the globe are worried about the erosion of their cultural ethos and values and finding it difficult in keeping their culture alive. In most cases, people living in an alien cultural environment are trying to preserve the eroding cultural practices and expressing their allegiance to the culture back home. They celebrate their festivals and rituals, as much as possible. Many have abandoned them just because it is not simply feasible. Many have tried to keep the traditions albeit in a distorted form. Nepalese living abroad want "national pride and sense of cultural unification", discerns a cultural activist.[15]

When Nepalese people settle abroad, their wish to get assimilated there confronts with the need for cultural identity. Unions are organized in social occasions and Nepalese festivals are celebrated collectively. In countries, where there is a sizeable presence, Nepalese organizations and associations are formed. Founded in 1960 in London, one of such organizations Yeti aims at promoting goodwill and cooperation among the Nepalese, preserving Nepali culture and tradition, and voicing Nepali aspirations. Yeti has always shown "solidarity and compassion" towards Nepal and the Nepalese people in time of needs, and is "fully aware of the tide of change, that is taking place around", claims its website. In futuristic note, it aims "to equip for the next millenium and to cater future generation", says its website..

---

[15] Chintamani Yogi, Principal of Hindu Vidaypeeth Nepal in *The Spotlight* (February 23-March –1, 2001)

The Association of Nepalis in the Americas (ANA), founded on July 1983, has grown steadily attracting a diverse membership that includes resident Nepalis in the Americas and many other scholars, scientists, and philanthropists who share an interest in the Nepali Culture and people. Among other things the purpose of the association is "to promote preservation of Nepali identity and culture in the Americas." They also aim at continuity and promotion of the cultural, religious, linguistic, historical, and educational heritage of Nepal.

There are also efforts to air Nepalese radio programs and television shows. Sagarmatha Television goes on air half an hour every Sunday in Washington DC. Everest Radio Times has started broadcasting Nepali program once in a week in London. A new Radio Dovan, airing Nepali program every Sunday was launched in Washington DC, in February 2001.

But the quest for cultural identity abroad gets diffused and people start to be assimilated in the place they live in the long run. If the people emigrated in their own generation still like to maintain the cultural links and try to establish Nepali identity, no later they become dismayed as their children prefer to abandon their cultural legacy and quickly adopt to the new cultural environment.

THE RECEIVING END OF CULTURE

Nepalese people, like the people of the rest of the world, are also being engulfed by the phenomenon of global change called "globalization". As a buzzword in the contemporary writings, in speeches and in even scholarly works, globalization has been used without much clarity in definitions. Economically, It has been described as the internationalization of the capital, technology and the human labor removing national boundaries as impediments to flow of capital, goods and services (Hochschild, 1998). In social perspective, it is a process, in which the social life is increasingly affected by international influences based on everything from political and trade ties to shared music, clothing and mass media. In the cultural sense, it means free movement of attitudes, values, norms, lifestyles, and culture across the cultural boundaries, which sometimes resemble national boundaries.

According to the World Culture Report (UNESCO, 2000), globalization offers both opportunities and threats to cultural diversity of various peoples around the world. "Those who are able to take an active part in global cultural exchange often experience culture as a process rather than a product, and their personal sense of cultural identity becomes a gateway of receptivity towards other cultures," writes UNESCO Director-General Koïchiro Matsuura in the preface to the report. "But for those who lack the means of exchange or of self-expression, or who experience globalization as an inexorable and alien process, there can be a retreat into a narrow sense of cultural identity that rejects diversity. When this negative reaction is exploited politically or exacerbated by other factors, culture swiftly becomes intertwined with conflict" (UNSECO, 2000).

Globalization may have helped in opening up new opportunities, particularly in the developing countries, in sharing of experiences and learning from one another's achievement and difficulties by cross-fertilization of ideas, cultural values and aspirations (Maskey, 1995). But it has also been blamed to have intensified poverty, unemployment, social disintegration, threats to human well being and environmental risks (Bhattachan, 1998). Some see globalization as an encroachment to national sovereignty of the less powerful by the more powerful countries (Bhaduri and Nayyar, quoted in Bhattachan, 1998). In fact, the globalization has made the culture of the smaller groups of people more vulnerable towards a more homogenous exposure. And there has started to be backlashes against the globalization of culture. The recent organized protests in Seattle (1999), Washington DC (2000), Prague (2000), and Davos (2001) against the WTO, IMF and the World Bank, were not only protests to the economic globalization, they were in part also the protests to resist what is seen as cultural imperialism.

Today, globalization has been criticized for its likeliness to induce the elements of *cultural imperialism* (transfer of money and resources from periphery to center and transfer of lifestyles from the center to the periphery), *domination* (culture imposed by transfer of money and resources), and *transculturation* (internationalization of culture e.g. pop music). The ever-increasing trend of globalization of culture presents a major challenge to traditions of social and cultural analyses developed and focused at the level of the nation state. In the cultural perspectives, globalization has been described as a worrisome phenomenon. Hochschild (1998) puts it like this:

This flow of culture across the borders would be something to celebrate, than (to) mourn, if ideas and images flowed both ways, instead of almost entirely from the US and Europe to the rest of the world. It would be something to celebrate if what crossed national boundaries most easily was the best of each culture and not the worst (Hochschild, 1998).

The annoying thing about globalization is that we are at the receiving end of the process. And this one-way process is given a rationale. Just as the 19th century colonialism was justified as the "white man's burden", the globalization is rationalized as "leveling the international playing field and allowing fair competition "(Hochschild, 1998). But the convulsions of the problems related to globalization and change have started to be discussed and considered for policy implications in many countries around the globe. Kennedy (1994) explains that:

> (T)here is clearly a broad and lively concern in many countries about where the world in general and one's own nation in particular are headed. Technological challenges, gender issues, migration, future of agriculture, environmental damage, the implication of globalization and the impact of all this upon policies, spending priorities, even values and culture are the subject of intense interest (Kennedy, 1994, p. 144).

Each of these effects is posing threats to the survival of discrete cultural processes such as that of Nepal. Though globalization has been perceived as inevitable, desirable and sacred, it is seen as advancing to engulf even the most remote people of the world in a suffocating embrace. Its cultural connotations are becoming costly to small countries with rich and diverse cultural heritage like Nepal.

It has been observed that the pace of globalization and its influence varies in different countries, societies and cultures. In Nepal, the all-pervasive influence of globalization has started to become subject of interest and academic inquiry. In introduction to an article in a book (Dahal, ed. 1998) on impact of globalization in Nepal, Bhattachan articulates like this:

> "The fear of globalization has caught up Nepalese policy makers, planners, political leaders, intellectuals and laymen alike. Some Nepalese 'moths' have developed fatal attraction to the 'bright light' of

globalization but other Nepalese 'butterflies' are repelled by the stinky smell of capitalist corpse of globalization" (Bhattachan, 1998).

In Nepal, this subtle phenomenon of globalization had a backdoor entry in the name of liberalization of the economic policies. Mesmerized by the psyche that freer is better, economic liberalization was adopted and accepted in Nepalese, especially in the government's policy towards economy, state as a sanctimonious slogan. As the economic liberalization and opening up the economy started, the tentacles of globalization gradually entered into the lives of the Nepalese people in the form of consumer culture. While the conventional phenomenon of modernization, and Westernization were already gripping the culture of the Nepalese people, the spread of globalization further intensified the process of homogenization of the Nepalese culture.

Today such a homogenization has been viewed as the foundation of what is called the "end of history" of mankind's ideological evolution towards the universalization of the Western liberal democracy. In defense to his thesis, Francis Fukuyama has said:

"Technology makes possible the limitless accumulation of wealth; and this satisfaction of an ever-expanding set of human desires. This process guarantees an increasing homogenization of all human societies, regardless of their historical rights or cultural inheritances. All countries undergoing economic modernization must increasingly resemble one another; unity on the basis of a centralized state; urbanize, replace traditional forms of societal organization like tribe, sect and family with economically rational based on function and efficiency and provide for the universal education of their citizens. Such societies have become increasingly linked with one another through global markets and the spread of a universal consumer culture" (Fukuyama, 1992, p. xiv-xv).

Fukuyama has said that liberal democracy demands liberal culture. The demand for education and labor mobility decreases the coherence of community- and the social connection becomes unstable as the "sense of identity provided by regionalism and localism diminishes": (Fukuyama, 1992, p. 325).

What Fukuyama could did not explain, though, was that the diverse ethnic and indigenous groups of people such as that of Nepal lack the economic and political clout and resources to support their struggle for a say in shaping their destiny and future even in the liberal democratic framework. In fact, the capitalist marketplace is not friendlier for disadvantaged groups of people and the liberal economic principles do not provide automatic support for traditional communities.

As cultural identities are becoming meaningful to most people world over, they are discerning their old identities and reinventing ethnicity. In defense of his thesis propounded in his famous book *Clash of Civilizations,* Huntington has explained, "there will be no universal civilization and Westernization of non-western cultures."

"In the post-Cold War world, the most important distinctions among the people are not ideological, political or economic. They are cultural. People and nations are attempting to answer a basic human question: Who are we? And they are answering that question in the traditional way, by reference to the things that mean the most to them: ancestry, religion, language, history, values, customs, institutions. People identify with cultural groups: tribes, ethnic groups, religious communities, nations, and, at the broadest level, civilizations" (Huntington, 1998).

Huntington has discerned that the global politics is being "reconfigured along cultural lines", as peoples and countries with similar cultures are coming together and as political boundaries are being redrawn to coincide with cultural ones (Huntington, 1996). He has argued that people ally based on "blood and belief, faith and family", and rally with those with similar ancestry, religion, language, values and institutions and distance themselves from those with different ones. That makes issues of identity and grouping together in terms of ethnicity, religions and civilizations highly relevant. Culture is said to be emerging as the third force determining the destiny and status of a nation in the world after market and military strength, the market having the possibility to replace the military strength. But people can respond to such changes positively, *if they so choose,* though the culture imposes barriers to such change, because an impending transformation threatens existing habits, ways of life, beliefs, and social prejudices (Kennedy, 1994).

While the Nepalese culture also continues to borrow, adopt and incorporate some elements of the outside civilizations, at the same time, the Nepalese culture has also rejected, resisted and abandoned some aspects of the global changes. The "cultural areas" with some common historical experiences and relatively distinctive patterns of social behavior have shown differing responses to globalization pressures beyond the local and national resistance. The cultural processes such as that of Nepal have responded to the phenomenon of globalization with much resistance at the conceptual level and much passion at the psychological level. Though Nepal represents unique case in this regard, Nepalese culture is in peril of being thrown into the global cultural junk box.

There is not enough literature on impact of globalization in Nepal. Bhattachan (1998) has identified some impacts of globalization in the Nepalese society and culture. He has blamed globalization for the development of "West-is-the-best-psyche", increasing rich-poor divide, growth of sandwiched institutions and cultures, rising individualism, brain and muscle drain, marginalization of women and children, exploitation of bio-diversity, loss of sovereignty, criminalization of politics, "cargo cult view" of development and growth of guerrilla warfare and insurgency. One may list several other influences and debate the exact nature of the influence in different communities and regions of the country. But there is no denying that globalization is bringing a lot of exposure and influence in the "Culture Shift" process in Nepal.

Identity at Stake

One of the most discernible trends of the "Culture Shift" in Nepal is the gradual loss and increasing search of the people's identity. With the evolution and expansion of the mass culture and the integration and assimilation of the discrete cultural phenomena into the mainstream society together with an increasing exposure to the modernization, Westernization and globalization, Nepalese people's identity is at stake. The crisis of identity is most evident among the various ethnic groups, who are minorities separately, but constitute a significant 35.6% of the total population. There is an upsurge of ethnicity and ethnic identity among the various linguistic, ethnic and regional minorities, especially after the democratic restoration in 1990. Identity crisis has been perceived in the growing awareness of ethnicity among the relatively larger and privileged ethnic groups of people like the Gurungs, the Limbus and the Newars. But the convulsions of change have also been experienced in the smaller ethnic groups of people, whose aspirations for identity has not yet been properly defined. Though culture has remained at the back seat of Nepal's politics, it has started to surface in the emerging politics of ethnicity and nationalism. And the problems of cultural disillusionment and threat to the survival of cultural diversity and invasion of alien culture have started to enter the mainstream politics as well. "It is every one's responsibility to save the country from cultural encroachment", said Madhav Kumar Nepal, General Secretary of Communist Party of Nepal (Unified Marxist Leninist), in his election speech[1].

EMERGING ETHNIC AWAKENING

The symptoms of the shaking identities among the people of Nepal are evident in the emerging politics of nationalism and ethnicity. In 1994, a National Convention of Ethnic Minorities and Nationalities

---

[1] *Gorkhapatra*, February 10, 1999

defined the term *Janjati* or "indigenous people", as people who were non-Hindu animist believers, who possessed a territory, and a language, who were deprived of tribal resources, who were denied of policy-making role, and who were egalitarian with no caste hierarchy. In 1996, a task force set up by the government added that the *Janajati* or the nationalities also have the characteristics such as a distinct collective identity, their own religion, tradition, culture and civilization, written or oral history, and "we-feeling". These definitions speak of the problems of identity, ethnicity and nationalism among the various ethnic minorities of Nepal.

Though the term *Janajati* is a new coinage, most of the ethnic minorities of Nepal had been grouped together as *Matwalis* or the alcohol-drinkers and the Hindu caste system had treated them as non-caste people. Included among them are the Magars, the Gurungs, the Thakalis, the Tamangs, the Rais, the Limbus, and the Tharus. In 1999, the Government recognized 61 nationalities, of which 21 from the Himalayas, 23 from the Hills, 7 from the Inner Terai and 10 from the Terai. *Janajati* has now become a palatable political vocabulary, which political organizations have translated as "nationalities" (Fisher, 1993). Their major concern is their unwillingness to be assimilated into the unified Nepalese culture, under the thesis of "cultural integration", which opposes the concept of a cultural pluralism.

But it is the absence of a decisive role in politics and government in modern Nepal, which has become a bone of contention in the rising trend of ethnicity and nationalism. In its introductory brochure, the National Committee for Development of Nationalities has blamed the "failure of the centrally formulated development programs, which was only a gesture of compassion, to evaluate of conventional knowledge, skills and life-style of the indigenous people" for undermining the upliftment of the socio-economic status of such nationalities.

In the political ferment since 1990, the ethnic minorities are demanding ethnic, religious and linguistic equality, opposing the caste system, Nepali language and "Hindu hegemony" (Gurung, 1997). Their demands include proportional representation and regional autonomy and economic demands include better access and fair share of the state's resources. Other ethnopolitical demands include call for recognition of all the "separate national identity" and 'right to self determination' of all Nepal's ethnic groups. Some like Khagendra Jung Gurung, leader of Nepal Rashtriya Janjati Party, have advocated that the country should be "divided into a dozen ethnic regions" (Gellner et al, 1997, p. 61).

Although the mainstream political discourse in Nepal, especially after 1990, regards "nationalism", as a politically correct and positive vocabulary (Gellner, 1997, p. 10), the politics of culture focussed on ethnic nationalism is not widely appreciated. It is seen as an effort to divide the ethnic and religious harmony that has existed in the country for centuries. Even the constitution, which is supposed to espouse the provisions of multi-ethnicity, pluralism and diversity, rejects the politics based on ethnicity and regionalism. Citing the constitutional clause, the Election Commission refused to recognize (1991) and register a few political parties, which had some ethnic flavor.[2]

The ethnic nationalism, a "politicized social consciousness centered upon ethnic identity" (Norbu, 1992), has started to appear as a political issue. The opposition against the domination of high caste Hindus, mainly Brahmans and Chhetris over the indigenous people and several ethnic groups of the "lower hierarchy" in the social structure has started to become visible. The ethnopolitical issues are gradually entering the mainstream political agenda.

During the Panchayat Period (1960-90), the freedom to express the ethnic demands and to raise voice against the discrimination existing in the society would be "denigrated as communal" (Baral, 1998). Even though, a coalition of various ethnic minorities emerged as *Magurali*, the acronym of four major Mongoloid ethnic group viz. Magar, Gurung, Rai and Limbu. This was later extended to include Sherpa and Tamang and the acronym was amended to *Sheta Magurali*. The voice of the ethnic minorities was a little bit articulated during the National Referendum (1979-80), when the Mongoloid ethnic groups "put up demands for declaring Nepal a secular state in addition to encouraging their language and culture" (Baral, 1998). However, such a group "could not be assertive after the return of the party-less Panchayat through the referendum" (Baral, 1998).

The restoration of democracy in 1990 unleashed the dormant energy of the ethnic minorities, as the new dispensation was more

---

[2] The Mongol National Organization and the Nepal Rashtriya Janjati Party, for example, were not registered "in accordance with the constitution" on the grounds that they were communal parties.

friendlier and open to the rights and problems of the ethnic minorities. Nepal was declared a multi-ethnic country and the constitution guaranteed the right of the people to promote their language, religion and culture. Among other things, the democratic framework allowed the formation of alliances and organizations among the ethnic minorities. Though the constitution has barred recognition of political parties on the ethnic, communal and regional basis, the liberal dispensation allowed the alliances and organizations to emerge without any hesitation.

The freer dispensation liberated the inertia of several political and social organizations of the ethnic groups in the banners like *Dalit*, *Janjati*, and *Mukti Morcha*. The growing awareness of identity of the ethnic groups and indigenous people has started to take a political shape. Many of these pressure groups and become active and influential in the political and cultural arena. *Nepal Bhasa Manka Khala* of Newars, *Langhali Association* of the Magars, *Tamu Dhim* of the Gurungs, *Thakali Sewa Kendriya Samiti* of Thakalis, and *Tharu Kalyan Karini Samiti* of Tharus have started to assert their political as well as cultural rights. Now, various ethnic groups of people have not only formed associations of their own, they have also started forming alliances. Several such associations have formed confederation like *Nepal Janajati Mahasangh*, which is a grand alliance of twenty-three ethnic associations. These ethnic organizations may have political objectives. But they are also motivated by the need to forge their collective cultural identity.

In the democratic constitution, Nepal was declared a "multi-ethnic, multi-linguistic" country. This was in itself a "dramatic departure from the government measures aimed at the homogenization of Nepalese society during the preceding decades" (Pfaff-Czarnecka, 1997). This declaration had found place in the constitution in a smooth manner, requiring no ethnic pressure or political agitation. That proves that the cultural diversity has been "a part of and is implicit in Nepal's historical legacy" (Sharma, 1997). But the ethnic minorities could not find the constitutional guarantees quite enough to dispel the discriminations and differences at the attitudinal level. Further, the constitutional provision of declaring Nepal a "Hindu kingdom", which appeared as a window-dressing, has raised some doubts among the ethnic minorities about the intention of the framers of the constitution.

In the post-democratic scenario, it is discerned that the minority groups are seeking to oppose *Bahunization* and *Sanskritization* of their culture, which has supposedly displaced "ethnic traditions by imposing Hindu culture and practices". Some people have started to boycott Hindu festivals like *Dashain*. Others burnt copies of a famous novel (*Sumnima*) by litterateur Bishweshwor Prasad Koirala alleging that the literary work was "racist" and "communal" against a particular (Kirant) community. Others, mainly activists of some of "nationalities and ethnic groups" have threatened to burn copies of Nepal's sacrosanct constitution to "mark their protest against its provision which declares Nepal a Hindu kingdom".[3]

Even the census taken after the democratic restoration was not seen as accommodating the interests of the ethnic minorities. It has been blamed that 1991 census has arbitrarily grouped some 86.5% people as Hindus, whereas many of the 35.6% ethnic minorities could be practicing their own religion, such as animism, Buddhism, shamanism etc. The census-taking methodology is supposedly manipulated by the state categorizing most ethnic minorities such as the Magars, the Rais, the Limbus and the Gurungs under Hindus. That is why the activists of some ethnic groups had demanded that there should be no categorization of people's caste, ethnicity, and religion in the national census of 2001. Such a categorization, according to them, would disrupt the traditional social framework. Some activists of the Kirants, on the other hand, wanted their religion to be categorized as "Kirant" in the census of 2001, instead of Hindus or "others", as was done in the previous census.

Now the ethnic issues have started to find place in the political discourse. A conscious "cultural nationalism" seems to be in the making. This politics of ethnicity is being espoused by the promoters of the new paradigms of development, which focuses on participation and upliftment of the marginalized population. It is also contributed by the entrepreneurs, who tend to support their own people committing more resources for their empowerment and employing people from their own ethnic groups. Even the donors, who prefer to have direct access, through the local NGOs, to the disadvantaged and neglected population are contributing to this process. The leaders of major political parties, who tend to use

---

[3] *The Spotlight*, February 12-18, 1999

ethnic minorities as vote-banks, are also fuelling the politicizing of the ethnic issues. It is being used as a strong political resource by the leaders of the ethnic groups in an effort to gain power in the existing political discourse serving as intermediaries.

Although the constitution has openly rejected any politics based on ethnicity, there are some political parties with hidden ethnopolitical agenda. Most of the Nepal's political parties have not espoused any specific cultural policies, except that they would promote the traditional culture and preserve the diversity and the heritage. Some, mainly the mainstream Communist Parties, have advocated *janapakshiya sanskriti* (people's culture), which is portrayed as egalitarian, liberal, reformative and changing culture preserving the old diversities and rights of the ethnic minorities.

But the state's response to the ethnopolitical demands is only lukewarm. In 1992, the government appointed a committee for formulating a "national cultural policy". But hardly anything was suggested, let alone implemented. In 1994, Radio Nepal, the state-owned broadcast, started to air news in twelve ethnic languages amidst controversy over inclusion of Sanskrit in the list. The criteria adopted were to include the language, which was spoken by more than 1% of the total population. It was announced in 1995 that a "Nationalities Academy" would be set up. But a charter remains to be legislated. In 1996, a report on the ethnic minorities was brought. A Nationalities Development Committee has been instituted in 1997. In 1999, the government approved a list of 61 *Janjatis*, which includes all major ethnic groups of Nepal, declared a national policy towards the ethnic minorities, which said the ethnic minorities should not be treated in the sense of charities and welfare, but they should be able to participate in the mainstream of the national development, utilizing their talents with high morale. But these declarations are not quite enough and the cultural problems of the ethnic minorities remain to be well articulated in the national political discourse.

To summarize, the emerging ethnopolitics is centered around the recognition of equality and freedom of all ethnic languages, demand for equal opportunities, especially in the employment in the government, and greater freedom to all customs, traditions and religions.

Cultural diversity had always been a cherished concept in Nepal. King Prithvi Narayan Shah had said that Nepal is a "garden of 4 *varna* and 36 *jats*, which is equivalent to four castes and 36 ethnic minorities respectively. That has been labeled as a concept of `Garden Nation', which assumes that the nation is made of people of different ethnicity, tribes and castes, just like a garden is a flower of different species. King Prithvi Narayan recruited people from all ethnic backgrounds in his army and civil service. Even after securing victory over the Kathmandu Valley, the King allowed the culture of the Newars to flourish and did not wish to enforce the Gorkhali culture to the people of the valley. The Ranas, who came to power in 1846, were kind of indifferent to the cultural diversity and they allowed the customs of the various ethnic groups. Though the Civil Code introduced in 1856 by Jung Bahadur Rana, the first Rana Prime Minister, legalized the Hindu caste system, it said that the ethnic groups would be allowed to observe their traditions and customs.

During the Panchayat era, "unity in diversity" among the various ethnic and caste structures was a nice slogan to conceal the agenda of the "integration policy", which sought to assimilate the cultural diversity of various ethnic groups into the mainstream culture of the majority Hindus. King Mahendra had initiated an ethnic integration outlawing the caste system legislating the New Civil Code in 1962 and introducing the resettlement of hill people in the Terai. The late King had divided the administrative zones in such a way that almost every zone included the Himalayas, the mountains and the Terai, hoping such a vertical division of the zones would allow the people scattered in the various zones to intermingle among themselves. The late king also started appointing people from different ethnic groups in high administrative positions to balance their representation. A few ethnic activists were absorbed in administrative and political appointments such as Zonal Commissioners. This was aimed at integrating different groups of people, who were isolated geographically in the entire history. That effort is now criticized as a state-imposed domination from the *Parbatiya* Khas and Brahmans over the ethnic minorities imposing Hinduism, Nepali language and uniform culture to all the ethnic minorities of Nepal.

During the Panchayat regime (1962-1990), which focused on the homogenization of the society through abolition of the traditional caste-framework with the provision of the New Civil Code, the politics of culture was suppressed because opposition to the Brahma-Chhetri dominated state would be construed as opposition to the Panchayat system. Some ethnic activists had formed ethnic alliance such as *Magurali*, naming their organization from the acronym of their ethnic groups (Magar, Gurung, Rai and Limbus). But the activists were very much underground and their organization was not overtly active. The state remained a guardian of the Hindu kingdom, conducting Sanskrit schools, donating to the Hindu temples, protecting the sacred cow and royal adherence to various elaborate Hindu rituals.

Today, it may not be so easy to let all the flowers bloom in this garden to all castes and tribes. The garden nation is now becoming a "burden nation". How to tend this garden? asks Sharma (1992). "The old Nepali axiom of encouraging varied flowers to bloom in the garden of the nation, common to its people, though an ideal proposition, is not easy to implement", says Jagadish Rana (1995. P. 117). The ethnic diversity is being portrayed as a liability to the country.

With the awakening of ethnopolitics, people have started to talk about the difficulties in ethnic harmony. Though politics of culture had never achieved high profile significance in Nepal, the division of *Jat* (caste) and *Jati* (ethnic minorities) seems to have occupied a significant place in the politics of culture. Unlike in other South Asian Countries, where ethnic tension has been evident to the surface, there is no significant separatist movement present in Nepal (Ahmed, 1996, p. 14-15). But some have started to say that ethnic tension could also surface in Nepal as it has been in the case outside the Nepalese territory, e.g. in Darjeeling and Bhutan.

But the ethnic problem is sometimes said to be overstated. As Dahal (1995) has discerned, "ethnic politics has no base as the grass-roots level and pose no immediate danger to political stability and national integration". And the "worst fears of some commentators about the politicization of culture may well prove to be unfounded" (Gellner, 1997, p. 28). This may be justified by the fact that the advocators of the ethnic politics do not enjoy much popular support. For example, *Rashtriya Janamukti Party*, which contested in the 1991 and 1994 election demanding quota representation for the members of various ethnic groups, not only failed to win a single seat in the House of Representatives, but got only around 1% of the popular vote in the both elections. Further, ethnicity has not entered the mainstream politics in Nepal, at least shown by the fact that ethnic populations have voted large parties, not individuals or parties which focus on ethnic demands. This phenomenon may be the direct result of high-caste domination in the major political parties of Nepal.

But the ethnopolitics is increasing on two major platforms. First, there is the freedom after restoration of democracy to put the otherwise unpopular demands that would be labeled as *Sampradayik* (communal) in the previous regime. Second, there is an urge to discover pride in one's own ethnic identity in the wake of loss of identity in globalizing and homogenizing world. But it is ironic that almost all ethnic politics spins around attack against the Hindu state, opposition to Sanskrit language, questioning the Brahman-Chhetri domination on the state affairs. But there is no backlash against the greater God, the Westernization and Globalization, which are also posing equally, if not more, suffocating embrace against the culture of the diverse ethnic groups of people.

ASPIRATIONS FOR IDENTITY

Convulsions of change and aspirations for identity have been studied in some micro studies focused at some communities and to some ethnic groups of people. There are various such studies available. Shigeru Iijima investigated *Hinduization* of a Himalayan tribe in Nepal (1963). Rosser (1966) studied "social mobility" in the Newar caste system. Hitchock (1966) assessed the changes and improvements of Magar status in his *Magars of Banyan Hill.* Caplan (1970) focused on the linkage between culture and politics in a community in relation to the land reform policy. Jones (1976) examined *Sanskritization* (spread of Hindu influence over ethnic non-Hindus) in Eastern Nepal. Iijima (1977) studied "ecology, economy and cultural change" among the Thakalis. Cox (1989) observed the political language of Hindu norms in Langtang Tibetans as a perspective on *Sanskritization.* Bista (1987) examined the process of *Nepalization* in Gandaki area. Dahal (1985) conducted an ethnographic study of social change among the *Athpahariya Rai* of Dhankuta, east Nepal. Gaenszle (1986) observed Hinduization among the *Mewahang Rai.* Continuity and socio-cultural change among the Thakalis have been studied (Messerschmidt, 1988). Gaenszle (in Toffin, 1990, pp 117-123) also explored the ways in which *Muddum* (oral tradition) of the *Mewahang Rai* in Central Arun Valley has been subject to change. Gurung (1994) has studied the process of identification and "*Sanskritization*" among the Duras of west Nepal and "modernization of economy" in a Chepang Village. Gellner (1986) compared the ancient and modern Newar identity in terms of the language, caste, religion and territory. Allen (1997) studied the social and economic change among Thulung Rai. McDonaugh (1997) investigated changes in the dynamics of land distribution and access and its social patterns among the Dangaura Tharus of the Dang Valley. There might be a few more examples. Though these studies do not reflect the nature of change in the culture of the people of Nepal as a whole, they signal that the ethnic minorities of Nepal are ready to respond to the demand for change and are asserting their cultural identities.

Aspirations and search of identity is evident in almost all communities. Even the Newars, relatively better off people in terms of their access to resources and powers of the state, the identity crisis is being expressed in their alliance with the *Janjatis*. *Nepal Bhasha Manka Khala*, a famous Newar linguistic and political organization, is now a member of *Nepal Janajati Mahasangh*, a federation of ethnic minorities in Nepal. Despite the fact that Newars continue to enjoy economic, political and administrative power (they are 5% in population and 35% in government jobs), Newars have aligned themselves as *Janjati*, claiming to be among those exploited by the Hindu majority (Sharma, 1997). There was a disillusionment as to whether Newars should be included in the list of *janjatis* (indigenous people), especially in the list of backward ones, because they constitute one of the most financially forward people in the country.[4] This confusion was further aggravated when the Government, at the recommendation of a committee formed to look after the affairs of the ethnic minorities, included the Newars in the list of 61 various ethnic groups of people, only to drop them from the list a year after, in 2000.

Among the Newars, the people with long-standing traditions and culture and a definite role in the making of the nation, art and craft of the country, the pride in ethnicity was compromised with the Gorkhali conquest of the Kathmandu Valley in 1768. Though the Kings of modern Nepal allowed the Newar cultural traditions to

---

[4] NESAC (1998), *Nepal: Human Development Report*, Nepal South Asia Center, Kathmandu

continue and even flourish, the Newars started to feel alienated. This was aggravated by the domination of the Parbatiya Brahman and Chettrirs, who subsequently migrated to the Kathmandu Valley, in the affairs of the state. Some Newars did gain prominence in the business sector and some even advanced to higher positions in the royal court and in the government bureaucracy. But with the increasing influx of migrant population into the Kathmandu Valley, the Newars started to feel a threat to their identity. They felt their language and culture was being encroached upon. The Newar resentment against this started with the demands for the recognition of *Nepal Bhasa* (Newari language) by the state and recognition of the *Nepal Sambat,* the Newar calendar era.[5] They also started voicing their grievance the domination of people other than Newars in Nepal's politics and bureaucracy. Today, most Newars in Kathmandu valley, even in Newar-only villages have become bilingual (Gellner, 1997, p. 155). Newars today feel that their social and cultural fabric of life is slowly being destroyed. They feel displaced, alienated in their own home due to the rush of immigrants in Kathmandu. That is not only "robbing Newars of their jobs, open space and unpolluted civic life", it is also destroying their cultures treating them as "dwindling specimen of aborigines deserving to be confined to the slum areas of Ason and the vegetable markets of Kathmandu" (Malla, 1992).

But the Newars were relatively late to react to the ethno-political activism compared to other indigenous people. During the Panchayat era, Newars expressed their demands for the recognition of their Newar language and Nepal Sambat, the Newar calendar era, through the linguistic organizations such as *Nepal Bhasha Manka Khala*. One of its prominent articulators, Padma Ratna Tuladhar would later become an influential politician, who would be elected to Nepal's parliament at least three times. Most Newars actively participated in the anti-establishment campaign, which culminated into the participation of Newar youths in the *Jana Andolan* (1990) to restore democracy in Nepal. In the democratic dispensation, the

---

[5] Nepal Sambat got an indirect recognition in 1999 as the government declared its founder Sankhadhar Sakh as one of the Rashtriya Bibhuti (national heroes). Launched on October 20, 879 AD, Nepal Sambat is said to have been in official use until 1903, when then Prime Minister Chandra Shamsher Rana replaced it with the Bikram Sambat, which is in universal use in Nepal, these days.

Newars continue to express opposition to the state and the establishment by supporting the communists (Gellner, 1997), which is evident by the election to the House of Representatives in the Kathmandu Valley in 1991, 1994 and 1999.

Identity crisis is more evident among the Newars outside Kathmandu Valley. As Newars dispersed from the Kathmandu Valley and started to settle in hill bazaars and district headquarters, in search of opportunities for business, their identity became diffused. As the Newar Diaspora continued, they assimilated in the *parbatiya* language and culture. Newars in many district headquarters have retained hardly any noticeable Newar culture. They hardly speak Newari speak as they are fluent in Nepali language and they observe the mainstream Hindu culture of the area.

Time will show, where Newars will stand in their search of identity. But their struggle for forging a new identity in the new democratic dispensation does not go unnoticed.

The story of the Gurung identity is no less different. Macfarlane (1997) identified the "cultural pressures" in the Gurungs, comparing the difference in the Gurung culture in 1968 and 1992. In 1968, most Gurungs were living in a village. In 1992, they were living in Nepali towns. Then, agriculture or army was the main occupation. "Various paid jobs" had become common in 1992. Then, most Gurungs were seen wearing Gurung clothes. In 1992, they wore "Nepali" clothes. In 1992, the Gurungs identified themselves as Nepali, whereas they would identify themselves as the "Gurungs" in 1968. Their popular institution called Rodi had given way to "leisure groups". The "cultural stress" among Gurungs is said to be stemming from "growing threat from and dominance by Hinduism and Buddhism, which threaten to the old unwritten shamanic religion of the Gurungs". Further, there is the loss of the long-standing political autonomy of the Gurungs to "rapid political centralization and mobilization" (Macfarlane, 1997). This speaks of the increasing stake in the Gurung identity, especially in the villages.

(T)he spread of Nepali medium teaching, the effects of the radio, the growing dominance of the town have all eroded the language and culture. The cultural pressures which coincide with the forceful introduction of consumer capitalism, ostentatious tourism, foreign aid projects, television and radio, are apparent in a variety of ways. There is a loss of confidence in the value of Gurung traditions and culture, a revolution of rising expectations, a growing frustration and disillusionment (Macfarlane, 1997. p. 187).

Until 1970s, on return from the military service as Gurkha, the Gurungs used to retire in the villages. Many of them would get elected as the representatives of village level committees, and some to the higher levels. In the decades of eighties, the Gurungs, mainly the ex-Gurkhas, started to prefer to live in urban areas like Kathmandu, Pokhara, Dharan or even in Indian cities. In the recent years, they shifted towards the search of work in security agencies abroad in countries like Singapore, Malaysia, and Canada. Today, many Gurungs are leaving their villages for good. And the cultural connections have become diffused and somewhat de-linked from the past traditions, institutions and beliefs. With this trauma of loss, alienation and diffusion of the culture, the Gurungs, who constitute 2.4% of the total population, are evidently in search of their identity. New cultural groups are being formed. Associations have emerged. Works of scholarly contribution have been written on Gurung history and tradition. They have revived *Loshar*, a traditional festival (Gurung, 1997). The identity has taken shape in the names as they have started to prefer to call themselves *"Tamu"* and name their ethnic organization as *Tamu Dhin*, which has been playing a key role in the revival of the Gurung identity.

In eastern Nepal, the Limbus, people known for their rich cultural and linguistic heritage, are also in search of their cultural, religious and linguistic identity. They are reconstructing their language, history and culture. Some Limbu activists and researchers have ventured to compile the famous *Mundhum*, which is also known as the Veda of the Karants, as much of it remains as oral traditions practiced by the Phedangbas, the Limbu priests. Other are advocating to boycott the Hindu festivals like Dashain in the belief that the Hindu culture was imposed upon the Limbus in the process of Sanskritization and Brahmanization of several indigenous people. The Limbu resentment against the domination of the Khas and Brahmans started with the gradual encroachment of the Limbuan area and with the abolishment of their famous *Kipat* system of rights to the land. Today, the Limbus oppose the abolition of the *kipat* labeling that as "internal colonization" by the migrant population in the ethnic areas.

Apart from opposing the *Sanskritization* and *Hinduization* of their culture, some Limbus have also started to demand a separate homeland. *Limbuan Mukti Morcha* is one such organization committed to the Limbu cause. In search their identity, the Limbus played important role in the formation of the alliance between various ethnic minorities. The first ever alliance of the ethnic minorities in the form of Magurali included the Limbus along with the Magars, Gurungs and the Rais. Today, the Limbus have joined the federation of *Janjati* demanding greater freedom and concessions to the ethnic minorities. The Limbu people, who constitute 1.6% of the total population of Nepal, are in the forefront of the movement among the people seeking their own identity, preserving their own culture and religion.

Among the Magars, yet another ethnic group of the hilly areas, the search of identity is being expressed in their desire to assert their own traditional customs. Among other things, the Magars are seeking to employ their own priests, the "Bhusals", instead of the Brahmans to conduct their rituals. The Magars, who were pushed to observe Hinduism, especially after the unification of Nepal and who were Sanskritized as evident by their adoption of Chhetri such names such as Thapa and Basnet, are also seeking to establish their own Shamanic and animist religions. In the recent census (2001), the Magars have sought to assert their identity putting "Magar" as a separate category in their religion, instead of categorizing themselves as Hindus, as in the earlier census. Like other Janjatis, the Magaras have also established their own "Langhali" society, which aims at the upliftment of the Magar culture and society, and have joined the coalition of the ethnic minorities, first in the Magurali and now in the federation of the ethnic minorities.

The predominant Rai people in the Khumbuan ares of east Nepal are "trying to dig into the history and traditions and establish a distinct Rai culture" (Rana, J. S. in Rana & Dhungel, 1998, p. 42). Some Rai scholars are compiling their dictionaries and vocabularies. The Thakalis, who have responded to the changing times removing practices such as marriages by capture, abandoning Brahman priests and the Brahman rituals, are seeking to reorient their identities. Following the increase on tourism since 1970s in Thak Khola area of Mustang, the Thakalis, who used to be traditionally dependent upon the salt-trade and agriculture, have started to focus on services catering to the tourists opening hotels, and selling of tourist items.

They are also trying to seek their identity in their ability to provide superior quality services to the tourists and compete in their businesses.

The search of identity among the Tharus, the indigenous inhabitants of the Terai and some river valleys, is also becoming pronounced. In Chitwan valley, it has been observed that the lives and cultures of the Tharus has been enormously altered by the influx of migrants from all over the kingdom. The migrants, especially the hill people "grabbed large tracts of Tharu land" and imposed several values on them. The Tharus, who had started to use the rituals of the hill people employing Brahmin priests for performing Hindu rituals, have also started to look back on their values and customs. For example, the statute of *Tharu Welfare Committee* aims at looking after the welfare of the natives, eradicating illiteracy, doing away with the useless and destructive traditions and mistakes ingrained in the traditional way of life and improving the economic situation (Boker in Toffin, 1990, p. 241).

The Tharu culture and traditions in Dang and Deukhuri valley is also at jeopardy. The Tharu community there is greatly concerned at the loss of their traditions and culture. Their traditional dances, festivals and music is getting less and less common. For example, *Badka Nach*, one of the most famous Tharu dances, was last played in Dang some twenty-five years ago[6]. Similarly, traditional Tharu dances like *Sakhiya*, *Abadha* and *Goriya* are not being performed in Dang district. *Jhumara*, *Chhokara* and *Mohatiya* dances are getting less common.

Among the Tharus of Dang and Deukhuri Valleys, the search of identity has been expressed by their desire to struggle against the local landlords. The land reforms in the 1960s and the malaria control in the 1970s had a lot of influence in the Tharu community in Dang valley. These events not only resulted into the increasing *pahari* (hill men) immigration to Dang valley, it exerted pressure on the Tharu community who were pushed further west in Kailali and Kanchanpur areas. The Pahari *jamindars* (hill landlords) gradually took control of a lot of the Tharu land and intruded the Tharu culture. In the eighties and nineties, the Tharus in Dang Valley witnessed "Nepalization" with the Nepali language, metropolitan patterns of dress, and popular

---

[6] *Gorkhapatra*, Ashwin 13, 2053 BS (1996)

media-based culture "all gaining ground at the expense of Tharu traditions" (McDonaugh, 1997. p. 297).

Today, the Tharus have lent a broad-based recognition and support to a local Non-government organization called Backwards Society Education (BASE). As Nepal's largest local NGO, the BASE and its promoter Dilli Bahadur Chaudhari have helped arouse the awareness of the Tharus. Through its work on non-formal education, the BASE has also been supporting the disadvantaged Tharu farmers and landless Tharu households and the organization of Tharu cultural communities to preserve their culture. This has also generated wider implication in the politics of the culture in the area.

Among the indicators of the struggle for identity among the Tharus is their opposition to *kamaiya pratha*, the bonded labor system. Thanks to their sustained movement supported by the networks of the non-government organizations, the Kamaiyas or the bonded-laborers have now been freed. Though the Tharu identity and ethnicity has been described as a "vague, slippery, and rapidly changing notion" and there is "not enough evidence to substantiate generalization" (McDonaugh, 1997), the Tharu ethnicity and identity is an emerging reality. The Thaurs, who constitute 6.5% of the total population of Nepal, are in the increasing search of reviving their culture and identity.

The *Madhesiyas*, as the people living in the Terai are generically known, are also struggling for their identity and role in the state affairs. Though most Madhesiyas or the people of Terai are not grouped under the "ethnic minorities" and "nationalities", their aspiration and struggle for identity resembles to that of the ethnic minorities. Conventionally, the Madhesiyas identity used to seen in their darkish skin, their habits of chewing beetle leaves, their Terai dialect closer to Hindi, their *dhoti* or a *Khadi* cloth, and a multi-purpose towel *Gamchha* carried around on all occasions. Today, all these denigrate a *Madhesiya* person. The search of identity among the Madhesiyas today revolve around the struggle to preserve their languages, traditional practices and culture, and the wider questions of citizenship, and representation to the government bureaucracy, and political framework. They also seek the state's increased involvement and commitment to protect the integrity and dignity of the Terai people. This has been reflected in their new political aspirations in the democratic framework in various ways.

During the Panchayat era, the concept of Nepali nationalism, which was promoted for the sake of "national integration", had become a strange concept to people of the Terai. Many of them had not seen its symbols such as the national bird *Danphe*, a Himalayan pheasant, the national flower rhododendron, a hill plant. Many did not know how to speak Nepali language. Instead, they spoke a local dialect, which had closer affinity to Hindi than to Nepali. But the Terai people could not voice their concerns, as it could be construed as anti-national and anti-Panchayat activity.

Today, the Madhesiya identity is taking the shape of a "Terai Nationalism". Though politics based on *Madhesiya* identity is not gaining popular support,[7] their grievance is being heard more progressively and more prominently. The *Madhesiya* identity is very much in ferment and taking a political shape. Nepal Sadbhavana Party, the major advocate of the *Madhesiya* cause, continues to hold demonstrations and stage hunger strikes demanding the liberal citizenship laws, wider representation in bureaucracy, and equal treatment to the *Madhesiya* population. It speaks of the Terai people's grievances and their lack of equal say and opportunity in the affairs of the state. The under-representation of Terai population in the Nepalese army and in the civil service is cited to prove such discrimination. These issues are raised to increase political aspiration and support. The next government, said the slogan of Nepal Sadbhabhana Party in their election pledge (1999) should be a "government of the exploited, the ethnic minorities, and the *Madhesiya*s".[8] Though this was not to be, the political aspirations are still there. The Terai people are in search of a new identity, which is different from the hill culture, which they hardly wish to conform to.

The case of search for identity among the people of the Terai has been best demonstrated in the case of the Maithali-speaking populations of the Central and eastern Nepal Terai. Their Mithila Culture, one of the prominent in the Nepal Terai because of its long history of over 5,000 years, also faces the threat to its identity. The

---

[7] It is evident by the fact that their representation in the parliament is far lower than the Madhesiya population and that in fact Nepal Sadbhabana Party, an advocate of Madhesiya cause, has been reduced to 5 seats in 1999 from 9 in 1991 in the House of Representatives. That support was reduced to 3 seats in the 1994.

[8] *The Rising Nepal*, February 7, 1999

search of identity in the Maithali-speaking people is becoming painful as they were alienated by the symbolic construction of Nepali nationhood (Gellner, et. at. 1997, p. 240). Like the other Terai people, Maithali-speaking people felt as "second-class citizens in their own country" (Gaige, 1975). There were several intrusions, particularly from the Nepali state, in the Maithali culture in Janakpur area. In Janakpur, the centre of Maithali culture, the pagoda style *Bibah Mandap* built during the Panchayat period, is not only alien to the surroundings and nearby Janaki temple because of its odd design, it also stands to the "humiliation" of Maithali cultural identity because it demands that Maithali culture fit into the hill culture forms (Burkert, 1997). Another uninvited intrusion in the Maithali culture is the statue of Nepali poet Bhanu Bhakta Acharya at a central chowk of Janakpur city, which is the center of Maithali civilization and new name of the old Mithila, the capital of Videha. The statue stands as symbol of cultural domination ignoring the importance of Maithali literature and its famous poet Vidyapati.[9] This provokes resentment. An all party meet has decided to erect Vidyapati's statue in place of Bhanu Bhakta's.

With the revival of Maithali identity and increase of the political power after the advent of democracy in 1990, there may not be another pagoda, or a statue of a hill poet in the area. The Maithali-speaking people have the "conviction" that in the new democratic framework, after 1990s, their cultural eminence can be regained and their access to power reclaimed (Burkert, 1997). But their aspirations for a distinctive place in the cultural scenario of the country will not be met easily.

Today, the revival of cultural identity of Maithali people has also culminated into a master plan for the development of religious sites and preservation their cultural heritage as the Greater Janakpur Development Project. Among other things, the project plans to make a 93-km *Parikrama* ring-road in the route of the religious sites

---

[9] Maithali poet Vidyapati is known for his 14th century writings at the royal court of Mithila. Most of his writings, including *Likhanawali, Purush Parikhsa, Dan Bakyabali, Goraksha Bijaya, Bhu-Parikrama* etc. are in Sanskrit. His *Padawali* the sole book in the Maithali language. But there are more than three hundred popular Maithali songs to his credit. Some of Vidyapati's manuscripts are preserved in the National Museum. His exact date of his birth has not been ascertained.

in the area. Nepali Congress youth leader and one-time Minister Bimalendra Nidhi, son of late Congress leader Mahendra Narayan Nidhi, is trying to promote a Maharshi Janak University in Janakpurdham, probably in view of the promoting the Maithali heritage. The Janakpur Municipal Corporation had even started to use Maithali as an additional official language apart from Nepali, until the decision was stayed by the Supreme Court in 1999.

But the diffused Maithali identity will not just be fulfilled by a news cast on the state radio once a day in Maithali language, a few primary schools which teach Maithali language, and by a Vidyapati statue in Janakpur town crossing. There are other subtle issues as well.

Among the concerns in the decay of the Mithila culture is the loss of their art and craft. Cultural artifacts are either being distorted or abandoned. Maithali dances and songs have been either abandoned or distorted. Silver ornaments, which used to be the conspicuous Maithali cultural artifacts, are also disappearing. Among the most famous cultural objects of the area is their Mithila art, which is also facing the threat of extinction. Mithila art, which is famous for the traditional paintings of elephants, peacocks and other village deities and objects, has become almost obsolete. Thanks to some foreign promoters, the art produced by Maithali women have reached the outside world as Mithila art. The Maithali culture dating from the Ramayana period has been changing its face due to invasion of the forces of modernization and lack of preservation.

The search and aspirations for identity is also reflected in the growing social organizations of the people of the Terai. The Nepal Vainshya Welfare Association with central office in Janakpur seeks to connect the business people in all Terai districts. *Chitragupta Sewa Samiti*, the organization of Kayasthas is another such organization in the Terai. Their cultural aspiration may be seen in the national politics, or at least at the politics of the culture in the country in the time to come.

Among other minority ethnic groups scattered throughout the country, there are convulsions of change. But the aspirations for identity have not been very well articulated. Among the Chepangs, one of the most let-behind minority ethnic groups (population about 40,000), who live mostly in the hilly Mahabharata mountain ranges of central Nepal, the contact with outsiders, mostly in the forms of various development programs such as the Praja Development Program initiated by government in 1976, have posed cultural homogenization, imposed inferiority, economic vulnerability, and diffused the tribal autonomy. The outside interventions in the name of development projects aimed at uplifting them have not been highly successful in removing the hardships in the lives of the Chepangs. These programs, in fact, have imposed a syndrome of dependency among them. It has been argued that the aspirations for better living standards among the Chepangs cannot be compromised in the name of the preservation of their culture and traditions. In any case, they are already loosing their language and culture and are in transitional period losing their own community structure unable to cope fully with the changing realities

The Duras, an indigenous tribe of vanishing people inhabiting around Dura Danda of Lamjung District in central Nepal, want to save their culture and identity in the wake of increasing consumerism and demonstration effect. Observing a few Hindu festivals including *Chaitra Dashain* and adopting the social customs and rituals and the values and norms of the Brahmins, the Dura culture was already vulnerable to the process of *Sanskritization*. Fruther, they were also being attracted to the culture of the Gurungs in order to be considered for the recruitment in the British and Indian armies (Gurung, *ibid*). Now, they are realizing the external threats in their culture, the Duras are trying to preserve their cultural identity. They want to save their Dura language, which has a written script and which used to be spoken until a few generations ago, but is seldom spoken these days as most Duras have been naturalized with the Nepali language or the language of the area. They want to preserve their traditional costume of Dura (*Bhoto, Kachhad, Jarkot*) and their traditional ornaments, which are becoming rare as the Dura youths are being increasingly allured to the modern clothing. Their rich dance tradition is also on the decline. Among other things, lack of preservation and poor research and study are the major cause of the decline of the indigenous Dura culture as was discussed by sociologists in a seminar organized by the Royal Nepalese Academy in March 1997.

Yet another group of people, who face a similar identity crisis is the Majhis. In a meeting held in Kathmandu, the Majhis expressed that their traditional occupation has been invaded and threatened by the recent development activities.[10] They not only voiced their concerns they also constituted as Central Committee to look after their own welfare. The Majhis, who used to make living by fishing and boating along the river banks of Sunkoshi, Tamakoshi, Tamor and Saptakoshi in the eastern hilly region of Nepal, have been exposed to construction of bridges and development of new fishing techniques in their areas. Though their population hardly exceeds 50,000 (1991 Census), they have their own language and culture, which is being threatened by outside influences. Many Majhis have been displaced from their traditional habitats and some have resorted to take jobs in the carpet industry in Kathmandu valley, as their traditional occupation of fishing and boating is in jeopardy. Like Majhis, the Danuwars living in the erstwhile malaria-infested jungles of the Terai and Inner Terai river valleys are also exposed to other cultures and are in need of preserving their identity. Though the Tharus, Danuwars and Majhi had retained their distinctiveness as the relatively mobile Brahmans and Chhetris would not interfere with them for the fear of malaria, they have been exposed to outside influences after the eradication of the disease in the 1906s.

There are people like *Gaines* (traditional folk singers), *Rajis* and Honey-Hunters, whose traditional lifestyles are no longer viable during the socio-economic changes. *Surel,* a minority tribe living in and around Dolkha district, are in the verge of extinction[11] and are abandoning their own culture. Their number has been reduced to mere 500-600. Increasingly exposed to dynamism and modernism, the Surels are mixing with other tribes and are migrating to other areas. Similar concerns could be expressed regarding the Rautes, Kusunda, Hayu and several other ethnic minorities of Nepal.

It has become evident that the aspirations for identity and preservation of their traditional culture among Nepal's 61 nationalities or ethnic groups varies to a great extent. Some are too small in number. For example, the National Committee for the Development of Nationalities says there are only 400 Bankariyas, 900 Rautes, and 700 Kisans. Others like the Thintan, the Topkegola and the Marphali are confined to only one village each and are named after that. In some cases, their population may be relatively

---

[10] *Kantipur,* Chaitra 8, 2053 BS (1997)

[11] *Gorkhapatra,* September 24, 1996

sizeable, such as in the case of the Thani (30,000) and the Chhantyal (20,000). But their aspiration for identity is not well pronounced. Even the Tamangs, Nepal's largest ethnic group comprising 7.2% of the total population, are relatively less interested in the rise of ethnicity and nationalism. But they not only dislike to be identified with their quintessential soberness and simplicity, with their not-very fluent Nepali, and with their bodily uncleanliness, they have been struggling to create a new space for them in the cultural mosaic of the country. In the urban areas such as Kathmandu, where they have been coming for employment either pushing a cart or driving a three-wheeler tempo, or working as a porter or household help, they prefer to be identified with their mountain culture and least like to be diffused in the cities.

The aspirations of identity, role and status is not limited to the ethnic minorities or "nationalities", as they have been called. Even Hindu Dalits, the oppressed and bottom-end people who have not been identified with the ethnic minorities, have started to voice the domination against them. The Dalits, who count for more than five million, of which most are illiterate[12] and poor, voice against the neglect and rejection of the state in many ways. In its introductory brochure, the Nepal National Depressed Welfare Organization, a coalition of the Dalits, says:

> The backwarded Dalit community has been kept far behind the normal line politically, socially, economically and religiously. Social status of this community has gained the respect less than of an animal by culture. We feel extremely sorry to say the truth that the system of untouchability has made Dalits inhuman in every respect. The so-called upper caste people have no concerns about the problems of Dalits. In fact, this situation of Dalit has become a privilege for them. There is no seat for Dalits in the House of Representatives, which has 205 seats and the Upper House has 2 nominated seats from Dalits at present. None of Dalits is represented in the local political authorities in villages and district level. No Dalits has been placed, by political appointment, in bureaucracy and administrative authorities".

Today, the Dalits are demanding a greater representation and recognition in the state affairs. They want to remove the attitudinal

---

[12] Nepal Human Development Report (1999) says the adult literacy rate among the Dalits is 16%, as against the national average of 48%.

barriers to untouchability and discriminations against them. They are seeking new identities. Many of the Dalits have even renamed themselves or obscured their surnames in order to remove the traditional biases associated with their traditional names. They are in the process of constructing their new identity in the pluralistic and democratic framework, which is supposed to remove all the barriers for their entry into the mainstream culture. Unfortunately, despite all the spread of mass culture and homogenization of the minority groups, the process of change among the Dalits has been relatively slow, mainly because of their poor socio-economic status and relatively weaker access to education.

THE MELTING POTS

In the ferment of the changes taking places in various places in Nepal, mainly the interaction between different communities and ethnic groups, is the creation of "melting pots" of culture. As the geographical, spatial and cultural barriers to interaction were removed allowing people to move in all directions, several such new melting pots were created. Chitwan, also referred to as the "seventy-sixth district" because of the presence here of a large number of settlers from all over the kingdom, has been one such "melting pot of change". The melting pot process is more evident in Chitwan than in other places because of a fast demographic transition there as people from all over the country have settled into the valley. This process was intensified after the eradication of malaria and introduction of Rapti Valley development plan. Such melting pot processes are also evident in the Kathmandu Valley and the entire belt of the Terai in the central and eastern Nepal.

Two major phenomena that have been contributing to the creation of the so-called "melting pots" are urbanization and the eradication of malaria. Both had huge impact in the dispersion of populations. As the valleys formerly deserted were free of the fears of the disease and as more land was available due to land reforms and clearing of the forests, there was new rush for resettlement. Migrants from the hilly region started to pour in the inner Terai valleys changing the ethnic pattern there. This not only changed the ethnic pattern in the inner Terai valleys, they also cleared forests for agriculture. In the Terai, the real momentum to such intermixing was created by the policy of resettlement of the hill people in the Terai.

The melting pot process was augmented by the most discernible shift in the demographic characteristics, mainly a boom in the population and a changing pattern of ethnic mosaic. Throughout the history, diversity of ethnic patterns, linguistic groups and religious sects was diversity was maintained due to the presence of several small principalities and kingdoms in various pockets of the country. For example, there were three kingdoms in Kathmandu Valley , 22 in Karnali Basin, 24 Gandaki Basin, and a few more in the Eastern Nepal until the unification of Nepal in 1768. The rugged terrain, the particular habitat preferences of certain communities and the policy of isolation adopted by the state for several centuries had helped maintain discrete cultural diversity among different communities and regions. But increasing patterns of mobility, increased inter-ethnic contacts with better roads, communication, air services and economic realities have reshaped the ethnic diversity, especially in the urban areas. Much of that is due to economic and political compulsions and policies adopted by the state. But a lot of attitudinal shift is also contributing to the transformation. And the changing habitat psychology has in turn brought more shifts in the culture of the people of Nepal. Although there is a marked cultural attachment to some areas, people are migrating to other areas due to better economic opportunities and due to the availability of the development infrastructure.

The history of Nepal proves that people of the mountainous region, especially Brahmans and Chhetris were highly mobile, and the eastward trek of the Khas people is well known. The Brahmans and the Khas were supposed to have entered Nepal from western region. The Khas lived in Jumla area of Karnali basin and expanded to all over the kingdom. Today, a large number of people from the mountains are migrating to the Terai and many other are concentrating in the urban areas like Kathmandu. Historically, Nepalese people were highly mobile. About a quarter of the total population of Nepal is continuously moving, especially during the winter season (Hagen, 1961; Gurung, 1968). "The poor agricultural land, low productivity, lack of alternative employment other than agricultural, lack of market, and high population pressure on the land have forced people to make seasonal trips to other parts of Nepal, particularly to the towns near the southern border" (Karan & Ishi, 1996). But many such migrants got attracted to the southern plains and have started to settle there permanently.

The changing mosaic is seen in the increasing percentage of the Terai population. The official census data shows Terai is swelling and in terms of population. In 1942, only one out of three people in Nepal lived in Terai. In 1991, nearly half (47%) lived in the southern plains of the country. The fattening of Terai population has been attributed several reasons. Anthropologists distinguish them as "push" factors, which displaces the people from the hills, and the "pull" factors, which attracts them to the Terai. The push factors include small holdings, insufficient food, lack of transport and communication facilities, lack of employment, poor health care and education facilities, indebtedness, natural calamities, and social stigma, whereas the pull factors include the resettlement program, eradication of malaria, better health, education, transport and communication facilities, opportunity for employment, attractions of friends and relatives, abundance of the productive areas, fertility of the soil and the easier way of life. (Regmi, 1999, p. 46). In the rural hilly region, as the land gets divided there is not enough food to keep them engaged and opportunities become inadequate. Thus, the desire to go out of the village becomes relevant. Some attribute the population growth in the Terai to the immigration from across the southern border, which is open and porous. Eradication of malaria, government policy of resettlement and rehabilitation of "land-less settlers", and opening of north-south road linkages and zoning of the Terai into vertical hill-Terai administrative regions are also major causes in the shift. Migration from the hills to Terai had started with the eradication of malaria and with the state-sponsored resettlement[13] plans during the Panchayat period. But it was accelerated by growing economic hardships and lack of opportunities arising out of population pressure in the hills (Gurung, 1998). This process was augmented after the construction of road and communication networks, which was developed more easily in the Terai than in the hills. After all, most people in the hills always

---

[13] The resettlement of landless people in the areas created after clearing the Terai jungles was a new ferment in the Terai. That would create a distinctive category of landless settles, called locally as *Sukumbasi*. They have not only put a pressure on the local environment, they are also a cultural drag in the local area.

believed that the Terai, so-called granary of Nepal, was a land of opportunity and life was much easier there.

When people from the hills and mountains poured into Terai, which used to be ethnically and culturally distinct from the rest of the country, it exerted visible influences in the culture of the Terai. People's interaction has produced a quite different subculture in Terai regions. Terai, which was inhabited by mostly *Madheshiya* is now becoming highly multi-cultural. In places like Jhapa, Sunsari and Morang districts, the migrants from hilly areas have highly populated the area. In the last three decades or so, people from hills have migrated to Terai in large proportions and changed the face of the Terai. Ethnic composition is changing and people's interaction has produced a quite different subculture in Terai regions, especially in the eastern Terai.

Racial composition of most Nepalese cities is also very much changing. For example, Kathmandu, Bhaktapur and Patan, three cities in the Kathmandu Valley, used to be predominantly Newar cities. So were several district headquarters, where the Newars were concentrated in most compact settlements and densely populated hilly bazaars, where there was high potential for trade. But this has ceased to be visible due to changing demographic and economic characteristics of the people. Kathmandu, mostly a Newar inhabitation until a few decades earlier, has now become highly multi-cultural. People from all over the kingdom are pouring into the capital in search of better opportunities. A small city of some 250,000 people in the 1970s, Kathmandu has grown into a modern metropolis of over one million people. Most of the new populations are migrants from outside the valley. Kathmandu valley is being converted into a culturally- amalgamated zones as all Nepalis coming from different zones are settling in and around the valley, says Professor Baral (1998).

As no further land is available for cultivation, young men in the villages are forced to leave and find temporary employment in the cities and urban areas. It is called "land push effect". It is not only the push, "city-pull" also constantly attracts young people to the urban area. Enchanted by the modernity, physical amenities, and opportunities, the youth swarm into the city centers. With immigrants from all over the country settling in Kathmandu, the ethnic composition has been altered while the valley's culture has started to erode.

Even in the hills, the continuous intermixing of various groups of people has been changing the ethnic mosaic. Many of Nepal's ethnic and linguistic groups have gradually adopted Hindu tradition and Indo-Aryan culture and Nepali language. With "no visible resistance to this process of assimilation and Nepalization" (Amatya, 1996), the cultural mosaic is getting homogenized.

There used to be three distinct categories of subculture in Nepal. They were the *Himalayan culture* in the high mountains influenced by Tibetan Buddhism and Tibetan language, *Hill culture* comprising of different ethnic mosaic of mixed Tibeto-Burman and Indo-Aryan groups, and *Terai Culture* dominated and influenced by the Indian Hindu culture of northern India. But such a categorization no more holds in a true sense. Although, much of the sub-cultural practices can be discerned, a discrete cultural division is increasingly becoming difficult to make. People are intermixing. A large number of Himalayan people have settled in the hilly areas and mountain valleys, whereas an increasing number of the hill people have settled in the Terai. People in all the three subcultures are in a continuous process of *Nepalization*, while continuously being exposed to Indianization, globalization and Westernization.

Further, the migratory trend from the hill to the Terai and from the rural to the urban areas is likely to continue. Roads and air links, better employment opportunities, access to modern amenities of life in the urban areas, have contributed to such migration. Though such mixing and contact may be good for so-called national integration, the process of assimilation has posed threats to the loss of distinct cultural identity and diversity of the Nepalese people.

But some tend to question the notion that the people of Nepal are undergoing a "melting pot process". "Have they formed a melting pot with cultural uniformity or a salad bowl with different cultures?", ask Karan & Ishii (1996, p. 171). Though they tend to approve the melting pot process in the small towns in the middle mountains, and new settlements along the motorable roads, Karan & Ishii suggest that a large segment of population in Kathmandu Valley and even in Terai have retained their distinct cultural identity without any visible diffusion into a homogenous pattern.

That is true in the sense that neither people migrating to Kathmandu from outside the valley are seen copying the Newar culture nor those from the mountains settling in the Terai have adopted the Terai rituals, clothes, language and other customs. There the transformation process has been characterized as "salad bowl" type (Karan & Ishii, 1996), in which "different ethnic groups keep their identities and their cultures." In whatever degree it is present, the "melting pot process", an increasing mix of different ethnic minorities with the dominant caste, is bringing about intermixing of their culture and is contributing to a certain degree of homogeneity in the society.

THE WEAKENING DIVIDE

The identity crisis has also been evident by the weakening of the traditional distinction of people on the basis of their region, ethnicity, and religion. The traditional antagonism and rivalry between different group of people is becoming blurred as the society is heading towards homogenization.

Regionalism has been a strong basis of structural differentiation of the Nepalese society. For example, the distinction between people living in the hills (*Parbate*), urban areas (*Shahariya*), suburbs (*Kanthe*), Terai plains (*Madheshiya*), eastern region (*Purbiya*), western region (*Paschima*), and regions adjoining Tibetan region (*Bhote*) used to be a strong basis for people's identity. Even in the Kathmandu Valley, which conventionally allowed a lot of intermixing of people from different regions, there used to be a great distinction and difference among the hill (*parbate*), urban (*shahariya*) and suburban people (*kanthe*). There existed a kind of unseen antagonism among these different groups of people. *Shahariya* (urban) people thought they were civilized better and were more intelligent and affluent than the others. *Parbate* people thought they knew the facts and hardships of life better than the other two. *Kanthe* people used to think they are aware of the advantages of the both. There used to be in general a derogating attitude towards each other among the three groups of people. This generalization seems to have lost its significance since many people of these different groups have greatly mixed with each other by marriage and residences especially in the new localities of the valley. The "chronic rivalry between the *Upadhyaya* and *Kumain* Brahmins with respect to the caste superiority" (Varya, n.d., p. 378) that existed earlier, also seems to be decreasing.

There used to be a big divide between people of different geographical and regional groupings. People around Karnali basin, termed generically as *Jumli* by the people of the east, were considered backward and derogated by the rest. The people of the region called the eastern Nepalese people as *Gorkhali*. There also used to be a mutually derogatory attitude between the *Parbatiya* and *Madhesiya* people. But such divide is weakening as people are being mobile and many have moved across the areas they were traditionally identified with. The broad division of the Nepalese people on the basis of their habitat in the different geographical regions is seen to be diluting. Though the division of people in the Himali, Hilly and Terai are still identifiable, the "north-south migration and spread of transport and communication have considerably diluted such identities", writes Professor Lok Raj Baral (1998).

People's identity, these days, is not necessarily reflected from the region where they live. For example, Kirants (Rai and Limbu) people are no more confined to *Kirant Pradesh*. The Rai have scattered outside what is known as *Majh Kirant* (middle Kirant) and Limbu outside *Pallo Kirant* (the other Kirant). Increasing number of Rais, Limbus and Gurungs are now settling in the city centers (e.g. Pokhara and Dharan) and district headquarters in the hilly region. Newars, once concentrated mainly in Kathmandu Valley, have dispersed to various headquarters of most hill districts, where they are mostly engaged in trading and business.

Though there are a number of ethnic groups specific to the Terai (*Tharu, Rajbanshi, Satar, Ahirs, Danuwar, Dhimal, Musahar* etc.) and around the Himalayas (*Sherpas, Tamangs, Gurungs*), many people have moved across such traditional habitat zones and are no more identifiable with the place they come from. Brahmans, Chhetris and Thakuris, who were traditionally mobile along the hilly areas, have now settled not only in most of the mountainous and hilly areas, they can be seen in the Terai and even in the most urban centers.

While the distinction and identity on the traditional basis of ethnicity, region and culture is becoming weaker, there is the emergence of the division based on the attitude and the economy. At attitudinal level, there is an increasing distinction between "us" and "them". According to Bista (1991) the concept of "*Afno Manchhe*", an institution of "one's own people", has become a strong basis for differentiation among the Nepalese people. Though the memberships to the *Afno Manchhe* is largely based on kinship, regional and ethnic affinity, an increasingly economic grouping is also emerging on the basis of "give and take". As people are becoming highly individualized, such groupings have started to be very fluid and dynamic concepts.

Earlier, the surname of a person used to suggest where the person has come from. For example Bhatta used to be a Brahmin from farwestern Nepal, and Prasai a Kumain Brahmin from the far-east area. People used references on people's habitation and there used to be very frequent generalizations and references on stereotypes based on people's habitation. These distinctions today only add to confusions.

There also used to be a vast difference in the attitudes, beliefs and value systems of rural and urban people. But due to an increasing urbanization and the influence of mass media and transport as well as communication has made the divide less visible and distinct. The traditional structure was not only ethnic, but also highly differentiated into urban and rural lifestyles. Kathmandu Valley, which has been the melting pot of ancient and medieval civilizations, had developed an extremely urban culture with residences built in compact cities. Newars, the majority of the inhabitants of the city, had developed their own culture with much of skill and proficiency in trade, business, and craft and art. This was not shared with rural people because lack of communication and contact. A great deal of structural differentiation had developed. But today with an increasing contact between the people and an ongoing influx of people from the rural areas into urban centers like Kathmandu, the rural-urban structure is also being challenged and weakened. But it is increasingly becoming difficult to identify people on the basis their castes, ethnicity, surname or geographic habitation. A great deal of mobility and change in the economic and social status of the people is contributing to this.

At present only 14% of the total population in Nepal resides in cities, but if the rapid rate of urbanization is left unchecked, the figure is bound to shoot up in a few years' time, writes a weekly[14]quoting a government report. With the current growth rate of the urban population at 5.8%, Nepal's urban population will pass three million-mark by the year 2002, and will reach 6.8 million by 2010. That may not be a big number and urbanization may not be a big menace in quantitative terms. But in Nepal's emerging shantytowns, where the pressures of the population have already reached a threshold,

---

[14] *The Spotlight* (December 19-25, 1997)

increasing population and a dynamic interaction among people from various regions and ethnic groups is bound to exert qualitative changes. Today, Nepalese cities are not only becoming centers for commercial and industrial development. They are also becoming the "focal points", and "melting pots" for cultural change.

The principal motivator is an economic one. People are pouring into big cities in order to seek better opportunities in terms of jobs and access to better amenities of life. Increasing industrialization focused in the urban centers is major drive for the urbanization. This has created a very fast integration of the various ethnic and cultural groups people into the mainstream of urban people. Thus, people are abandoning their rural and tribal culture in order to be assimilated into the urban lives. In the urban culture of anonymity, people are loosing their identities and being massefied towards homogeneity. The shift from rural to urban culture is increasingly becoming common in search of education, job and business opportunities. Furthermore, settling in an urban area and adopting an urban life is being seen something of higher economic and social status.

Urbanization poses one of the strongest challenges to the preservation of the cultural identity and diversity. As economic growth accelerates, people migrate across their cultural boundaries. They start to perceive threats to their cultural identity and feel endangered and beleaguered. The urban anonymity gives temptation to break the cultural rules while the cultural identity becomes diffused and homogenized. Sometimes such a condition invites the interest in "the back to the roots" connections. People start finding their linkages and cultural identities. Similar interest groups are formed and organizations created. *Samparka Samitis* of various districts in Kathmandu, caste-based or sub-caste organizations like *Sudhar Samitis* start becoming the converging places to forge the lost identities.

Though most youngsters from the rural areas go to the urban areas and abroad with best hopes and a lot of expectations, they don't always bring the best of the fortunes. Unlike a few decades earlier, the progress and advancement in education and jobs is not certain. Today, the youngsters who go to urban areas selling some property or borrowing from others, don't always succeed in their academic pursuit. Difficulty with competitions, irregularities of the academic sessions, and intermittent strikes and student politics makes their academic pursuit chaotic. If they do complete the academic study, they will only fare a mediocre performance, as they will have to compete with the ones who had better education backgrounds available in the urban areas. Even if they achieve some success and fare better in the academics, jobs are not always assured. They do not know what to expect and which career to plan. Many such youngsters, dismayed by the problems like these and tired of competition, will retire back to the village only to discover that they are not even ready to be helping hands of the household jobs and work related to agriculture. Many such youth remain unemployed, and turn to intermittent politics. With their dreams cherished around Indian movies, aspirations to look modern with sunglasses, jeans, and hats, they start ridiculing the village life. They loose the sense of belonging to the place they were born and grown up. Many go back to the cities to look for work of "lesser category", anything to survive, despite their education does not match the same.

Those who come to the cities without much of expectations are relatively better off. Whether they start as drivers of buses, trucks, taxis and tempos (auto-rickshaws), or find jobs as construction workers, *bhariya* (the porters) or *"thelawala"* (cart pushing jobs), they find the cities still more attractive than the villages. They cherish the city life, despite all the odds and difficulties, and contribute to the weakening of the rural-urban divide. When they go back home, they become the carriers of the consumer culture of the cities, as they bring gadgets and modern things to the rural areas. And they start to diffuse the difference between the rural and urban areas.

DIVERSITY AT RISK

Nepal is a country of great cultural diversity. For a country of small size, the presence of traditional ethnic, cultural and linguistic diversity is something to wonder about. There are more than five dozen ethnic groups of people, plus various Hindu castes, each offering diverse cultural traditions and heritage. They speak at least forty different languages and who observe a myriad of cultural practices, worship various gods and goddesses, and celebrate various colorful festivals. Though majority people are Hindus, there are followers of Hinduism, Islam, Christianity and several other religions such as Bonpo, animism and nature worship. Numerous festivals are observed to mark different cultural and religious occasion by each community. As Nepal's 22.5 million people liver under diverse geographical and environmental conditions, from the hot tropical climate of the Terai plains to the snow-covered mountains in the Himalayas, their culture is accustomed to the climatic and environmental variations. In the highlands connecting the Himalayas, the highest mountains of the world, live the Sherpas, who are known for their cultural resemblance to the Tibetans. There are ethnic groups of the Gurung, the Rai, the Magars etc., who are famous for their martial qualities and unique culture, distributed in the middle hills. In Kathmandu Valley and some district headquarters live the famous and culturally rich Newar people. Brahmans and Chhetris are dispersed throughout the country, especially in the hilly region. The Terai plains are inhabited by some ethnic groups such as Tharu and several other *Madhesiya* people. All these people exhibit a great diversity in their languages, costume, occupations and arts.   This diversity or pluralism in the culture is something to cherish about and a good asset of Nepal. But the same is at risk due to a host of factors.

The cultural diversity started to be threatened with the traditional dynamism such as Sanskritization and Hinduization. In that, the various ethnic groups of people were encouraged to copy the culture of the upper-caste Brahman-Chhetris. Then came the process of Nepalization, which led to the emergence of a pan-Nepali culture diffusing the diversity of various groups if people.

Among them was the rise of Nepali nationalism, which has been labeled as an ideological tool devised by the Brahmin-Chhetri for domination against the ethnic minorities. With "the monarchy, Hinduism and the Nepali language considered as the triumvirate of the official Nepali nationalism" (Burghart, 1996), the state sought to impose "unity in diversity" and aimed at cultural integration of the diverse ethnic groups of people into the mainstream culture. The composite Nepalese identity was often portrayed as that of the majority Brahman Chhetris. Though being Nepali meant different things to different people (Whelpton, 1997), there was no such thing as a Nepali culture, save a composite culture of various ethnic groups and the "dominant" Brahman-Chhetris.

Even the development of a pan-Nepalese culture and identity served to diffuse the cultural diversity, mainly because the culture of the Brahman-Chhetris, instead of the various ethnic groups, was adopted as symbols of the pan-Nepalese culture. The cultural identities and symbols of various ethnic groups are rarely adopted by the state as the national cultural identity and symbols. Except that Royal Nepal Academy projected Newari Kumari and Charya dances as the national classical dances, a Bhadgaon Newar's cap or Palpali *dhaka* cap is worn by bureaucrats or politicians as national headgear, and the Sherpa women dress is worn by the staff in the fashionable hotels, and by the female staff on board the Royal Nepal Airlines, the cultural symbols of the ethnic groups is hardly adopted for reflecting the pan-Nepali identity. This reluctance to pick up the symbols of the diverse ethnic groups of people has also served to diffuse the cultural diversity in the country. It has been balmed that the state in the past did not encourage the symbols of the various ethnic groups of people to promote the national identity.[15] Instead, the protagonists of pan-Nepali culture promoted the Nepali language and Hinduism as the state religion, and the cultural symbols of Hindus, not that of various ethnic groups. That is why, Bhattachan (1998), says that the pan-Nepali culture is that of "internal colonizers". But he concedes even the "imposed pan-Nepali culture has received a serious blow from globalization or from powerful external cultural invasion" (Bhattachan, ibid.). The pan-Nepalese culture itself is being engulfed by the expansion of global culture and the pan-Nepali identity is succumbing to the alarming spread of the tentacles of globalization and homogenization of culture.

While the ethnic minorities are reinventing their cultural identities, the pan-Nepali cultural identities and symbols are being reshaped and reoriented. Today, the Nepalese people are reinventing their identities and their culture. Though the links to the past have weakened, a search of reviving the cultural ethos is also on the making. In the struggle for asserting the ethnic rights, in the

---

[15] For example, it has been blamed that dresses imported from abroad were adopted as national dress, instead of the dress of one of the ethnic groups of Nepal. The men's *daura-suruwal* came from the Rajasthnai influence, and the coat (jacket) seems to have been introduced after Jung Bahadur Rana's Europe tour. Even the Bhadgaon cap seems to be have been popularized after the Muslim caps, especially during the Prime Ministership of Chandra Shamsher Rana. And the women's *saree* is a distinct Indian thing (Shailendra K. Upadhyaya, in *Himal*).

opposition to the caste-based social structure, in absorbing the Western consumer culture, there is a drive for reinventing the Nepalese culture.

With the advance of global forces like communication and craze for things from abroad, it has not only become difficult to preserve the national cultural identity, the cultural diversity and pluralism that has existed over centuries is also being challenged. While the identity of various people is at stake, the cultural diversity of Nepal is no less exposed to threats. Professor Khanal has put this like this:

> Science and economics are not only sublimating the world into unity but also pushing it down into uniformity, This applies to culture also, Even in the developed countries, culture is unable to keep pace with the spreading pop culture, Mass culture and mass consumption have gone hand in hand. Regional and international integration, which is more advanced in developed societies has encouraged and reinforced the same trend. This uniformity of pop music, commercial painting, instant food, advertisement literature threatens to engulf developed and developing societies alike. Ugliness in this development lies in its disinclination to tolerate and accommodate active diversity, which alone gives life to unity (Khanal, 1996, pp. 43-44).

As we are heading towards a more homogenized consumer culture, the ethnic diversity has started to merge in the mainstream culture which infuses alien things quiet easily as its own values. Though the polymorphous structure the society and its diverse cultural traditions have provided a favorable atmosphere for the flourishing of a pluralistic democratic society in the recently introduced political framework, the homogenization of the culture at the global scale has started to pose threats to Nepal's cultural diversity. Borrowed habits, behavior and norms have started to chase out the traditional cultural diversity. Despite sporadic efforts to salvage the sinking ship of the culture, the cry against the crisis in the culture has become a loosing battle. Politicians speak of the need to preserve the Nepalese culture. But that just becomes a piece of rhetoric. Non-government organizations and some activists organize seminars on the need for protecting the heritage. But very little is achieved on the ground.

The Nepalese people are constantly at jeopardy of loosing "cultural sovereignty" that they had been exercising over more than two millennia. Nepalese people have started to allow and accept diffusion of the Nepalese culture into a global homogenous culture that is in the process of emerging. All these outside contact and influences have made 'direct and indirect, and positive as well as negative impacts on individuals, family, community and the nation as a whole", speaks Bhattachan (1998). Nepali identity, which is built upon diversity and multi-ethnicity, is at the risk of being succumbed to the emerging trends of homogenization. The pace of globalization, modernization and Westernization, and the increasing clout of the cultural offensive through the mass media, technology, entertainment and information industry, is being seen as a formidable challenge for the preservation of the cultural diversity in Nepal.

A Hierarchy Rejected

Nepalese society has been always described as hierarchical, structured and caste-based. Scholars have gone to the extent that they described people with the caste system as *Homo hierarchicus* (Dumont, 1970). Some described *Homo hierarchicus nepalensis* as a separate cultural subspecies (Fisher, 1978). Anthropologists continue to conceptualize hierarchy in the Nepalese society on the basis of the caste structure. There is no denying that the traditional Nepalese society was a hierarchical one. There used to be a vertical integration supported by the caste system and the economic class structure and there was a huge distance in terms of power, status and prestige between the people of the lowest rung of the hierarchy and that of the highest. But these traditional notions caste hierarchy in the Nepalese society has been challenged. "While caste continues to be a social fact of Nepali society", says Onta-Bhatta (1996), "its logic is *no longer* the paramount determiner of national, cultural, and social hierarchy in Nepal today".

Diffusion of cultural identity and flattening of the traditional social hierarchy had started to be reported in Nepal as early as 1975. In a study of an administrative town in far-western Nepal, it was noted that there was no cultural plurality and that the various castes and different ethnic groups of people had assimilated into a "uniform set of customary practices". People spoke Nepali as the first language, wore same dresses, celebrated the same festivals and household rites, and utilized same category of ritual specialists and so on (Caplan, 1975). This seems to be applying to many small towns in the middle mountains, including new settlements springing up along the motorable roads (Karan & Ishii, 1996). Karan and Ishii (1996) have said, a system founded on hierarchy is considerably diluted and is gradually being replaced by the notion of "separate but equal".

Nepal's famous anthropologist Dor Bahadur Bista, who in his earlier ethnography (Bista, 1967) had adopted the traditional classification of the Nepalese society on the basis of the caste system following the pattern adopted by the foreign scholars, has also challenged the notion of traditional hierarchy in the Nepalese society in his later works. "It seems rather odd to continue to discuss the structure of Nepalese society along these lines for ever", concedes Bista (in Malla, 1989, p. 172). "Much of it is in ferment, partly by design and partly by spontaneous process of change" (Bista, 1989).

Even the concept of "Sanskritization", which assumes that the 'low caste' people attempt to raise their status by adopting the values, rituals, eating habits and dress of the upper castes, shows that the caste system is not static, but fluid and dynamic organization allowing social mobility from the within. That also favors the argument that the traditional hierarchy in the Nepalese society has been challenged by both the traditional dynamism such as Sanskritization or Hinduization and by the modern dynamism such Westernization, modernization and globalization.

With unprecedented changes in people's social, economic, cultural, and political imperatives and aspirations, the traditional caste structure has been challenged, both at the popular and the attitudinal level. The culture shift is being geared towards the weakening of the traditional social hierarchy and structure. The traditional structure is waning and new social framework, which is based on an increasingly economic hierarchy, is being shaped.

The Nepalese society was without much rigid structure and hierarchy before the structuring of the Nepalese society began in the Kathmandu Valley in the fourteenth century and in Gorkha in the seventeenth century. With the advise of Maithali Brahmins of India, who had influence in the royal court, King Jayasthiti Malla (1382-1395) introduced the caste-system based on the principles of division of labor and occupations along Hindu social structure then prevailing in some parts of India. In Gorkha, the predecessor of modern Nepal, King Ram Shah (1606-1636) introduced the structured and ascriptive caste structure in the form of his social engineering. These two efforts were so influential in shaping the Nepali society that the caste system later on was encoded into common laws. Prime Minister Jung Bahadur Rana developed and introduced rigorous codes of social conduct and hierarchical caste structure in the *Muluki Ain* (Civil Code, 1854). Although the Civil Code would not apply to some communities, who had their own codes of conduct, it created tremendous impact in the social structure until it was challenged after the introduction of democracy in 1950, when the Rana family autocracy was thrown away by a strong popular revolution. The caste structure was only to be outlawed by the New Civil Code in 1963. The New Civil Code (1963) was a bold step in de-recognizing the hierarchical caste system. That was a landmark legal instrument in the state-imposed changes in the social structure. It was in this legal instrument that the state support for the caste-system was withdrawn. The traditional norms of untouchability, marriages, and contacts between different groups of peoples, and the vertical social hierarchy was challenged. The effort was to integrate the horizontal structure into a non-hierarchical egalitarian caste-less structure.

Another milestone in the social change was laid with the introduction of the *Land Reforms* that regulated the size holdings of the agricultural land. This program challenged the traditional social hierarchy and patronizing practice on the basis of land holdings, and helped tenants materialize their rights challenging the traditional social structure.

In the last four or five decades, the traditional values supporting hierarchical social structure has also been challenged due to "the widespread exposure to different social and political systems around the world through modern media, education and contact with the people from outside of Nepal" (Bista, ibid.). An increasing contact among different ethnic and geographic groups of people and external contacts with people from abroad has brought several changes in the social structure along the diffusion of the caste-based social hierarchy.

Traditionally, the Nepalese society aimed at "vertical integration", in which people would fit into the caste structure from the highest and lowest strata. The hierarchical structure prevailed mainly because people lived in isolated river valleys and mountain slopes without much of interaction and contact with people from different regions. And the caste structure prevailed because the ruling elite continued to support it. The traditional structure was maintained in the interest of the upper castes, who had a great influence, if not control, over the affairs of the state. With an increasing trend towards horizontal integration, especially in major urban areas, it is becoming difficult to distinguish people on the basis of their caste. Patronizing, which was characteristic of the hierarchical society is gradually decreasing as the society is integrating horizontally. Although it is a long way to go to classlessness, much of the conventional patronizing in the traditional hierarchical society is gradually fading.

Traditionally, the Nepalese society had mostly remained fragmented and isolated. The feudal rulers had kept the society fragmented vertically and horizontally in order to be able to maintain law and order and collection of revenues exploiting the natural resources (Bista, 1989). "In course of time, the fragmentation of the society began to affect the mind and the thinking process of the people. People got used to think in terms of very restricted small groups as their only reference of being their own people" (Bista, in Malla 1989, p. 176). But today many Nepali people are hardly confined to their own ethnic and regional group for a cultural affiliation. People are crossing the boundaries to exert their influence, both political and economic, in the changing society.

Today, most Nepalese people have started to disregard the traditional social caste structure. The caste based on religion and division of labor has started to disintegrate. People have started to accept the emergence of an economic class, of the *haves* and the *have nots*. With the classification of the rich and poor, the economic extremes and gaps are increasing.

This is not to suggest that the traditional caste structure has disappeared. Although the traditional caste system has been challenged legally and rationally, the caste structure is still practiced and existing in Nepal. Although the traditional Hindu law based on the caste system has been outlawed, the caste system still exists as an important aspect of the Nepalese social life. The caste system is still haunting Nepalese society in one way or the other. "The old structure and frame of caste principles and of social hierarchy are still there in skeletal form, although they are ignored, bypassed and snubbed, whenever they have stood on the way of the innovative people of the new generation with ideas different from those of seniors, elders or community leaders", says Bista (in Malla, 1989).

But the traditional rules and practices are changing. People are no more strictly ranked from the highest to the lowest castes. Not all Brahmins today are regarded as priestly people to be respected by the people of other castes. Nor many of them continue to be dominantly involved in studying the religion and performing the religious rites. Chhetris, supposed to be rulers, protectors of people and defenders of the nation, are not confined to the army and police services. Similarly, it is not restricted to Vainsyas when it comes to doing business and farming. "Shudras", the so-called service people, are expanding their sphere activities all sectors of economy and education.

In fact, people's anonymity in the urban life has made the idea of one's caste trivial and obsolete. No one is really bothered to seek to know other's caste as they used to be interested in people's caste identification asking "which caste do you belong to?" (*kasma hunu hunchha ?*), some decades ago.

The emerging politics of ethnicity and nationalism may have made the old distinctions reappear in the politics of culture in the form of Janjajti versus the Hindus, as is evident in the voicing of the cultural aspirations among the various ethnic groups of people. But it has also served to challenge the notion of the caste system, rejecting the Hindus social organization as the basis of the differentiation between peoples. The emerging empowerment of the so called low-caste people, popularly called as "*Dalits*" in the new democratic set-up has also liberated the desire to social classlessness and degeneration of the traditional hierarchical structure of the Nepalese society. Exercising their clout through ballot and new pluralistic democratic framework, the people of the so-called lower castes have increasingly become able to exert their influence and demand for social equality. The belief in the caste system is slipping, especially among educated and urban Nepalese people. Today, politics, education and economics, not caste, account for the inequalities among the Nepalese people.

THE DEGRADED NOBLE HOUSE

In the traditional structure, the caste purity used to be given a lot of significance in the Nepali society. There used to be a strict taboo on marriages between men and women of different castes. Caste consciousness used to be very important social consideration in social behavior and relations among people. For example, consuming alcohol or chicken, drinking or eating with an "untouchable person", marrying with a partner of "lower hierarchy", used to be an act to degrade one's caste (*Jat Phalne*). But this belief is gradually disappearing, especially in the urban areas. Even in the rural areas, the concept abstaining from drinking alcohol is no more a strong consideration for retaining one's caste. Untouchability has been generally abandoned in the urban areas. A definite cultural pattern against untouchability is emerging even in the rural areas. The concept of untouchability is no longer a strong barrier to the social development and towards the formation of an egalitarian and democratic society.

Marrying a partner of "lower" caste used to significantly alter people's social prestige and status in the society in rural as well as in the urban areas. Though inter-caste marriage have not been very common, the caste-barrier in marrying has ceased to be a very strong consideration for retaining one's own caste belongingness. In the traditional Nepalese society, caste degradation, i.e. lowering of one's caste used to be a common practice. People could be downgraded if they married a "lower-caste". Among Brahmans, there used to be a system of caste-downgrading based on the marriages. Brahmans used to establish and maintain purity of their clan. They didn't easily mix with other tribes and castes. For a Brahman, marrying non-Brahman woman was almost unthinkable. But modern Nepalese Brahmans don't hesitate in inter-caste marriages. Brahmans, who used to exercise most rigorous abstinence and frequent ablutions, are abandoning these practices. Caste purity is no longer given a strong cultural significance.

Among most people, the superiority among castes and clans used to be determined by the level of strictness in adhering to some traditions. A noble house used to be the one with people who were strict to most social customs, who followed the exact rules for family alliance and who worked less and enjoyed more. *Kul Gharana* used to be a typical concept in the Hindu value systems. A good *Kul Gharana* (noble house) was the one, which had accumulated a lot of wealth, which restricted any changes in the superstitious traditions. People sought to find and verify the status of *Kul Gharana* establishing family linkages, marital relationships and even business partnerships. That concept is gradually fading away with the emergence of neo-economic classes and weakening of the social caste hierarchy. A new *Kul Gharana* is emerging, an economic one.

Today, a noble house is one, which is rich and affluent, which has access to political power and economic resources, which is modern and Westernized, which disregards the traditional culture, and which regards culture and religion as something of the domain of the priests and Brahmans.

Dor Bahadur Bista describes the influence of and indoctrination over other castes and non-caste (*Janjati*) by Brahmans as *Bahunism* and defines it as "socio-economic alliance and superiority" of the

Brahmans over non-Brahmans, mainly the various ethnic groups of people (Bista, 1991). Contrary to views that Brahmanhood is a symbol of indifference to worldly power and material advantage, Brahmans in Nepal are said to have exercised the political and economic clout to dominate other castes and non-caste people. This is not to deny that there did not exist any Brahminical hierarchy and superiority. However, the Brahmin hierarchy has been facing strong challenges and is not existing in the state Bista has ascribed. Varya writes on the waning of Brahmin influence in Nepal :

> The Brahminical hierarchy had long been unchallenged with its predominance in the social life of the Nepalese people through out the Malla, Shah and Rana regimes as well as its existence of immense political influence in the periods like those of Jung Bahadur and others. Although eccelesiasticism was their main profession, they began to take up official works also later one. But after the debacle of Ranarchy in 1951, the superiority of Brahmans which was unquestionable in the Nepalese communities before 1951 has been on the wane (Varya, n. d. p. 379).

The Brahminical system and hierarchy has been opposed, criticized and disregarded lately. There is "considerable evidence of resentment, even among some communities that have nominally adopted Hinduism, against the enforcement of such Brahmanic principles as the ban on cow-slaughters and the consumption of alcoholic beverages, and the rigid caste purification rites" (Rose, 1971, p. 8). Opposition by people like Gurungs, Magars and Limbus against the "Brahmin dominance" is taking the form of a cultural movement. People are starting to talk something like abandonment of Hindu festival *Dashain* and opposing use of Sanskrit curricula and even Sanskrit news aired by the radio, all supposed to have designed by the Brahmins to exert their cultural influence.

The Brahmin influence and their supremacy over the rest of the society is gradually waning. Many Hindu cultural practices, rituals, customs and traditions have been ridiculed, abandoned and even opposed because they are thought to be devised by the Brahmans to continue to exert their influence over the society. Today, a Brahmin is a subject of ridicule in the society, not the symbol of authority and power, as it used to be in the supreme old days of Brahminhood. A Brahman is being portrayed as a timid, god-fearing, and weak person in the society. Although Brahmans continue to be one of the largest groups of people with comparatively larger share in the bureaucracy and politics, they no longer represent the dominant caste. The "elitist approach" of Brahminhood is also waning due to declining interest in the priesthood and spirituality practiced by the Brahmans. The Brahminical order that lasted for centuries is on the decay.

The comparatively larger share of Brahmans in political, parties, in the parliament, in the government bureaucracy tends underscore the poor, weak, timid and marginalized Brahmans, who have no access to power and resources. It is only some leaders and activists, who have happened to be enlightened due to the access to education to be in the forefront of the political movements such as that of 1950 and1990. Therefore, they are better represented in the political parties thus resulting in the higher representation of the Brahmans in the politics.

In fact, Brahmin domination was never to the scale it is generally attributed to. How come the timid and god-fearing Brahmans were supposed to be the culprits of cultural domination? How could they spread their influence by just officiating some rites, wearing some saffron robes and carrying some religious books? If anything has suffered most in the era of ethnopolitics, it is the image of Brahmans, says Sharma (1997). *Bahunbad* has become a political vocabulary palatable to the ethnic activists and scholarly writers. All Brahmans are portrayed as perpetrators of Hindu dominance or even "colonization" of non-Hindu ethnic groups dominating the sate politics and therefore controlling resources. This often ignores that the privileged Brahmans, who are part of the ruling class, are only a small minority of the greater population of Brahmans in Nepal and that Brahmans were mobile throughout the history and didn't have any specific habitats to exert their influence.

Yet another major factor causing the decline of the Brahman influence is the increasing neglect by the anthropological studies and foreign scholars, who have proven tendencies to favor the ethnic minorities they have studied and patronized them as opposed to the *Parbatiya* hill culture of the Brahmans (Sharma, 1997). Today, a common stereotype of a Brahman is portrayed as a "greedy priest", "a crafty village money lender, a stealer of other's land, (one) who shuns rough and dirty work, carries with him an air of haughtiness, and is presumptuous and patronizing" (Sharma, 1997). And "this is the image often sold to the outside audience", much without substance and ignoring the weak and marginalized Brahmans, who never had any role whatsoever in the "dominance or colonizing" of the non-Hindus in Nepal. One cannot disagree that the influence of Brahminical order is declining in the society, which is rejecting the traditional hierarchy based on caste and religion.

THE HIERARCHY OF MONEY

As the traditionally vertical social caste structure is gradually disappearing, a new class structure is emerging: an economic one. People are increasingly becoming more and more differentiated by their economic status, not the social position. The difference between the rich and poor is increasing. The "haves" and "have- nots" have become the facts of life. A new class, which is named "new rich" class is emerging in the urban centers and even in some rural areas.

Until some decades ago, the upper economic class used to be the ruling families of Ranas, Thakuris, and a few landlords in the Terai, and a few businessmen in Kathmandu and other regional cities. But new economic orientation has seen emergence of new rich families. The increase in the "fast and easy money" due to corruption has created an entirely new generation of richer people. The other group of the affluent class is the business people, who are in constant upward surge of richness and accumulation of material wealth.

People living in subsistence in rural areas and people living on physical labor or fixed wages are the ones who are becoming poorer. That is mainly due to the decline in real wages as the economy goes on devaluating itself and as the purchasing power of money drops while the level of income remains static or increases negligibly. On the other hand, the number of people living in small cities and shantytowns and slums is also increasing. This is redefining the social values and the traditional roles and respect people attached to each other in terms of the social hierarchy.

An expanding economic class, often labeled as "middle class" or "new rich class", is an emerging phenomenon in Nepal. Today the influence of the middle class people in increasing. They are represented in parliament. They run political parties and are most numbered people in the bureaucracy. They are the majority among the so-called intellectuals, academicians and the professionals. They also cover most of the small enterprises and large portion of agricultural land in the country.

On the contrast, a rich class, with their status symbols such as elegantly-built house with modern kitchen, bedroom, living and bathrooms, few cars, children studying abroad, engagement in one or several industries or in the business, access to a range of modern utilities like air-conditioning, and the ability to buy professional and intellectual people and a range of bureaucrats and politicians, continue to exert influence in their profit making activities and share in the state's resources. Several rich people have patronized several poor and middle-class people. They shape the policies at least the ones that influence or affect them. And people and society at large give them respect and regard, just because of their economic status.

Despite vociferous support for "poverty alleviation" and to the upliftment of the "poor, and marginalized" people, the gap between the Haves and Have Nots is increasing. Rich and affluent are getting richer leaving the poor people marginalized. Bhattachan blames globalization for the "increasing rich-poor divide". A "handful of big business houses and rich families are getting richer, middle class families are slowly increasing, and an overwhelming majority of people who come under a lower class are getting poorer day by day." (Bhattachan, 1998). Though the young people possess egalitarian dreams, the gap and the difference between the rich and the poor is increasing.[1] The hierarchy of money is becoming more and more evident.

THE CARRIERS OF CULTURE CHANGE

In 1959, B. P. Koirala, Nepal's first elected prime minister and a revolutionary and socialist thinker, wanted every Nepali family to be prosperous in fifteen years with a nicely built house, 4 bighas of rice farm (*khet*), a cow and all of their children going to schools. Those were the symbols of a typical middle class then. But today, the middle class is a dynamic concept. It is the class of an upwardly mobile people, which has crossed all traditional barriers for making progress. Today, the

---

[1] According to Nepal Human Development Report (1999), 36% of the total population was absolutely poor in 1977. That has increased to 42% in 1998. The unjust land distribution also justifies the gap. The top 5% of the population controls 40% of the agricultural land, whereas the bottom 60% shares only 20%.

typical middle class status symbols include a nicely-built house in a major town, children studying in private English-medium schools, access to basic modern utilities like television, and some members associated with some business, bureaucracy or some level of politics.

It is this emerging class of people, who are becoming the agents of cultural change and deterioration in the country. They are the consumer class, which wants to act rich demonstrating their wealth and success as their new lifestyles. This burgeoning middle class has loosened it strict moral code. There is a strong doctrinal bias towards the self and one's family. This group of people has become highly self-centered and, in that pursuit, does not distinguish between moral and amoral, god and bad, and between correct and incorrect. They have very little concern towards others, and there is a blurring sense of obligation to the society. They exhibit a deliberate withdrawal from a constructive interference in the societal affairs. They have an insatiable desire to make money, using all means. They do not hesitate to consume at the expense of others. Whether it is siphoning drinking water with a pump or jumping a queue in public places, it is this middle class people, who are not hesitating doing things at the cost of the others. They are viewing individual or their family as the microcosm.

They are known for their capacity to resistance to authority and to bend the rules. They possess an outspokenness to criticize anybody. Doing things of interest without having to wait, getting personal business expedited and exacting preference to services even in the market places are some of the obvious things. The average middle class Nepalis are believer of a short cut and quick-fix solution. They skip rituals and abandon the traditions. This mentality is increasingly becoming the average mentality of the Nepalese, as they are the most numbered people in the politics, in business and in bureaucracy. They are capturing the agenda of the nation in political movements, intellectual debates, social changes, and economic transformation. There is a craze for upward mobility in *Jagir*, in business and in politics.

But they are least bothered about the deteriorating culture. Today, this middle class is continuously aping the snob values and mock culture abandoning the treasured traditions. On top of all, it is this middle class, which rejects all forms of traditional social and economic hierarchy.

Breakdown of the Family

Nepalese society always had a "pronounced familial core" (Sharma, 1973). Family used to be a quintessential social unit and center of all cultural and economic activities, relations and celebrations. The extended family had been the primary agent of education and the basis of the social organization. Nepali citizens inherited their knowledge of religion, economics, politics, castes and class from the large extended family. People accepted uncritically the precept of the all-powerful family. The members of the extended family used to continue the profession inherited from the household. The writ of the head of the family reigned supreme in the management of the family (Sharma, 1973, p. x). Though many communities even today have the same household pattern as in the past, this all-powerful family is a falling bastion. There is an increasing trend that large and extended families are breaking or disintegrating into smaller nuclear units. Breakdowns of the large extended cohesive families that lived in close proximity to each other into unclear one have been made possible by the exodus of many people from the villages to the urban centers in the search of jobs and better opportunities, the need to live elsewhere, and influence of global trend towards a nuclear family.

. The influence of the monolithic family seems to be on the decline not only in relation to the individuals. The family's influence on the society also seems to be decreasing. The breakdown of the extended families into nuclear units and development of new areas of settlement of less cohesive groups of people has changed the social dynamism and the maintenance of cultural practices of the area. This has accelerated the process of "Culture Shift". It is obvious that once the large extended families start to disintegrate, the burden of continuing the cultural practices of the extended families becomes too costly to the new nuclear families and the individuals. This breakdown becomes heavily burdensome in maintaining the cultural traditions. A nuclear family living on fixed income in a rented house in a city is hardly expected to have a family priest to come to perform regular family rites. It is neither feasible for them to visit their extended family living in a far away village on each major festival. Even a visit during Dashain, the biggest of Nepalese festivals, will have to curtailed or planned once every two or three years. These problems force the smarter families to abandon many of the cultural practices. Further, they question several cultural rites and customs in terms of economic rationality. Even if people have managed to continue such traditions, the underlying principles of such practices are being questioned and new idealism is being developed in the modern economic reality.

At first, people in the rural areas leave their children and spouse behind and go for searching opportunities in the urban areas. As soon as they find some job or business, they bring their spouses and children leaving their parents and other members of the joint family behind. Linkage is maintained by occasional visits, money sent on some occasions, shared interest in the management of property and the like. But the greatest blow of separation goes to the culture. Family rites are either missed or ignored. It is not feasible to have a family priest to visit the houses on various occasions in the urban areas. Festivals come and go but seldom attract the zeal and enthusiasm as it did in the villages.

The first generation nuclear families in Nepal are the civil servants, who have left behind their parents and other members of the extended family. As their jobs demanded mobility, it was not possible to bring along all the family members. Similar mobility is being observed among the people in the private businesses and even among the employees of the private sector. Nuclearity becomes compulsion, not choice, when one has to keep moving around. Emerging smarter families in Nepal are not even "nuclear families" in the strictest sense of the term. Though residential nuclearity is there, the Nepalese nuclear families continue to maintain ties with the extended families. What becomes disconnected is the sense of belongingness, the shared values of family as a monolithic cultural unit, and the continuation of the mutual support in the extended families. The nuclear family becomes the sole spectator of disappearing cultural bond that used to exist in the extended families.

Such a breakdown of the cultural bond of the monolithic family has also been signaled by the increase in the number of street children[1] in Nepal's cities. "Contrary to the popular conception of strong family values and relationships in Nepal', writes Onta (1995), "street children

---

[1] According a NGO, there were 500 street children in 1990 and the number had reached 1500 in 1993 (CWIN)

have left their home primarily because of breakdown in their family support system, domestic violence and parental neglect and abuse".

The shift towards the nuclear family has put enormous pressures to young couples. Apart from having to manage to live in isolation from the joint family, the nuclear families have become increasingly vulnerable to the anxieties of child rearing. They also face the problem of alienation from their own culture as they lag behind in their capacity to meet social and cultural obligations. Visiting relatives and friends, attending ceremonies, and performing and continuing cultural practices has become increasingly stressful to the people in nuclear families. The cultural burden, which was shared by the large joint families, is falling upon the smarter families. Young Nepalese couples are finding themselves trapped between respecting the old custom and adopting modernity. And people are finding themselves in an extremely difficult cultural transition.

CURTAILING KIDS

Until a few decades ago, many Nepalese people used to believe they had little control over how many children they could get. The number of children one could "get" was believed to be under the "mercy of the God". People used to consider it as "sin" to control the number of children by artificial means. There used to be a widespread belief that larger the number of kids better the prosperity of a family. That is why people were blessed to have their numerous children reach everywhere. There was widespread belief in sayings such as *Santanle Dandakanda Dhakos* (May one's offspring reach everywhere), and *Praja Phailiyos* (let the population expand). There was a very poor awareness of the methods and reliability of the family planning techniques. The appropriateness of artificial birth control was questioned in moral terms. That had made controlling the number of children unthinkable.

But this attitude and situation has been totally reversed. Today, most people in the urban areas prefer two or three children. It is not only economic reality that has made the "fewer-child option" mandatory. The attitude of the today's Nepalese parents is changing towards a smarter family. The new parents in the urban families have accepted and rationalized family planning. Curtailing the number of kids has become a voluntary and conscious choice. As people are choosing smarter families and as access to education and family planning techniques is increasing, most people are favoring to have less than three children. Education, among other things, has served as the best contraceptive, which is being evident by the fact that no educated couples are choosing to have more than two or three children, these days. Economic compulsions and the burden of child rearing do not allow the increasingly nuclear and educated families to have more than tow children. Yet another dimension of the smarter families is the increasing exit of women from the household to work in different walks of life. With women going out from their homes, it has become an imperative to curtail the number of children to make the families smarter.

Even in the rural areas, with increasing access of family planning and birth control techniques, there is a trend towards curtailing the number of kids per family. "Small is beautiful" seems to the preference even in rural families. As the number of children people desire depends upon their social, economic and cultural factors, the couples are believed to be interested in less number of children. The norms for smaller family size are underway due to successful implementation of family planning, the economic imperatives and the change of attitude at all levels. Though this has yet to score at the official census until that of 1991, which shows the population growth in Nepal at 2.1% per annum, it will not be too far when it will be reflected in the demographic statistics as well.

THE AGED ABANDONED

The senior and old citizens are the people who are facing serious problems due to break up of joint families into nuclear units. Although most Nepalese think it is their duty to look after their parents, this practice is gradually fading and the older people are getting abandoned. As the members of a family leave their home one by one in pursuit of education, jobs and other opportunities, a traumatic process of adjustment begins for the elderly parents, left behind in the rural villages. They not only experience the feeling of loss, separation and void, their lives become culturally insecure. Without their offspring to take care, the anxiety of being abandoned at the old age becomes a reality, which shatters the ideals of the extended families.

Though the reason is mainly economic, an increasing level of attitudinal detachment from the older generation is also contributing to the state of the elderly. With disintegrating interest in the old and traditional family ties and inadequate provisions to take care of the elderly people at the community level, the fate of the old people has been worsening due to their abandonment by the people of the smarter families. Though there have been recent efforts to introduce a namesake social security of the elderly people, including a small old-age pension, the problem of the old people is getting worse.

Traditionally, people used to invest in their children, mainly for the education of their male children, so that they could grow up, earn and take care of their parents at the old age. The concept of being taken care by one's offspring, especially y the male one, at one's old age was built upon the concept of the extended families in the traditional Nepalese society. People were trained to take care of their parents when they got old and it was supposed to be a moral social duty. But the young people are getting less and less interested in their parents and the old people. In the pursuance of their career and economic survival, the people of the smarter families are abandoning old people, mainly their parents and grandparents, behind. It is not only economic burden that taking care of the elderly has become a less desirable and less important task for the younger people these days, a lot of attitudinal dimension is also contributing to the neglect of the senior citizens of the country.

Disinterest in the things of the past, loss of relevance to the values and norms of the old times, and increasing generation gaps are mainly responsible for such neglects. When a young boy is more interested in the Disney than his grandfather's *Dantyakatha* (folk stories), when the music, fashion and sports replace the never-ending discussion of the land-prices and nice old times, and when carnivals and street festivals become more important than *jatras* and pilgrimages, the old are subject of ridicule and neglect. There have been some initiatives to open some old age homes in some urban areas. But not all of the Nepalese old-age homes have enough occupants. Old-aged people still prefer to stay behind neglected and abandoned rather than join these social institutions, which are yet to become culturally acceptable.

THE *PER CAPITA* CULTURE

In the traditional Hindu framework of the hierarchical society, Nepalese individuals were subordinated to the authorities of the traditional families, the village chieftains and the caste belonging. There used to be distinction between the "superior" and "inferior" castes and tribes, where individual identity was often surrendered to the caste identity. Further, there used to be a strong sense of collectivism among the peoples of same family, caste, ethic group, or a region. As a result, the progress made by an individual was shunned and was often grouped together with that of the family, caste, ethnic group, or the region the person came from. The individuals of the "lower caste" were forced with sanctions against adopting the status symbols of the "higher caste", thus shunning the individual competence and capability. Individuals were forced to adopt the occupations, rituals and cultural practices that specifically identified them with their family, caste or even a village. The elder or senior male members of the family used to decide in favor of the individuals of the family including the adults. There used to be very limited choice available to the individuals from among the diversity of the cultural practices. The actions and behaviors of the individuals in the traditional Nepalese framework was severely constrained and controlled by the rules and practices of the group into which the individual was born. And the subordination of the individual to the group was accepted and even coerced upon people.

With the advent of democracy and recognition of individual freedom as a cardinal value system, the individuals in the Nepalese society have started to make their choices of their own. This has greatly challenged the continuation of the traditional group norms and the culture thereof.

Individualism is evident in the urban areas, especially among the educated people, where the traditional social, cultural and religious institutions are gradually disappearing. The institution of family and the writ of the head of the family and respect to the elders and seniors is declining. Individualism is not only supported by the imported values from the Western freedom, but new economic realities and the breakdown of the monolithic family structures into nuclear units has also spearheaded the emergence of the individualism in the Nepalese society. As Nepalese people are becoming more and more individualized, the Nepalese culture has started to be a per capita thing, just as income or production.

But the worrying aspect of the rise in the individualism is the apathy of the individuals to the culture. It is the emerging new individuals, who are courageous to break the norms and rules of traditions and bend the culture for individual convenience. They break away from the group norms and the group culture of the family, society and the nation altogether. Perhaps due to an increasing apathy of the individuals to the group norms and behavior, the interest in community work for culture preservation has become a disappearing activity.

The Crumbling Heritage

In the four-way crossing at Old Baneshwor in Kathmandu, an old abandoned building is falling apart. The tiled roof has collapsed completely. The carved wooden windows have disappeared. The wall is being gradually leveled to the ground. On top of the frame of the building, there is a huge colorful banner of a Hindi movie. This old *Pati*, a public rest-house built for travelers and pilgrims, was occupied by some shopkeepers and vendors until it started to crumble. When they abandoned it, nobody ever ventured to repair it, nor anybody ever raised a voice against the condition of disrepair. This traditional building was left to crumble due to neglect, disrepair and a callous attitude of the denizens, who live around.

This Pati in Old Baneswor is not the only traditional building in Kathmandu Valley, which is falling prey to encroachment, neglect and disrepair. In Kathmandu Valley, the seat of six World Heritages sites and numerous temples and shrines, architectural structures, waterspouts and courtyards, the state of deterioration of the traditional cultural heritage is becoming serious. Nepal's rich cultural heritage, which was handed down from generations and which has survived through the ages because it used to be attached to the lives of people, seems to be crumbling. Until quite recently, heritage used to be a part of the people's daily lives the heritage value was part of the culture. But nowadays, "the pressures of population growth, uncontrolled development, poverty, tourism, inadequate legislation, and social breakdown have all contributed to a perilous situation for the continuation of living heritage", concedes a government report (IUCN/HMGN, 1992).

The conditions of our heritage are declining day after day. Temples are decaying due to lack of maintenance. Images are being stolen from the shrines of worships, artistic artifacts are getting lost and dilapidated and there is an increasing encroachment of the heritage sites. Many temples and shrines are seen being fallen apart and being dilapidated. Once landmark monuments are being buried under an expanding and indiscriminate "concrete jungle". With the growing forces of modernization, globalization, negligence, and economic compulsions, the Nepalese heritage, is being decayed.

INSTITUTIONS INEFFECTIVE

One of the problems regarding the crumbling of heritage sites is the breakdown of *Guthis*, the traditional institutions for maintaining cultural heritage with a trust-fund system. Introduced by the Lichhavis as "Gosthi" (a meeting for a particular purpose), Guthis were institutionalized during the Malla Period. The Guthis not only used to give people a sense of group identity and entertainment, it also laid down the rules and group norms for the continuation of heritage. With the nationalization of *Guthis* introducing a government owned corporation (*Guthi Sansthan*) in 1964, the local initiative for the preservation of the heritage and traditions, have been shunned. In fact, the corporation was formed to look after and regularize the Guthi institutions. But they hardly achieved anything significant in the continuation of the heritage because the corporation itself became overwhelmed by too many things to look after. The *Guthi Sansthan* lacks the capacity to take care of them, even if some degree of genuine interest to protect them exists.

Besides, the local populace has developed a callous attitude towards the traditional heritage. Instead of protecting the cultural monuments and institutions thereof, people have not hesitated to grab and encroach upon the *Guthi* land of various religious shrines. As people's belief and interest in the religious and cultural traditions is fading, some people don't hesitate to grab land from religious shrines and several other religious *Guthis*. Today, the *Guthi Sansthan* is a weak spectator of the encroachment of various religious sites. As a result of encroachment of *Guthi* land, the resources for holding festivals, *jatras* and community activities have been constrained and many such activities have been abandoned.

Heritage conservation has been pushed outside from the people's main economic agenda. People have not been able to afford the conservation of heritage at the expense of their living. Indiscriminate expansion of urban areas, loss of collective identity of people in the overpopulated areas, heterogeneous development without considering the cultural heritage conservation, capture of heritage sites for personal use, increasing attraction to modern concrete structures, and ineffective planning and controls are largely responsible for the loss of quality of heritage in major areas. Furthermore, the Nepalese education mechanism ignores the importance of cultural values and heritage preservation. Introduction of external values, pressures of market economy along with slow breakdown of religious values are also responsible for the heritage decline.

But it the neglect, disrepair, and encroachment, which is causing the decline of the heritage. Some attribute the lack of "viable institutions to guide, conserve and promote the 'polychromatic culture' and the rich cultural heritage of Nepal" (Rana, in Rana & Dhungel, eds., 1998). The encroachment of the cultural heritage sites is so evident that many such sites are either getting shrunk or are being dwarfed by the outside intrusion. If the land and buildings of the heritage sites have not been converted into personal property, vendors and shopkeepers have occupied them temporarily for commercial and even residential purposes. "Almost all the historical as well as national monuments are not only houses of the gods and goddess, but also the resting place of the street dogs, beggars and travelers" writes Amatya (1991).

Values and social structures, which have developed and supported the heritage, are being influenced by pervasive destructive process, both from within and outside the society. Not only is the diverse heritage under threat, much of the same has been already lost and disappeared due to lack of concerted conservation efforts. Heritage in Nepal is declining mainly due to absence of the notion that the heritage is a continuum of cultural expansion from rural to urban areas, which is not a museum of protected things but part of people's lives. It is hardly appreciated that heritage conservation is a system of inter-linked elements, players and forces and it remains to be fully recognized that the heritage will not be conserved by wishful thinking, scientific registers or by romantic notions by narrow interest groups, whether led by Nepalese or foreign donors (IUCN/HMGN, 1992). It has not been properly recognized that heritage conservation cannot be imposed on an unwilling population and that it must reflect the prevailing socio-economic conditions.

The conservationist and heritage activists have been raising increasing concerns regarding the crumbling of cultural heritage in Nepal. Some activists organize lucrative seminars in cozy hotel conference rooms. But they lack a widespread support. There is a very poor financial and moral support and weak awareness of the intrinsic cultural values. The preservation of valuable cultural heritage has become a lesser priority.

Furthermore, heritage conservation has been determined and led by foreign aided projects without an adequate participation and awareness of the local population. Though the government has developed concerted Master Plans for preservation of some monuments and heritage sites, the implementation is very weak because participation of people is not very enthusiastic. There were also master plans prepared (1977) for the conservation of the cultural heritage of the Kathmandu Valley. But according to Amatya (1991), the same could not be implemented for "paucity of funds". Amatya also lists such preservation activities that were carried out under the initiatives of the government-owned Department of Archaeology. There have been some efforts made to conserve the traditional values of the heritage sites. Restoration of Bhaktapur town including its cultural buildings is one such example. Similarly, efforts have been made to restore historical monuments and preserve heritage site with the assistance of various donor countries and international agencies. Master plans and projects have been developed and implemented. Conservation efforts by the Lumbini Development Trust, Pashupati Area Development Fund, and Greater Janakpur Development Project, are some good examples. Besides, lone Ancient Monuments Preservation Act (1956), a name-sake Department of Archaeology and now the Ministry of Culture and Tourism and the already ineffective *Guthi Sansthan* and their occasional efforts preservation of the heritage sites are not quite enough.

The destruction and deterioration is in such a vast scale that little efforts like these have hardly been able to prevent the decline of the cultural heritage. The government does not have adequate funds, neither has there been adequate initiatives to arouse a sense of preservation in the local communities. Breakdown of the large extended joint families into squatter nuclear units have also made maintenance of heritage much more problematic. But the broken historical links between and cultural objects and the community have jeopardized the continuation of the cultural heritage in Nepal.

Even the World Heritage Sites, which there are eight in Nepal, seven of them in Kathmandu Valley itself, are not spared from the neglect, encroachment, and callous attitude. Apart from the deteriorating condition of World Heritage Sites, illegal construction of high rise buildings in and around them areas has threatened the very existence of monuments. It has reached to such a critical stage in some sites that the UNESCO, which is responsible for declaring the World Heritage Sites, has warned that it would remove some of the Nepalese sites from the World Heritage List, if the sites are not maintained according to the world preservation standards.

There are namesake norms adopted by the government to protect the World Heritage Sites in Nepal. It restricts the construction of new buildings at certain distance and height from the declared world heritage monuments. The odd Nepal Heritage Act also does not allow construction of any house or commercial building above 35 feet high. Further, the Building Code introduced by the Department of Archaeology in 1979 also underlines certain reservations regarding building construction in these areas. Apart from height and distance, one has to strictly maintain certain traditional architecture like traditional windows, doors, rooftops, tiles, traditional bricks, etc while building private houses around the heritage sites. But these norms rather exist in the paper and are hardly seen translated into implementation.

For example, in Hanumandhoka and Bouddhanath, two of Kathmandu's famous heritage sites, buildings in the surroundings have exceeded the prescribed height. The encroachment upon the heritage land is also visible in the latter. Buildings, which do not meet the prescribed criteria, have mushroomed in the area. What defaces these areas, more than anything else, is the erection of matchbox style multi-story building with concrete structures. Whereas there is the lack of cooperation and interest from the public, the mechanism for monitoring the government-introduced codes and norms also seems to be hardly effective.

THE GODS EXILED

In August 1999, a Los Angeles-based antique collector returned back three stolen images of different Hindu deities, including a 9th century Buddha from Vichy Bahal (stolen in 1982), a 10th century Garudasana Vishnu from Hyumat Tol (stolen in the 1970s), a 12th century mutilated head of Saraswoti from Pharping (stolen in the 1980s) and a 14th century Surya from Panauti. The return by unnamed collector was inspired by Lain Singh Bangdel's book on the stolen images of Nepal. In another case, some sixteen similar images, said to be left unclaimed at London's Heathrow airport, were retrieved back in April 1996.

But these are only isolated cases. Most of the images of the gods and goddess exiled or stolen from their original places, never return. In fact, no one really knows how many are actually lost. Today, there are many temples and shrines without the sacred and beautiful images. Bangdel, in his book *The Stolen Images of Nepal,* has listed the catalogue of images lost from shrines in Nepal. He has documented with photographs some 140 stolen statues from Nepal's various temples.

Several shrines are left image-less and unattended by the public for this reason. Once popular deities in Nepal are now resting in the rooms of private collectors or museums. A popular joke about the stolen images is that the Gods and Goddesses are tired of sitting idle in the shrines are on a sightseeing vacation abroad.

Almost all of the Nepalese statuary and sculpture, that has some antiquity, found in the Western museums and private collectors are stolen property of Nepal. "Every piece of ancient religious statuary from Kathmandu Valley sits today in the West is stolen property", writes Kanak Mani Dixit. "The gods must be returned from their exile, and until such time, those who presently hold them are mere custodians."

> The process of idol theft started soon after Nepal shed up the Rana era and opened up to the world in the late 1950s. Western connoisseurs of Orient art came upon a valley which hosted a treasure trove of iconography in stone, bronze and wood- the artistic outpouring of the valley's prosperous and accomplished culture going back beyond the 5th century".. "There is now, more than ever, a need for community activists, archeologists, and other public and private custodians of Nepal's heritage to work together to actively seek the return of sculptural heritage that is today scattered throughout the West.. Besides, seeking the return of the stolen cultural property, it is important to note that a loud and visible campaign would force down the value of artifacts to destroy the future market..[1] (Dixit, 1999).

Idol-lifting may be "demand-driven", as suggested by some scholars, in the sense that the Western collectors want to get them at all costs,

---

[1] Kanakmani Dixit in *Himal,* October 1999, p. 8.

including paying the price for the smuggled items. But it is also the callous attitude of the people and the lack of continuity of the living heritage, which is sending the gods and goddess in exile. Further, weak social institutions and poor social leadership for the protection of the heritage compound the scene.

Nepal's famous images lay in museums and private collections world over, not in the shrines and temple they are supposed to be. There is a Standing Buddha (591 AD), the earliest dated bronze image of Nepal, at Cleveland Museum of Art, USA. A 9th century *Vishnu Vishwarupa* rests in Boston Museum of Fine Arts. Jack Zimmermann collection in New York keeps a *Garudasana Vishnu* (1004 AD). British Museum in London houses several images including a 12th century *Tara.* "A few Nepalese bronzes belonging to the Lichhavi Period are found in Western Museums. And among them, the *Bodhisatwa* with *Vajrapurusa* from the Los Angeles County Museum of Art, *Vajrapani* from Pan Asian Collection, New York, and the seated Buddha from the Boston Museum of Fine Arts, are some of the best examples", writes Bangdel (in Malla, 1989, p. 416-417). There is the 900-old sculpture of of Uma-Maheswor from Dhulikhel at the Museum fur Indische Kunst in Berlin. A 15th-century Laxmi-Narayan was included in the 1990 sales catalogue of the Sothby's (Dixit, *ibid*). No one really knows if many of them were not stolen or not smuggled out of Nepal.

These are only examples. There are several other art pieces lying in the private collections and museums abroad. "Since the 1960s, thousands upon thousands of stone sculptures have disappeared in this manner from the temples, monasteries, fields and forests of Kathmandu Valley and nearby towns", writes Dixit in *Himal.* "The only way devotees can view these deities is by travelling across the oceans to see them displayed, spot-lit and isolated in private drawing-room pedestals and museum niches. Other remain locked up in storage vaults, and quite safe still turn up for sale, advertised in glossy magazines specializing in oriental art" (Dixit, *ibid*). This reflects how grave is the problem of the lost images and how inconsiderate we have been towards our cultural heritage. Is not it a funny situation where one has to go to the Western museums and request private collectors in order to study the Nepalese art?

Like Bangdel has written in his book, for generations and centuries, the stolen images were worshipped and venerated by people of Nepal offering flower, vermilion powder and sweets, in times of happiness and in times of sorrow, with great pomp and festivity. When the devotees and people of the country are deprived of their gods and goddesses, their "heart-bleeds". "The stealing of such religious images is an atrocity, a serious crime which the civilized world should take steps to stop".

THE PLIGHT OF POLLUTED WATERS

In a drama staged by some school children in Kathmandu, a very dirtily dressed woman named Bagmati was not allowed in the court of Lord Indra, King of Gods, because she was very stinking so badly that she could pollute the kingdom of Gods. And she was complaining that it was "human" species, which had forced her to live in that pitiful condition. The school children were very right in showcasing the state of one of the most sacred rivers in Nepal. The impact of environmental degradation on the culture and the cultural heritage of Nepal be could not be exemplified better.

Today, Bagmati River, which flows by the holiest Hindu shrine of Pashupatinath, is the mixture of effluents or carpet washing and sewage from upstream localities. People can hardly believe it as a sacred river and very few actually dare to take a dip in the "holy water", whereas taking a holy dip used to be a pious work of the most devotees during their pilgrimage to the temple of Pashupatinath until some decades ago.

Lately, an effort has been initiated to dig a tunnel beneath the Bagmati River to allow the sewage and effluent to bypass the holy shrine of Pashupatinath. But the implementation is very slow ad no one actually knows what it would look like after the completion of the work. This will be a test case for the Nepalese people's commitment for heritage conservation, for there isn't any more pressing and worst scenario than this one.

Similarly the plight of other sacred rivers Vishnumati is very painful, in the sense that there has not been an effort to clean it. The story of Kathmandu's other rivers such as Manohara, Dhobikhola and especially Tukucha is more disgustin, because they have been converted into sewage channels.

Even the waterspouts, which the only source of drinking, washing and cleaning water in the urban areas until very recently, have become the sites for dumping garbage and sewage and many of them have dried out. These waterspouts were the architectural achievements of the medieval and even ancient Nepal and were associated with the daily lives of the people. Many were site of fairs and holy bathing and even sacred idol washing on various occasions. People used to take initiative to preserve and keep these spouts clean. Kings used to construct waterspout as pious acts. But these architectural and the cultural heritage of the history are vanishing because of lack of necessary maintenance. But these stone water taps of majestic beauty are now becoming sites for piling garbage and accumulating the sewage in many localities. Encroachment of the tap area is increasing. Many such sources of clean drinking water are not operating. According to one report (1995), out of 130 stone taps in Kathmandu, only 30 are operational. Most sources of water to such taps have dried up. The famous example is Sundhara, the best known water golden waterspout in the heart of Kathmandu. Some years ago, the water source there had dried up after a public undertaking dug the nearby area for the construction of its business complex. With increasingly large number of residents getting piped-water supply, the use of such traditional taps is declining and the sites are being abandoned. In some cases, the sunken places around taps are filled by sewage from the local areas, and sometimes by solid garbage.

The plight of numerous ancient ponds of cultural significance in Kathmandu valley is no less different. Ancient and medieval kings and court-men used to dig ponds for pious work. Those ponds were tied with the lives of people because they provided water for cleaning, washing, drinking and even for recreating. Many of them were associated with several legends and some are linked to the festivals. In some, the local deities used to be taken to holy dips. Taudhaha, the reminiscent of legendary Lake *Naghrad,* the draining of which believed to have created the Kathmandu Valley, has been associated with the legends of the famous *Karkotak Naga,* a serpent king, who is said to have donated the diamond-studded vest of Lord Machhendranath, which is exhibited each year in the festival *Bhotojatra,* in Patan. There are legends and history associated with Ranipokhari of Kathmandu, and *Taba Pokhari* of Bhaktapur.

But these ponds have been abandoned and are out of public use. Several such ponds are sites for accumulating the sewage of the local area. In several others, the outside area is encroached and engulfed by brick-box houses. An effort to encroach the western side of

Ranipokhari, a famous pond at the heart of Kathmandu, was thwarted in November 2000 after a public uproar. The interesting side of this story is that the construction of the business complex there was initiated by a public undertaking, which was supposed to be maintaining such sites. Not only is the religious and cultural importance of such heritage being lost away, even the commercial and day-to-day use of the sanctitious ponds is declining.

In Janakpurdham, a city with numerous ponds of religious significance, the condition of the sacred water tanks is not less painful. Apart from the encroachment to the scared ponds, the continuing flow of sewage and industrial effluence into the ponds has altogether changed the scared image of the city's water containers. It is these sacred ponds, where the pious devotees take holy ablutions and come to worship their deities. Several thousand devotes take holy dips in these ponds during the famous festival of *Chhath*, in which the people of the areas make offering to the Sun god.

MODERNIZATION INTERFERING WITH HERITAGE

A story in a local weekly[2] said that the temple of *Amar Narayan* in Tansen, the headquarters of Palpa district, west Nepal, was being modernized. Built in 1806 by war hero Amar Singh Thapa and full of historical and cultural artifacts, the temple structure was reinforced by cement and iron grills, and its *Tunals* and struts were painted with enamel.

While the neglect of the local population has left the heritage to crumble in some cases, inappropriate conservation efforts have distorted the original face and value of the heritage in some others. In many cases, the enthusiasm to preserve the heritage has resulted in distortion of the original art form. At others, efforts to build new cultural structures have de-linked the traditions associated with such sites.

Today, such "inappropriate and modern materials such as cement, ceramic tile, marble, and corrugated metal sheets have been introduced" in building temples and for preserving ancient monuments and shrines (Amatya, 1991). In some shrines, the votaries offer some bells or add some structures, which are completely disregarding the

---

[2] *Bimarsha*, September 9, 1994

aesthetics of the ancient art form and sometimes the historical character of the heritage itself becomes lost in such a process, says Amatya (1991).

In Deughat, a well-known pilgrimage center at the confluence of Kali Gandaki and Trishuli rivers, a newly constructed temple, poses a conspicuous oddity in the environment of the area, which consists of mainly small shrines and *ashrams*. Besides the several small temples including that of *Laxmi Narayana*, *Satya Narayana* and *Kurma Avatar* (tortoise incarnation of Lord Vishnu), there are several *ashrams* and *kutis* where sages and saints stay in order to devote their lives to the God. Most of these structures are constructed out of wood and rocks and have either thatched or slated roofs. These little buildings remind us of the *Satya Yuga*, the famous Hindu age of truth and benevolence, when religion and truth was practiced as a way of life. Many old people have come here to reside in the *ashrams* in order to spend their time in the devotion of Lord Vishnu. They have clad themselves in saffron robes and are seen walking around in the narrow pavement. There are *Tulsi Maths* (small mounds for planting the sacred herb *Tulsi*) in front of each of the *Kutis*. Several saints are seen sitting in *Dhuni* (the continuous burning of fire-logs) and religious rites are seen being performed in some places. Recitals of sacred *Mantras* and *Bhajans* can be heard in some places. Cows are seen every where and there is no trace of modernization. This area could constitute an ideal location for a representative Hindu way of life for people and tourist to come and see. But this new temple looks so ugly and this spoils the beauty of the area so much that, it is almost shocking to a visitor. This new temple of *Harihar Vishnu* is a huge double-story structure with shining white marbles and Moslem style domes on the top. This temple must have been built recently with a lot of amount raised from the wealthy business people in Chitwan area. It looks modern but ugly. Inside the temple, the main image is locked inside a iron-grill gate. It is not only the deity, which is in prison, even the heritage tradition is held hostage by such indiscriminate modernization.

In Bhaktapur, a big satellite antenna stands by a stone statue of Garuda, a mythological half-man-half-bird guardian of *Vaisnavite* temples worshipped as the vehicle of Lord Vishnu. Such indiscriminate modernizing of the heritage sites and encroachment of the heritage sites and shrines has not only spoiled the beauty of the area, but has also posed risk to the invaluable treasures. The introduction of modern structures and services has caused significant deterioration in the historic character of the heritage sites. Overhead electrical wiring, poles and suspended transformers in the vicinity of the monuments are not only intrusive to the heritage value, they also pose a risk of fire to the shrines. The installation of dish antennae, telephone and TV cables, as well as street-lighting equipment on historic facades is defacing their originality. The cutting of pavement to install underground services, with subsequent sub-standard restoration, has also led to rapid deterioration of the heritage sites. Building houses and modern structures without considering the aesthetic and cultural value of the heritage sites is becoming very much common. People are encroaching the traditional land and property of the religious shrines and heritage sites. This is not only due to lack of the government action. But the attitude towards the cultural sites is also seems to be changing towards negligence and disregard. In other places, people have erected new temples and shrines in contrast departure from the traditions of building religious shrines in the country.

Yet another factor defacing the cultural values of the heritage is the indiscriminate advertising with the posters, banners, and hoarding boards. The craze for advertising has become so pervasive that there are banners and hoarding boards of consumer items everywhere. Advertising materials can even seen on top of the rural houses along the beneath the cable car en route to the temple of *Manakamana*, a famous deity in the central hilly area west of Kathmandu. So much so that, even the temple premises have been invaded by the advertising banners and boards of consumer products. Some years ago, the pollution was restricted to the expansion of the lodges and the *Bhattis* (shops which sell liquor) in areas adjoining the temple, a famous pilgrimage center in Central Nepal. This has abated since the construction of the cable car connecting to the temple site. But the conspicuous hoarding advertisement signs including that of alcoholic beverages right at the temple premises still continue to bewilder the devotees, who visit there.

This kind of cultural pollution has not only threatened the religious and cultural values, but it has also spoiled the beauty of the area. Similar pollution of cultural sites can also be seen elsewhere, especially in an around the Kathmandu Valley. The encroachment of advertising materials not only defaces the heritage areas, it also reduces the importance of the sites to commercial use minimizing its heritage value..

FADING FESTIVALS

Some years ago, a feature article in a local daily stated that the interest in Kathmandu to celebrate the famous *Gaijatra* festival was decreasing. In the last two decades or so, less and less number of people are sending boys dressed as cows to commemorate their dead relatives during the year. This may have been brought about by the decreasing population of the holy cow in the Kathmandu Valley, which is unable sustain the bovine population because of increasing urbanization. But the changing economic and cultural imperatives and values have been pushing the festivals outside the people's priorities. The loss of interest to celebrate *Gaijatra*, in which the whole Kathmandu Valley used to be in festive mood until very recently, is not an exception. The loss of interest in celebrating the traditional festival, fairs and worships seems to be declining in general, mainly urban areas. The interest on tradition and festivals is fading. The festivals are losing their charm and they little fascinate people as they used to do sometime ago.

A headline in a local daily[3] reported that "the Jubilation of *Bibah Panchami* is waning". In Janakpurdham, the fifth day of the bright lunar fortnight in the month of December is observed as *Bibah Panchami*, to commemorate the auspicious wedding of Lord Rama and his consort Sita. There used to be a huge fair held jubilantly with much of fanfare and religious activities. As the religious festival of Janakpurdham known for processions and fairs, *Bibah Panchami* used to be celebrated with much of fanfare until some decades ago. Pilgrims used to congregate here from places in India and adjoining regions of Janakpurdham. Several theaters and drama groups, circus and theatrical performances etc. were used to be organized. Vendors used to come all the way from Ludhiana and Delhi of India. The festive activity used to last for about a month. But that is now the celebration has started to be done as a mere formality and there is no such fanfare. The loss of interest in such a huge cultural event, which has been there for centuries, is a distinct pattern of the Culture Shift in Nepal.

---

[3] *Kantipur*, December 4, 1994

"Festivals are waning in their importance", concedes a government report. "The cultural significance of festivals has been influenced by outside pressures, which keep people away from traditional belief and associated performances. As a result, the visits by pilgrims and other worshippers to various sites are less of a cultural event than a modern distortion of cheap entertainment, and the festivals as a result become a less important feature of Nepali life" (IUCN/HMGN, 1992).

FORGOTTEN CALENDARS

Hindu lunar calendar, known popularly as *Panchanga,* used to occupy very important place in the way of life and cultural and religious activities in Nepal. Named after the five things that had special significance in human life (the day, the date, the location of the moon, and the place of planets), *Panchanga* system of lunar calendar, lists days, months, weeks, hours and moments, that are either auspicious or inauspicious for human beings. People's daily rhythm corresponded to the lunar cycle. People used to abide by the rule and norms on the days and dates according to this calendar system. People used to seek advises from a priest about an auspicious day to start to a pilgrimage or to initiate a cultural rite. Every Nepalese household used to keep a *Panchanga* calendar, which also used to give them the sense of time and divine programming. Hindu astrological predictions were so accurate that eclipses and several other celestial events could be timed almost exactly.

But with the advent of modern Western calendar system and with a gradual dissociation with the traditional rhythm of life, Nepalese people hardly continue to do their daily chores and rituals in accordance with the lunar calendar system. It is becoming quite unusual for Nepalese people to ask for an advise for an auspicious days. Though people still look for auspicious days to start building a house or performing a cultural ceremony like a wedding, very rarely they consult the traditional lunar calendar to do most of other cultural errands. Most people are increasingly attracted to the glossy charts of the western Christian era. Even the Nepali calendar of Bikram Sambat, which is 57 years ahead of the Christian calendar era, and which is still used in the official correspondence in Nepal, seems to have lost relevance to many a modernized Nepalese people living in Kathmandu and around the globe.

Festivals like *Balachaturdashi, Nagapanchami, Rakshabandahan*, which used to be celebrated jubilantly with much of fanfare and festivities, have now been reduced to mere formalities. On festive occasions these days, people dislike taking a dip in the "holy water" of Bagmati and other sacred rivers in Kathmandu. It is not only because the river is getting too much polluted, but largely because people's interest on festive and religious activities is waning. People are altogether entering into a seemingly new cultural transition. The cultural and festive activities in most parts of the country are held with less fanfare and enthusiasm than it used to a couple of decades ago. People's active and enthusiastic participation in festivals and cultural activities has been considerably decreasing. The festive dances and unique *jatras* of Kathmandu valley, which were celebrated jubilantly throughout the year, have either disappeared or have been reduced to rituals and formalities. Several traditional practices have either already disappeared or stopped being performed. At times, festivals were regarded as "foundation" of the Nepalese society. Today, people's zeal and enthusiasm for such festivities is nothing but declining.

Even *Indrajatra*, the premier festival of Kathmandu, is losing its enthusiasm and it has been reduced to a mere formality, writes a columnist.[4] The tradition of the famous Tripurasundari dance held on the occasion has disappeared. Earlier, there was the tradition of slaughtering a male-buffalo on all seven days of Indrajatra. These days, only one is offered. Further, the practice of erecting the statue of *Indrayani* in each Tole in Kathmandu during the festival has almost vanished.

The loss of interest in some of the festivals is also being assisted by the recent opposition to some of the festival alleging there are the festivals of the Hindu Brahman Chhetris, not that of the ethnic minorities. Lately, the activists people of certain ethnic groups have started campaigning to abandon celebrating Hindu festivals like *Dashain* and *Tihar*. That may be labeled as "politically motivated" blamed as "ethnopolitics". But the challenge to the traditional Hindu festivals has raised the question on their universality in the country. It has started to be blamed that these festivals have been imposed upon indigenous people by the immigrant Hindus, mainly Brahmans. Though this change has not yet taken visible shape, and rejection of *Dashain* has

---

[4] Kusum Bhattarai in *Khabarpatrika*, September 21, 1999

been mostly symbolic, the importance of festivals are being questioned by applying political, religious, economic and even cultural rationality.

UNFASTENING LEGENDS

Legends that have been binding people together with religious and cultural belief are unfastening. Myths and legends that have been followed as reality earnestly and venerably have now lost their significance. People have lost interests on festivals and ceremonies based on such myths and legends. Festivals based on legends and stories are becoming less popular. Be it a legend of the lost and found vest of Lord *Machhendranath*, that of *Karkotak Naga*, demons *Balasur* and *Ghantakarna*, legends and myths have started to bring fewer impacts and influences in the people's lives.

Today, it is quite usual for many young people in Patan not to know about the origin and significance of Red *Macchendranath's* chariot festival and the exhibition of the vest (*Bhotojatra*). Oral traditions such as story telling are dying. With outside influences, the social values and culture embedded in those traditions are lost. Even though all temples and places have their own stories, which keep their history alive, these folk tales are infrequently published (IUCN/HMGN, 1992, p. 13). Forget about the strong oral tradition of telling stories from *Dantyakatha* and *Panchatantra*, which were both entertaining as well as instructive.

A local daily had reported in 1994, that the yearly *Dattatraya* festival of Bhaktapur did not take place that year. This *Jatra* is held on the day following *Gaijatra*. But that year, the department of archaeology, which has kept the costumes and materials taken out in procession of the deity, kept the things locked in the *Bhaktapur Durbar*. And the tradition stopped. Many other deities are kept captive in their shrines instead of being traditionally carried out in public processions.

In 1989, a tradition of more than 400 years was broken as the yearly *Ashtamatrika* dance of Patan was discontinued because of "lack of funds". Traditionally, the colorful dance of the eight masked mother goddesses (*Brahmayani, Maheswori, Kumari, Vaisnavi, Varahi, Indrayani, Chamunda* and *Mahalaxmi*), which used to be held amidst melodious traditional music and fanfare of the local people, was institutionalized under a *Guthi*, a traditional cooperative, which used to get revenue from its land plots in Kathmandu Valley. After the land of the Guthi was transferred to the *Guthi Sansthan*, the public corporation for overseeing the affairs of the *Guthis*, in 1964, there was a scarcity of resources for funding such dances and cultural activities. The *Ashtamatrika* dance got funds from Patan municipality for a few years. Then that stopped. It takes a lot of money to prepare the gorgeous masks and dresses and other decoration for the dance. Musical instruments cost money. Without money, the activity stopped. The mother goddesses disappeared from the streets of the old city. No one knows, when they will dance again. There are only some examples. Today, there are many traditional *jatras* and festivals, which are being abandoned because of lack of funds or lack of community interest.

In other cases, the essence and merit of the festivals have changed and the events have taken altogether a new cultural shape. In his popular TV comedy soap "*Hijo Aajaka Kura*", Santosh Pant, a well known comedian, satires how people observe festivals like Tihar abandoning the original quest of the festivals. In Tihar, the festivals of lights, the young people have abandoned the traditional tune "*Deusi*" and "*Bhailo*" songs and instead started to mix modern and western music. Neither they tell that "we are sent by Bali Raja". In some extreme cases, as in Santosh Pant's comedy show, the youth use the collected money to drink beer and disturb other groups going door to door in the traditional fashion. In fact, today, most of the young people play *Deusi* for the money they get not for its cultural significance. Further, the practice of gambling in Tihar is on the rise, while shopping sweetmeats and flower garlands is on the decline. Interestingly, use of firecrackers smuggled in from India, which used to be rare, is becoming more and popular, despite the ban imposed by the state.

Enthusiasm in celebrating a festive occasion may be observed in some cases. But the inner motive for such enthusiasm may be a different one. For example, cheering students along the Highways in the Terai erect barricades and collect money from drivers of buses, trucks, cars and motorcycles in the name of Saraswoti Puja. In Kathmandu, young children frenziedly extort money from by-passers and drivers for "cremating *Ghantakarna*", a legendary and infamous demon. In Tihar, young people move around singing *Bhailo* and *Deusi* in a very festive mood. But the motive may not be to get the religious merit but to collect money for fun. In Holi, the Hindu festival of colors, young students (mostly boys) throw water balloons jubilantly at women passing by or at the buses and cars. In Tij, many young men visit the festive sites such as Pashupanitnath along with the women. The motive, in these cases, are different, that of teasing or flirting with young women. Festivals like these are being celebrated albeit with different connotations.

THE UPSURGE OF UGLINESS

If anything is defacing the cultural heritage of Nepal, it is the upsurge of ugliness. In the expanding slums in urban areas, all the aesthetic sense manifested in the traditional Nepalese art and architecture is being jettisoned. The jungle of signboards of all sizes, colors and sizes with incorrectly spelt names, various wall graffiti and posters, gaudy posters from the Hind and Nepali movies, gawky advertisement boards and neon signs continue to deface Nepalese towns and cities. In the urban concrete jungle, the original beauty of a templescape or a traditional temple courtyard have now been confined rarely to a few places of historical interest.

The ugliness is not just confined to outside world. People's inner sense of aesthetics is being lost. The ugly dresses, which do not conform to the local culture, have been accepted easily. By adopting the ugliest kinds of imported junk food and dress, people are defacing their own culture with ugliness. Brass and bronze kitchenware has given way to steel, glass and plastics. Modern synthetic and acrylic clothes have replaced the traditional textiles and home-woven clothes. Women use plastic flowers to beautify their living rooms. People attend marriage parties in gaudiest suits, instead of the traditional Nepali dresses. Children wear shoes that spark and make every irritating noise at every step. Cacophonic band music is blasted during the weddings imitating the phony Hindi songs. People blast ugliest songs and irrelevant music through loudspeakers on every occasions, disregarding the peace of others. People erect ugly pandals and welcome gates and decorate them with mismatching colors and lights to demonstrate their wealth and status. But they do not realize the dearth of cultural values.

People pollute the shrines adding ugly, unimpressive and mismatching structures form their ill-earned money to purchase the divine pardon for the sins they have committed. Others erect whole new temples without considering the heritage values in the surrounding area. People also buy the commercial portraits of gods and goddesses, which perpetuate a pervasive sense of ugliness lacking even a trace of a sense of aesthetics. In a country, where artistic and aesthetic heritage used to so much well developed, it is this ugliness, which is defacing the cultural heritage.

Anarchic Architecture

If architecture is frozen art, the treasure of Nepalese traditional architecture, which is famous for picturesque pagodas, majestic palaces, and numerous indigenous housing structures, is gradually melting. Traditional style and norms of construction are gradually disappearing. The beauty and originality of Nepali architecture is being replaced by brick box type houses and concrete structures expanding in the fastest ever rate, mainly in Kathmandu Valley. While the treasures of ancient architectural knowledge are being forgotten, alien architectural styles are invading the Nepalese architecture. The traditional Nepalese architecture, which was successful to create so many beautiful pagodas and shrines, is now forgotten and the modern Nepalese architecture is becoming anarchic.

MUZAFFARPUR IN THE MAKING

Until a few decades ago, the dominant architectural structures in Kathmandu Valley used to be the majestic pagodas and omnipresent shrines. The typical scene in a village and even in the urban areas used to be a conspicuous temple or a shrine built in pagoda style tapering amidst the lush green fields and brick-red houses. But this picture is changing very fast, especially in urban areas, due to expansion of modern housing. Indiscriminate housing without considering the beauty of traditional Nepalese architecture has spoiled the beauty of urban areas, which are fast turning into slums. In Kathmandu Valley, "once fertile land has now grown into ugly concrete jungle completely destroying the scenic beauty and skyline dominated by pagodas", writes a commentator in a local fortnightly magazine.[1] The traditional "templescape" in Kathmandu Valley is being taken over by the expanding "concretescape".

The haphazard expansion and unplanned urbanization has not only spoiled the physical beauty of the city, it has also degraded the

---

[1] Paudel, Keshab (1996), Culture: Setting a Course for Nowhere, *The Spotlight* (Sep 6-12, 1996), Kathmandu.

cultural quality of the architecture and the Nepalese art. For some years between 1975 and 1980, there used to be construction norms requiring the buildings in Kathmandu Valley to have Nepalese style slanted rooftops and to have red bricks exposed outside, at least in the front part of the house. But that could not be implemented, mainly due to absence of rigorous building codes and the unlimited pressure of construction of new houses in the urban areas for residential and commercial purposes. Similarly, there are norms restricting the height of commercial buildings to be built around the monument sites. But multi-story buildings higher than the temples are being built in such designated areas. Today, palatial modern buildings are sprouting like mushrooms everywhere, irrespective of the location of temples, shrines and traditional monuments. The ineffective implementation of these norms has spoiled the architectural beauty of the city in an irreversible way.

One of the most direct threats to the traditional Nepalese architecture comes from the lack of planning, zoning and construction norms. That is compounded by the callous attitude of the people towards the built heritage:

> Modern Nepal suffers from a lack of planning and zoning. People are permitted to build whatever they like. Thus industries, shops, family residences, restaurants, temples can exist everywhere and anywhere. The Nepalese don't seem to see the danger of factories and shops eroding the temples. Nor do most see a need to reconstruct decaying temples. Many decaying temples are demolished and replaced with cement box-like houses or commercial buildings (Josephson, 1998).

To prevent the haphazard expansion of the residential areas in Kathmandu Valley, there were some efforts to introduce planned housing in some areas like Kuleswor, Golphutar, Dullu, Gongabu and Bhainsepati. But these town planning initiatives where not only highly inadequate and painfully slow in implementation to meet the increasing demand, they were also out of reach of the emerging middle class, which continued to pour into the Kathmandu Valley in search of education, jobs, and business opportunities.

So the housing expanded in whatever or wherever there was a possibility. The expansion did not even spare the lowlands in the banks of three main rivers of the valley, Bagmati, Vishnumati and Dhobikhola. Once protected for cultivation because of high soil fertility, these low-lying area have now been taken over mostly by the people of the emerging middle class, who are in need of cheap housing in the Kathmandu Valley as they are new economic migrants to the city. If the present haphazard urbanization continues, Kathmandu Valley, once the seat of living heritage, "will turn into a concrete slum", warns Poudel.[2]

In Kathmandu Valley, the Newar towns used to set up with a good sense of planning. Highlands were allocated for settlement and lowlands for farming. The city center used to be designed in intricate patterns and there used to spaces allocated for courtyards, temples, public gatherings, markets and the like. Streets, though narrow, used to be paved and kept clean. But this conventional wisdom seems to have disappeared, even among the Newar settlements, especially among the newly expanding suburbs.

The haphazard urbanization is not only spoiling the aesthetic beauty of our ancient cities, it has also led to the destruction of the natural, and cultural heritage, at the same time polluting the environment very badly. Even the famous Basantapur Durbar Square, which is in the protected zone in the heart of Kathmandu, is not spared:

> We are sad to notice that today around the monument areas, for example Basantapur Durbar Square, which is the heart of the Nepalese architecture, many new ugly buildings are coming up in numbers, which spoil the whole divine atmosphere, environment, landscape and the beauty of the area. The sky-kissing Gajuras of our temples and stupas are slowly pushed into the background by the mass of these tall giant modern buildings. Even the beautiful aerial view of the valley is marred by these ugly projections. It is very dangerous that the foreign architecture is dominating the whole valley (Amatya, 1991).

Similarly disappointing views can been seen around the most beautiful temples and traditional courtyards in Kathmandu Valley, which was once described by a visitor as a place "where there are more religious buildings than houses". Except in the Durbar Squares, some temple courtyards, and some thoroughfares of old parts of Kathmandu, Patan and Bhaktapur, where it is still common to come across a pagoda, a shrine, a traditional water tank or a rest house (*Paati*), the traditional

---

[2] In *The Spotlight*, September 11, 1998

architectural structure is rarely seen in the new parts of the cities. All one can see in the newly expanded areas is the concrete structures.

A typical Newari house in Kathmandu Valley used to be built on a rectangular base, two to three stories high, crowned with double-pitched tile roof, ornately carved wooden beams, pillars, windows and doors, and wooden struts supporting the slanting roofs. But this architecture is now restricted to some exclusive Newar suburbs like Panauti, Banepa, Harisiddhi, Bode, Thimi near Kathmandu Valley.

In the cities, new constructions even among Newars don't follow the old and traditional architecture. The principal reason is the attraction towards and demonstration effect of the modern concrete housing. The second is an economic one. The traditional housing is an expensive venture since it requires a lot of wood and art work which is getting more and more expensive these days. Traditional houses are gradually being replaced with matchbox type concrete structure that has not only spoiled the beauty of a town but also lost the architectural heritage.

Some traditional housing and the templescape are saved in Bhaktapur, the oldest city in Kathmandu Valley. Nyatapola is still the highest structure and many other pagoda roofs look prominent in the city. But new concrete buildings replacing the beautiful Newar traditional houses along the old brick-paved Bhaktapur streets is spoiling the entire scenic beauty of the old medieval town. Patan, the town of the craftsmen, "is being taken over by spindly skyscrapers built on tiny plots of sub-divided land", writes a columnist: [3]

Aged buildings with frescos, latticed windows and fired-brick fonts come down in a flurry of centuries-old dust and in their places shoot up multistoried cement boxes with ubiquitous steel shutters on the ground floor. Billboards of Pepsi and Coca-Cola block views of stupas, political graffiti deface temple walls, and banners of assorted beers and lotteries festoon the narrow gullies. Patan gets to look more and more like India's provincial town of Muzaffurpur or Gorakhpur.

This "anarchic" state of architecture owes to the lack of proper building codes and implementation strategy in the part of the state. But it is also the callous attitude of the people, who do not wish to retain the

---

[3] Shrestha, Bijaya Lal (1991), "Patan: A City No More Shining", *Himal* (May/June 1991)

traditional norms in their craze for modernization. Furthermore, the construction in the traditional norms is not only highly expensive, it is all the more difficult in the competitive market, which sells more attractive materials for cheaper prices.

The uncontrolled expansion of concrete buildings in Kathmandu valley has not only spoiled the beauty of the towns, it has also put a large number of people at risk to the earthquakes, especially in the narrow streets, where escape in the event of a big disaster is extremely difficult. Pagodas and even ordinary buildings of the medieval period were highly resistant to earthquakes because they were constructed with inter-linked wooden struts and wooden support at roofs and wall corners. The expansion of the concrete jungle has completely forgotten the conventional wisdom and traditional art at the same time. The haphazard expansion has created confusion regarding our ancient arts, culture and tradition. The cultural harmony with regards to architecture is at jeopardy.

The alarming nature of expansion is not that the concretescape is expanding, but it is that the preservation and expansion of the cultural heritage has almost stopped. Many temples can been seen with emerging trees from the rooftops, broken walls and lost images. The fundamental characteristics of the Nepalese architecture, be it a towering pagoda or an ordinary house, thatched hut or a traditional mud-brick house, included slanting roof, exposed red wall bricks, carved windows, separate story carnations, high plinth level, tile columns, and use of a lot of wooden struts and beams. But these are becoming rare.

An official report (IUCN/HMGN, 1992) concedes that the trend of architectural development in Nepal does not blend with various built heritage of Nepal such as temples, shrines, Durbar Squares, Bahals, Ghats etc. It also says that many traditional building skills are declining, and in some cases, have disappeared due to lack of popular demand and lack of economic viability. The report further adds that building materials of the past like large size timber, high quality bricks, and brass and other materials are no longer available, and that the traditional technology has been unable to compete with industrialized processes.

Traditional Nepali architecture, especially the construction of temples and monasteries, was based on manuals called *Vastu Shashtra*, the science of architecture. Even cities used to be designed on the basis of these treatises. The three cities of Kathmandu, Bhaktapur and

Lalitpur- were "planned in accordance with the basic *Mandala* principles as described in the town-planning treatises of *Manasara* and were planned to resemble specific religious objects to ensure constant protection by the gods and goddesses, and to ensure health, wealth and prosperity of the cities' inhabitants (Karan & Ishii, 1996, p. 191). Kathmandu was designed in the shape of a sword of the goddess *Mahalaxmi*, and Patan like that of Buddha's *Dharma Wheel.* The town planning consisted of the innate sense of aesthetics, a natural rhythmic articulation of objects and a concerted effort to preserve the tradition. *Vastu Shashtras* had laid down principles of harmonious construction on the basis of topography, the constellations, planetary positions of the sun and the moon. The most important buildings were constructed on most auspicious places. Cities were designed in intricate grid pattern, where specific constructions were made at certain allocated places.

There used to be much more detailed plans and architectural designs available for traditional buildings. Traditional architecture (*Vastukala*) used to be a great science and art and subject of a lot of devotion and study. This knowledge was preserved for centuries and applied by the rulers and residents alike for centuries. But this treasure of knowledge is now limited to some never consulted documents being eaten by moths. The rich treasures have seldom been utilized in planning new cities and modern houses.

In the medieval Kathmandu, towns were intricately designed with a mesh of residence, Bahals, Bahis, and Chowks. Town planners conceived the necessity of *Pati* and *Dharmashala* (public rest places), *Dabali* (places for drama and theatre show). There were several waterspouts, ponds, and open spaces (e.g. Lagankhel, Tundikhel). All of these were highly useful and were associated with the daily lives of people. Some of these were used for organizing community cultural activities, mainly rituals and feasts.

But many of these cultural sites are being occupied or encroached indiscriminately. This is changing the cultural landscape and spoiling the vernacular architecture in the valley. The concretescape is not only prevalent in the areas, which are expanding. But traditional building in the core city areas of Patan, Kathmandu, Bhaktapur and Kirtipur are also being demolished and new concrete-brick boxes are being erected in their place. In some places such as Kirtipur, Harisiddhi and Thimi, there still remain intermittent latticed windows and wooden struts along with old brick walls. But the new concrete structures are outnumbering the traditional architectural structures.

ARCHITECTURAL INVASIONS

Although pagodas dominated the Nepalese temple architecture, many architectural styles were introduced in Nepal in different epochs of the history. The Indian *Shikhara* style of architecture, which is usually built on a square base with a dome which represents a folded umbrella, was introduced as early as the sixteenth century in temples such as Krishna Mandir (built in 1583) and Mahabouddha (built 1636) of Patan.

Though some temples were built in Muslim type domes during the Malla Period (c. 1200-1768), the Muslim architecture was brought to Kathmandu only in the 19th century by the Ranas. For example, the temple of Kalamochan, built in 1884 by Jung Bahadur Rana, has a lot of Muslim architectural influence. Moghul type temples are also found around Pashupatinath complex and in the middle of Rani Pokhari, in the temple of Bala Narayana. Much of traditional and Moghul architecture was constructed in what has been described as "ill-advised architectural marriages" (Josephson, 1988). The famous Dharahara, built by Bhimsen Thapa, was also an imitation to Muslim style minaret. Some architectural motifs, cuspid arches and cypress columns, give evidence of Muslim influence in Nepali architecture (Josephson, *ibid.,* 1988).

Decaying of the traditional architecture in Nepal began as the Rana administrators started to introduce European style palaces. On his return (1851) from a tour of Europe, Prime Minister Jung Bahadur Rana initiated construction of British style palaces. Ranas adopted this style of architecture in erecting their residences and office buildings. Chadra Shamsher Rana constructed the famous Singhadurbar,[4] which now houses the secretariat complex of the government and the most prominent of all such buildings. Though this majestic building adds to the architectural beauty of Kathmandu, it rarely has rarely anything that depicts a Nepali style. Western style big halls with huge crystal chandeliers and round columns and pillars are the main features. There

---

[4] Built in 1901, Singhadurbar was destroyed partially in a fire in 1973 and a part of it was rebuilt., to a some extent, to the original specification. According to a legend, it took 27 months to complete its construction and there were 404 rooms originally.

are several such structures in Kathmandu. Typically named as Durbars after the person who built them, they have "extravagant tastes: huge crystal chandeliers, plate-glass, bronze nymphs, billiard tables, Victorian bric-a-bracs, grandfather clocks, and other exotic items carried on men's backs" (Josephson, 1988, p. 55). Examples include Keshar Mahal, Shital Niwas, Baghdarbar, Harihar Bhawan, Lal Darbar, etc. Similar influence can be seen in other architectural structures. For example, Ghantaghar, the clock-tower of Kathmandu, was built by Bir Shamsher Rana as an imitation of Britain's Big Ben. These new styles of construction retarded the interest in the traditional architecture in Kathmandu valley.

The loss of traditional beauty of the Nepalese architecture is not only common in urban areas. Even in district headquarters in the hilly regions, new ugly construction are increasing in the name of modernization. Instead of the traditional two or three storey houses with slanting roofs, new brick-box concrete structures are becoming omnipresent in the small towns and market centers een in the rurla areas. In Syangja, a hilly district in central Nepal, for example, the round thatched huts, which used to be common, are now disappearing.[5]

The Kathmandu Valley is traditionally famous for people skilled in masonry, carpentry and crafts. They knew how to build temples, Bihars and monasteries. Beautifully carved windows and doors and wooden beams in the traditional structures were the creative art of the people in the valley. But today people from outside the valley do much of the jobs related to building houses. A large number of masons and carpenters are coming to the valley to seek jobs in the new type of construction. Kathmandu Valley, which was once famous for skilled construction workers, is importing construction labors from India and southern plains. This has not only flooded cheap labor in Kathmandu valley, it has also gradually lost the well known skills of artistic constructions. The interest for building traditional houses is fading as the attraction for modern engineered houses do not give enough room for Nepali designs. Today, only a few hotels, resorts, a few private bungalows are being built in traditional styles. Most of the private residences are following matchbox concrete structures. The Nepalese architecture is becoming anarchic.

---

[5] *Kantipur*, December 2, 1996

A Different Entertainment

With the invasion of the satellite television, round the clock broadcasts of the FM channels, opening of several dancing restaurants and discotheques, and emergence of a new culture of drinking, gambling and partying, the traditional forms of Nepalese entertainment is changing rapidly. Nepalese people are gradually abandoning the traditional forms of entertainment such as celebrating various festivals, organizing family unions and feasts, drinking home made liquors, and going to various fairs (*melas* and *jatras*), singing folk songs, playing traditional musical instruments, and watching the traditional dances. While traditional institutions like Rodighar are on decay and the folk musical traditions are being obsolete, signs of copying the Western entertainment culture. Increasingly, an "Hungama Culture", an upbeat entertainment with loud music, wild dances and a lot of partying, is becoming the Nepalese method of entertainment. The culture of drinking, gambling, and partying, which used to be restricted in some festive occasions and a few communities, is now gripping the entire society. Further, partying for one reason or another, and traveling for fun and for pleasure, Nepalese people are seeking different new forms of entertainment and escapes from daily chores of life.

THE HOUSE ARREST

If only one thing is to be attributed to the Culture Shift, one would tend to name the satellite television. The numerous channels available through the satellite television have not only offered information, images and entertainment unknown to the Nepalese people a few decades ago, it has infused an altogether new culture of entertainment in the Nepalese society. With the access to the magic box expanding to an increasingly large number of people in the country, Nepalese people are being exposed to a plethora of entertainment, information, images and events. The invasion from the sky has become so much pervasive that many Nepalese people, especially the youngsters in the urban areas are increasingly becoming "TV addicts". Even the people of older generations are becoming "house arrest" as the captive audiences of the television. With the increasing access to the magic box, the Nepalese people have been increasingly falling prey to the ever-expanding doses of the television. Today, while the youngsters watch the television for their favorite MTV V-Jays, for the mock wrestling shows, several countdown shows and hip-shaking numbers from the movie world and Indipop songs, they hardly realize that they are being trapped in an inescapable "TV culture". Today, television, more than anything else, has been instrumental in shaping the minds and mood of the Nepalese people at a much greater pace than ever before. The television has shaped new values, norms and lifestyles of the people, especially among the younger generations.

Though the satellite television is available only in Kathmandu and a few urban areas, and is accessible to a limited percentage of population, its impact has been gradually increasing. "Even Kathmandu has cable", wrote John Naisbitt in his *Megatrends Asia.* "At the beginning of 1995, about 1,000 homes there could choose among 16 different channels. Prazwol Pradhan, the person who brought cable to Kathmandu, intends to grow the industry into a satellite broadcasting hub rivaling Hong Kong and Singapore", wrote Naisbitt (1996). A regional hub may be a distant thing. But by the beginning of 2001, most of the people in Kathmandu Valley have already an access to more than thirty channels offered by several cable TV providers. Space Time Network, a cable provider in Nepal covering areas such as Kathmandu, Narayangadh, Dang, Butwal, Pokhara etc, was expanding its 22 channels first to 30 and then to 51, its co-chairperson Jamim Shah had been quoted some time in 1999. Besides, some people have put separate disc antennae, which can access to the satellite TV without the need to connect through a cable. In the district towns and marketplaces and places near the highways, one can see the TV antennae sprouting from several houses. Even some relatively poor households have access to TV in such places.

As the television has started to be permanent feature in most of the urban middle class people, it is gripping the culture of "enfotainment", a combination of entertainment and information. The round-the-clock shows on everything humanly possible things have been shaping the minds and moods of the Nepalese people, especially of the youngsters, for it is easier to change their fertile minds. The television has not only contributed to the eroding of the traditional values, it has crated new kinds of dreams and aspirations among the people. Though many young Nepalese people's dreams are not fully defined and understood, their "want-to-be" are the personalities either from the sport or from the entertainment world from abroad, not the national heroes of fame. The Nepalese youngsters are growing idolizing WWF and *Baywatch* stars, MTV V- jays, and Bollywood stars. For young Nepalese girls, their want-to-be are characters from Indian cinema, not the daughters of Nepalese fame. Madonna and Madhuri Dixit become the role models, not Pasang Lhamu (the woman climber to Mt. Everest) and Parijat (novelist of literary fame). Shahrukh Khan and Rhitik Roshan[1] become their heroes instead of Tenjing Norgay, the Nepali hero to reach the top of Mt. Everest for the first time and war-hero Amar Singh Thapa. Observing some "autographs", kind of small journals where the youngsters exchange words on their friendship and things of their interest, likes and dislikes, this author was astounded to find that most of the school children, aged between 10 and 14, had their favorite songs, movies and personalities either from the Hollywood or from Indian cinema. None of the several autographs had stated a Nepali movie as their best liked movie, and a Nepali person as their role model.

No wonder the youngster watch the Indian movies and their dance numbers feverishly. Despite the fact that some informative material is offered by some channels, youngsters opt for the action-packed movies, bare-leg dances and countdown shows, which are being aired by one of the several channels round the clock. Choice is fun and it is nice to be able to surf several channels in the television. But people are getting more of the same in more than three dozen channels that are being made available. Except for occasional news, a few comedy shows such as that of Santosh Pant, Nepalese viewers of television hardly control their instincts to opt for one of several satellite channels. Today, the viewers in the Nepalese homes are hooked to one of the several comedy shows, countdown shows, and soap operas offered by outside channels. These shows plus the numerous advertisement materials continuously air materials stuffed with vulgarity, which is not particularly suitable in the Nepalese culture.

---

[1] The liking was so obsessive that many youngsters went to the streets in Kathmandu protesting violently, when they were hurt by an unconfirmed report in November 2001 that this Indian actor had said something against the Nepal and the Nepalese people.

The latest invention of "game-show" is mesmerizing the Nepalese viewers, just as it has done to the Indian viewers.

Though the television could become instrumental in disseminating the traditional values, if properly inculcated in the shows, even the Nepal Television, which has been owned by the state, has not been able to do so. The Nepal Television does not promote the ugly and lewd shows. But there is a tendency to copy the countdown shows, soap operas, and talk-shows, which tend to engage the youngsters and elders alike. Further, the Nepali channel does not provide the attraction offered by the satellite channels, which blast continuously focusing on the youngsters. One of the reasons of increasing attractions to the non-Nepali channels is the lack of attraction, glamour, competitiveness and quality of the Nepalese national TV programs. But it is the passion for consumer styles and Western culture that attracts people to dozens of outside channels. On top of that, even Nepal TV broadcasts Hindi movies, Indian pop songs and numbers of Hindi serials, which sport violence, revenge and erotic and obscene images quite unpalatable to the traditional norms of the Nepalese society, but wildly welcomed by the Nepalese youngsters. "Nepal Television's two most popular programs are a Pakistani serial on Tuesday evening and Hindi film on Saturday afternoon", wrote Suman Pradhan some years ago.[2]

Nepal television is not even in the satellite. Hence it does not reach a larger audience in Nepal, let alone to the populations of the so-called Nepalese Diaspora. Lately, the Shangri-La channel is trying to deliver Nepalese programs but it also relies on programs developed elsewhere and does not feed genuinely qualitative Nepalese product. They use the "lull time" as they air programs when the Nepal Television is free.

Though the television programs Nepalese people get today has a strong middle-class bias, no one is out of the reach and influence of the television. The programs are heavily loaded with advertisements for products and services beyond the reach of the majority of the poor people, and soap operas focusing on the middle-class and rich class problems. But even in the rural areas, the reach to the magic box is increasing as is seen by television antennae sprouting on rooftops along the major highways and around areas where

---

electricity has reached already. A few well-to-dos are even seen sporting a satellite disc.

The magic box was introduced in Nepal in the 1980s. Since then, a whole generation of youngsters, which can be said as TV Generation, has grown up adjusting their lives with the patterns of the TV. Today, the expansion of the network of several television channels has greatly influenced the peoples' choices, especially of the youngsters. Ranging from the pantheon of the pop stars to the latest Hindi movie songs in the countdown shows, Nepalese youngsters are spending a lot of time and energy to watch these channels. With shows aired on cartoons, sports, music, movies, science fiction, and other forms of entertainment, the kids of TV *Generation* are facing a real stress to manage to watch them. They are not only fed with the junk that they merely need, they are becoming victims to indoctrination of strange values and beliefs which contravene to their own culture and traditions.

Parents of the school-going children in Kathmandu receive complaints from the class teachers about their children not doing the homework properly. At home, the children are having difficulty to manage with watching several serials and episodes along with fist-fight melodrama and twist torso dance and serials of cartoons and other shows and doing their homework. Parents blame the schools for giving too much homework, not the over-dozed television. In some families, the parent-kid relationship is getting strained because of the former not letting the kids watch the TV programs they would like to view. Children become elusive when parents start to restrict TV hours on them. If it is entertainment for youngsters, restricting TV hours is one of the anxieties of the parents and it is one of fiercest battles fought at home. Moreover, the impact of the TV is falling out upon the Nepalese of the new generations. And even the social bond of the family gets weakened.

As the Nepalese children are increasingly becoming prisoners of the television, they start to do funny things under the influence of the TV programs they watch. Some quickly learn the violence and resort to fighting at schools and at home. Thanks we do not have any freaky stories of children resorting to violence using guns in the schools. Watching several fistfight and revenge-centered Indian movies, the Nepalese children are increasingly becoming more and more and revenge-seeking. Some attribute the fighting at schools, at the streets and at home among the kids of new generation to the movies and other shows in the television. Indiscriminate cinemas showing violent and sexist images are said to be menacing the social order of the younger generation. Violent and erotic movies and serials requiring parental guidance and even restriction against viewing are shown indiscriminately at all hours of the day and is instantly available to all the children and elders alike. Such indiscriminate pollution of the TV has been putting tremendous pressures on the people of the young generation. It is often becoming too late when people realize that the TV their children are getting is overdosed and is not conducive for a fair mental and psychological development of the kids. The "TV Generation" has not only become violent, they have become highly vulnerable to insecurities and burdens of life that adults are supposed to take care of. For example, the scene of violence, deaths, killings, murders, terrorism, etc. are putting impact upon kids to think extra burdens.

For the children of the Culture Shift era, it is becoming increasingly difficult to cope with the television culture. They are finding it extremely difficult to distinguish the right choice between the values, norms, and attitudes of their elders and that sported by these numerous shows. For many children of the TV generation, it has been a source frustration, mainly because of their inability to cope with the TV image of the youngsters, who are portrayed as ultra smart, extrovert, and always romantic, singing and dancing with friends of opposite sex, an experience which they find difficult to realize in their own life. Such stereotype images, imposed upon the youngsters, have led to their desperation and agony.

THE HUNGAMA CULTURE

A 1996 listing of the Nepalese song albums showed that five out of top ten albums had English names like *Legendary Mingle*, *The Steel Wheels*, *The Move Priyasi-2*, *Neva Beatles*, and *Rhythm*. These albums were the songs of young Nepalese artists, who create Western style pop music, which is in increasing popularity in Nepal. Until a few years ago, the popular songs used to be famous Nepali folk songs or modern melodious songs sung by such singers as Kumar Basnet, Narayan Gopal, Tara Devi, and Aruna Lama. But today gone are the days of folk songs. The emerging pop groups in Kathmandu are busy producing several pop style Nepali albums. In fact, the number of such groups has risen geometrically over past five years or so. According to a write-up,[3] more than 500 musical groups have been established in Nepal. Hardly anyone has any doubt that most of them are modern Nepali pop music bands instituted by some enthusiastic Nepalese youths, who feverishly copy the styles of the popular Western music.

As the pop version of the Nepalese music is being accepted among the youth, it is heralding a subtle deterioration of the Nepalese musical tradition. It has not only made Nepalese music dry and tasteless, it has sidelined the traditions of Nepalese folk music and instruments such as *Sarangi, Murchunga, Shahanai,* and *Madal.* Instead, loud bands of drums and electric guitar and computer automated organs have taken over the traditional Nepalese music, which has numbers available according to the seasons, months, festive occasions and even the hour of the day. Apart from that, the pop culture is making the Nepalese youths disoriented from originality and creativity. "All these pop singers are doing is remixing the traditional Nepali songs with Western versions and a lot of their work lack any trace of creativity and originality", complains Kumar Basnet, one of the best known popularizer of folk Nepalese music. This is heralding a new phenomenon in the Culture Shift era, which is becoming very much obsessed with the pop music. To lovers of originality of the folk Nepalese songs, the growth of the Nepali pop industry is sending a blow. But to the increasingly numerous young listeners of pop song, this is "booming" of Nepali music. Nabin Bhattarai, an emerging pop singer of *Smriti* and *Samjhana* fame, for example has "positively changed the people's attitude towards the pop music", says another modern singer Ram Krishna Dhakal.

Influenced by the popularity of music channels such as *MTV,* these Nepalese youths are seeking to create their own version of the Nepalese pop music. Today, they are getting attracted to rocks, raps, jazz, rhapsody and Bhangras instead of *Jhyaure, Maruni, Sorathi,* and several other folk songs and music.

Nepalese entertainment market has always been flooded with Hindi songs, movies and entertainment magazines. But the popularity of the Hindi film music and emerging "Indipop" songs is also supplemented by the round-the-clock broadcasts of the several FM channels, apart from the numerous satellite TV channels. Besides,

---

[3] *Kantipur,* Jul 24,1999

even the state-owned Radio Nepal and Nepal Television also broadcast Hindi songs at the request of the young men and women, who write to them and watch or listen to such programs regularly.

Another interesting phenomenon in the entertainment industry in Kathmandu is the proliferation of *Gajal* restaurants, which are small eating-out places where some professional singers and musicians perform while the customers eat and drink. Although *Gajals* are outside Nepalese cultural norms and alien to Nepalese musical tradition, their popularity has increased due to the commercialization of Gajals, which have become palatable for people, who want entertainment while eating out. A lot of what is called *Gajal* in Kathmandu's numerous restaurants is not the traditional music but the Hindi movie songs and some popular Nepali numbers. Nepalese *Gajal* outfits have commercialized in a populist and cheap musicals, which are not compatible to the traditions of the Nepali music. Lately, many of these self-styled restaurants have converted themselves into "dancing restaurants", which have become quite popular in the nightlife of Kathmandu Valley. One regular visitor to such restaurants told this author, there were 80 such restaurants in the beginning of 2000. In many such restaurants, young men and women in revealing costumes perform twist-torso dance while the customers, mainly Nepalese young men aged between 25 and 35, eat, drink a lot, and watch the dances with a lot of enthusiasm. It is this group of young men, who wish to freak out with a relatively easily earned disposable money, which has contributed to the growth of the "Hungama Culture".

And the latest arrivals in the scene are several discotheques, mainly in Kathmandu and in Pokhara. Alien to the Nepalese youngsters until a few decades ago, and restricted to few big hotels until very recently, the emerging new discotheques have now become new venues for expressing the attitudes of the young generations, especially their desire to be abreast with the Western pop culture. Going to disco has become a new subculture in the night life of the Nepalese youths, especially in the Kathmandu Valley. With a little more disposable income and a passion towards the Western culture, the Nepalese youngsters not only seek entertainment in these dancing outfits. They also seek to express their attitude and up-to-dateness with the modern versions of the lifestyles available in Nepal. The Nepalese people, especially the upwardly mobile youngsters in the urban areas, are slowly imitating the "pub and pop culture." In several discotheques that are coming up, Nepalese youngsters dance in latest "hits" from Bollywod and the MTV. There is an increasing rush of the youngsters in the pubs, discotheques and dancing restaurants, despite the exorbitant prices. In many such places, the presence of young girls is increasing. It can be said that a new "night life" is emerging in Kathmandu.

Another late comer in the entertainment world is the *FM* radio broadcast. Until the time of this writing, there were as many as seven FM channels aired in Kathmandu. And there were proposals for airing the same in other towns like Biratnagar and such far-flung places as Kanchanpur, in the far-west. The FM has not only become a very popular mode of entertainment, especially among the young people, it has become a kind of new revolution in the entertainment world in Kathmandu. This has certainly generated a *"FM Generation"* in Kathmandu, as described in a cover story of a weekly magazine.[4] Increasing popularity of the FM, as evident by the large umber of calls made to *FM* station by the fans of Nepali, Hindi and English pop songs, illustrates this.

Though there was an initial uproar against the conduct of the many FM programs, especially in its use of the English medium, the FM has now been accepted and socialized in the Valley. But the impact created by these FM channels in the Nepalese culture and traditions remains to be fully understood. Some Nepalese intellectuals and critics had criticized the *FM* as a "wrong start". Some said that the *FM* was been a source of "cultural pollution" in the Kathmandu Valley. Others blamed the FM for creating a generation, which was being spoilt in the addiction to the music and to the pop culture. The channel has definitely challenged Nepalese language, culture, customs and traditions in an unprecedented manner. There is no denying that *FM* and its programs on Western music and discussion on various subjects has augmented the process of *"cultural invasion"* already in the process of entering into the Nepalese households courtesy the satellite TV. The FM channels have increasingly "sidelined" the Nepalese musical traditions and entertainment in the country. What is becoming popular is loud musical bands, hip-hop Hindi songs "remixed" from the original chirpy versions. What rocks you is a *Bhangra* or a rap, the MTV releases or the latest music from Hindi cine world. The FM has

---

[4] *The Spotlight* (May 29-June 4, 1998)

contributed to the success of the so-called "*hungama culture*", in which people who do not like it are also becoming the captive audience.

Whether we accept or not, the teenager's hearts in Kathmandu Valley beat with the music and never-ending discussions aired by the FM channels, almost round the clock. It is this electronic media which plays Nepali, Hindi and English songs, launches discussions with callers, mainly young ones, shares jokes with its listeners, and becomes the themes of the youngsters' lives. The numerous conductors of the *FM* channels focus on the young people. These young Nepalese fans can be heard dedicating songs to their friends and loved ones. Among the things discussed in the *FM* also includes the sacrosanct sex and the "relationships", which were a kind of taboo in the society until the arrival of the FM.

There are positive aspects of these channels as well. At least, that is the belief of the majority of the urban Nepalese youths. Many youngsters believe that the FM channels have made them confident, abreast with the changing values and times, and conversant in the English language, simultaneously. Others say, the FM provides the youngsters some say in the society, which traditionally had very little scope for the young people to be heard of. The FM channels have also served as a "counseling forum"[5] to the Nepalese youths, who are otherwise, confused, dismayed and frustrated in the changing times. Besides, the FM has become a pass-time for Kathmandu's homebound teenagers, especially girls, who lack a mechanism for informal socializing interactions other than the colleges and noisy pubs and discotheques.

But the FM delivers less information and serious talk and focuses on "too much snob entertainment". The commerce will only allow the programs to remain "hot cakes", which means you air more entertainment and lighter content than any serious stuff. After all, the youngsters, today, are not after the serious business. Theirs is a generation, which lives to enjoy. And FM catches this mentality, of a generation, which is crazy after something, which does not have anything, but still appealing to them. At least, it is true with the popular rap, *Bhangra*, and "Indipop" songs, which really don't carry a lot of meaning. Fast beat and senseless lyrics are elements of making entertainment attractive in the new pop culture. A whole new breed of

---

synthesized music and new breed of remix orchestration is becoming increasingly popular, neglecting the originality and melody of the traditional Nepali instruments.

This onslaught is casting a huge shadow on the folk traditions of Nepal's various ethnic groups. The rich cultural heritage of folklore, which are suited to festivals, fairs, and rituals, has been encroached upon mercilessly by the new pop culture. Even the traditions of classical Nepalese music, which used to be patronized in the royal courts, is facing this fate in the wake of gradual eclipsing by the Western pop culture.

Some people call it "cultural terrorism", i.e. threat to the existing cultural harmony and peace from an alien and threatening element as the people and the state have no control over things like satellite broadcasting from the space. The cultural heritage with regards to traditional modes of entertainment is in jeopardy. Gone are the days of *dabali nach*, where the colorful dramas and dances depicting the glory of the past were performed. Forgotten are the treasures of Nepalese art of entertainment, which was blended with the people's lives and their styles of entertainment.

The Hungama Culture is not just confined to Kathmandu. In places like Dharan, Pokhara and Biratnagar, the Western pop music and westernized Nepali pop music is increasingly becoming popular. In Biratnagar, an emerging group called Twenty First Century Media International organized a show called "Live 2100 Watts", a musical program which some 8000 people watched the heated pop show for 5 uninterrupted hours despite the cold waves in the month of December, 1997, reported a weekly.[6] Back in villages, the traditional institutions of Rodighar are becoming vulnerable and film music from Bollywood's Hindi cinema is becoming increasingly sung and popular.

The growth of the Hungama Culture is also contributed by the growing size of the Nepalese film industry. Though the appetite for Hindi movies and songs has not abated, Nepalese people are also witnessing the growth of their own Nepali film industry with a lot of zeal and enthusiasm. Some three decades ago, Nepal used to produce hardly one or two movies in two to three years. Today, more than 30 celluloid movies are released each year. On top of that, several movies in the video-film category are produced and shown in several video halls in major towns in Nepal. Today, the Nepalese film industry has

---

[6] *Saptahik*, Kantipur Publications, Kathmandu, January 16, 1998

been successful to create a pantheon of its own stars. A plethora of songs and characters have been popularized. Though Nepalese movie industry is pretty much independent, it has copied several things including the technical inputs from Bombay, the movie capital of India popularly named as Bollywood. But what is copied is not the quality of performance and the art, but the fist-fights and melodrama of revengeful stories and thip-thud dances with hundred men and women dancing together like in a physical training course. The copying goes to so much so that Kathmandu is known as self-styled *"Kollywood"* after Bollywood, the Bombay version of Hollywood. In this process, the huge treasure of Nepalese performing art is getting diffused and homogenized with the Bollywood formulae. Instead of creating its own space in the culture, the Nepalese film industry has been an extended version of the Hindi cinema. The Nepalese movie industry has not been successful in inculcating the Nepalese morals and values through the world of cinema. It has served to disseminate the latest in the world of fashion, music, fad, and glamour from the India's movie capital Bombay, now known as Mumbai.

There have been a few efforts to produce genuinely Nepali movies. Yadav Kharel's *Prem Pinda* (1994) and Nir Shah's *Basanti* (2000) are some good examples. But the success rate is not quite high. What sells is the Bombay style action-packed and revengeful stories with a lot of hip-shaking dances. Though the impact of Hindi movies is far more prominent than that of Nepali ones, Nepali celluloid and lately Video movies have all but contributed to the deterioration of the rich tradition of the Nepali performing entertainment. They have also infused alien values and elements of artificiality and glamour in the lives of the youngsters.

RODIGHAR RUINED

While the Hungama culture grips the nation, the traditional institutions and practices of entertainment and socializing get the severest blow. Foremost of them is the Gurung institution of entertainment called *Rodighar*, which used to serve as a nightclub, a center for chit-chatting, singing, dancing and drinking. This traditional institution of entertainment is being abandoned for people are abandoning their original culture. Many Gurung families have migrated to towns and are leaving the villages for good. In the urban areas, where the most families of the Gurungs retired from military services abroad are living, the Gurung youngsters are choosing to modern Western entertainment, mainly in the pop songs, dancing restaurants and the discotheques. Many play modern musical instruments and are members of groups or bands, which perform metallic instruments. Instead of learning to play the traditional flute and *Madal*, they are learning the electric guitars and loud drums. Some of the Gurung youth living in the urban areas haven't even seen a *Rodighar*, which used to a symbol of identity in the Gurung villages. Today, Rodi is regarded as something of a village. In cities Pokhara, where there is a sizeable population of the Gurungs, some Rodi institutions do exist in the city. But the membership is small and the interest in the institution is decreasing, save representing these institutions as clubs in some non-traditional performances. Even in the Gurung villages in the rural areas, the traditional recreational institutions of Rodighar are disappearing. The traditional Rodi institutions have been replaced by recreational institutions called "Mother Groups" (Gurung, 1994).

Today, it is not only Rodighar that has been ruined. Several traditional community organizations for entertainment are also on the decline. This is evident in the decreasing role of the traditional Guthis for running several festive activities. The traditional Guthis are still practiced in some communities such as the Newars and the Thakalis. But they are no more the pivotal institutions to organize, run and preserve the traditional institutions of entertainment. With the breakdown of community, the traditional music and dances performed in temples and localities are also on the decline. For example in Bhaktapur, out of 60 performing musical groups, barely a few are surviving today and the rest are gradually disappearing (IUCN/HMGN, 1992).

The "Culture Shift" is equally blatant to the traditional dances. For example, *Ghatu*, a popular dance for the last four centuries of the Magars and Gurungs in Gorkha, Lamjung, Kaski and Dhadhing district of central Nepal, is being endangered. Very few villages in the area have kept the tradition of the dances alive. Decreasing popularity of the local folk dances and increasing attraction to the Western style music and dance have reduced the relevance of the traditional dances. These days, the *Ghatu* dance is just practiced by people of the old age, not by the youngsters, who are increasingly attracted to the Western music and dance, writes a columnist.[7] Today, many Nepali folk dances are only preserved by some performing artists at the Royal Nepalese Academy, not performed by the people at fairs and festivities.

Nepalese stage dramas that used to be popular form of entertainment are also on the decay. The royal courts used to patronize such artists. Some Kings even wrote plays and even performed them. The traditional *dabalis,* an elevated place in the center of the town for holding such stage art, are now either encroached or used for some other purposes. With emergence of other forms of performing entertainment like the rock bands and movies, the artistic dispensation of the stage art is declining. No wonder the iron-gate of Rashtriya Nachghar, the country's national performing art theater, remains closed most of time and there have been hardly any major performances there after Devkota's *Muna Madan* some decades ago.

The encroachment to the traditions of the Nepalese entertainment is also evident in the folk musical instruments. In an around *Ghandruk* area in Annapurna region, Kaski district, there is a threat to survival of Nepali folk musical instruments like *Madal, Damphu, Jhyali, Karnal,* and *Khainjadi,* reported a weekly.

The loss of the folk musical instruments is linked with the loss of the traditional professions based on making and playing such music. Many people like *Gaines* have abandoned their traditional profession of singing and playing *Sarangi* in search of livelihood. Bewildered in the choice of professions, many have left their traditions and lost the traditional skills and efficiency. There is a menace to the continuity of the heritage in the folk musical instruments.

Until a few decades ago, the wedding ceremonies used to employ the traditional *Panchebaja* played by the occupational caste of *Darji.* With increasing popularity of "Band Music", people have almost ceased to use *Panchebaja* on auspicious occasions like weddings. The "*Band-Baja*" has become a symbol of affluence and modernization, which has taken place of the traditional auspicious musical orchestra.

Today, many folk musical instruments are catered to the curio vendors in tourist destinations. Many folk musicians and makers of the instruments have abandoned the profession due to invasion of modern musical instruments. People have abandoned playing

---

[7] Juddha B. Gurung in *Saptahik,* Kantipur Publications (January 16, 1998)

instruments like *Narasingha, Damaha* and *Jhyali* mainly because they are out of practice and also because they are not easily available at the local markets.

Even the most popular *dhime baja* of the Kathmandu Newars seems to be disappearing. Earlier played extensively on festivals and religious occasions, especially by Jyapu community in the Kathmandu Valley, *dhime baja* used to be a cultural symbol of the Newar festivities. Because of invasion of modern musical instruments and increasing popularity of the band music, the traditional musical instruments like *dhime baja,* have been pushed to the back seat.

A NEW CULT IN THE MAKING

Some six men, between twenty-five and fifty years, are in their routine "marriage" session, a popular card game introduced in the area, some years ago. One is a local schoolteacher, one is the member of the Village Development Committee, another is a local contractor, and another the rural shopkeeper. By the evening time, each payer has already sipped a few glasses of country liquor and the conversation has started to become vulgar. Bitter words are exchanged on each other's political associations, and source of earnings. But the overall aura is that of great sense of humor and fun. A phenomenon in the Nepalese entertainment that is emerging in the urban as well as rural areas can be labeled as the "cult of gambling and drinking". Playing cards and drinking have become so much associated with the lives of people, especially male members of the Nepalese society that they have become an obsession of many people, and many other have become addicted to the same.

Some decades ago drinking alcohol was a privilege of a few people who were classified as *Matwali,* the alcohol drinkers, and the same used to be a taboo among the people of so called higher castes like Brahmins and even some Chhetris. *Tagadharis,* the sacrosanct thread wearing Brahmans and Chhetris, were not supposed to consume the "filthy drink". Today, this has been totally rejected. Only very pious and religious-minded people, like priests, do not consume alcohol because it is unacceptable according to customs. But in new generation, even among the Brahmins, drinking alcohol has been widely accepted and rationalized in the last few decades. Many young people regard drinking alcohol as the best form of entertainment. Drinking alcohol has been not only acceptable and socially correct behavior, it has even become imperative for socializing and entertaining people.

Alcohol has so much permeated the lives of people these days that socialization has almost become rare without the "filthy" drink. In rural areas, the indiscriminate consumption of the local and homemade liquor has made nuisance to the public life. This coupled with the perennial culture of playing cards as gambling has spoiled the whole atmosphere of the rural villages, where life used to be close to nature and remained rustic otherwise. In urban areas, alcohol has become a status symbol of the emerging middle class and the *noveaux riches*. Thanks to the several beer and liquor products that are available at every shop, and the presence of ubiquitous vendors every nook and corner of the country. People have such an easy access to a variety of liquor that its influence in the Nepalese people's lives has become a remarkable cultural phenomenon. It is sarcastically said, alcoholic beverages can be purchased more easily than the milk, which used to be a kind of scarce resource commodity in Kathmandu until some years ago.

Gambling has been a part of Nepalese people's lives for a long time and it continues to be so. In the rural areas, the most popular form of entertainment for men is drinking *Rakshi* and playing cards. Playing cards and gambling used to be legitimized by the government in earlier periods. Until very recently, gambling used to be free on certain days of the years, in *Kojagrat Purnima,* the last day of *Dashain* festival, and on the three days of *Tihar.* Though gambling has been made illegal, the slow poison of gambling and drinking is engulfing the people in the urban as well as rural areas.

In Kathmandu, some neo-rich people sneak into one of the several casinos quietly in guise of Indians to satisfy their craze for gambling (Nepalese are not legally allowed to enter the casinos). Others enjoy the perennial card game called "marriage" (mistaken for mirage). But in the rural areas, people play cards openly. They do so not only for gambling, but also for entertainment, social contact, pastime, and many times by compulsion of being in certain companionship. Card games called *Paploo* reached its peak of popularity in Nepal in the decade of the eighties. Today *Marriage* is becoming popular. Time and again, people have invented and adopted different card games. In the old days, people and the royal court officials used to play a typically Nepali gamble called *Pasa.* This had tradition in the royal courts and religious stories. Other forms of gambling like lotteries and *Langur Burja*, which used to be popular in Kathmandu valley, has been albeit on the decline. The cult of card playing seems to be in the increasing trends. To many civil servants in Kathmandu, playing cards remains as the only pastime and entertainment on holidays. And in the rural areas, the drinking and card playing has become a social malaise and source of erosion of physical as well as moral capital. It has become so much pervasive that some village women have organized themselves to put pressure against the men for abandoning the card playing and drinking. In some hilly districts, especially in the western Nepal, these women's groups have become successful in banning the sale, production and consumption of various alcoholic drinks from the district altogether.

While every one is becoming more social and entertainment-oriented, the habit of partying is being very common, especially to the *noveaux riches* in Kathmandu. Emergence of a range of "clubs" and "exclusive member" parties and increase in the offer made by party providers are indirect indicators. But if you live in Kathmandu you can never miss such wild manifestations of the extravagance and outgoing culture, which is emerging among the otherwise shy and introvert Nepalese people with regards to partying. Starting from rice-feeding rituals to birthday celebrations, the cultural ethos are blended into the party culture adopted from abroad. What is served is not the traditional cuisine, but expensive drinks and recipe imported from abroad. And you are injected with a whole lot of non-conventional music and often asked to "belly-dance" in those pieces you have never heard of. This mood of partying is also reflected in the large crowds in any activity that has entertainment in it. Fashion shows, street festivals, fairs, music shows and the like attract a large number of young people. All of this has a kind of partying culture attached to the attitude of the emerging new class status symbols, especially in the urban areas.

Items featuring in a fair organized to mark the Dashain festival in Kathmandu in 1996 included "rice beer drinking", "momo-eating", "tube-light dance shows", "Nepali Rock Concert", "Music Jam Session" etc. This illustrates the choice of the people towards new types of entertainment, which is strange to the Nepalese traditional entertainment practices. Though the cultural connection of rituals of life are disappearing, the partying associated with the same is nothing but increasing. Today, people may ignore a ritual. But the occasion may be celebrated wildly, inviting several guests and partying, especially among the affluent circles. The core of culture has shifted to entertainment, not the merit of the occasion.

The culture of partying and drinking goes to the extent that people tend to say *"Surya Ast, Nepal Mast"*, meaning the Nepalese people will be on their full swing on the culture of partying and drinking, as soon as the sun sets. This culture is complimented by the numerous bars, dancing restaurants, discotheques, and the similar kind of places, especially in the capital city. Even in the villages, the mood of enjoying drinking local homemade liquor takes the shape of a party culture.

THE NEW ESCAPE FOR ENTERTAINMENT

While everything else is changing, so is people's orientation towards travel and tourism. Perhaps inspired by the growing tourism industry and demonstration effect of the modern lifestyles, Nepalese people are seeking more and more opportunities for travelling both within and abroad. An entirely new Nepali traveler species is on the making. The traditional Nepalese travelling used to be limited to visit to the traditional pilgrimage centers such as *Char Dham* in India. From the villages, people used to go to a town in the Terai or to the capital for one reason or the other. But the new Nepalese traveler is a person, who seeks an escape from the "house arrest" of the television and enjoy the nuclearity of the "smart family". This is the person of a burgeoning middle class with moderate disposable incomes and busy lifestyles. He or she seeks to maximize time with his or her family in travel and who wants to copy global lifestyles, who considers travel as the most important form of entertainment to break away from the monotony of the work. The average Nepali traveler today is not just a pilgrim and a trader, but a tourist, an adventurer, and a pleasure-seeker combined. Whether it is the pilgrimage to the temple of *Manakamana* (lately, the opening of the cable car route has further added to the swarm of visitors), a sojourn to Pokhara, or safari to Chitwan, the new Nepalese traveler seeks religious merit, entertainment, pleasure, sight seeing and time together with the family. As more incomes are available for travelling, as the attitude of pleasure seeking invades people's hectic lifestyles, the upwardly mobile Nepalese people see real satisfaction in going around, at least to the destination, they finds affordable. Thanks to the numerous bus services, domestic airlines that serve more than 42 destinations, and a burgeoning tourist industry, which is willing to cater to the domestic tourists. For those who can afford, a trip to Indian cities and pilgrimage centers and destinations in Thailand, Hong Kong and Singapore are also not very far. There may be an element of business here and element of religion there. But the burgeoning Nepalese travelers are starting to realize that travelling is the best way to be abreast with the world.

This desire of going around is complimented by competitive fairs and package tours, aggressive marketing advertisements, and the emerging nuclear status of the families, where cost of travel suddenly becomes not only affordable, but also justifiable. Above all, one wants to be seen as being affluent and to signal that one has accomplished something. Travelling could become one way of ding that.

Motives may be different. But the influences are generated from the burgeoning tourist industry in the country as well. After all, copying of the global lifestyle could begin from copying the tourists one could see around. Further, due to the intrusion of the television, which has kept people in "house arrest" as they are glued to their television sets watching the round-the-clock shows of all kinds, there is the growing pursuit of leisure and need go out. It can be safely assumed that a large number of the Nepalese people are becoming outgoing. As families are becoming nuclear, the desire and affordability of the out-going culture and enjoying pleasure of the leisure time is becoming evident in the people's lifestyles. The claustrophobic existence and people's homebound values are now changing for an outside-oriented entertainment. Saving for future generations has been taken over by spending for the enjoyment of leisure time and entertainment. While one of the reasons for the growth of the outward-orientation in the entertainment of the people is the availability of a "disposable income", the attitude of copying the global lifestyles and an escape from the "claustrophobic existence" has been mainly responsible for the emergence of the new Nepalese traveler.

The Harbinger of Change

Whereas nearly half of Nepal's twenty two million people still remain illiterate, education has been one of the most important factors contributing to the Culture Shift in Nepal. Education has not only opened up avenues for new beliefs, thoughts, scientific interpretation of the world and natural phenomena, it has also initiated a process of "de-traditionalization", which has generated an unprecedented momentum in the loss of the culture in Nepal. People are not only abandoning superstitions and myths, they have been copying lifestyles and wisdom from the contacts with different ethnic and cultural groups as well as with people from abroad due to increase in educational activities.

Proliferation of the private schooling institutions, increasing emphasis on paper certificates, deteriorating academic standards, and hiking commercialization have widened the gaps between the traditional and modern schooling in Nepal. With increasing number of Nepalese youngsters studying in English medium "boarding schools" and an alarming exodus of Nepalese neo-rich kids abroad in search of "quality education", the education psychology has undergone a dramatic change in the last two decades or so. Today, education is one of the major factors contributing to the copying of the lifestyles and culture of West. It is being realized that opportunities in education and benefits thereof have been achieved at the cost of the traditional art and culture. Today, education has only forced people to reject their own culture and traditions, it has also created a new group of frustrated people and has become a source of disillusionment among the youth in Nepal.

THE FORGOTTEN WISDOM

Perhaps no other change is more harmful to the traditional culture and lifestyles of people than the changes in education. What is lost in the process of modernization of education is the merits of the traditional education system. Nepalese people have almost abandoned traditional Hindu and Buddhist way, style and philosophy of education. All the conventional wisdom and heritage with regards to education is almost vanishing. People interested and involved in traditional way of education are becoming rare. Efforts to preserve traditional values of education are becoming very weak or non-existing. A vast treasure of ancestral and traditional knowledge and wisdom has been dubbed as "filthy superstition" and have been dumped out from the current usage due to an increasing hatred towards the past heritage and knowledge, wrote a columnist in a local newspaper.

Education in the traditional Hindu society used to be a social system and way of life. Hindu social organization based on the concept of *Ashrams* used to have profound influence on the nature of education in the Nepalese society. Schooling used to be compared to *Brahmacharya Ashram*, in which the method of management of education was focused at *Gurukul* as a social institution and teaching and studying was regarded as a sanctitious vocation. Although most of Hindu teaching focused on *Dharma Shashtra* (religious science), ancient Hindu teaching also consisted of subjects like *Vyakarna* (grammar), *Nirukta* (etymology), *Tarka Shashtra* (science of logic), *Jyotisha* (astrology), *Ganit* (arithmetic), *Nitishashtra* (science of ethics), *Dhanurvidya* (science of archery), *Ayurvidya* (science of life), etc. But the traditional concepts of education have now become confined to the texts of the ancient knowledge and people are abandoning the traditional treasure of knowledge and merit of such a form of education. Today's schooling based on Western education system abandons the cultural values of centuries. With an increasing popularity of natural sciences, business studies and computer science, priority of the youngsters is getting away from the merits of the traditional teachings on various subjects. Education is not paying as much respect and prestige in the society as it used to in earlier periods.

At *Gurukul*, traditional Hindu institutions of education, the students were supposed to beg alms for themselves. There used to be rules regarding the hours of study, times and nature of meals, codes of dressing, methods of greeting teachers and the staff, abandonment of luxuries. Even the children of rich and affluent families had to undergo such rigorous educational lives. They were supposed to eat simple food, live in the huts, walk bare foot and wear simple dresses. There exited a belief that education could only be achieved under hardship and an egalitarian environment. *Panchatantra*, a Hindu religious text of moral studies, has listed five symptoms and characteristics of a good student: *Alpahari* (eating little), *Grihatyagi* (leaving one's house), *Swananindra* (a dog's sleep), *Bakodhyanam* (an egret's concentration), and *Kakachesta* (a crow's intention). Hindu educational psychology was built upon the morals of economic and physical hardships and concentration as well as wisdom of the pupils. Today, these characteristics are ridiculed and thought to be applicable only to Brahmans who study Sanskrit and Vedas. Many students are not even aware of such characteristics. Concepts like this sound funny and ridiculous to most Nepalese youths studying in the numerous English medium schools, which are sprouting like anything in the urban areas. Instead, the parents of the school going children wish to demonstrate their wealth and give their children every kind of luxury they can afford. Though a new era of enlightenment is on the making, the conventional wisdom is being forgotten.

THE CREDENTIAL INFLATION

Education in Nepal has been extremely credentialized. People have started to focus in academic paper certificates as the ultimate objective of their study, not the quality of the academic pursuits accrued from such degrees. Certificates are supposed to be the signboards of ability to know, perform, manage and lead. That is why several people have completed more than one. It is not that there is a demand of people with these academic backgrounds. But there is high recognition to credentials. Proliferation of the schooling institutions is one of the major factors responsible for inflation in the quality of education. Though the number seems to be increasing, the quality of education seems to be declining.

Cases of fraudulent certificates imported from across the border also represent the extent of credentialism as the core element of education psychology in Nepal. Time and again, Tribhuvan University and other academic institutions disclose the fake certificates of students at school and especially higher education level. These certificates are mainly made and sold in the territories adjoining Nepal's border. People are trying to fake the presence of certificates since that is considered a tool to get into entry into the civil service and for getting admissions in courses which require high percentages of marks. Today fake certificates are bought for getting scholarships, admission to colleges, getting better jobs and many other advantages accrued from a certificate of an academic degree. This has wrought the ethical decay in the society.

But the decay in education is not just confined to the fake certificates, there is a whole new culture of cheating seems to be emerging. A feature article puts it well:

> "If there is a first prize to be given for the primary reason of the degeneration of Nepalese culture, then it could be easily awarded to the education. The child is taught to acquire knowledge only to pass exams and those exams appear to be the be-all and end-all of existence. The education has taken on a commercial character. The teacher encourages the students to enroll in private coaching classes with himself or herself. The system of private tuition or coaching is the beginning of corruption of the public life, in which students learn to bribe the teachers. If it is not the leaked question papers, the students who have gone for tuition are given preferred ranking. Besides that, cheating in examinations are rampant in universities and schools. One can imagine the moral fibre of a student who starts learning cheating in the schools and fooling the examiners to get high scores." [1]

Students at all level of educational institutions desire to achieve higher percentage of marks. The motive is to do better in the exams, not to acquire the knowledge. Teaching at all levels discourages independent thinking other than the school texts and shuns the growth of inquisitive, experimental and analytical faculty of mind. The objective of education of any level seems to be to prepare to a level just next in the educational hierarchy, not the scholastic merit of each grade.

And the whole educated elite seems to have been gripped by a "percentage anxiety", *i.e.* a desire to achieve higher percentage in academic examinations. Success in the academic is world is measured by the percentage of marks obtained in the examinations. The entire system of education is examination-oriented and the "percentage culture" is reinforced by the highly competitive environment in getting admissions, jobs, and tests like the GRE, GMAT, TOEFL etc, which are required for entry into many foreign schools. These certificates are regarded as good as passports to the Western education institutions. Performing better in these tests has become

---

[1] *The Kathmandu Post*, February 20, 1998

the nightmares of many Nepalese students. Some succeed. But many fail and remain frustrated.

With changing definition of jobs and transformation in the skills required for a new array of emerging occupations, the credentials that are produced in the Nepalese academic institutions are being unable to cope with the pace of change. Credential inflation, the need for higher and better qualifications, is changing the education psyche of the people. As the jobs and people are becoming mobile, and as styles of training are always on the need for modification, and as unemployment trend is on the rise, the value of certificates of academic performance is becoming less and less important. With the competitive schooling, the need for high academic performance wit higher percentage of marks in the schools and colleges have preoccupied the motives of the students and their parents.

Education is also contributing to the increasing disillusionment of the Nepalese youth. First, there is no direct relevance between the education they get everywhere (thanks to several colleges that have opened in such far-flung places as Panchthar and Jumla) and the career they wish to pursue. Many end up doing jobs not related to their training in the schools and colleges. Others remain unemployed. Second, as the educated masses do not wish to go back to the toil of the fields, and they have nothing else to do, they remain disillusioned. Some join such activities as the Maoists-led "People's War", which gives them a sense of identity and a forum to express their resentment against the establishment.

"A well established boarding school with over 300 students in Naxal is for sale", read an advertisement in a local daily some time ago. There was another notice, in which a business partner to invest in a "boarding school" was wanted. These are symptoms of high degree of profit-orientation and commercialization of education in urban Nepal. With the privatization of schooling, education has become a commodity to be retailed in the market. Although, the schooling institutions are required by law to be non-profit and are exempt from income and other taxes, they are run and operated like business in order to make profit as the government has started to recognize the private schools as enterprises. In Kathmandu and many other urban centers, the children of the rich and affluent and even of the middle class people are sent to such private boarding schools where profit, not the quality of education, is the motive. The social motive for education is on the decline. The government has allowed that schools could be registered as a private business company and could be taxed. In the wake of privatization in every sector, the government has sought to encourage the private sector involvement in the country's education sector. This has ushered the growth and expansion of private educational institutions. Seven hundred new private schools were established between 1990 and 1995 and these accounted for 30% of total enrollment of school children in Nepal, says a write-up.[2]

Nepalese education psychology does not support free schooling. Although most government schools, which run "free education", are packed with non-fee paying students, most people prefer to send their children to fee-paying private schools. Sending children to government sponsored schools is considered an act of low economic status and prestige compared to sending kids to highly expensive schools. The most prestigious one could be sending the pupils abroad. The psychology of "expensive is better" prevails in education along with other aspects of Nepalese consumer behavior. In Kathmandu, one of topical issues of discussion is a good school for one's children. Parents dream, compete, use their connection and even money for better education for their children. In a few schools that are known to have good education standards, people crowd with their children seeking admission. The schools extort quite a big amount in terms of fees and supplementary charges. Yet the standard of education is not coming up to the expectations.

Most Nepalese people view education as an instrument for earning and making living. People invest in their children's education in order "to make them able to earn". Very rarely is education viewed as something to achieve scholastic achievement. Education is mostly viewed as something, which helps people to grow to be able to make money.

Yet another trend that suggests the adaptability of the education system to the economic orientation is the proliferation of the computer training centers, language institutes, driving institutes etc. in Kathmandu and major urban centers. As many and more youngsters learn to click the mouse and "surf" the net, as increasingly large new job ads demand experience with "interface" and "keyboarding skills", the attraction for such new training is all but justified according to the

---

[2] Subba, Phanindra (1996), Education in the Market Place, *The Rising Nepal* (September 13, 1996)

principles of market forces. But an attitudinal dimension is also there. Increasingly large number of youngsters think it is imperative to learn driving, computers, and English language to be abreast with the modernism and not to be alienated from their peers, who talk, speak and consume the chips live in an increasingly mobile society. Many other join these courses hoping to go abroad in search of jobs. All of that has brought a decay in the education standards and psychology.

Further, the credential inflation is also brought about by the proliferation of the schooling institutions in the country. Today, schools and colleges have been opened in all major towns and even far -flung districts of the country. Unlike the other development extension programs, which saw a lot of resistance from the local elite, the expansion of the schools in the rural areas was received with a lot of enthusiasm. One of the main reasons was that the setting up of the schools was in the advantage of the rural elite, who would otherwise have to send their children to Kathmandu or to the Indian cities. Thus educational institutions sprang everywhere, disregarding the availability of the teachers, and physical as well as academic and financial resources. That brought the spread of low quality education, which contributed to the so-called credential inflation.

In Kathmandu Valley and major urban centers, the growth of private "boarding schools" became popular for their English medium and smart uniforms, despite the lofty fees, which was hardly affordable. Thus, schooling started to be a status symbol and the people's place the social hierarchy started to be determined on the basis of which schools they sent their children for education. The poor families sent their children to the government schools, where teaching quality was often compromised for low fees. A little richer and so-called "middle class" people sent their children to the private boarding schools. The richest rung sought the status sending their wards abroad, at first to Indian town and later to the West, mainly to the United States. This would later take the shape of an "education exodus".

THE EDUCATION EXODUS

If anything is luring the Nepalese youth out of the country, it is the pursuit of higher education in a foreign country. Increasingly large number of Nepalese students are studying in various colleges abroad. Many seek admissions in medicine, engineering and computer science. There is increasing popularity in disciplines like environment science, and business administration. High priority destinations are the United States of America, and Australia. But there are other countries like India, Pakistan, Bangladesh, Thailand, Russia, The Philippines, etc.[3] Some of the private institutions in these countries charge hefty tuition plus other fees. It may be a good sign that the Nepalese people are investing in their human capital. But the flight of economic capital and the eventual possibility of the absorption of the Nepalese talent abroad through such opportunities is creating a painstaking void in the Nepalese education scenario.

Even those, who complete studies in Nepal, tend to go abroad to find jobs. Today we produce doctors who prefer to serve in Massachusetts, not Mugu. We train engineers who prefer to build expressways in Bangkok, not a rural road in Banke. Our professionals and geniuses succumb to the West, and our institutions go into entropy and decay. There is some serious lapse in our education system and psychology.

In the rural areas, the exodus to urban areas in search of jobs and education has been depriving the human resources there. In fact, in the rural areas, education has become an active source of depriving physical labor from the traditional work force. If one is educated, the general tendency is to go to look for *Jagir*, a salary position, where there is believed to less work and more benefits. Once a young man or a woman gets the high school education in a rural village, she or he is an educated person. The next logical step is to leave the village for an urban area or the capital city to look for jobs because there is no labor dignity for educated people to work in the paddy fields. Working on physical labor is considered a job of the non-educated people. This has not only to do with the work ethic, but with the education system as a whole as well.

The foundation of the education system is so week that people can not start their own work or jobs after completing a certain level of study. The aim of a level of education is to prepare the students for

---

[3] According to a source (*Khabarpatrika*, Ashoj 4, 2056 BS) quoting the Ministry of Education, some 1383 students went to various countries for self-financed studies in the year 2055 BS. It is possible that many cases go unrecorded.

the level just above that. If people complete school, their aim is to get into the college for higher studies. There is very little people can achieve in their practical lives once they complete a certain level of education.

Traditionally, education used to be the prerogative of the upper classes and a powerful symbol of status (Bista, 1991, p. 6). But an increasing access of increasingly large number of people to schooling has averted the work ethic. With an access to even school level of education, youngsters have abandoned their traditional professions and have shied away from physical labor. Access to modern schooling has also put the profession and occupations related to the traditional art and craft at jeopardy. The new Nepalese students, who have done modern schooling, hardly wish to go back to the traditional professions of their ancestors. And the heritage of centuries is allowed to decay and disappear.

DETERIORATING MORAL FIBER

Father of a ten year old boy was in trouble. His son, who averaged in the schools, had started getting into problems. Sometimes he used to hit his friends. Sometimes, he was caught stealing books and pens from his friends. At others, he ran away from the school. Then the teachers complained to his father. This baffled father didn't know how to respond with his son. Mixed with some satire in the contemporary society, he said, "If I ask my son not to do so (his bad deeds), he will be bullied and dominated by others and it will be difficult for him to survive in today's world, where peoples are losing ethics in the battles of their own economic existence". "If I ask him to continue whatever he is doing now, how can I do so being a father, who is supposed to teach good ethical values to his children". The problem was not about the difficulties of raising the children, it was about educating them ethics. The overall moral fabric of the Nepalese society is deteriorating due to an increasing acceptance and institutionalization of corruption and decreasing interest in the traditional values and norms. The education system has contributed to degrading the moral capital of the Nepalese people. A moral bankruptcy is being unleashed in the Nepalese society, which was built upon a strong ethical values.

The traditional Hindu system of education used to focus upon the moral character building as one of the most important aspects of education along with the development of the intellect of the student. A whole set of moral culture, values and norms used to be imparted to the pupils. That used to be bases of their lives. This used to give profound impact in traditional Hindu society. Hindu system of education was based on a strong self-control mechanism. Very little punishment was required and used. However, the teachers could use a rod and a rope to punish the pupils if they committed things unacceptable. One of the aims of education used to be to develop the capability to control the sensory organs. The students were supposed to abandon *Kama* (lust), *Krodh* (anger), *Lobha* (greed), *Harsha* (joy), *Mada* (conceit) and *Mana* (vanity). Hindu education system used to be the strict adherence of celibacy (*Brahmacharya*) while at school. This used to be a strong moral value, which could never be broken. *Brahmacharya* used to be so important in the education system that this term later used to be a synonym of a student.

But the modern schooling have been grossly incapable to share the moral education to the students. The decline in the ethical standards is not due to the education system only. A number of other work and wealth related ethics, developed at home and at work places as well, is also contributing to the deterioration of the moral fiber. Children learn the parental ethic while they are growing and living together with their parents while continuing the schools.

Modern schooling in Nepal has completely forgotten the advantages and concepts of traditional educational system and moral character building therein. There are a few Sanskrit schools funded by the government. But people feel ashamed of studying there and it is not seen as a good form of education. A large number of Nepalese students are taught in modern "boarding schools" and some Christian missionary schools, where they hardly get any education about their own cultural heritage. They don't know the meaning of much of the traditional heritage they are supposed to inherit from their ancestors.

Modern Nepalese education system does not emphasize on traditional cultural values. Neither does it impart the heritage education, conservation, and continuation. Education is mostly based on the Western ethics and is a mere replica of the Western learning process approach. It ignores the national and cultural parameters. Students are rarely exposed to the richness of Nepali culture. Neither are they made aware of the cultural values and significance associated with the heritage. Modern schooling is de-linked with the preservation of the ancient culture and heritage. It ignores the merit and importance of ethics. People who respect and admire the good morality are ridiculed and viewed as anti-modern and less civilized. It has become counter-productive to cultural values and norms as well to the preservation of the society's moral fiber. This has started a process of de-traditionalization.

Schooling has produced several changes, especially in the rural communities. According to an unpublished report (Koirala, 1995), schooling has become an instrument to reproduce the larger society by nurturing gender inequality, and sustaining ethnic oppression, casteism and class values through both its explicit and hidden curriculum. It has imposed Western values of modernization (individualism and competitiveness), encouraged brain drain, and produced unemployed graduates, produced "safe" and docile citizen instead of making them liberated human beings. It has produced culturally alienated personalities and generated modernism at the cost of cultural, linguistic and humanistic repression.

Institutes of education sector in Nepal have lately been engulfed by anarchy. There are continuing nuisances in the shrines of learning. Student protests, strikes, lockouts, and politics have become common. Lack of discipline, disrespect of the teachers, harassment of the woman teachers and girl students by their male counterparts is becoming increasingly common. Since the shrines of learning are being turned into shrines of learning disrespect and hooliganism, the culture is bound to be affected.

Outside the schools, the society's moral fiber is no less deteriorated. A satirical essay[4] on the contemporary Nepalese society stated a few "diseases" that have plagued the Nepalese people. *Honestophobia* (fearing the honest people), *thought pollution* (indoctrination of political ideology in each individual), *moneyitis* (believing only in money and classifying people by their wealth), *oldmania* (increasing hatred towards the things of the past), according to the humorist were the national malaise. He is perhaps right.

Corruption in the ethics enter people's lives as students try to cheat in the examinations, when intellectuals resort to plagiarism in writing books and articles, and when fake certificates are bought from across the border.

---

[4] *Kantipur*, Falgun 30, 2053 BS (1997)

THE INTELLECTUAL APATHY

The decay in the cultural values and ancient heritage is also augmented by the apathy of the so-called intellectuals in the country. The emergence and reshaping of the intellectual institution is contributing to the culture shift in Nepal especially in shaping the values, attitudes, beliefs and level of response to the problems of cultural deterioration. These self-styled "buddhijibis' act tall against ordinary citizens in all affairs of the state and tend to prescribe their "one best way" in everything. But they have failed to deliver anything in the preservation of the cultural identity and the ancient heritage in the country. Today, an increasingly large number of people in the intelligentsia are becoming obsessed with their personal successes and are less caring about the society as a whole. Instead of being modest and humble to their achievements in their respective fields, the intellectuals have turned arrogant and are increasingly acting proud, willing to display their wisdom and looking down upon other people who they think don't have that level of wisdom. The Nepalese "intellectuals" today are increasingly developing an impulse to send explicit or implicit symbols and messages signifying their smartness, power, status, and achievement, while they are becoming highly apathetic to their own culture, tradition and heritage.

The status of the so-called intellectuals as a moral agent or a catalyst in the social process is being faded. Hardly any people who claim to be "intellectual" think they shoulder the responsibility of the moral agent. Neither are they seen as public's memory or a repository of the universal interests of all the citizens, as intellectual institution used to be entrusted with a few decades earlier.

The intellectuals *(Buddhijibis)* are unique people in Nepal. They possess a great deal of outspokenness and ability to criticize the rest of the world. They are people with one or other profession having achieved somewhat fame and recognition. They appear regularly in television to comment on topical issues. They are instantly referred to when there is a problem or a controversy. Different newspapers and tabloids keep interviewing them. They can issue statements on any issues and speak instantly on any subject on the earth. If nothing is on the air, they can write articles in the local newspapers.

There are various types of intellectuals. One group always rejects a new idea. This display of intellectual fundamentalism, i.e. the emphasis of "one-best-way", is the source of the disillusionment and frustrations in the Nepalese society. These intellectual fundamentals instantly reject a new idea and immediately put forward their hypotheses, as if they have readymade answers to most mundane problems. In fact, every one knows how to criticize, but no one knows what needs to be done. To many Nepalese intellectuals, if you don't criticize, you loose your outspokenness and loose your intellectuality.

The other group is the chameleons, who change colors seasonally and are extremely flexible to the need of the situation. Particularly, they change sides in politics depending upon who is in the power, which they have a high degree genuflection to. Opportunism is the core of their moral. And this breed seems to be increasing. The determining factor for their flexibility is their personal benefits and gains. Though many have lost the moral quality, they can influence political and social issues from their *Kothe Gaff*, the living room discussions, write-ups in the local tabloids, speeches in the seminars, and appearance in the magic box, the television.

What is worrisome is the ongoing erosion of the intellectual quality. Previously people used to write books and scholarly works. Now they write short articles on issues, which are obvious. Very rarely they raise issues. The middle pages of daily newspapers and several columns of weekly tabloids carry several such articles. Yet another erosion in the intellectual value system is the emergence of self-aggrandizement. Whereas the real intellectuals are supposed to exhibit simplicity, modesty and humbleness, the neo-intellectuals are more and more showing that they are great, that they have accomplished many things, and that they have outsmarted others. Self-praise, if not self-prophecy, is the ulterior motive of many such intellectuals, these days.

The worse side of the intellectual behavior affecting the culture is that they discuss every thing but the cultural enrichment. Intellectual debate is either philosophical or political. It is usually trivial to advocate the traditional norms and values because that is hardly seen as being intellectual. In the old times, discussing about the cultural heritage and rich cultural practices and citing examples from Sanskrit verses used to be a symbol of access to a lot of knowledge and intellectual capability. Today, that hardly represents one's intellectual capability. A quote from English saying is preferred to that from the Hindu epic *Mahabharat*.

It is generally true that many intellectuals are not aware of their role in the ensuing Culture Shift in the country. People are increasingly happy to think and talk about what is going wrong, with the nation, the politicians, and "others". But no one hardly thinks and bothers about what is wrong with oneself, and how one can contribute to the society at large. General attitude is that of blaming others, which is central to most Nepali conversations. But no one critically examines one's own role in the guilt or in the things that are going wrong.

Asked about this country's future, most of the so-called intellectuals give a blunt negative and pessimistic answer. Many tend to blame politicians. People's pessimism is so marked that many Nepalese intellectuals do not allow positive comments on any issue that confronts the society.

In the old Hindu as well as Buddhist traditions, a wise person used to be usually a person, who spent most of the time studying and practicing religion and philosophy. Scholars used to give lectures and speeches on their respective religious, philosophical and spiritual merits. Today, a wise person is usually one, who has completed a high academic degree, preferably a Ph.D. A more sophisticated educated elite would be one, who has completed higher education from the west, e.g. the United States and can speak fluently in English on some of the contemporary subjects. People aspire and try to get degrees not in order to gain access to the academic knowledge in a particular field, but to obtain a special recognition in the society. There is a general complex among the intelligentsia that getting the sanctitious degrees is getting access to the highest echelon of the educated elite. The average Nepalese concept of a wise person is tilting towards one, who knows the time, locale and circumstances (*Desh-Kala-Paristhiti*) very well, one who is fit to every circumstance. The merit of intellectuality and wisdom is also sloping down. This is affecting the overall educational ethic and psychology and is contributing to the Culture Shift in a larger perspective.

The Linguistic Landscape

Language has been one of the distinct platforms in the making of the identities of people, especially of various ethnic groups, and in the phenomenon of the Culture Shift in Nepal. For a multi-ethnic and multi-linguistic country like Nepal, language has become the prime mover of the cultural awakening and differences among the people. In fact, many of the culture related movements are focused around the language, which has become a major resource in the "politics of culture" that is the making in Nepal. There are demands for the recognition of ethnic languages. Some of the aspirations of the language movement are reflected in the constitution of the kingdom of Nepal (1991) in the sense that the constitution declares Nepal a multi-linguistic country and requires the state to promote all the ethnic languages. While several dialects and regional languages are in the verge of extinction, a new movement for linguistic revivalism is also on the making. Many ethnic activists are reinventing their languages, reconstructing scripts, grammar, vocabularies, dictionaries and even literature. Others are demanding greater recognition to their languages. As Sanskrit is being forgotten and confined to the books of rituals and religion, use of English is intensifying among the emerging rich class in the urban society. Nepali is not only neglected, it is gradually changing towards a sycophantic dialect. Hindi is becoming increasingly palatable as movies from "Bollywood" are invading people's perception of entertainment.

People of Nepal, influenced by the patronization of the rulers and immigrants, have time and again, adopted and abandoned languages. The Lichhavis brought and introduced classical Sanskrit from *Vaisali* in India and replaced the language spoken by Kirants, who were at the helm of the affairs of the country then. They adopted and patronized the language. The first documented evidence of written script of Sanskrit in Nepal is in the *Changu Narayan* inscription (dated 464 AD). The Brahamans helped proliferate this language as the medium of religious code. Sanskrit later became the language both of Hinduism and Buddhism. This is evident from the fact that all the ancient sacred texts of both Mahayana Buddhism and Hinduism found in Nepal are in

Sanskrit (Malla, 1989, p. 446). Sanskrit remained the language of religious and royal ceremonies until the advent of Newari during the Malla period. Newari language was "instituted as a rival" of Sanskrit language during the early Malla Period (1200-1482 AD) and it became the language of literature under the court patronage only after the restoration of Malla dynasty in the second half of the fourteenth century (Malla, 1989). Newari became the official language of the royal courts during the reign of King Yaksha Malla (1412-82). Malla kings also used a lot of Urdu words in their courts under an influence from Moslem rulers in contemporary India. They were fond of adopting and learning different languages. They started to adopt such languages as Bengali and Maithali (Malla, 1989, p. 447). King Pratap Malla of Kantipur is said to have been master of fifteen different languages. His polyglot inscription in front of Hanumandhoka, Kathmandu, is regarded as one of the most difficult and undecipherable.

Modern Nepali language developed from *Khas Kura*, a language spoken originally by *Khas* people of Karnali region. After unification of Nepal and conquest of the Kathmandu Valley, *Khas Kura* written in *Devanagari* script replaced Newari (Malla, 1989, p. 447). At first, the Khas language was used for administrative communications. Then, it was picked up as a common medium of communication between different groups of people, who needed a common language to communicate with each other after the unification. Also known as *Parbatiya*, and *Gorkhali* until 1933, *Khas Kura* later started to be known as Nepali. Although originally prevalent in the hilly region, with modernization and spread of communication and adoption by the state as a national language, Nepali became *lingua franca* and penetrated the Terai and the Himalayas.

CRISES IN THE ETHNIC LANGUAGES

With about 70 mutually unintelligible languages spoken in Nepal within its present day boundaries (Malla, 1989, p. 49), multi-lingualism is the characteristics of the Nepalese society. Languages of four different families including Sino-Tibetan (56), Indo-European (14), *Dravidian* (Jhangar), and *Austro-Asiatic* (Satar) are spoken in Nepal. Though some of these languages are spoken by a relatively a large number of people, many of these languages are spoken by less than one percent of the total population of Nepal. The mere fact that there are so few speakers tells us that some of these languages are very vulnerable in their very existence. Many such languages are being lost in the process of integration to the mainstream Nepali and other dominant languages. Hamilton (1989) mentioned that Nepali made a rapid progress in "extinguishing the aboriginal dialects of the mountains". Dr. Chaitanya Subba, Secretary of National Indigenous Development Committee, is quoted as saying "about 18 to 19 different ethnic languages are on the verge of being extinct while 29 others do not have the tradition of script"[1] hence vulnerable to disappear.

Even Gurung language, which is a major ethnic language, is not supported by evidence to have a written script. There have been claims of existence and destruction of the Gurung script in the 17th century Gorkha. Tamu Kyui (Gurung language) has been said to be in danger of dying out (Des Chene, 1996) as reflected in the national census. In 1961, three were 111,963 people who spoke Gurung language. In 1981, the number had decreased to 80,958, whereas the overall population was shown to be growing. If we disregard the chances of error in the census taking, this represents a big change since the population of Nepal has doubled in that period. Concerns are expressed about the loss of Gurung language in magazines promoting Gurung culture (*Rodhi, Tamu Sum Tam* etc.). It is said that the Gurung language is being lost, it remains unwritten and, is not taught, and not valued (Des Chene, 1996, p. 130).

As the Tamu or Gurung Diaspora continues and as Gurungs continue to stay outside their village mostly after joining the military (both national and abroad), the loss of language has been further aggravated. And the second generation Gurungs, who have lived outside their villages, will have higher tendency of abandoning their mother tongue.

A study on Gurung culture of Gandaki region (Gurung in Toffin, 1993 p. 132-138) states the Gurungs of the region "forgot their language and traditional manner after coming into contacts with other ethnic groups". This reflects how different linguistic composition is either changing or disappearing in the course of cultural assimilation and integration. This is true with several other tribal dialects, which don't even have their own script and written literature. Much of the

---

[1] *The Spotlight*, October 30, 1998

linguistic heritage has either become extinct or is in the verge of extinction.

The state policy in the past was not particularly friendly to the ethnic languages. For example, the education policy during the Panchayat regime actively discouraged schooling in ethnic or local languages in order to promote Nepali, as a policy of "integration" espoused by the state. This caused steady decline in the local languages and many children grew up adopting Nepali as their first language abandoning their ethnic tongue.

People gradually abandoned their languages and adopted Nepali as *lingua franca* succumbing to the pressure of "national integration" as speaking an ethnic language would constitute a shame or an embarrassment to many educated elite. If government statistics is to be believed, only 19.5 % of total population used to speak Nepali in 1952/54, whereas the census of 1991 shows Nepali-speaking population has risen to 50.3%. On the other hand, 22.2% of people used to speak one of 17 Tibeto-Burman languages, the languages of ethnic minorities in 1952/54. In 1991 census, that figure has been seen dropping to 17.2%, a decline by 5%. Though this may be a marginal change, the indications are there that the ethnic languages are loosing the popularity as spoken languages. Many have resorted to *lingua franca* Nepali.

There has been a "greater incidence of bilingualism and weakening of linguistic homogeneity" of the lowland Terai especially due to the resettlement and land distribution in the region (Malla, 1989, p. 453). There are similar trends in the hilly region, where several ethnic groups have started to become bilingual or have even abandoned their own ethnic languages. "This tendency is most pronounced in the western hills among the Gurungs, the Magars and the Thakalis" and among the people in the eastern hills (Malla, 1989). There are a number of reasons.

"First, Nepali has been a *lingua franca* throughout the hills for some time. Secondly, it has been the language of social prestige in terms of civil or military or police service-mostly military, either in the Nepalese army or the Gorkha Rifles of India or Britain. Thirdly, in terms of literacy and availability of printed materials there is no scope for minority languages of the hills. Finally, as the national language has been identified with Nepal's increasing aspirations towards nationhood, any attempt at language loyalty or revival is often interpreted as communalism or tribalism" (Malla, ibid.).

As most linguistic communities are very small and as there are very little incentives and opportunities to continue to study their own language even up to the primary level of schooling, the links with the past are weakening and people are starting to forget their own language. The linguistic diversity of the people of Nepal is at stake.

Even with Newari, which has retained its own script, developed much of literature and has a big linguistic community, and which is taught in the university, most Newari speaking people, especially those living outside Kathmandu Valley and those in bureaucracy are becoming increasingly bilingual with Nepali. Recently, there has been "a growing tendency among the middle class Newar parents to use Nepali while communicating with their children, though they themselves may still continue to use Newari while communicating in their peer groups" (Malla, 1989, p. 455). Many Newars, who have left Kathmandu Valley, have adopted Nepali as their mother tongues. Today, Newar activists in Kathmandu Valley have been successfully campaigning the politics of language via their unique organization called *Nepal Bhasha Manka Khala*, which would become a strong political organization in the Valley's politics.

Despite all that, some ethnic communities have started to look back at their own language. Many *Janajati* language activists have started to publish their own magazines in their own language. Some such mouthpieces include *Tharu Sanskriti* (Tharus), *Tamun* (Gurungs), *Khanglo* (Thakalis), *Paru-hang* (Kirants), *Kiran* (pan-ethnic) and *Chhahara* (pan-ethnic). They are creating dictionaries and grammars and basic texts for education. There are "striking parallels between the efforts that went into promotion of Nepali language and culture in the first half of this century... and the efforts of *janajatis* today" (Des Chene, 1996). Language in the post-*andolan* politics has become an "acid test of the seriousness of the state's said commitment to the cultural diversity and equalization opportunity for *janjatis* (Des Chene, 1996, p. 128). Despite recent moves allowing primary schooling in the mother tongue ethnic languages and policy of airing radio news in eight ethnic languages, the ethnic languages are not in the state of recovery of the perennial loss they have witnessed in the history of Nepal.

Despite the recognition given by the constitution (1990) as *rashtriya bhasha* (languages of the nation), ethnic languages are still considered other languages and don't enjoy the status of Nepali, which is called *rashtra bhasha*, the national language. Recognizing ethnic languages only as other languages is a "point of bitterness and taken as a measure of bad faith and disinterest in the presentation of minority languages" (Des Chene, 1996). The constitution is said to have treated the ethnic languages or *janjati bhasha* as the second class status. The multi-cultural and mutli-linguistic rhetoric is pronounced in the constitution, in election manifestos, and in ministerial speeches. But the translation of the same into policy and programs to the benefit of the ethnic minority remains to be achieved. Whereas the issue of language is usually labeled as "politicizing" of the language by *janjatis*, the language activism is hardly perceived as a cultural necessity in the wake of the identity crisis experienced by the ethnic minorities.

The shifting landscape in the languages is evident in the politics of culture based on language as a political resource. Language today has become a major parameter of the politics of culture. Ethnic activists have not only demanded a greater freedom to their languages, they have asked that the state adopt promotional policies to each of them. Though the constitution (1990) recognizes Nepal as a "multi-linguistic and multi-ethnic" country, politics of language is not confined to the state recognition. It is strikingly connected to people's identity and the trend of cultural revivalism, which is taking shape in Nepal, especially among the ethnic minorities.

The state support for the promotion of ethnic languages is all but very feeble. Apart from the publishing of *Sayaparti*, a multi-lingual journal dedicated to "national languages, literatures and cultures" by the Royal Nepal Academy, the commitment made by the post-*andolan* government to set up a *Janjati* Academy remains to be fully accomplished. The airing of news in Radio Nepal eight minority languages and filming of some telefilms in these languages in the Nepal Television were welcome steps, but the appropriate support to develop these languages is yet to be realized to the expectations of the *Janjati* activists. The constitution has allowed primary schooling in all *rashtriya bhasha* (the languages of the nation). This has enthused local activists of various ethnic groups to start such schools. But their expectation for the state's support in developing textbooks, providing financial resources and in appointing teachers remains to be fulfilled. Thus the primary teaching in the local languages has become burdensome to may ethnic groups. In the rural villages, where ethnic minorities are concentrated, teaching and learning Nepali is preferred over the ethnic languages. But in the small towns and cities, where there are diffused populations of various ethnic groups of people, the ethnic languages are gradually being abandoned, especially by the young people, who have increasing access to education in Nepali and English.

Leaving apart Newari and Maithali, most other ethnic languages don't have enough literature. Some don't' even have a written form. Other lack their dictionaries and grammar. But the activists of the revivalism era have recognized the importance of their language and are developing their own dictionaries and grammars.[2] Despite of the passion towards English and universalization of Nepali, the activists have produced periodicals in their own languages. Some have developed their own script and some are creating literature.

Regional languages, which were suppressed in the name of nationalism, have been recognized by the Constitution (1990). In an unprecedented gesture, Radio Nepal has started broadcasting since August 14, 1994 the news in eight minority languages (Rai, Gurung, Magar, Limbu, Tamang, Awadhi, Bhojpuri, Tharu) apart from Newari that was on air since 1990 and Maithali since 1993.

Though there is a sketchy state support to the regional languages, the recognition itself and the pro-language cultural policy, is heralding the revival of the languages, which are on the verge of extinction from the usage and literature point of view. This "dramatic shift in the official policy" (Gellner, 1997 in Gellner *et. al* ed., 1997, p. 6), may be a cause for euphoria for a while. But their actual development and their revival will be a long march ahead given the amount of damage already incurred to these languages.

It is not only the state policy that is solely responsible for the decay in the regional languages. For many Nepalis today their local language and traditions have "no particular value" and are "a disadvantage in the highly competitive scramble for employment and survival" (Gellner, 1997, p. 20). Further the local languages are so much divided by dialect, there is much of controversy which one to learn leading to the logical conclusion that another connecting thread could be searched in the Nepali language.

In an effort to revive the regional and ethnic languages, some Municipalities started to recognize the regional languages. Newari in

---

[2] Though assisted by outsiders, a 2,400-word Dhimal dictionary, compiled by Suyoyoshi Toba, Japanese scholar and Honorary member of the Royal Nepalese Academy, and published in 1999 and a Dhimal grammar, being compiled by a Swiss linguist Catrherine Cuper Young are some examples.

Kathmandu and Maithali in Janakpurdham were introduced by the municipalities as "supplementary" official language. This move was stayed in April 1998 and eventually the use of ethnic languages other Nepali in the local bodies was essentially outlawed by the Supreme Court verdict on June 1, 1999. The verdict ordered that only the Nepalese language and *Devanagari* script could be officially recognized in accordance with the Constitution of the Kingdom of Nepal. But the Supreme Court order has not prevented the activists to pursue the policy of getting recognition of their languages. In Kathmandu, the Linguistic Rights Movement Committee (LMRC), an alliance formed to obtain the state recognition of the ethnic languages, called a "Valley Bandh" to protest of the verdict that outlawed ethnic languages being used as official language in the municipalities and other local bodies. They have demanded amendments in the Constitution to facilitate the use of languages other Nepali as official languages in the local bodies. The opposition and bitterness against decision to prevent the use of ethnic languages goes to the extent that Malla K Sunder, the coordinator of the LMRC, has asked how the ethnic languages could not be allowed, whereas Hindi has been allowed in the parliament.[3] The language activists are not only demanding the recognition of the ethnic languages in the municipalities. They are also demanding the removal of Sanskrit as a compulsory subject from the school curricula, and that all the local languages be given equal priority and access in the state media "without any discrimination". This represents a major shift in the support of the regional and ethnic languages. But this is labeled as a politics of language and the several languages and various dialects continue to be in threat of loss of interest and in some cases to the extent of extinction.

THE FORGOTTEN LANGUAGE

It is not only the ethnic languages that are loosing in the ensuing language battle. Sanskrit, the quintessential language, supposed to have been sponsored by the Brahmans and the state, is also in the decline and increasingly becoming a rare knowledge. Although it is known for its richness and invaluable hidden treasure, it has already become an

---

[3] *The Kathmandu Post*, August 12, 1999

obsolete language in terms of usage and general communication. These days, this language is being forgotten even in the scholastic studies. Today, Sanskrit is confined to some Hindu and Buddhist texts and rituals only.

According to traditional Hindu education system, Sanskrit used to be the language and medium of learning. Students were taught Sanskrit at *Gurukul.* Sanskrit was the language of religious texts and of performing the rituals. Its importance as the repository of religious knowledge and as Hindu heritage was never compromised. In fact, Sanskrit was not just a language, it was a way of life, history, a religious form of expression and many other things. Therefore abandoning Sanskrit education or promotion used to be out of contemporary thinking. But this is not the case with many intellectuals and planners who don't foresee direct benefit of educating Sanskrit in the schools. Therefore, the curriculum of Sanskrit language in the school level education has been actively curtailed down.

Sanskrit, a language of rich vocabulary and a language with much more ancient knowledge than many other languages in the world, is increasingly considered an obsolete and a language of rituals. People feel ashamed to use, understand or learn this language. The religious texts with depth of knowledge is considered to be confined to the sphere of the Brahmins performing the rituals and worships. Learning the depths of these treatises is seen going backwards and against the "modernization". People with advanced knowledge about the spiritual world also possess this intellectual apathy towards Sanskrit.

For several decades, many well known Nepali litterateurs Sanskritized Nepali language in the name of literary contribution. The trend became so powerful that it was almost impossible to write modern literary Nepali without using Sanskrit words and phrases. Many academic writing were seen citing Sanskrit verses to give examples and powerful expressions. Use of Sanskrit started to become so extensive that some litterateurs started to oppose the heavy use of Sanskrit vocabulary in Nepali literature. The movement was initiated in the 1950s by litterateurs Bal Krishna Pokharel, Taranath Sharma, Ballav Mani Dahal, and later supported by litterateur Mahananda Sapkota. Known as *Jharrobad*, the movement envisaged the use of pure Nepali lexicons and morphemes instead of foreign words, mainly Sanskrit. But this movement faced heavy criticism and was short-lived (Acharya, 1994, p. 85).

Today, people have started to challenge that everything written in Sanskrit is sacrosanct and have started to question the ideals and values developed during the Sanskrit era. A recent row (1995) over introduction of Sanskrit news by the radio Nepal is a case in point. The uproar against the news broadcast was focused on the lack of relevance of the language in present day Nepal and opposition to it was based on the belief that its promotion by the sate was tantamount to the state protection of Brahmin domination over other ethnic language. Though people no longer view the merit of airing Sanskrit to "purify one's soul", the battle for and against Sanskrit continues to be a bone of contention, albeit it is becoming a loosing battle.

Whereas the state is blamed to be espousing Sanskrit, the support to this ancient language is confined to teaching the language in a few government schools and airing news in Sanskrit over the Radio Nepal. Otherwise, the state support to Sanskrit is waning. Even Brahmans, who are supposed to the custodians of this language, do not seem to see any direct benefit from this language and are distancing from this language.

Though the government has been supposedly promoting Sanskrit and its institutions, the ancient language is loosing grounds and relevance. Some academic work and some teaching is going in the Mahendra Sanskrit University, the kingdom's premier institution for promoting Sanskrit. There are a few Sanskrit schools in some places. But there are not many students and the interest in the study of Sanskrit is waning. Radio Nepal, kingdom's state broadcast, offers morning prayers and news in Sanskrit. But that is being opposed as Bahunization. Despite its rich knowledge and heritage, the ancient language has become a source of controversy and is gradually loosing its authority, legitimacy and universality.

NEPALI NEGLECTED

Whereas it may sound like Nepali is achieving too much focus and attention, and is supposed to be major cause of the decline of the ethnic languages, there is a trend of the neglect of Nepali language and literature as well. Adoption of Nepali as a *lingua franca* may be blamed as one of the principal factors responsible for gradual decline of the ethnic languages in Nepal. But Nepali itself is on the decline due to increasing shifts towards other languages. Nepali has been actively screened out from various official communications. Seminars, training, newspaper articles and even speeches in Nepal are becoming common in English. Despite support of the state, movement of linguistic chauvinism by the Nepali literary figures and the all-powerful status of the language is declining. Nepali is increasingly slipping away from conversations, correspondence, business and day-to-day-use.

Nepali is the "national language" of Nepal. It is taught in all government schools. It is the medium of communication in the government offices and even government school curricula are mostly in this language. But it is a strange situation that Nepali should become a neglected language.   First, Nepali no longer continues to be the medium of teaching in most modern English schools, euphemistically called as "boarding schools". Nepali is taught as a course simply because it is required by the curricula. Second, learning Nepali is not considered something nice by the younger generations. Young people disown their language and some even dislike studying Nepali. Very rarely students take Nepali as a subject in the academic studies.

Despite the constitution reiterating Nepali as the national language (*rashtra bhasha*), the state support for Nepali is now confined to government offices, where Nepali has been assigned as the working language. Even public service examinations have withdrawn Nepali as a curriculum. In 1993, Nepali was screened out from the Public Service Commission curricula for civil service examinations. There was little uproar for some time and the issue subsided until the same was taken to the judiciary.

Among the modern youngsters, who take pride in speaking English, their tone of speaking Nepali has almost become Anglicized. Anglicization of Nepali pronunciation has become a kind of fashion among the youngsters, who prefer to perspire and roll their tongues even while speaking Nepali, creating a non-Nepali dialect, which is very much in the making. Further, there is an increasing passion towards English and there is an increasing bilingualism among the modern Kathmanduites, who can speak English as well as Nepali. Then there is another group of Nepalese who have settled abroad or has studied abroad. For this category, Nepali is hardly a language of communication, even at home.

Today, Nepali as a language, is sidelined also by the opposition of the ethnic minorities in the wake of revival of their own languages. And only some government institutions like the Royal Nepalese Academy have some concerns for promotion of Nepali. Every other quarter has left Nepali to wane. Even the Nepali linguistic and literary movement outside Nepal called as *Prabasi Sahitya*, in areas such as Darjeeling, and Assam, has also started to wane even after Nepali was recognized by the Indian constitution.

Yet another distortion to the Nepali language is seen in the significant trend, especially among the Kathmanduites, towards the sycophantic version of the language. During earlier periods, many residents of Kathmandu had adopted the royal version of the Nepali language because they had to deal with the royal family. Priests, palace officials and other associates in the royal court were required to use the royal language in the palace and to address the royal family and the Ranas. They gradually adopted this as a family language in order to have their children access to the royal palace. This practice in language has become so much pervasive in Kathmandu these days that every one is using the royal version of Nepali language, even if they have nothing to do with the royal family and the palace. This trend has so much invaded Nepali language that many people have taken it as a normal thing and they don't even notice it. In this, people tend to copy the formal elocution that uses extremely pleasing words to the person being addressed. Most verbs are used with *Baksyos*. For example eating (*Khanus*) becomes *Jyunar Garibaksyos* (please grace us by eating).

This trend in the distortion of the Nepali language is also related to the *Chakari* bureau-culture that continues to exist in Nepal. People used to take pride to show some kind of association with the royal court and the Rana administrators. That used to give status and satisfaction and even some kind of power to many people in Kathmandu. For that reason, people who were not used to use this form of elocution also started using this to praise and please the persons they were speaking with and this gradually developed as a bureau-language.

In the bureaucratic formality, language is one of the most widely misused things to please the boss. Employees flatteringly use *Hajur* and *Baksyos* while addressing their bosses. In fact, in most bureaucratic structures, it is very difficult not to use such flattering words. People are expected to use such language as a routine form of address in speech and the people who refuse to use this are very rare and are seen as rude and impolite. Using the flattering version of the Nepali at work and at home, people are perhaps trying to secure their status, politeness and good understanding. But this is spoiling the beauty of eloquence of the ordinary Nepali language.

Ironically, all the formal written language in the official correspondence even addressed to the seniors and bosses is regular and routine Nepali. The formal elocution copying the royal accent is not used while addressing younger and junior people. In any case, the trend of copying the royal language in a distorted version has spoiled its originality and eloquence and has developed as a corrupt version of the original Nepali language.

INTENSIFYING ENGLISH

It was a party of the upwardly mobile Nepalese men. There were about ten people assembled for their evening drinks at a local pub. By the time all the members had arrived, most people had already started speaking English. They had started using English greetings and English expressions in their conversation. In fact, no one seemed to be using Nepali neither anybody noticed it save the new comer, who felt awkward and instantly cut a joke, "my friends, let us please speak Nepali if we can". Every one laughed.

There is a strong evidence that more and more Nepalese people are adopting English as their language at their homes, workplaces, and at places of study. More and more people have started to understand, speak and use English language in place of Nepali and other ethnic languages. In Kathmandu, it has become a kind of fashion to be able to speak English and communicate in this language. It is with this fashion that there has been a rush in the so-called English medium schools. People are extremely conscious about their children's ability to speak English. In other words, the ability to speak English has been one of the key indicators of good education.

There may not be the usual confidence in English as a *lingua franca*. But you speak it to show your sophistication, to demonstrate that you are educated and knowledgeable. For many, the ability of speaking English is a status symbol. For many others, speaking local languages might even become a sign of backwardness. Though there are usual hesitations initially. But people use their chances to speak whenever then get one.

Many young and educated Nepalese are fond of speaking English. Listening to a group of young Nepalese students discussing among

themselves, one can find much of what they are talking is English.
Using English words and expressions is understood as some kind of
sophistication one has achieved during the education. Some may even
use a whole sentence of English in between Nepali words. In fact,
many such discussions sound like people are using English as the main
language adding some Nepali in between.

A whole new corpus of English writing is evolving in Nepal. In
fact, increasingly more and more works on Nepal and Nepali people is
becoming available in English language. People organize seminars,
write papers, discuss their ideas and write books in English language.
English-speaking ability has not only become essential for
communication and for being recognized, it has become a status
symbol for being recognized, especially among the professionals,
academicians and business people.

With proliferation of computer education and increasing attraction
to English-language courses, the access to the language is increasing. As
English-medium schools have mushroomed, as increasingly large
number of English-medium channels are available in Satellite TV, as
new English-language media is evolving, English has started to reach
the masses and no more a privilege of a "ruling" or "rich class" people.
Competence in English language has become sole yardstick to the
capability to perform in business, in government bureaucracy and in
the academia.

Several factors have contributed to the intensification of English in
the urban areas especially among the young people. Increasing number
of private boarding schools, hike in the need for English speaking jobs
(e.g. in the tourism industry), expansion of television channels like
CNN, BBC and Star TV, and lately the FM radio, and increasing
contacts abroad, have intensified the use of English in Nepal. Further,
the youngsters, who have dreamt of going abroad for anything, English
has become mandatory. Besides, the expansion of computer networks
and universalization of the Internet and email has made English a
language of the households in the urban areas.

THE HINDI *HUNGAMA*

Traditionally, Hindi language had a lot of influence in people's lives in
Nepal, especially in that of urban and educated people. People knew
Hindi mainly from their association with India during their study. Many

went to Benares, Patna, and Calcutta for higher studies. Others learnt it by way of contacts in pilgrimages, employment and in trade. These days, Hindi movies and television channels account for the spread of Hindi in Nepal than the traditional mechanisms. Hindi cinema sometimes is as popular in Nepal as it is in India. In the decades of the seventies, many young people used to even go to the Indian cities just in order to see a new Hindi movie. Film actors and actresses from Hindi movies in India are far more popular in Nepal than those from Nepalese movies. Film magazines and blow up posters of Hindi actresses and actors are sold and bought with fanfare everywhere in Nepal. There are popular melodies in Hindi and there are fans of old and new Hindi songs. Hindi music is played at parties, homes and in public places. People know words of several popular Hindi movies by heart and youngsters enjoy singing Hindi songs. India's Bollywood is the largest producer of cinema in the world, which has reached to the far-flung corners of world such as the South East and Middle-East Asia and Africa. Nepal cannot remain uninfluenced. Various cinema halls in Kathmandu show the latest releases of Hindi movies. Radio Nepal airs numerous Hindi songs. Nepal Television also sports Hindi songs intermittently. Numerous FM Channels in Kathmandu air Hindi songs round the clock.

Apart from the influence of the Hindi cinema world, there are influences of the Television Channels like *Doordarshan,* and *ZEE TV,* and Hindi newspapers and magazines, especially in the urban areas and areas adjoining Indian border. Besides, people learn Hindi during contacts with Indians vegetable vendors who have rushed into the valley in a large number. The influence is so much that many people use intermittent Hindi words while speaking Nepali and many others have corrupted Nepali language altogether using incorrect Hindi lexicons and morphemes.

Except people in the Terai areas adjoining India, very few Nepalese people speak Hindi in normal conversation except for purposes of satire or joke, though they comprehend the language very well. Occasionally, Hindi language also becomes a political resource. Nepal Sadbhabhana Party, which advocates the cause of the Madhesiyas, demands recognition of Hindi as one of the state languages, as it is supposed to be the medium of communication between different communities in the Terai. Its leader Gajendra Narayn Singh has spoken in Hindi the Nepalese parliament, demanding the recognition of the language on some occasions. Whether it is included in the constitution or not, Hindi is understood and admired by a relatively large umber of Nepalese people in the ongoing embrace of the Hindi Hungama.

Interestingly, even people in the rural areas, who have hardly come into contact with Hindi-speaking people, become mesmerized by the Indian cinema. They watch Hindi movies in the video played with the help of generators in the village stalls. And the returnees from the employment as Gurkha soldiers in the Indian army take it as pride to be able to speak Hindi in their distinct Lahure accent.

LEANING LITERATURE

Perhaps the talk of culture shift will be incomplete without the mention of Nepali literature, which has dramatically changed in the last couple of decades.Contemporary poetry and essays on Nepali literature and some novels reflects the mind and mood of the Nepalese people and the writers. Nepalese literature evolved around the sycophancy of the kings. The court poets called as *Bhats* used to write eulogy of the kings and praise their deeds. God and Hero-worshipping has been a trend in the early Nepali literature. Poets like Raghunath Panta, Subananda Das Yadunath Pokharel wrote about the personalities of the kings and powerful court officials, war deeds, and devotion to the gods (Subedi in Malla, 1989). Nepali literature, which evolved with poet Bhanubhakta Acharya's famous Hindu epic Ramayana in Nepali language, modernized in the era after the ousting of Rana regime in 1950. Several novels, epics and literary works were contributed by several writers. A whole new corpus of Nepali literature has developed with extensive writings in poetry and novels. But lately, it is observed that the interest in literary works is declining and so is the quality of the Nepalese literature.

Whatever little work is being added to the contemporary Nepali literature is demonstrating the amount of frustration and desperation in the young generation. Most people are writing about the state of non-achievement, frustration and something to ridicule or satire. Nepal has not seen great literary works in the last few decades. Except a few good novels and epics, there are hardly any writing, which can be labeled as a major literary contribution. Today, people write small poems (*muktaks*) in several tabloids, which represent the sentiments of the youngsters.

The unfulfilled dreams, departed souls, compulsions, defeated mindset and nostalgia of the village past are the dominant themes in such pieces that appear constantly in Kathmandu's tabloids.

Until some time ago, people used to admire poets, singers, comedians and religious leaders. Today, people like movie actors and actresses, political leaders and sports-persons have overshadowed them. This shift is perhaps due to declining interest in matters like art and literature and an increasing attraction towards things of "instant" appeal like sports, movie and politics. A great deal of these changes is obviously engineered by the mass media and the magic box, the television. With the advent of satellite TV, people have been increasingly hooked up to music, sports and movie channels. They have very little time to focus and generate interest in the literature. The erosion of people's interest in the literature is falling back upon people's intellectuality, morality and sensitivity towards the cultural heritage. Nepalese people are getting disinterested in the Nepalese literature and receiving less quality literature than they used to some time ago. Among other things, the education system in Nepal is also responsible for the shadowing of the Nepali literature, writes a columnist.[4] In an education system, in which all the school going youngsters aspire to become doctors and engineers, its is quite natural that literature is pushed to the back seat.

Further, the deterioration in the culture and moral fiber seems to have hurt the literature as well. In his sporadic poetry, senior civil servant Bimal Koirala writes against the corruption, "self-less lifestyles", moral deterioration, social distortions, escapist mentality, and attack of the Western culture on the Nepalese originality. That, perhaps, represents the mood of the Nepalese literature in relation to the ongoing cultural deterioration, at present.

---

[4] Manjushree Thapa, in *Himal Khabarpatrika*, 1-15 Falgun, 2057 BS (16-26 February, 2001).

The Development Drama

For decades since the 1950s, Nepal has been a stage for rehearsing the development drama. Various development models have been developed, tried and tested in the soil of this tiny Himalayan kingdom. Various jargons, concepts and theories of development have been formulated and applied. Once the focus was in the development of infrastructure. Then there was emphasis on regional development. Rural development was a buzzword for decades. Alleviation of poverty has been the focus of planners and development administrators for years. Ranging from basic needs to sustainability, human development to institution building, transfer of technology to people's participation, several themes remained prevalent for decades. This tiny kingdom has been a development laboratory.

Nepal's aspiration to modernize began with the out-throwing of the autocratic Rana rule and establishment of democracy in 1950. Ever since, development has been the pronounced emphasis of the political rhetoric, economic policies, intellectual discussions, bureaucratic endeavors, and the administration of foreign aid in Nepal (Pande in Malla, 1989, p. 275). It has also been the aspiration of the masses. It has permeated the lives and culture of the Nepalese people. Influenced by the rhetoric of the state-centered planning models of the socialist countries, and enchanted by the selling power of the plan objectives, Nepalese politicians and technocrats developed five-year plans one after another. Each espoused different objectives, priorities and outlay, which were never matched. Infrastructure would be developed. Regional imbalance would be ameliorated. Poverty would be alleviated. Employment would be generated and what not. Plan became document to sell aspirations and an instrument to disseminate the political rhetoric.

During the Panchayat regime, the entire state machinery was supposedly driven for the development. "Politics for development" was a pronounced slogan. But the Panchayat dream for a development utopia could not materialize due to lack of popular participation in the selection, execution and evaluation of the development activities. The restoration of multiparty democracy in 1990 allowed people to question the traditional concepts of development. It "unleashed forces to redefine the direction, contents and *modus operandi* of Nepal's development" (Sainju, in Maskay, ed. 1997). But it was like reinventing the wheel. Same old concepts were repackaged into new programs, which could seldom deliver to the expectations of people. Of all the effects of the poor performance of development programs in Nepal is the frustration arising out of failure to meet people's rising expectation, especially after the *Jana Andolan* of 1990.

This author tends to agree that "development" was a Western myth[1] and was a set of practices and belief that was woven into the fabric of the Western culture, aimed at manipulating the natural process in the poorer countries. Thus, the development model copied from the West was successful in transferring the goods, capital, technology, and various gadgets. But the same could not become highly successful in transferring the values of accomplishment, competition, and innovative culture that is supposed to be seen in the Western culture. One of the significant expectations was that the Western development philosophy would be replicated and reconstructed in the developing countries like Nepal. But this expectation was created without assessing whether the culture in the developing countries would permit such values to be copied.

Despite five decades of political rhetoric, economic efforts, plan hopes and pledges and plethora of development projects, development has remained a dream yet to be fulfilled. Nepal still remains one of the poorest countries in the world and development continues to be sold in political as well as economic arena of the country. Some villages near major urban areas have seen fruits of development. In Satungal, a village 7-km west of Kathmandu, for example, the most visible changes in the last four decades has been the "green revolution, monetization of their economy, spread of modernization, and a transformation of the traditional village structures" (Karan & Ishii, 1996, p. 165-169). But most other villages in the rural areas of the country have yet to reap the benefits of the same.

---

[1] Trucker, Vincent, "The Myth of Development: A Critique of Economic Discourse", in Ronaldo Munick and Denis O'Hearn, eds. *Critical Development Theory* (1999), The University Press, Dhaka.

Some blame rampant corruption for this failure. Others flay lack of "good governance". The conventional excuses for the poor state of development used to be the land-locked condition and difficult topography. Today new jargons like lack of sustainability, poor institutional development, weaker popular participation have been invented for explaining the dismal performance of the development programs. Several other factors have been attributed for the failure of development in Nepal. Ineffective plan machinery, top-down donor-driven planning processes, ignorance of local cultural variables and importance of participation of the beneficiaries, *ad hocism* in selection of projects and over dependence upon foreign aid are more frequently cited ones.

Dor Bahadur Bista blames the culture of "fatalism", the belief that one's destiny is controlled by an external fate, and "Bahuism", the dominance of Brahman-Chhetris over the diverse ethnic groups of peple, to be retarding the development. Other cultural variables like the caste structure are also said to be retarding the pace of development. As the Nepalese society fragmented with various castes and ethnic groups, the motivation for innovation and progress was shunned. The feudal rulers preferred to retain the horizontal and vertical fragmentation of the people of Nepal in order to enable themselves to maintain the law and order and collect the revenue exploiting the natural resources. "Even the progress of the most highly developed material culture and a rich and colorful urban way of Kathmandu valley was frozen at the level, which was allowed to degenerate" (Bista, 1989).

Though the efforts to achieve development did not register a significant pattern in the economic upliftment if the people, its influence in the culture started to become visible. Pondering over *"Nepal's Failed Development"*, bureaucrat-turned social activist Devendra Raj Pandey has said, "the failure to develop despite all efforts, accumulated due to cumulative grievances and neglect, has begun to transform into a large issue of ethnic tension, communal competition and other forms of social stress" (Pandey, 1999). The growing disillusionment and frustration on the failure of development has bearing on the culture. Some have started to say that development has begun to "disrupt the social fabric" (Shrestha, 1997). Instead of transforming life of majority of people, five decades old development efforts have but delivered butter to a small section of population living around urban areas and added misery to majority of citizens elsewhere, laments Shrestha (1997) in his book *In the Name of Development*. This notion seems to have got a widespread recognition. In an introduction to the "Strategy for the New Millenium", the Federation of Nepalese Chambers of Commerce and Industry (FNCCI) had written in February 1999:

> Despite Nepal's nearly half a century of experiments and efforts towards enhancing basic quality of life and livelihood of its populace, the preparedness for its entry into the New Millenium is bloated with deep resentment and defeat. Nearly half of the population still live(s) in absolute poverty and illiteracy. Economic fundamentals are weak and deteriorating. The GDP growth rate is showing steady decline. The farm sector, the mainstay of Nepali population, is virtually stagnant. The performance of small non-farm sector is also not encouraging.

But development still continues to be the rhetoric in the politics, in planning and in academic vocabulary. Despite all this neglect, failure and disillusionment, many Nepalese people have not completely erased their "pipe dream" for development. There still exists a "cargo-cult view of about-to-arrive development", which means that people still possess a "widespread belief that the cargo ship carrying foreign aid, technology, democracy, human rights and other necessary supplies of modernism and development, piloted by Western development experts, will arrive and all the citizens will be able to live happily ever after in the 'never never land' of development", writes Bhattachan (1998). This "cargo cult" was sold during the Panchayat regime and is being sold even after the advent of multi-party democracy. But the "cargo has not arrived and people's hopes are still alive." (Bhattachan, 1998). And despite relentless efforts to develop, stagnation remains. Nepal's economy rallies with the "Sitting Ducks" of South Asia, unlike the "Flying Geese" of the South East Asia, says Dr. Harka Bahadur Gurung (Gurung, 1997).

Even though the efforts to develop did not go without any achievements. Major breakthroughs were achieved in road construction, communications, literacy rates and health services (Karan & Ishi, 1996). If the government statistics is to believed, conceivably outstanding infrastructure has been created in the last few decades. Roads have been built. Airports have been constructed.

Communication system has been improved. Hospitals drinking water and schools have become available to many.

With intense debate over priorities, loggerheads at who is to get what, and changing paradigms and modalities of development, hospitals are built, irrigation canals dug, water pipes laid down, and saplings are planted. But the doctor is never present. Teachers are rarely available or textbooks seldom sent. Water does not flow in the canals and the taps. The road is washed away by the rain. The development effort goes in vain.

Despite all that, Nepalese villages in the rural areas are not left untouched by the flags of modernism and development. The local costumes, languages, eating and living habits, and way of thinking has been subjected to changes in the villages as well. Plastic pouches and electronic gadgets have invaded the villages like anything. Modernism comes in the villages in the beer bottles, the noodles-packets, and branded items. The cultural value that had remained intact is being diluted. People are depending their meager resources to consume things from urban areas and abroad. If all this is not enough to satisfy, many village youths go to cities in search of jobs. Hardly any adult males are seen in many Nepalese villages. They have eluded their places in search of modernity and opportunities.

Though Nepal is comparatively less developed than other Western societies, there have been instances when Nepal had achieved much more advanced level of development. "At a time when most of the Western society was primitive and living in hovels, the Nepalese had already developed an urban culture with a highly advanced technology of building temples, palaces, *viharas*, technique of bronze work, stone sculpture *etc.*" (Bista in Malla, 1989, p. 174). At that time, the development was indigenous and built upon the values of traditions and the culture. But the present race for development is culturally dissociated with the values of people and unleashing an attack on the culture of the people. Today, the efforts to develop and modernize pose direct threats to the preservation of the cultural heritage. As the resources available have been committed to development and modernization, the conventional methods of preserving the heritage have become unsustainable.

Whereas development has been a function of the culture of the people, infusion of development has, no doubt, induced a lot of shift in the culture as well. When small farmers form groups of five to nine and take loans in joint responsibility, the group norm gets reshaped. When water starts to flow from the tap in front of the house instead of having to carrying it from a rivulet half-hour away, the work ethic and the pace of life is bound to be affected.

THE ALL EMBRACING GOVERNMENT

Among the major impacts on the people's ideology on development is the creation of the notion that the development is a function of the government. As the government machinery started to plan, propagate and execute the development activities, the people started to assume that development is a responsibility of the government. Expansion of development works made the government an all-embracing agent of carrying the progress vehicle. Every area of activity carried out as development started to be considered the function of the government. The state rhetoric of development deteriorated the community's faith on the capacity to make progress on their own. Everything starting from sanitation in one's courtyard to the protection of jungles in the villages, began to be a government activity. Even the preservation of the cultural heritage was pushed to the government.

There are several reasons for the growth of such a notion. First, the nationalization of guthis, which were very important institutions responsible for holding community activities, shunned the local initiatives for community participation in the same. Second, the political leaders and bureaucrats educated from India, in those days of Indian independence swallowed much of the Nehruvian philosophy that the government was an all-powerful machine for converting the hopes of millions into reality. Third, the ambitious plans put forward by the government started to sound that development is beyond the capacity of the communities. Fourth, the Nepalese politicians, bureaucrats, intelligentsia and academicians sought the reason of failure of development in the government's capacity to deliver. Lastly, early foreign assistance programs focused on government sponsored projects disregarding the local capacity and initiatives. These notions solidified the concept of all-embracing and all-powerful government. The expectation that every thing should be delivered by the government was also generated by the callousness of the intellectuals and the burgeoning middle class in the country. Their ability to demand anything from the state and their smartness to criticize the government, when delivery fails, augmented the notion that the government is the sole producer of all the amenities people were supposed to get.

The all-embracing government psyche has so much dominated the national mood that people blame all failures and mistakes of the society to the government. It is with this psyche that even the democratically elected governments, which were expected to deliver good governance fulfilling the wish of the people, could hardly meet such expectations and successive governments have been criticized for failing to deliver. One time bureaucrat Kul Shekhar Sharma attributes the failure in the post *jana andolan*-scenario to the lack of "good governance". He cites "excessive indulgence in political issues for holding on to power, the utter neglect of the real business of governance, political instability due to unprincipled alliances, continuation of misrule and rampant corruption, poor reforms in the political party structures, lack of a visionary and exemplary political leadership, and inadequate reforms in the labyrinthine structure and rules of bureaucracy" as barriers to good governance in the country (Sharma, 1998).

The belief in the all-embracing capacity of the government was reinforced, as there were proliferation of the development projects. Each development activity of the government, which was discrete and demanded a separate and specific treatment and which could not be dealt with routine government department, started to be named as a project. With increasing infusion of foreign aid, expansion of government and non-government activities in all spheres of human life, projects became formidable realities in the development psychology of the Nepalese people.

Ideally, projects would be instituted in activities, which had definite objectives, time frame, separate existence and definite output. But the proliferation was so pervasive that every activity started to be a project. Even the preservation of the cultural heritage, which was being done at the people's own initiatives, started to depend on the foreign aided projects.

Along with the projects came a few experts from the donor countries or institutions, a few imported jeeps, dozen of computers and never-ending reports on things hardly accomplished. For politicians, the projects served as recruitment centers their relatives and political workers from the constituencies. For businessmen and contractors, they became the institutions for minting money, if they could win those contracts. For engineers and the administrators of the projects, they constituted the ladder to rise to the top and build a house in Kathmandu every time a project was executed.

The craze for development projects became so pervasive that they were accepted without assessing adequate alternatives. Sometimes, good projects were selected, but never implemented. Some were implemented, but were hardly completed. Even if some were completed, there was no mechanism for repair and maintenance. As soon as the foreign staff left, the projects began to falter. Others continued bulging and increasing assuming the shape and qualities of the government departments. A category of permanent project staff started to be rotated between various projects.

Then, the projects became centralized technocratic exercise. Local population was seldom consulted, let alone allowed to participate in decision making and benefit sharing. Programs and budget failed to reflect the reality of the local cultural conditions. Hardly any projects were sustainable and manageable by the local population. They mostly ignored the conventional wisdom and resourcefulness of the local populations. Many adopted the technology alien to the people.

Despite all these, the development projects *did* bring some degree of efficiency, accountability and program-orientation in the development programs instituted by the government. But the proliferation of the development projects in Nepal infused a receiver-mentality and created a high degree of social acceptance of corruption. Though they were the backbones of the development plans and governments' willpower to deliver, the projects created a psyche that anything that is good comes from the government and from outside support only. Such a mentality, created by the proliferation of the development projects, brought an entirely new dimension to the development psyche to the Nepalese people. As not all of the projects and actions of the all-embracing government were successful and as they could not fulfil the expectations of the people, the development itself started to be questioned. People not only developed a skepticism regarding the government's capability to implement the development programs properly. They also started to be dubious about their own traditional methods of self-help and community work. That heralded an escapist mentality from the social and community level responsibilities, as people started to expect the government to do the jobs they were doing on their own. That applied to the conservation of the cultural heritage as well.

THE DEVELOPMENT PSYCHE

The stage of economic and cultural development in Nepal may be a product of Nepalese people's beliefs, attitudes, behaviors, thoughts, values and norms. But the aspiration of development has also influenced the Nepalese culture. Progress in education, communication, and employment pattern, brought about by development has imposed several changes in the culture of the people.

In his *Fatalism and Development,* Dor Bahadur Bista (1991) isolated "fatalism" as one of key factors that are retarding and diminishing development in Nepal. Saying "the culture of fatalism devalues the concept of productivity", Bista (1991) argued that values of fatalism (belief that one has no personal control over one's life circumstances but is determined through a divine external agency) is conflicting with development and achievement motivation and devastating effect on the "work ethic". He further argued that the ascriptive caste system and social hierarchy, prevalent in Nepal, was not conducive to the concept of development. Bista also deplored "*Bahunism'* (syndrome of cultural configurations along the principle of caste system introduced by Brahmans in the medieval period) as anti-developmental. He further argued patronization and the subculture of one's own people (*Afno Manchhe*) as natural form of social organization formed by traded privileges and factionalism, breeds corruption and malfunctioning of development.

One may tend to agree to these notions. But attitudinal and behavioral variables of development in Nepal have been changing. Values and institutions with regards to development have been shifting. While the existing values systems of fatalism, *Bahunism,* caste structure, institutions of *Chakari* and *Afno Manchhe* have profound impacts upon development, the emergence of new economic classes, the changing work and wealth ethic, the breakdown of traditional joint families into nuclear units, and increasing contacts abroad have reversed the traditional explanation of development psychology in Nepal.

Although fatalism has been a barrier to innovation and development, there are trends, which suggest people are increasingly becoming achievement-oriented. It is becoming very difficult to discern fatalistic belief in Nepalese youths, who are becoming motivated for personal achievement. There are trends, which suggest people are willing to shape their own destinies. An influx to the urban areas from rural villages, exodus of young people abroad in search of opportunities, and an increasing number of entrepreneurial activities suggest this hypothesis. The shift to nuclear families and individualism also signals that many people have abandoned much of the fatalistic belief.

But the development psyche of dependence and fatalism is being augmented by the increasing trend of over-dependence to foreign aid in Nepal. Social institutions, government structures and political parties often bring forward programs anticipating some kind of foreign assistance. It has become impossible to think about a project without having a foreign assistance element. Plans are made, projects are formulated and programs are developed taking into account that there will be some kind of foreign assistance. This applies not only to the government structures. Even the non-government organizations make their plans, programs and activities taking into account the anticipated foreign assistance element.

The foreign assistance has become so pervasive that only the World Bank, since it entered into "partnership" with Nepal in 1969, has spent some 1.31 billion US dollars in several projects in agriculture, irrigation, transportation, energy telecommunications water supply, sanitation, forestry, poverty alleviation and human resource development. Today, no development activity in Nepal is free from foreign aid. Ranging from economic liberalization to supply of iodized salt, everything comes though the magic channel. People anticipate, accept and appreciate the foreign aid. There is very little political or intellectual opposition to any kind of foreign assistance.

But despite the decades of injection of foreign aid, Nepal still remains one of the poorest countries in the world. Today, foreign aid has injected "receiver mentality" among the people and institutions in Nepal. There is a gradual growth of a "dependency syndrome", which has been built around and exaggerated by foreign aid. This mentality has struck deep into the core of Nepali life and has eroded the traditional concept and significance of self-reliance in the country. It has created an assumption that foreign aid is a perpetual source of funding Nepal's development programs.

Foreign assistance in Nepal has been shifting from one trend to another. In the 1950s, foreign aid came in the form of an assistance as a token goodwill and cooperation. There was increased capital investment in institution-building and infrastructure building in the 1960s. In 1970s, the shift was focused on beneficiaries, the rural poor. The trend in the 1980s focused on economic growth and restructuring, macro-economic reforms. In the 1990s, the foreign assistance is being diverted towards human and social development.

Apart from assisting to meet the scarcity of capital and foreign exchange, foreign aid may have helped expedite Nepal's economic growth, introduce the technology, expand planning and project management capability, acquire skills, build infrastructure, develop human resources, utilize ideal natural resources, expand non-governmental organizations, build confidence for foreign investors, and the like. But the negative consequences like the increasing dependency and likelihood of the country's falling into "debt trap", politicizing of social life, introduction of inappropriate technology, and making the economy high cost have made foreign aid a burdensome venture.

Despite the dismal impact of foreign aid in the economic development front, there is a strong cultural and attitudinal dimension infused by foreign aid in Nepal over the last five decades. There have been an emergence of a mentality that everything that comes under the umbrella and banner of foreign assistance should be accepted, despite the fact that the same may come for experimentation. Bista (1991) has vividly put the implications of foreign assistance in Nepal, especially on the receiver-mentality it has created.

> In its most blatant form this perversion manifests itself in the expectation of foreign aid as a divinely instigated redistribution. The peculiar geo-political situation of Nepal has helped its elite to develop an attitude of acceptance and of adaptation to any influence from outside. On the other hand, a sense of equanimity has also provided a measure to resilience, which has helped Nepal maintain its independent and sovereign status. Ironically, the same background congenial for the infusion of fatalistic principle that conditions the attitude towards foreign aid today. In the present context aid become merely something that is justly due to Nepal and not a resource that is meant to be considered seriously and used productively (Bista, 1991).

The passive and donor-driven foreign assistance has resulted in the adoption of ambitious goals and targets, which has resulted at the frustration among the people when the success of such programs are at high stake. Ready acceptance of foreign aid in areas outside government's priorities, has developed a mentality that foreign assistance should be accepted in anything, because "it's free".

Further, the donor-imposed conditions like preference to technical assistance as a major block of aid has been a substituting and demoralizing the local talent in the country. The focus on commodity and services tied to donor country's own products has been imposing binding conditions to buy good and services from the donor country is going to the benefit of the private sector of the donor-countries not to the Nepalese people, who are supposed to be beneficiaries. There is also a tendency to a high level of flow-back in terms of consultancy, procurement of goods and services from the donor country. There is an apprehension that foreign aid does not trickle down effectively to the target groups and as much as 60% of the total assistance drives back to the donor countries (Dahal, 1998). Some even have doubts that the aid is reaching the real beneficiaries at all. 'In Nepal, the extent of foreign involvement in the national development effort is so great that, in some schemes, it is genuinely difficult to discern whether the real beneficiaries are even intended to the Nepalese poor or whether, in fact, the whole exercise has been designed around the needs and interests of expatriate corporations." (Hancock, 1989, quoted in Dahal, 1998).

Many donor-driven projects are accepted without adequate consideration to the local needs. Foreign aid has also introduced *ad hocism* in the execution of development program since projects are accepted without taking into consideration of the adequate number of alternatives. Foreign assistance has also introduced duplication and proliferation of projects, which are sometimes carried despite lack of sound financial proposals. Many grant projects ignoring the recurring local costs have been becoming unsustainable and eventually being unsuccessful. Several ill-conceived foreign aided projects have been dragging countries meager resources and thus becoming the burden to the local capacity.

Inability to decrease dependency on foreign aid as a perpetual source of funding development projects has created a mounting external debt crisis. Though a bulk loan is concessional, commercial loans tied up with projects is mounting. There is a heavy repayment burden on national revenue. If this trend continues, it is not impossible for Nepal to fall under an irreversible "debt trap".

The foreign aided development projects have also infused problems like deterioration of financial discipline, mainly as corruption and commission on procurement. They have also created a pessimistic approach to development and sense of dependence and tendency to seek foreign aid even for small projects within national capacity.

Partners to Nepal's development programs and economic cooperation, in their review of the economy and in their declarations in the aid consortium meetings, have been increasingly moving outside the realm of the core economic policies. They have started to focus on such issues as corruption, political instability, child labor, women trafficking, environmental degradation, and neutrality of bureaucracy as conditions to their aid programs. Not that these issues are not real and do not deserve discussion. But it indicates that donor countries and agencies are concerned on political, ecological and cultural parameters more than economic ones. By way of imposing such conditions, donors have been able to influence the direction of Nepal's policy agenda. As there is no domestically designed version of development programs, including those espoused by the successive versions of five-year plans, it is the donor ideas which are repackaged into development programs.

Though some degree of "receiver mentality" and practice of asking favors existed in the Nepalese society by way of traditions and culture, that had not distorted the cultural values. In fact, there are deep rooted-traditions and philosophies regarding the habit and practice of begging alms and living a saintly lifestyle, especially for abandonment of the materialistic world. According to Hindu social organization (*Varnashram*), there used to be a stage called Sanyas, in which people spent their lives living on cottages begging alms. During *Vratabandha*, one of the most important rituals of life among the Hinuds, the young men are asked to beg alms from their parents and close relatives as an initiation to the practice of begging. This ritual heralds the child's entry on Brahmacharya Ashram, in which he is supposed to beg alms for himself and for his teacher during his stay at Gurukul, the traditional school of learning. Long-haired ascetics called Yogis, clad in saffron loincloths, go door to door begging alms for their daily meals and for performing religious rites. Ordinary people take pride in donating and consider it a duty to donate to the saints.

Though the tradition of begging alms and donating still continues, the intent is now being distorted. The charity and benevolence of donating the rice and coins, that used to exist earlier, is almost vanishing. Today, one can see beggars around most tourist places and temples. Others expose their bodily distortions and diseases to exact money from the visitors and by-passers. The Gaines, who used to sing the glorious rulers and heroic deeds and love stories and exposing the ridicules of the society going village to village playing their *Sarangi*, today crowd the tourist sites for money. The receiver mentality has been reinforced by the wave of modernization and development.

THE THIRD FORCE

While the government, particularly its bureaucracy, is supposed to shoulder the major responsibility for development, and private sector to take care of the economy, a third sector, the non-governmental organizations (NGO), has emerged significantly in the development scenario in Nepal. So-called non-government organizations, which constitute a major part of the "civil society" have nearly outnumbered the government offices and are of every type and category. There are non-government organizations in activities ranging from raising awareness to alleviating rural poverty, from educating the children to raising the status of women, from environment conservation to rural development, and from health services to drug abuse control etc. "In the aggregate", writes Devendra Raj Pandey (1999), "the non-government organizations sector has been able to graduate to a countervailing force to compliment the role of the government in development to establish checks against anti-democratic and anti-people politics, tendencies and actions."

Social service as a concept has deep-rooted traditions in Nepal. People used to organize cooperatives (*Guthis*) for constructing and maintaining temples, rest-houses, water spouts, and for running festivals and *Jatras*. Though these *Guthis* and financial cooperatives are still common among many people in different parts of the country, their role and clout to influence the culture and heritage has been grossly sidelined dwarfed by the mushrooming of the non-governmental sector of the professional non-government organizations.

These days, non-government organizations have become buzzwords synonymous to social service and social development. Whereas many of the non-governmental organizations have been instrumental in speeding the "vehicle of development", many are viewed by the public as money-making institutions and are criticized as "begging bowls" and as a "front for siphoning off dollars". But the international development agencies and institutions are actively encouraging them as vehicles for social and human development. Among the donors, the non-government organizations are accepted as good mechanism for funding development programs since they are easy to handle and are accountable to the donor needs.

With the advent of democracy in the country, organizing is accepted and guaranteed as a fundamental right. Non-government organizations are taking the advantage of this new philosophy. Diversification of interests, professional groups and associations are among other things that have contributed to the development of such organizations. Though the mushrooming of non-government organizations has definitely helped to some extent to the social development in certain sectors, their growth has contributed to the Culture Shift in the very fragile social, cultural and economic structure of the country.

Social service these days is viewed as a lucrative vocation and there is a gradual decline in the spirit of service. Instead, these are viewed as one of the fastest-growing institutions for easy money making, especially among the educated elite of the urban areas. This fact is well proved by the concentration of more than 90% of the country's 4,500 non-government organizations operating in and around Kathmandu and other urban centers. There are definitely some exceptions to this rule of money making. There are a few real social service agencies, which have earned high reputation in their activities to reach the needy people..

Several non-government organizations are registered by people of a closed group, with one authoritative member who rarely delegates authority and members are usually other members of the family of an extended form of the leader. Many non-government organizations leaders are promoters of their professional interest rather than the concern of beneficiaries, although they are objectively focused to the "marginalized and "disadvantaged" beneficiaries.

Though the proliferation of non-government organizations has helped raise activities related to human rights, ecological activism,, and other grassroots empowerment, it has created a "dependency syndrome" and a "receiver-mentality" among many communities. On the other hand, the non-government organizations have overshadowed the energy, talent and creativity of traditional community organizations and self-help groups including *Guthis*, which were the major institutions responsible for the continuation of the cultural heritage.

Among the cultural impacts of the Non-Government Organizations is their impetus to the "back-to-the-roots" movement. As they advocate development policies such as people's participation, community development, empowerment etc., they give a boost to the cultural empowerment of the people in rural and marginalized areas. The non-government organizations along with their foreign partners, have been bringing a culture of accountability, and an awareness of helping the marginalized and disadvantaged people. This may have enriched the cause of deprived people. But, at the same time, it has increased the expectations the erstwhile underdogs, who are feeling disillusioned and frustrated as the expectations have been hardly met. At the same time, they also make social activities a high cost affair because they pay higher salary and allowances and spend more on office overheads. The foreign funding agencies, which seek to by-pass the bureaucratic hurdles of the state, establish direct contacts to the people through the non-government organizations. As many ethnic groups come into contact with the donors and the non-government organizations willing to help them in their development endeavors, their new partners hardly involve the local people in preservation of their culture. In fact, in the wrath of the development, they become the sole spectators of the decay in their culture and traditions.

Even in the overall cause of the development, these emerging bodies have hardly become effective. Most of the Nepalese non-government organizations are only working in periphery and have not yet been the mainstream of development and service delivery agencies. Their coverage is very sketchy. They tend to focus on roadside projects that too in fair weather. Further, the amount of resources at their disposal is very small.

But the most frightening of all deteriorating trends in the non-government organizations is their neglect and callous attitude towards the cultural heritage. Though a few non-government organizations have become highly visible in advocacy and awareness, the voice for cultural preservation is nothing more than sketchy. Some have become vocal against the trends of globalization. Others organize a few seminars in cozy hotel conference rooms. There are, in fact, very few committed to heritage conservation.

Further, the non-governmental organizations along with the media, professional associations and the intellectuals, also called collectively as the civil society, today have been dominated by the so-called people of the "middle class" and emerging rich class. As it is this group of people, who are becoming more and more self-centered, hedonistic and escapist in the social responsibilities, it is no wonder that the civil society at large is callous towards the ongoing deterioration of the culture in the country. In principle, they may be advocating the cause of the poor, downtrodden and underprivileged groups of people. But deep in their motives, save for few exceptions, lies their own professional development, if they are not all out for making a living selling the slogans of upliftment of the under-represented people and their culture.

The Pollution of Culture

In the Culture Shift era, it is politics, more than anything else, which accounts for the shaping of new values and ideologies of the people. After the advent of democratic form of governance, the ideas of multi-culturalism, pluralism, egalitarianism, fundamental freedoms and universal human rights have found place in the constitution, law of the land, policy commitments of the state, and in the day-to-day academic vocabulary. These ideas and principles have even seeped into the foundations of the ideology of the Nepalese people. While the new dispensation has liberated the dormant energy of erstwhile underdogs and underprivileged people, it has also unleashed a flood of new expectations. But the pollution in the politics, especially the creeping culture of corruption and an increasing perception of failure to delivery has become a source of increasing disillusionment of the intelligentsia as well as the masses. In a society, fragmented horizontally as well as vertically, because of the traditional (such as caste system) and the new differences (economic gaps), an agenda of egalitarianism is being sold as a pipe dream, but without much fruition. Further, politicization of every sphere of human activity, has eroded the traditional bondage between the peoples, who are increasingly becoming polarized along the ideology of the mainstream political parties. As the political superstructure moulds the culture of a country, the pollution in the culture of politics has also started a pollution of the popular culture in the country.

THE DISILLUSIONMENT ERA

In the last half-century, Nepalese people have witnessed four constitutions, three regimes, more than twenty-five government changes and several political upheavals. There have been people's movements and revolutions and rise and fall and rise of democracy. Each had profound impact in the people's understanding about the political power, the attitude towards governance, and nature of people's control over the political process. These changes also had bearing in the culture of the people of Nepal.

It was the revolution of 1950, which strongly shaped the Nepali society at all levels. The revolution (*Sat Salko Kranti*) not only ended Nepal's centuries old "self-imposed isolation", it unleashed the traditional dormant feeling of the oppressed and underdogs into the mainstream politics. People could voice their concerns openly. They could join political parties and cast their ballot for the choice of their political representatives. Much of that freedom was withdrawn during the Panchayat regime (1962-1990), which tried to introduce its own version of utopia in a restricted political environment. Even the Panchayat system had become successful in transferring the system's identity crisis on to the intelligentsia, who tried to justify the existence of the polity in terms of its relevance to the socio-cultural norms of the times and the system showed itself to be flexible enough to incorporate contemporary changes, which in fact it did only ostensibly (Subedi, 1996). Then came the National Referendum (1980), which allowed people to vote for a choice of the political system. That gave people "freedom for open discussions, meetings, campaigns and raising slogans for expressing their political views".[1]

But the most significant of all changes was the introduction of democracy following the People's Movement (*Jana Andolan*) in the 1990s. The political dispensation that was brought after the movement has unleashed the political consciousness of the people, who are increasingly become aware of their rights and privileges as individuals and as groups. The "people's movement of 1990 was an event of such magnitude that its echoes and ripples are still rebounding uneasily off the many facets of Nepal's socio-political landscape", observed a researcher[2]. The democratization of the polity since the 1990s has certainly led to a higher level of political consciousness, more informed political discourse, and possibly, more intense political participation", says the Nepal Human Development Report (1998).[3]

---

[1] Dor Bahadur Bista in Malla, Kamal Prakash (1989), *Nepal: Perspectives in Continuity and Change*, Centre for Nepal and Asian Studies, Tribhuvan University, Nepal (p. 171)

[2] Lietchy, Mark (1996) Paying for Modernity: Women and the Discourse of Freedom in Kathmandu, *Studies in Nepalese History and Society* (June 1996), vol. 1, no. 1, Mandala Book Point.

[3] *Nepal: Human Development Report (1998)*, Nepal South Asia Center, Kathmandu

As the political superstructure moulds the culture, the introduction of democracy has done so in many ways. Democracy has not only given people a free voice and choice of their own representatives in the affairs of the government, it has exposed the pluralistic concerns, which otherwise used to be blamed as communal. Professional association and non-government organizations have become vocal and visible. More importantly, women and other disadvantaged groups have found ways to voice discriminations against them.

Though the majority of the Nepalese people have expressed faith in the political system,[4] there is a growing disillusionment about the state of politics and governance in general and the frequent changes in the government and failure to deliver in particular. As all combinations including a majority, a minority, and coalitions of all sorts are criticized to have failed to deliver the "public goods", people's faith in politics is all but flattering. The never-ending combinations and permutations to form the coalitions and even the single party governments have failed to fulfill people's expectations. "People have started to express openly in tea-stalls, in village *chautaras*, and local *bhattis* and in academic circles, a dire need of an alternative, a savior to get the nation out of this political imbroglio, a political party which a clean (and) strong leadership and the requisite political will to actually bell the cat", wrote a columnist.[5]

While politics pollutes every sphere of human life, while politicians become adversarial and resort to sloganeering distributing hopes and aspirations, and as corruption pervades the society, the commoner, who is supposed to exercise the sovereignty, becomes the passive sufferer. As the least powerful person lying in the lowest rung of political and economic hierarchy, quite opposite to what is conceived in the constitution and ideals of the political system, the ordinary people can hardly exercise their constitutional power to mark the system work in the their favor. Election after election, the ballot pledges and commitments are never fulfilled. The people get dismayed, confused

---

[4] The South Asian Human Development Report (1999) says 69% of the surveyed Nepalese people expressed faith in the political system. This was found to be highest in the South Asia.
[5] Gurung, Maitalal (1998), Ready for Clean Green Revolution?, *Spotlight*, The National Newsmagazine. November 28-December 4, 1997;

and disillusioned. It is not only the masses who are disillusioned. The fragility of the political system and ineffective delivery of goods and services to the people has also dismayed the political leaders.

Despite all that, every aspect of the society is influenced by the politics, which has corrupted the societal thinking, customs, values, norms, behavior and activities. Schools and universities, the shrines of learning, are breeding grounds for political fries. Teaching and studying is second to politics. Students unions propagate and advocate more the political ideology of the party they represent than the rights of the students, which they are supposed to look after. It is not only students who are actively political. Teachers, medical doctors, lawyers, journalists, litterateurs, and even civil servants have become highly political after the advent of democracy in 1990. Even appointments in places like university, academy of arts and literature and science and technology are said to be not free from political biases.

Whether it is good or bad, the Nepalese people's interest in the politics is much higher than their concern towards their own cultural pride and values. People understand, like and enjoy talking and discussing politics. Most Nepalese people keep active understanding of the current political events and scenario. The so-called intellectuals are even more political than ordinary people, and many of them are politically biased to one side or the other. Though these intellectuals cannot live without discussing politics, it is this group of people, which criticizes the politics and the politicians most. But it is also said that many Nepalese intellectuals are no more interested in the day to day political problems of their fellow compatriots, whereas they have developed a passion for the Western music, songs, dance, sports and life styles.[6]

The ordinary people in the urban areas take a lot of interest in the politics because they have the access to the information. Whereas the individuals in the cities have become highly economic-minded due to pressures of competition, free market economy and anxiety for survival, in groups, they have become highly political. Even in the rural communities, people discuss and live in politics and the political

---

[6] Bhattachan, Krishna B. (1998), Globalization and its impacts on Nepalese Society and Culture, in Dahal, Madan ed. (1998), *Impact of Globalization in Nepal*, Nepal Foundation for Advanced Studies, Kathmandu.

gridlock always fascinates the people. That is evident in the local tea stall talks, where the polarization of people along the mainstream political parties can be easily visible.

Though there is a craze for politics in general, many young people today disapprove all kinds of politicians. Criticizing politicians is a routine matter of discussion among people of all walks of life. People discount political performance. *Jun Jogi Aaye Pani Kanai Chireko* (Every saint has forked ears), goes a popular saying implying that politicians are all the same and that they are slave to the culture of nepotism, non-performance and corruption. This has led to a kind of apathy towards politics, though the same becomes a subject of never-ending discussions. Today, there is a great deal of anxiety over the state of political affairs. People criticize political institutions and their leaders for inefficiency and corruption. Non-performance of the political leadership is a common *Kothe Gaff* (living-room talk) and tea-stall agenda. In overheard comments and in daily conversations, people take political institutions as subject of ridicule and political leaders as corrupt or inefficient people. Pessimism about political performance is central to most such talks. Due to a widespread frustration, lack of optimism and non-performance of various sectors, people's attitude is gradually turning negative. Positive value system has been actively excluded from the mainstream attitude and values in Nepal. Some Nepalese "intellectuals", in a discussion, had expressed concern and anxiety over the state of politics in Nepal. Professor Y. N. Khanal, one of Nepal's best-known scholars, had summarized the mood of the discussion: [7]

> "Concern is expressed about the quality of political leadership, de-stabilizing and often irresponsible hang-over of agitation politics, tendency to wrest or vest power within the two major parties in extra-constitutional entities, hunger for power, fear of elections, vulgarization of electoral practices, false slogans and promises, general lack of progress and, above all, a gathering disillusionment among people with democracy itself."

One-time Speaker of the House of Representatives and one of the architects of the democratic constitution of Nepal, Daman Nath

---

[7] Khanal, Y. N. (1995) *Politics and Administration in Nepal,* Paper presented in a seminar, Public Administration Association of Nepal, Kathmandu.

Dhungana had summarized prevailing anxiety about the characteristics and culture of the contemporary Nepali politics: [8].

"(L)ack of commitment, morality and dedication among the leaders who are made out of long sacrifice and struggle for democracy; loss of memory of the hard days of struggle; abandonment of the values, norms and morals achieved out of life-time dedication; big gap between what is said and what is done; high degree of opportunism; more tilt towards individualism rather than institutionalism; craze for power and hunger for chair; lack of clean and moral public life; greed for property and earning from power; taking abuse of authority as a minor thing; accepting only oneself as right and others as wrong; etc."

On top of that, politics has been increasingly falling victim to mobocracy, criminalization and communalization. If people are able to create mobs and build pressures on institutions and other groups of people, they are definitely in a more advantageous position in order to secure their demands met than they are unable to do so. Parliamentarians have been abducted and kept captive in hotels in times like censure motions. Sometimes even the Ministers have 'fled' the country not sure of how they should vote in the no-confidence motions. Buying members to increase the numerical strength in the parliament had once become common, despite vocal opposition of the same by every party. In political institutions, mainly major political parties, the roles of the workers as mob and crowd has apparently out-powered their leaders. Lack of charismatic leaders in the contemporary politics is a major cause of frustrations expressed by many. The contemporary Nepalese politics is said to be lacking a visionary and charismatic leadership. In the years after restoration of democracy in 1990, the leaders, who fought for democracy, were expected to be competent and ethically suitable to look after the people's problems. But that expectation was only a wishful idea and unrealistic, writes Pratyuosh Onta.[9] Even some potent leaders are highly vulnerable to criticism and opposition and they have been ineffective to deliver leadership to the maddening crowds of the political workers. They suffer from political myopia and lack of capability to put forward a

---

[8] Quoted in *Kantipur*, November 9, 1995

[9] *Himal Khabarpatrika* (27 February-13 March 2001), quoting from a seminar.

futuristic vision. There does not exist any saying or declaration by any politician, who has put forward a vision for the next decade, let alone for the entire twenty first century, though the new century is often quoted in the political rhetoric. There is the fist-fight and bickering for the chair and the farthest thing the politicians have discerned is the next election. Such political myopia is bound to have influence in the contemporary Nepalese society. Without a visionary future, Nepalese society is heading towards a dark plunge without any direction. The lack of vision and mission has disillusioned the masses. Break-ups, ideological disillusion, frustrated workers, and hunger for power are haunting the Nepalese politics.

One of the manifestations of such disillusionment is the emergence of Maoist insurgency in the hilly districts of Nepal. A considerable section of the intellectuals, media and politicians have started to believe that the youths in the rural areas are being allured to fighting the guerilla war, not solely due to their belief in Maoism, but also due to a growing disillusionment among them.[10]

For those who have interest and stake in the parliamentary democracy, the source of disillusionment lies in possible corruption of the electoral process. In fact, the existence of desire of manipulating the elections in one's favor is justified by the fact that all major parties have made efforts to be in power while holding elections. For the common people, the ballot becomes only weapon left with them to avoid the feeling of powerlessness to change the state of political affairs. But for politicians, the manipulation of the election process has become a coveted desire. "Because of the imperative of electoral democracy, the culture that the political parties seem to understand that democracy is about winning elections, and for winning election, a party or a leader can stop as low as necessary and collect the wherewithal for personal and party uses", says bureaucrat-turned politician and writer Devendra Raj Pandey. "As a result, the misuse of office, the abuse of civil service, unholy alliances, and perhaps, direct rigging of the polls are all permissible." [11]

---

[10] According to the last official count, some 1600 people have succumbed to the five-year old "People's War" staged by the Maoists in Nepal.

[11] Pandey, Devendra Raj (1999), *Nepal's Failed Development*, Reflections on the mission and the maladies, Nepal South Asia Center, Kathmandu (p.106).

Even the various interest groups, which have been able to freely express their views and to exert influence into the political process in the new democratic dispensation, are not left without disillusionment. Read the inside columns written by various professionals in various Nepalese tabloids or listen to several seminars in various subjects being held in Kathmandu's cozy hotel rooms. This kind of dissatisfaction is reflected in the various strikes, *bandhs*, and *gheraos*, which are not always used only after all other lawful means have been exhausted. Some political groups call for strikes for very simple matters, which can be solved by simply talking with the ruling party or the authorities. Others simply issue statements in the mass media on any public or political international issue. In fact, for most of the politician statements are the only means of political activity. Many such statements are the accusation and counter-accusations common in the political scene. The war of words has become the main political game. But what is done is different from what is pledged. Though political activists enthusiastically deface public places with posters and graffiti, though they turn in thousands in public meetings and though they stone and burn vehicles and break street bars during protests, they do not always get the expected results. And that frustrates themselves and the masses.

THE EGALITARIAN AGENDA

Nationalism and egalitarianism are the two famous political agenda, which have a lot of implication in the dynamics of culture in Nepal. We have already discussed the role of *ethnic nationalism* in emerging stakes of identities and their demands for better share in the state, especially among various ethnic groups of people. A latest manifestation is the *regionalism*, among which, Terai nationalism and some liberation *Morchas* have somewhat shown the presence in the political landscape. There is also the dormant *Hindu nationalism*, which has not taken a visible shape, as in the case of adjacent India. Here we will discuss egalitarianism, the desire to be seen and treated at equal par with others, especially its impact in the making of ideology and culture of politics among the people of Nepal.

The egalitarian agenda is built in almost all political, social and economic aspirations of the Nepalese people. First of all, this dream is an outcome of the hierarchical and structured nature of the Nepalese society both in the term of social and economic differentiation. Today this aspiration is reflected in the "equality before law" and "freedom to equality" in the words of constitution. But these nice words are not quite enough. Inequalities and differences persist in the Nepal society. Therefore, people have perpetuated their egalitarian dream in the form of political ideologies and emerging cultural movements.

Among the various ethnic groups of people, now called as "nationalities", egalitarianism is considered a part of their social characteristics. In a definition of the ethnic nationalities, the listed characteristics include the presence of the "traditional social fabric based on equality". In fact, it is the desire to preserve that equality, which make the ethnic groups of people so conscious to assert their ethnic rights and identity.

Though the political parties in Nepal draw their ideology from different doctrinal sources[12], almost all political parties in the country have some kind of egalitarian concepts built in their ideology or program of action. Nepali Congress Party, one of the mainstream political parties in the democratic dispensation, states socialism as one of the three tenets of their political ideology, other two being nationalism and democracy. Nepal Communist Party, which is divided into several factions, aims at establishing a classless society. Parties or political groups demanding a greater freedom to ethnic minorities are also advocating the egalitarian cause. Egalitarianism remains as the dominant psyche of the contemporary Nepalese politics, despite the rise of liberalism and open market forces in the economic arena.

It is with this dream that the communists constitute a significant political force in the country. Even as the communist regimes were collapsing all over the world, the communists in Nepal were rallying along with the democratic forces to establish multi-party democracy in the country in 1990. Now they have become a major political force and have come to power, at least twice, in 1995 and 1997. They have formed the government, including their own and in coalition with others through parliamentary means.

Enchanted by the egalitarian dreams, many people in Nepal have become strong supporters the communist ideology. A large number of Nepalese people have chosen communists even in the choice of the ballot. One of the several factors behind the communist strength is the

[12] Rijal, Mukti (1999), Political Parties in Nepal: Test of Internal Party Democracy, *The Rising Nepal*, February 2, 1999, Kathmandu.

people's expectation of an egalitarian framework in the society. The others may be their *modus operandi* and the organization culture. In any case, the sickle and hammer has become the instrument for mass mobilization. Despite the fissiparous tendencies in the communist movement, with splinter groups supporting to various foreign models and personalities, people are being attracted to the ideals espoused by each.

Some youths have even been allured to the self-styled "people's war" called by yet another communist group, called Maoists. All of these movements are selling egalitarian dreams. But the rise of the Maoist "people's war" may also have been contributed by the growth of the disillusionment among the youngsters. The failure of constitutional forces to affect changes in the socio-political environment in order to meet the expectations of the poverty stricken masses has led to the guerilla insurgency organized by the Maoists, wrote a commentator.[13] Some say that the Maoist uprising not only owes to the egalitarian political dream machine, but they consider it as a social problem. The Maoist uprising, which has affected a third of the country's districts, is believed to be more of a social unrest than a political movement, wrote *Himal,* a fortnightly newsmagazine. In some hilly districts of Nepal, young men and women rally behind the Maoists in their desperate dream and search of equality in the society, doing away with the traditional hierarchies.

Disillusionment may be a new phenomenon. But egalitarianism has been the mainstream of the Nepalese political life in the last four decades. Even the Panchayat system had advocated for an "exploitation-free" society. It was during this period that the infamous Civil Code, which had legalized the caste system and hierarchies, was amended to bring about an egalitarian and horizontally integrated social structure. Further, the Panchayat also started a program of Land Reform, in which the excess arable land held by the aristocrats and landlords was confiscated and distributed to the landless people. Though the success of these programs is debatable, it cannot be denied that the system wanted to introduce some kind of equality removing the traditional hierarchies in the society.

---

[13] Chitra Krishna Tiwari in an essay in *The Spotlight* (January 29- February 4, 1999)

Today the egalitarian agenda is also espoused in the growing awareness and movement of the ethnic groups and the underprivileged people. The demand of the ethnic rights is also based on the concept of egalitarianism. That is why most of the organizations who claim to represent the "oppressed" (*Dalits*) and "ethnic minorities" (*Janjati*) have preferred to ally with the mainstream communist parties. In fact, one or other communist leadership mobilizes many such organizations. Even the ethnopolitical demands of the *janjatis* are based on the concept of egalitarianism, which is against the hierarchical structure supposedly espoused by the Hindus. While *Jat* is believed to be hierarchical and supposed to be opposing the egalitarisnism, *Jati* or *Janjati* is portrayed as egalitarian.

The dream for "equality" as envisaged in the constitution and the statutes of major parties have occupied the minds of the Nepalese people. Haunted by the economic differences, too much structural differentiation espoused by the caste system and sometimes religion, people have been increasingly allured to the theme that puts them in equal terms with other people. And the new democratic framework, which is based on the concept of pluralism and equality before law, has been reinforcing the idea of egalitarianism, in whatever extent it can. And wherever and whenever such an expectation has failed, it has led to the frustration and disillusionment of the masses.

Various developments in the fields of communication, patterns of power sharing and access to education might have eroded the traditional hierarchy in many ways. Despite all these, the Nepalese society is yet to witness their egalitarian dream fulfilled. Education, which is supposed to be removing superstitions and bringing about awareness on social ills, has not been able to bring adequate egalitarian changes. The opportunity for education introduced into a hierarchical social structure continues to be channeled to high castes. Today, rates of literacy and illiteracy among the various ethnic groups are prime indices of inequality. But yet another creator of the hierarchy, an economic divide, continues to haunt the Nepalese people, as we have discussed elsewhere.

But the most influential aspect of this egalitarian agenda is its wrath against the traditional culture built upon hierarchies of age, gender, and caste. Today, people not only find it rational to deplore the vertical fragmentation of the society on the basis of their age, gender, caste and economic differences, they also find it politically correct to deplore the traditional hierarchies. Whether it is good or bad, the egalitarian agenda is among the several new challenges to the culture and traditions in the country. This is one of the sources of the rising expectations and increasing disillusionment of the masses.

THE CULTURE OF CORRUPTION

One of the major polluters of the culture toady is the culture of corruption, which is creeping into all spheres of the national life. But it is the politics and bureaucracy, which accounts for the most of the corruption prevalent in the society.

In 1996, the Members of Parliament were given the treat to buy a vehicle under a privilege of almost no customs duty. Though this privilege has been withdrawn in 1999 after severe ridicule, criticism and the public uproar, this has become a subculture known in common vocabulary as the Pajero Culture,[14] which is synonymous to corruption in the Nepalese political vocabulary. The Pajero culture was probably the peak of the emergence of a rent seeking behavior, i.e. using the public chair for making personal benefits, in the contemporary politics. Politicians often get elected on a broad political platform, mostly in a party ticket. But no sooner they get elected, the need to nurse the constituency which keeps them tied up in petty interest of their actual and potential voters, becomes more important than ever before. From awarding contracts and jobs and channeling development projects, the politicians are constantly under pressure to maintain the backward linkage, which requires a lot of money. Thus, the culture of corruption becomes compulsive, not a choice.

Then, they accept kickbacks from sponsored business, collect large sums changing sides at critical junctures of politics. Surreptitious sources of incomes are believed to make their way as contracts are awarded, as permissions are granted, and as agreements are signed. As a journalist wrote somewhere, the politics has become a *carte blanche* for corruption. It is the breeding ground for the white crime, which is eating up the moral fiber of the society. That is why the ballot as sole weapon against the social malaise has become too weak to be effective. And the politicians who have resorted to the corrupt practices get re-

---

[14] Since most of the parliamentarians bought a Pajero Jeep each under this privilege, the whole issue of corruption in the politics has been often named as Pajero culture.

elected comfortably. Perhaps it was with this notion that Radha Raman Upadhyaya, one time chief commissioner of the Commission for Investigation of Abuse of Authority, the Nepali Ombudsman, had once said, "if you are to clean the Ganges, you have to start cleaning from *Gangotri*." He was quoting from an Indian rhetoric, implying that politics is the source of corruption and any remedy against this anti-social problem should begin from clean politics.

Many attribute social acceptance of corruption to the socio-cultural environment. There was the officer, who once said, "if you spent an evening in a *bhatti* (a local liquor bar), no body will believe you did not drink any alcoholic liquor but only had a glass of pure milk". He wanted to infer that if one is in a polluted environment such as corrupt politics or bureaucracy, there is no merit of being seen as non-corrupt. And there was another humorous officer who knew rates for the malpractice. Ten rupees for settling an electricity or telephone bill, a hundred for expediting a queue in government offices, 1, 000 for getting a driving license, 10,000 for expediting a citizenship certificate or for obtaining a fake academic certificate, 100,000 for getting an industrial license, 1 million for awarding a contract, 10 million for buying an airplane. Everywhere, from top to the bottom, rates reflect the acceptability and universality of corruption in the Nepalese society. "While corruption was limited to select families during the Rana regime and certain groups in single party during the Panchayat regime", says Gajendra Narayan Singh, President of Nepal Sadbhavana Party, "it has now trickled down to the people's level". Earning from corrupt practices is not only accepted, it has been a dream of many people. In government bureaucracies, there is an increasing pressure for getting an assignment where corruption runs high. The political leaders have acknowledged the widespread prevalence of corruption. "Corruption is a serious issue which has not only hampered the economic development and the appropriate use of resources", said Bharat Mohan Adhikari, Nepal's Finance Minister addressing a meeting of the donors in February 1999, "more importantly, it has torn the social fabric of building a decent society".

And the private sector has reasons to worry from this malaise. In an introduction to the Socio-Economic Summit for "Strategy for the New Millenium", the Federation of the Nepalese Chambers of Commerce and Industry (FNCCI) had said:

"The rising influence of criminal elements and Mafia gangs in the corridors of power are illustrious. Corollary to this, corruption has gained higher grounds resulting into ever bad allocation of scarce public resources, delays in project decision and execution, and harassment to investors".

But corruption has not left any sector. It is not just the politics and bureaucracy, which is the breeding ground for corruption. Corruption has pervaded all occupations, businesses, professions, services and even charities and the non-government organizations. When a doctor asks a patient at the government hospital to come the Nursing Home he or she works for better check up, when students cheat in their examinations, when teachers asks the students at schools to come for private tuition, when a butcher strikes his finger unnoticeably before he fills more flesh in the weighing balance, when the shopkeeper sells sugar at a different price when it is scarce, corruption enters people's lives in a subtle manner. But the loose social fabric is the major harbinger of corruption in the Nepalese society. Aditya Man Shrestha, a campaigner of Transparency International in Nepal calls it "bleeding mountains", which is a story of all-pervasive corruption, greed and misuse of power and resources.[15]

The driving force for the rise of corruption is the need to raise the living standards copying the Western standards and consumer culture. But ironically, the Western values against corruption and for performance and merit remains to be copied by the society, systematically. This is the problem with the Culture Shift, in which we copy the worse aspects of another culture and delay learning the positive sides of the same.

More than economic corruption, it is the corruption of the morality that is tearing the traditional fabric and culture of the Nepalese society. We have already discussed the deterioration of the moral fibre. Here it will suffice to conclude that the corruption of morality is the ultimate pollution of culture. And the contemporary political discourse in the country has not been able to correct this aberration. In fact, it is contributing to the further deterioration of the same.

---

[15] Shrestha, Aditya Man (1999), *Bleeding Mountains of Nepal*, Ekta Books, Kathmandu.

The Economic *Nirvana*

Though Nepal has been relatively late to adopt the quintessential doctrine of liberalization, privatization, and the open market economy, globalization had a backdoor entry in the country as the economic reforms initiated by the state in the decade of the 1980s in programs like the Structural Adjustment. Enchanted by the Western economic liberalism and wooed by the proponents of economic reforms as the panacea to the mundane problems, Nepalese technocrats and politicians adopted a path, in which the ultimate freedom known as market economy has been voiced as economic *nirvana* to solve every sort of difficulties. Though the aim was to push economic growth, to attract investment and to increase export, what was intruded along with liberalization of the import regime was a plethora of the consumer goods. This augmented, the insatiable desire to consume among the burgeoning Nepalese middle class fond of plastic gadgets. The consumer culture, thus created, enhanced the process of liberalization of economy to an indiscriminate liberalization of the culture. As market economy was adopted as the sacrosanct slogan, the Western consumer culture entered the lives of the Nepalese people under the liberal import regime pursued by the state. Liberal economy was welcomed by the middle class and intellectuals for its freedom letting people to consume as much as they could. This has significantly altered people's behavior and culture, their motivation for entrepreneurship, possession, achievement and success.

It was not only the desire to consume, which rose astronomically. A distinct hierarchy of money, and the mania to make money altered the traditional concepts business in Nepal and unleashed a new competition for upward mobility in the society. The ensuing entrepreneurial culture would see many Nepalese people, especially in the urban areas, swarming into new business activities, where the profit was quick and easy. This led to a culture of corruption in the Nepalese society. In the craze for earning and the spending spree and extravaganza, the material culture rose to its peak. Today, the focus of lives of many Nepalese people is shifting from leisure, merry making and religious emancipation to money-making, spending and consuming whatever is available and affordable with the disposable income thus generated with an insatiable desire to consume, a new morality of "utilitarianism" is emerging. The market forces, competition, privatization, and profit ethics have been shaping these shifts. With the rising role of money, and increase in corruption and frauds, people are increasingly leading their lives out of economic compulsions rather than out of social responsibilities. There is an increasing gap between the "haves" and the "have-nots". Whereas a distinct culture of poverty continues to haunt the lives of nearly two-thirds of the Nepalese people, a distinct middle class, which the carrier of the culture change is sort of emerging, especially in the urban areas and small towns. And there is a new breed of *noveaux riches,* who have been taking advantages of the liberal policies for making profit. They have not only rationalized their upward mobility under the new economic dispensation, which rewards entrepreneurship, they have also been able to bend the rules in their favor.

CHANGING FOCUS

During the ancient and medieval history, Nepalese culture was focused on religion and spiritualism. Economy was not the main focus and objective of the life. Culture was far more important than economy. There used to be a lot of surplus, which could be used in adding cultural monuments and maintaining the cultural and religious practices. Pious works and pilgrimage were quite affordable from the surplus. People observed religion as a basis of life and revered gods and goddesses on a routine basis. The kings used to take pride in conducting the religious performances or erecting new shrines. They preserved the traditions and the cultural heritage at all costs. The exemplary lives of the sages and saint always used to keep people inspired to religious observance.

Today the focus has reversed: people are paying more attention to economy than to the culture. Economic factor has become far more important than the culture. These days the economy dictates people's religious and cultural status. People have witnessed decreasing interests in the cultural and religious things that cost money. Cultural and religious needs and practices are being surrendered to economic obligations. Due to lack of observance of certain cultural and religious traditions, things are being thrown to museums and being abandoned to decay and disappear.

This change in the focus has been augmented by the outward-orientation in the economic policies of the state. As we attract tourists and investors, as we import consumer goods and technology, and as we seek development assistance and solicit foreign aid, the forces of globalization have the natural tendency to operate. Along with the policy of integrating our economy into that of the globe, we are letting global forces operate in this tiny country. When doing so we may be worried about our "economic sovereignty", but we hardly think about the effect of such polices on the culture. The costs of economic liberalization to the culture are yet to be known fully. Despite the numerous opportunities offered by globalization, and its child liberalization, the rationale is being questioned and a certain degree of backlash against this world phenomenon is emerging, as it is evident in various write-ups.[1]

Whereas 90 out of 100 people live in the rural areas and depend upon subsistence agriculture, a vibrant 10 percent enjoys the amenities of modern lives, mostly in the urban areas. While the rural sector is merely a subsistence economy, the modern urban economy is becoming vibrant and efficient. For the first time in 1996, the government budget speech acknowledged the existence of the two diverse sectors in the economy. One "rural sector" which needed intervention and subsidies and the fledgling "modern sector" which required competitive framework and less controls. And, again for the first time, two different sets of policies were recommended for the two different sectors. It was the first acknowledgment that the modern sector was an offshoot of the economic liberalization, globalization and outward-looking economic policies, which required separate response from the government than that recommended to the rural sector, where income and employment generation, subsidies and poverty alleviation were the main thrusts.

Because of programmed intervention and various socio-economic changes, the economy in the rural areas has also been gradually changes. Though the economy there in the villages is pre-dominantly agricultural, it no longer remains subsistence one. As new seeds, new crops and chemical fertilizers are available and as

---

[1] One such example is found in Dahal, Madan K. (1997), "Globalization and the Future of Nepalese Economy: Economic Nationalism Revisited", *The Political Economy of Small States*, Nepal Foundation for Advanced Studies (NEFAS) and Fredrich Ebert Strifftung (FES), Kathmandu

costs are involved in getting them and as the products are to be sold and inputs have to be bought, the village economy assumes a different character. A village economy getting more and more influenced and dependent on external factors, cannot be called "subsistent" in its primary sense any more.[2]

In a country, where people in rural areas bartered goods and services for survival, until a few decades ago, the expansion of a booming banking is bringing a profound impact on the people's idea of saving, investing and spending. They have expanded their activities to almost all the rural areas. The availability of credit is changing the life patterns of people and bringing a lot of shift in the traditional values with regard to money and work.

Until a few decades ago, the social prestige, status, recognition and honor used to be accorded on the basis of spiritual or religious superiority, good moral characteristics and ideals, and scholastic achievements. But these days, high status is achieved by three distinct symbols: wealth, success, and media coverage. If you are rich enough to send messages that you are rich, or if you have achieved a nation wide success in politics or in a profession, and if you mange to appear in the state and private media, you definitely have a higher status than most other people. A Nepali professor who had returned after several years abroad said: Nepalis have started to view and weigh everything in terms of money. Money has become the driving force of the Nepalese society. There is an increasing recognition of an "economic nirvana", which is in the making. Wealth, not moral, spiritual and scholastic superiority, is being recognized as a basis for superiority.

MONEY MANIA

The Nepalese society is gradually going extravagant. People are spending more and more on less and less important things. The spending spree has caught people, especially of the urban neo-rich class, who think spending as a status symbol. Many *noveaux riches* are willing to demonstrate their wealth by building expensive houses, buying good vehicles, wearing valuable ornaments and fashionable

---

[2] Euler, Claus (1984), Changing Patterns of a Subsistence Economy, *Contributions to Nepalese Studies*, vol. 11, no. 3. (August 1984), Centre for Nepal and Asian Studies, Tribhuvan University, Kathmandu.

dresses, and organizing expensive and frequent feasts and parties. The growing and influential "middle class" is also forced to spend more and more to save their so-called "ijjat", the prestige. And the poor are bound to do the same, even at the cost of borrowing. Although the economic rationality does not justify the ever- increasing spending spree, there are implicit cultural signals that people are sending by buying and spending more. Most Nepalese people's consumer behavior is not just economically rational, it is highly cultural and psychological. People who can not afford also spend with a lot of enthusiasm in certain cultural occasions, no matter how they have gathered the money from. In many cases, people borrow from their relatives or sell their assets to celebrate a cultural rite, perform a family ritual or to celebrate a feast.

Nepalese people, who have achieved some success and accomplished in economic and social status, like to be seen as if they are just back from or ready to go abroad. They will try to prove as if they just had met or are going to meet a very powerful and important person, and as if they have outsmarted other people telling them they were wrong and telling them something blunt. They also try to demonstrate as if they are in a big rush of time, as if they are the most sought-after, as if they are doing something really important, and as if they are the most sophisticated people in the society. People are constantly, whether consciously or not, trying to demonstrate and tell people their superiority in status and styles. All of that is due to their economic prowess, access to the material wealth and desire to copy the global lifestyles.

Soaring of the land prices and the spread of easy money in the economy are among the principal factors responsible for the increasing extravagance in the Nepalese society. There is no numerical representation of the rise in the land price in urban areas like Kathmandu. This has left unwarranted money at the hands of the people who were used to live a rustic lifestyle. It is this group of people, who can buy a lavish lifestyle selling a small piece of urban land. Today, the children of this category of people are studying in colleges and schools abroad at their personal expenses. They buy expensive jewelry and throw outlandish parties at social occasions.

The soaring prices have put much of impact on people's attitudes, norms and behaviors related to the economy, especially their consumer behavior, although, there is not much research in this area as well..

Although many old people admire the past and are never tired of speaking of the cheap prices of the previous era, average Nepalese consumer psychology increasingly supports the idea that "expensive is better". Though people continue to bargain for a few rupees in petty items like vegetables, they pay a lot of money for things that demonstrate prestige and status.

Today, earning money and spending more for things that can buy status and physical amenities have become the most important of life goal of most Nepalese people, especially of the younger generation. Making money is appreciated as a symbol of success. It does not matter how the money is made, it matters if one has become rich. These days, Nepalese wealth ethic permits fast money. People dream, believe and try for easy money. This includes earning from any means possible: corruption, black-marketing, smuggling and the like. Instances of rushes in the share market, financial companies, and real estate business, justify the quick and easy money mentality of the people. The *Get-rich-fast syndrome* is not only common in the politics and bureaucracy. Business folk also do not hesitate to extort as much money possible, whenever there is an opportunity. A growing focus on commercial sector rather than industry, which has usually longer return periods, shows that people aspire for quick money. There is no patience to wait for better returns. This myopic investment pattern has not only stunned growth pattern of the country, it has reversed the overall morality of the people. With the easy money, people are focusing to the refurbish their life styles buying plastic and electronic gadgets but loosing their moral character.

This has resulted in a situation, in which every body seems to be running after the money. As a result, economic anxiety seems to be the top most concern of the people today. Young men from rural districts come to Kathmandu in search of jobs. People from hills migrate to Terai to seek work. People in the urban areas try to secure investment into things that pay back. Youngsters are trying to go abroad to get better economic opportunities. Economic anxiety is on the top agenda of Nepalese people, these days. For people who do not have enough economic resources, there is the anxiety of survival. For people, who have access to wealth and resources, a secured environment for investment is of great concern. Inadequate opportunities and lack of continuity of policies and instability are some factors to name a few responsible for such a sense of the economic insecurity. The rising price levels, weakening purchasing power of the money, low increase in real wage rates, and the growth of unemployment have warranted economic insecurity, which has made most people vulnerable to even minor economic changes.[3] The anxiety is further aggravated by the emergence of a new economic hierarchy, spending spree of the people, and the get-rich fast syndrome that is gripping the Nepalese society.

Traditionally *Jagir* (salaried position) used to give status, money, power, and prestige. Today, business is increasingly becoming attractive. But getting into *Jagir* or business is highly competitive and uncertain. Thousands of applicants queue in public corporations and public service commission for a few vacancies. Educational institutions over produce graduates than can be absorbed by the government and private sector. Coping with competition is the biggest anxiety of young people today. Starting from entrance to colleges and universities and into getting into a job or starting a business, the environment is becoming competitive. People of newer generations are much more vulnerable to competition than those of the earlier ones, who have already settled in some economic activities.

Uncertainty of things is another major anxiety of our times. Most Nepalese people are highly anxious about the increasingly dynamic nature of the future. Uncertainty in political, economic and social life is making people's positions highly vulnerable. The anxiety of economic survival is the central theme of the culture shift era in Nepal.

CONSUMING THE WEST

Some call it "Coca-colization", some name it *Disney et. al.* and still others fear it as *Magna Mac.* Yet others would prefer to call it "Westoxication". Bhattachan names it "West-is-the best psyche".[4]

Today, the Nepalese people are being extremely catch-up with myth of the West. In the cities like Kathmandu, Pokhara, and

---

[3]   Nepal was not affected by the Southeast Asian crisis (1998-99), mainly because the Nepalese financial and capital market is not linked to the global system. And there was not much short-term foreign investment, which seems to be the immediate cause of the Southeast Asian crisis.

[4]   Bhattachan, Krishna B. (1998), Globalization and its impacts on Nepalese Society and Culture, in Dahal, Madan ed. (1998), *Impact of Globalization in Nepal*, Nepal Foundation for Advanced Studies, Kathmandu.

Dharan, the Nepalese youths are becoming fascinated with the Western consumer goods, pop music and the dress code. Most of the youth dress in jeans, and T-shirts. Among their popular dreams is going to the "US of A". Nepalese youths are falling prey to the cultural globalization, which has not spared the Himalayan kingdom. Though Asia is said to be "easternizing and, in fact "Asianizing",[5] the influence of the West continues in countries like Nepal is increasing. In fact, it is easier to discern Westernization in Nepal than it is to see Asianization. The West is entering Nepal in technology, in information, in consumer goods, and in the value systems.

Whether it is called "consumer culture" or "mercantilism", the impact of the Western consumerism is a sublime phenomenon that is gradually engulfing the Nepalese culture. When increasing number of foreign companies have expanded their products in the Nepalese market, they are not only imposing the consumer culture, they are also burdening the people from the anxiety of over-choice and over-competition. Today, Nepalese people consume the products from abroad like anything. Canned food, fast junk food, imported liquors, soft beverages are available almost everywhere. Many of these products, mainly the soft drinks like Coca Cola, liquors like San Miguel, Carlsberg, and electronic products like the Television have even reached the villages.[6] In Kathmandu Valley, the consumer culture is evident in the rising number of "departmental stores", which sport all kinds of consumer goods at competitive prices. The consumers today have not only a multiplicity and freedom of choice, they also have the freedom to demonstrate which products they want to be identified with. That is why the Western branded items are gradually finding place in the markets in the urban centers in Nepal.

Today the youngsters enjoy the Western culture listening to pop music, munching burgers and drinking Cocacola. They may not be falling prey to the "colonization" by *Disney et. al.*", which as supposed to be engulfing the global culture. But they are departing from their own culture and life styles and trying to copy global lifestyles, which is becoming pervasive.

[5] Naisbitt, John (1996), *Megatrends Asia*, Nicholas Brealey Publishing, London.

[6] Bhattachan, *ibid.*, op.cit. 1998

There have been efforts to assess how an increasingly consumer-oriented cultural economy begins to transform the language, logic, and symbols through which people understand themselves and their society's categories. Adopting "consumption" as a key "cultural dynamic" to show how Kathmandu's middle class "deploys a new sphere of consumer culture as it seeks to produce local cultural distinction", a researcher[7] has disapproved simplistic assumptions of global cultural homogenization and concept of "global village" arguing that the cultural outcome of globalization is a shared experience of political, commercial and cultural processes with continued production of difference within a new global cultural economy.

It is not only the consumerism, in which the "West is the best psyche" is operating. Today, most Nepalese youth are fans of the Western pop songs, and they dream to go to the West for studies, business and jobs. This has triggered a shrinking of the moral domain and rise of the greed. The desire to possess more and more have become the ultimate nirvana for the consumers. The middle class has become as "consumerist predator", which consumes anything new and modern at the expense of their own economy and culture. The consumer generation is witnessing a crippling ideological barrenness.

People of all income groups in Nepal vehemently practice the consumer culture and extravagance. *Noveaux riches* do it demonstrating their wealth and poor people hiding their poverty. Starting from a wedding party to a birthday celebration, extravagant parties have become common. People send implicit symbols of their being abreast with the latest fashion putting expensive designer clothes from the fashion world. Anything that is new in the list of imported things are bought with much of rejoice and fanfare.

An alarming influx of things from abroad, especially the West has not fulfilled people's insatiable desire to consume. Nepalese people are increasingly consuming the West, their goods and services, and their culture, but not ready to achieve their progress and prosperity yet. Though things like fast food places have yet to flood the Nepalese markets, they have started to arrive in Kathmandu. And Nepalese youths have welcomed them with a great zeal and enthusiasm. Many Nepalese youngsters, who welcome things from abroad like anything,

---

[7] Liechty, Mark (1997), *Consumer Culture in Kathmandu*, Internet Website http://iias/leidenuniv.nl /iiasn6/south/liechty.html

have cheered the opening of the fast food outlets with positive response.

Yet another cultural infusion from the West is evident in the field of music. Western pop music has become highly popular these days among the Nepalese youths. Lately, the FM radio broadcast has added impetus for such an influx in among the urban youths. But it is not just the music and food, which is being consumed by the Nepalese people with a lot of appreciation, the values and norms of individualism and consumerism is also on the rise.

There is not only the innate desire to consume, the obsession to possess more and more is also rising. The "materialistic pursuit" is on the perpetual rise. Despite the sign of visible success in the sense that more people have their own houses, more people can afford to buy the electronic and plastic gadgets, and more people own cars, people's endless desire to multiply the possession of the materialistic things continues. Along with the desire for material culture, there is the utter insensibility to the social and moral causes. People are in the ultimate pursuit of hedonism, the pursuit of materialistic consumption, which has been largely assisted by the liberal economic regime for the consumer goods. Plus the disposable income generated by a range of economic activities has allowed the people to consume more and more.

Though the passion towards the things from the West is evident in the urban areas, it is no less true with various ethnic groups of people even in the rural areas. There may be differences in the degree of acceptance depending upon the generation, gender, economic class, relative distance from an urban area. But almost all people have started to develop the "West is Best Psyche". And the Western Consumer goods have started to be liked everywhere. In the urban areas, it may come as market economy. But in the rural areas, it comes attached to foreign aid, and development projects and influx of tourists.

But one thing is almost certain. The callous copying of the myth of the West is going to lead to the loss or erosion of or own traditions and culture. The Western culture may have started a homogenization of our culture. But it has not reduced the gaps between the rich and poor. Neither it has reduced the difference between the men and women, and between the caste and ethnic groups of people.

THE NEPAL INC.

Yet another emerging phenomenon, which is shaping the Nepalese culture, is the emergence of Nepal Inc., the growth of corporate Nepal. Perhaps the most evident of all changes in Nepalese economy in the last four decades is the growth of a powerful private sector. Nepal's corporate growth owes mainly to the liberal economic policies adopted by the state since the 1990s. The opening of finance companies and private airlines spurred the growth at the beginning. By the time of this writing, there are more than seven joint venture banks with foreign equity. Many private airlines fly to different destinations in Nepal and some even fly abroad (e.g. Necon Air). Joint-venture projects in industry are increasing.

This robust growth of the Nepal Inc. also owes to the outward-orientation of the Nepalese economy. A strong corporate sector is emerging in Nepal in view of Nepal's location between two of the world's largest markets, that of India and China, wrote a columnist.[8] For example, Dabur-Nepal, which specializes on Ayurvedic products and Nepal Lever, a subsidiary of Hindustan Level Ltd., are successful enterprises established in view of the proximity to the Indian market. A large number of carpet and ready made garment industries were established eyeing the export market in the West. The hotels and airlines were aimed at meeting the demand of the burgeoning tourist industry in the country.

But even internally, the growth of private enterprises has been significant. Some companies have become big enough to have their own listings in the Nepal's nascent capital market. Surya Tobacco Company, with a total transaction of Rs 250 crore (1998), is one of Nepal's largest private sector enterprises, for example. Other big names in the Nepalese private sector such as Hulas Steel, Jyoti Spinning, Necon Air, Soaltee Hotel Ltd., Bhrikuti Pulp and Paper Ltd. Nepal Thai Foods, Gorkha Brewery etc. are also doing well. There are industries producing cigarettes, brewery, cotton threads, vegetable ghee, textiles, and sugar. Private sector enterprise in the tourism industry is also well-developed. Thanks to the liberal economic policy adopted by the government and overall business-friendly environment in the country.

---

[8] Sudip Ghosh in *The Times of India*, September 27, 1998

Before the 1950s, the domain of the private sector used to be confined in some terraced paddy fields and some kind of trading in some items of daily necessities, mainly in the form of barter. Most other goods and services were produced and provided at the public or community level. Ranging from the construction of a canal to erecting an oil-crush mill, activities used to be public and communitarian. Either the community or the government was the sole provider of the services. Today the growth of the private sector has taken almost all such activities, This has exposed Nepalese people to a relentless competition and people are finding it extremely difficult to cope with the growth of the unrestricted market competition.

The growth of the private sector is also an indication of the achievement, oriented entrepreneurial culture in the country. In country, in which most people believed in fatalism (Bista, 1991), the growth of entrepreneurship shows a great deal of change in the work culture in relation to the economy. Though most of the private sector activities have been somewhat dominated by businessmen of Indian origin, there is no dearth of successful Nepalese entrepreneurs. Such successes are demonstrated in the tourism industry, in financial sector, private airlines, ad the carpet industry. Lately, such enterprising activities are also seen in the Nepalese movie industry. Hardly a few Nepali movies were produced each year until two decades ago. Today, Nepal's private sector alone produce over thirty films, each year. Tourism sector has also seen private enterprises with the rise of travel agencies, hotels and associated business in the tourism industry. And Nepal's big business houses have started to look for a vision beyond the twentieth century. "As this century draws to a close, Chaudhary Group Nepal is ready to meet the challenges of the new millenium", reads an advertisement of the group. Chaudhary Group also 'envisions reaching the top of every market it serves" and is "committed for excellence of perfection" and will use "its vitality as a large corporate entity".

There are big business houses like Golchhas, Jyotis, Kedia etc. Each of them has contributed to the growth of Nepal Inc. which is in the making. Today, the business community in Nepal has assumed the "responsibility and moral mandate to propel the nation ahead" and to "drive the national cause forward". That was pledged by the Federation of the Nepalese Chambers of Commerce and Industry (FNCCI) in the Socio-Economic Summit Nepal (1999) for framing the "*Strategy for the*

New Millenium". "It has become imperative for the Nepalese business community to look for the critical aspects of development endeavor with the long term perspective with a view to arriving on a consensus on the strategy to identify ways and means to recharge the engine of growth and prosperity of the nation at this crossroad", the FNCCI had said.

The growth of a relatively robust private sector may be a nice thing to rejoice economically, for it provides unique opportunities for employment, income generation and better access to education and physical amenities to the otherwise deprive people of the country. But the worrying side of it has started to be seen in the deterioration of the culture. As urbanization fueled by industrialization has pulled the people from villages to towns and cities in search of jobs, the process has unleashed a process of deterioration of the culture of the people. Kathmandu's growing carpet and garment industry alone employs some 400,000 people, mostly young men and women from the rural villages. These youngsters are hardly expected to continue the culture of the village past, as they come to cities for work. Instead, they are allured by the Hindi movies, Indian fashion in Kathmandu. Go to one of numerous cinema halls that have sprung in the Kathmandu Valley to witness the increasing presence of the village youngsters employed by the growing Nepal Inc. It is not just their own culture, which deteriorates. These new comers also exert a tremendous pressure in the built heritage of the urban areas, which has already reached a threshold for lack of preservation and a callous attitude of the denizens.

THE CULTURE OF POVERTY

Whereas the growth of the Nepal Inc. may be a matter to appreciate and celebrate, it is painful that the culture of poverty continues to perpetuate in Nepal. In a chapter to the World Culture Report on the issue of culture and poverty Professor Rodolfo Stavenhagen argues that there are implicit and explicit values associated with the concept of poverty and that the definition and measurement of poverty itself is a "complex and multidimensional phenomenon" associated with the culture of the people.[9]

---

[9] UNESCO (2000), *World Culture Report*

In Nepal, traditionally, the Hindu philosophy of the "sanctification of the poor" (*e.g.* Sudama in *Mahabharata*) had led to the acceptance of poverty as a sacred and moral thing. As there was enough surplus in agriculture, people living in poverty were assisted by those who could afford in the form of donations and patronizing the poor. Several poor families used to spin around the service of one or two rich families in the village or even in the cities. Plus, there used to be a whole breed of the so-called Yogis, who spent their lives begging alms, as a style of living. Living in the perpetual culture of poverty, that of begging for daily meals, the Yogis could command a lot of respect in the society.

But today, the links between the culture and poverty has been reversed. Not only the economic compulsions have dissociated people with their heritage, there is a continuous pressure upon people to abandon the belief in the merits of cultural practices, as poverty and deprivation continues to haunt them. When people cannot afford to live and survive, they can hardly be expected to adhere to the cultural credo, let alone contribute to the preservation of the heritage.

Since people's lifestyles and economic activities are inextricably linked to the observance and adherence to cultural practices, poverty and poor economic status has aggravated the deterioration of the culture. For example, pilgrimages to religious shrines located far away are out of question if the economic status of the people does not support that. Family rites cost money. A lot of resources are required for inviting guests, offering gifts, and performing rituals. Some families have been indebted because of the extravagant spending on cultural rites. In a wedding, a small family spends much more irrationally than an economic scale would permit. In several occasions, people have to invite their relatives, offer various kinds of gifts, feed them and bear the cost of different things. This and a lot more other things cost money. Some families go permanently indebted and are not in a position to continue the cultural traditions.

The culture of poverty has become institutionalized among the permanent underclass of poverty-stricken people. There are cultural restrictions and sanctions against people who can not afford to pay. In Nepal, the culture of poverty is becoming increasingly acceptable. People are being quickly socialized into the values and attitudes of being poor. There is a rise in the cash economy, where people earn instantaneous wages and there is no certainty about the future. Economic security of the future is seldom thought and planned. The poor people are expanding in population because more people are becoming poor and because there is a high birth rate among the poverty stricken people. Many people have accepted poverty as the cultural characteristics. Poverty is inherited and the cycle of self-deprivation self- perpetuating.

Elsewhere, we have discussed the phenomenal emergence of a "new rich class" in the Nepalese society. A new "poor class", the class of urban poor, is also emerging. Increasing number of the urban destitute are seen by the rise of squatters, the increasing number of street children and the number of people dependent on physical labor. The rich and even the emerging middle class people have also contributed to the perpetual culture of poverty in the country. People's attitude towards the poor has been that of indifference: take as little notice of the poverty as possible, ignore poor and their problems, disregard the destitute and discount their problems. This "other Nepal", that of poverty, squalor, hunger, and diseases, is ignored by the most people of the middle or emerging new rich class and many so-called intellectuals. And the culture of poverty continues.

But it is the poor people, who are the sole custodians of the folk culture and traditions. Their dances today, their music, their belief to religion, their enthusiasm to celebrate festivals, *melas* and *jatras* and their relation to the nature have some what saved the culture in the rural areas.

OCCUPATIONAL SHIFTS

A look at the advertisements in the contemporary leading newspapers in Kathmandu reflect the general trend of the emerging new occupations: computer training, driving courses, secretarial sciences, language training and "study abroads", which are dominating the scene signaling emergence of new occupations. With the changing patterns of market economy, increasingly large number of people are adopting new professions. Several new professions and occupations are emerging while traditional occupations and jobs are disappearing. Farming, which used to be the main occupation of most people in Kathmandu Valley and which was associated with the lifestyle, culture, and traditions of the people, has been a declining occupation. With expansion of the "concrete jungle" and soaring of land prices, the agricultural land of Kathmandu Valley has been transforming into residential slums and people's occupation has been shifting dominantly from farming to business.

Since traditional art and craft is dying, people have abandoned the traditional professions. An increasing access to modern technology and education has produced options for people to adopt new professions and abandon older ones. People are no more maintaining the family business that transcended from generations. The transfer of skills that was required to provide continuity for the craft and art has been interrupted due to changing economic preferences and educational accesses. The Nepalese schools don't promote traditional craft and art. This has brought a perilous impact in the traditional art and craft of the people.

Whether it is the scroll-painting of Solukhumbu or Khukuri making of Bhojpur, blanket weaving of Okhaldhunga or pottery of Thimi, and mask-making of Kathmandu Valley and the cap making of Palpa, the craft is gradually dying. It is saved only to cater the needs of the tourists interested in the local craft. As people are getting into the industrial labor, the traditional employment pattern is no more sustainable. This trauma has put several professions in jeopardy. Especially several traditional professions like carpenting, sculpting and architecture are at risk by this kind of shift.

Pottery, which used to be a sound occupation for many people, mainly some Newars and *Kumhals,* has been threatened by people's decreasing interest in earthenware and flooding of market with cheap plastic-ware. Loss of aesthetic and artistic part in the earthenware, metal-craft and woodcraft is significantly altering the scope of art and craft and the occupations thereof. In Bhaktapur, *Kumhals,* the occupational caste of potters, are realizing that their profession is at jeopardy. Plastic and steel-ware is replacing the demand for pottery. Demand for traditional Newari pottery-ware like *Soma, Anti* (liquor serving pot) *Thapincha* and *Hansi* (alcohol brewing pot) has almost disappeared. Places that were used to extract clay for making pottery have now been crowded with expansion of housing. Many young potters in the area have now been attracted towards modern ceramics instead of the traditional pottery business. The traditional art and beauty of earthenware is at stake and so is its occupation.

The loss of traditional arts and craft is also conditioned by the advancement of technology. Local necessities used to be met with traditional skills and resources. The artisan's dexterity continued to flourish to cater the needs of the people. But the conventional skills and technology is at crucial crossroads. Import of modern technology is threatening the existence of traditional arts and craft and making many jobs and occupations obsolete.

The traditional technology not only used to be the national heritage of the country, the same used to be a very wise way of giving jobs to people, making efficient use of natural resources and developing the local creativity. But the new technology entering Nepal in the name of technology transfer, appropriate technology, intermediate technology, and even rural technology is greatly replacing the local talent and creativity. A lot of traditional technology being used for household works, agriculture, housing, metal works, water management, health, cloth making etc. has been changing due to the adoption of new technology. Development of new technology coupled with lack of preservation has resulted in the loss of the cultural heritage with regards to traditional technology and the occupations and jobs thereof.

Bronze craftsmanship, which used to be famous in Kathmandu Valley is also vanishing slowly. There are very few people today who really know the art of bronze embossing.[10] Though there is a flourishing demand for the metal craft in the market abroad, the rising cost of metals, wax and charcoal is turning the metal casting business into a more and more costly affair.[11]

The local demand for brass-ware like *Ankhora, Karuwa, Surahi,* and dinner plates is also declining because they are getting costlier and less attractive compared to the china, plastic-ware and steel-ware imported from abroad or manufactured locally. Palpa, which was popular for making and marketing *Karuwa*, a metal vase, is no more a city, which enthusiastically produces the water container. Whereas until a few decades earlier, almost every house in Tansen's Taksar Tol used to make Karuwas, there are today only three families who are devoted to it, reported a weekly tabloid in Kathmandu. [12]

---

[10] Amatya, Saphalya (1991), *Art and Culture of Nepal*, Nirala Series-12, Nirala Publications, New Delhi

[11] Gajurel and Vaidya (1984), *The Traditional Technology of Nepal*, Ratna Pustak Bhandar, Kathmandu (p.12).

[12] *Deshantar*, Chaitra 4, 2053 BS (1997)

The woodcraft is also in fast decay. Surviving wood carvers are not well versed in their art. It is becoming highly expensive to use carved windows and struts at buildings. There is not much demand of the woodcraft in the local market, except for some tourist shops and some export to the foreign countries. Nepal's traditional brick and tile industry, which produced a artistic heritage in the country, has also seen setback due to increasing number of concrete structures, which seldom require the traditional bricks and tiles. This has resulted in the gradual loss of art and craft manufacturing the traditional bricks and tiles.

Weaving cotton clothes used to be so much associated with the people's lives in Kathmandu that some Newar people used to gift weaving accessories in dowry to a newly wed women. This custom does not hold any significance today as weaving has almost disappeared in most households of Kathmandu Valley. Weaving clothes is no more a lucrative business due to the availability of cheaper machine spun and synthetic clothes and ready-made garments in the local market. According to the official statistics, only 8,717 people in 192 establishments were weaving and spinning textiles in 1994. Similarly, the use of coarse cotton cloth *Bhangra* in the hilly region has been reduced to a much smaller scale. Technology for making such coarse cotton cloth and its dyeing is no more common in the hilly areas. The demand for coarse woolen rugs (*Radi, Pakhi*) is also declining. People are being attracted to linoleum, and acrylic rugs imported from abroad. Yet another setback in the traditional technology is the ruining of the business of making traditional Nepalese paper from a plant called Lokta (*Daphnea papyracia*). Though there is some demand for such paper, much of the same has been replaced by modern paper, which has become cheaper and easily available these days.

Technology for fermenting, wine making and brewery is also being declined due to increase in demand for modern liquors and beers in the Nepalese market. Local liquor is less enthusiastically consumed than the imported one, though the later is much more expensive.

The traditional technology for tanning, manure production, preparing par-boiled rice, processing dry food, milk churning, preparing tobacco, fishing, etc. are gradually disappearing from the village scenes. Similarly, the technology of bullock carts, water mills, incense making, etc. is also becoming irrelevant or obsolete, thus making people's lives much more different than it used to be a decade or two earlier.

There has also been a remarkable departure in occupations and their traditional caste. With increasing access to education, contact with the outside world, new economic realities, changing face of technology, some occupations have bee unable to perpetuate the links between the caste and occupations.

Among Chepangs, the shift is from a forestry-adaptation to secondary agriculture.[13] Rautes, who are the last nomadic tribes of Nepal, are gradually adopting agriculture as their professions. Large number of Brahmans, who only had adopted priesthood as their professions are now adopting farming and trade for living. People like Gaines and Honey-hunters no more find their professions and occupations feasible in today's changing circumstances. In the new economic dispensation, people's occupation, as every thing else, is changing.

---

13 Gurung, Ganesh M. (1994), *Indigenous People: Mobilization and Change*, Kathmandu

Changing Manners

When Gopikrishna Pokharel came to Kathmandu some twenty years ago, he used to speak a clear village accent from the eastern Nepal. While in conversation, he used to wave his hand with numerous gestures,. He had wild laughs and he used to pat his friends at their back, whistle a lot, and sometimes sing the famous *larke joban* song. He enjoyed large quantity of *dal-bhat* with ghee. He used to drink tea with a funny sound of 'shrrrp'. He had never tasted alcohol. He used to meet his friends and relatives without any advance notices. He had a great sense of humor and very casual attitude towards the worldly things.

Today a senior civil servant in government bureaucracy, Gopi Krishna speaks with a subtle artificial voice in English mixed tone. He has learnt to eat less and avoid fatty food, including his famous favorite ghee. He is a fan of 'jasmine tea', which he drinks without making a noise. He enjoys drinking a few pegs of whisky at parties and at home. At his office, Gopi Krishna sits in his revolving chair with a frowny poker face, which does not communicate his mood. He hardly meets any people without appointment. His informality, ever-chattering and ever-friendly habit is hardly noticed.

Gopikrishna is only an example and he represents a burgeoning class of people, who have undergone startling transformation in their manners. The Nepalese mannerism has undergone stunning metamorphosis in the past few decades. That is mainly due to changes in the family structures, changing work and wealth ethic, changing gender roles, invention of new institutions, changes in the value systems, redefinition of sycophancy and power worship, rise of individualism, the weakening of social hierarchy and emergence of new economic classes. Today, the people do not find themselves comfortable with the traditional mannerism of the past. They are increasingly abreast with the imported culture, instead of the traditional belongingness, and respect of the seniors. Even the form of greetings such as Namaste have given way to the culture of "Hi-Hello", and shaking hands oddly as ridiculed by a TV showman.

Several traditional rules of manners are being replaced with new ones. The pace of life of the people is not only becoming faster. People are becoming increasingly programmed and instantaneous. While an increasing urban indifference is making people self-centered, people's mannerism with regard to food and their health consciousness is changing dramatically. People are not only exposed to the world of glamour, they are also being succumbed to alien mannerism.

THE FAST LANE

Due to the economic compulsion of having to cope with the competitive environment, increasingly large number of Nepalese people are forced to taking faster paces in their lives. People are becoming much more hectic than they used to be a decade or two earlier. There is much bigger rush in the peak hours in Kathmandu and other urban centers. People commuting from long distances for job, business or studies have become common.

The usual relaxed attitude, appearance and value system is changing very rapidly. People are increasingly under the pressure of time. Managing time has been anxiety of an increasingly large number of Nepalese people, especially of the younger generation. Being "busy" has not only become a status symbol, it has become a fact of life. People have certainly become more active, occupied, and restless than ever before.

Among other things, the "Get Rich Fast Syndrome" has put people in much more strained speed. The earning craze and spending spree is getting faster. The race is on and people are increasingly competing to get more from less in less time. Nepalese people have started to realize that time is a resource and that it should be saved and spent like money.

Catching a public transport, shopping at crowded market places, getting things done at different places of interest and having to manage time for the kids and parents has started to become more stressful than it used to be. Even in the rural areas, the pace of life has become somewhat faster. Mail comes faster. People have quicker access to hospitals schools and means of communication. The pace of life is shifting to the fast lane.

Nepalese people in the urban areas are becoming more and more programmed. People's work, leisure, holiday, business, and social occasions are being scheduled under intense pressure of time. Seeking appointments to visit a friend, a relative or a client, making plans in advance to accomplish certain things and splitting time between work, entertainment, family and academic activity or business is becoming difficult for many Nepalese people.

Until a few decades ago, social visits to friends and families used to be very unscheduled. But a lot of planing in advance is becoming common. Casual visits are getting less preferred by people, who are becoming highly programmed in their work and public life. When friends or relatives arrive without prior notice, they are less warmly welcomed and their visit is less enthusiastically appreciated than it used to be done before. Unlike the host family hiding their schedule or anything that used to be unpleasant to the visitors, unprogramed visitors are not supposed to be as warmly welcome as the same used to be until a few decades ago when people used to be more relaxed and used to have more time to entertain the casual visitors. Programming and appointments have been common for friendly visits and even for family unions.

A few decades ago, people used to visit their friends and relatives' on their own convenience rather than that of the visited. Such visits used to be informally exchanged. The number of such informal visits is decreasing. It is no more regarded as highly courteous and desirable to reciprocate such visits. The new generation is becoming increasingly programmed than people used to be a few decades earlier.

"Nepali Time" used to be a ridicule concept about the late coming behavior of Nepalese people. People used to accept, anticipate and plan late arrivals to meetings, seminars and appointments. There used to be a relaxed attitude towards a point of time and a short delay was usually justified and excused easily. The pace of life used to be very slow. Except for the hectic businesspersons, people seldom felt pressured by the time. But due to an increasing shift towards the fast lane and program orientation, people are becoming more punctual and conscious of time planning.

Many Nepalese vehemently believe that they had much better and easier time in the past. People refer to cheap prices, low population pressures and cleaner environment as merits of the past in their own life-time. Things of past are usually discussed in terms of prices and the legends and stories of the rulers and the chieftains. Many people, who had witnessed Rana regime, are fond of talking about the glory and the glamour of the Rana administrators rather than autocratic rule they perpetuated for 104 years. A large number of Nepalese people are very much past-oriented. They love past time fun stories, look backward to enjoy, and seek constantly to rationalize their past instead of looking towards the future. One major reason for such past-orientation is the degree of difficulty being faced by people in the rapidly changing and uncertain environment today.

There is no strong evidence as to how Nepalese people deal and react with future. For many young people, future is highly uncertain, unknown and something, which does not exist. There are two broad categories of people who give typical reaction to the future perspective. One is the religious minded older people. For them, securing a good future is often interpreted as obtaining an easy access to the heaven (*Vaikuntha*) through religious merit. It is for this reason that people usually become pious when they get old. In the eastern Nepal Terai and hills, many old people are adopting *Vaisnavism* (worship of Vishnu) when they get old. They abstain from consuming "filthy food" like fish, meat and onion, cook their own meal and spend most of their time in devotional prayer to Lord Vishnu. They are constantly trying to achieve religious merit, the liberation from worldly affairs into a more secured future, i.e. the access to the world of the god. The religious observance is strictly a pattern of behaviors that is future-oriented.

Another group of people that is future-oriented is the youths who are in constant search for a better career and personal success. For this reason, young people have been trying to go abroad in search of jobs, education opportunities and the like. For this category of people, investing for future is common and future-orientation guides their every sort of behavior. The value system for this category of people is increasingly future-oriented.

But these are the two extremes of the hyperbole. Another major bulk of Nepalese people is becoming instantaneous. People have been subjected to so much pressures of the present that they hardly think of the past and the future. The "get-rich-fast" wealth ethic is increasingly making people more and more instantaneous. People want to do something quick and instant. Patience is very rare. That's why most people invest in quick businesses rather than in long term entrepreneurial activities like industries. This category of people are hardly accustomed to plan or think about a year later, let alone plan about the next generation. This is also because the future is highly uncertain due to such elements like political instability, lack of consistency in the government's policy and action, continuous change in the price and the market structure and a high degree of dynamism in the society. For an average Nepalese person, future is very bleak and uncertain. The unpredictability element in the future is believed to be so high that it is highly irrational to plan for the future. That demands a rational action, that of instant response.

But it is the Western consumerism that demands instantaneous response than anything else. As the consumerism costs it for today, the tendency to save for future is waning, while it is becoming difficult to remember and look back at one's past.

THE URBAN INDIFFERENCE

Nepalese people are known to be of highly cooperative and of helping attitude. But the urban civilization has induced much of indifference in people's attitudes towards others. Many people used to gather around with willingness to help and assist once they came across an accident or something of human tragedy. But many people have started to ignore an accident, an unconscious person, or an event, which they come across. This attitude of indifference is a symptom of increasing degree of individualism in the society, mainly in urban areas. Not a single soul will come and help unless people can prove they have some interest in the problem.

Nepalese people have been commended for their hospitality, generosity and courteousness. There used to be high regard for guests from abroad. Though, this may be found, to some extent, in the rural areas, most of the people in the urban areas have lost this tradition. People have seen transformation in their traditions with regards to mannerism and have westernized themselves in etiquette.

Today, many Nepalese people are not as friendly and hospitable to unfamiliar persons as they used to be a decade or two ago. Although, it is quite common in the rural areas to get generous smile in every eye contact, in urban areas, people have increasingly started to ignore the unacquainted persons. Even in regular tourist destinations and sites where people from abroad used to attract a lot of attention and interest among the Nepalese people, people have started to be indifferent towards the tourists. Tourists are no more seen as strangers, and as subjects of amusement to kids, youngsters and adults alike, as they used to be earlier. Neither are they viewed as *Mleksha* and "untouchable", as they were believed some time ago.

It is becoming increasingly difficult to see ready smile among many urban Nepalese people. People are increasingly becoming less generous, and less concerned about others. Self-centered activities are becoming increasingly common.

The urban callousness is best seen among the people, who drive their cars in the cities like Kathmandu. As more and more Nepalese people have started to possess and drive vehicles of their own, their behavior to the fellow urban residents has been distorted in a manner, which does not suit the Nepalese mannerism. The possessing or driving one's own vehicle has not only become a kind of a necessity, it has also become a status symbol for the upwardly mobile Nepalese people, especially in the urban areas. With an access to increasing access to more and more disposable incomes, many Nepalese neo-rich people have been able to afford to keep their own vehicles. As the number of vehicles increases in the congested roads of Kathmandu, the behavior of the Nepalese drivers becomes a despicable mannerism.

People on the wheels are seen to be constantly outsmarting others. Whether refusing to let others pass or overtaking in the narrow stretches, they are demonstrating their superiority to others without a slightest consideration of the convenience of the others. This sort of callousness has made driving in Nepal, especially in Kathmandu increasingly risky. With increasing traffic congestion and lighter nerve of most people coupled with a kind of recklessness, driving has been testing the people's patience, which is becoming very fragile. Especially when there is a traffic jam, drivers have the tendency to go into the congestion rather than to wait. Honking is such situation is very high and this can be highly frustrating to most people. Motorcyclists are in the category of drivers who are extremely reckless and impatient in such situations.

There is not only the mad rush in the traffic in the urban areas. Even in the highways, people block traffic for hours if there has been a minor accident. People spread things in the roads for drying and even for thrashing the grains. Speeding buses look like they are readying for a take-off. One can cross road from anywhere even in the main roads. To the amusement of the tourists and locals alike, cows, dogs and other animals wander in the middle of the roads. Thanks to the congestion on cities like Kathmandu, there is no need the speed limits, hence fewer accidents.

It is not just driving. Playing smart and doing things wrong ways have become a common behavior pattern, especially among the urban middle class. Among many well-to-do and educated urban residents, disobeying rules and regulations is increasingly considered as smartness and bravery. If one is able to get hold of something either by jumping the queue or by using some personal contact, he or she is seen as very efficient and smart person. People who are smart enough to disobey rules and regulations and who can get things done that way are admired by friends and relatives and are sometimes sought for help in similar occasions. We are so smart with rules and regulations that we know them very well. Then only we would know we are smarting them out.

Young people enjoy fooling others. If one is able to fool a bus conductor or a movie theater gate keeper to manage to ride or to see a movie without paying, one is considered smart. Young people admire such behavior and assume this in order to win cheer-mates. The socially wrong things are being accepted and portrayed as right. We are upbringing a generation with entirely new set of values. The values of indifference and disrespect of the sentiments of others.

EATING CHICKEN IN A HIDEOUT

Not long time ago, a group of young boys, aged between fourteen and nineteen, had assembled in a hideout in a forest nearby their village in an eastern hilly district of Nepal. Most of them were Brahmins. They were preparing to slaughter a chicken and cook its delicacy. In their village, in 1970s, consuming chicken was a taboo, especially for Brahmins. It was considered an act of shedding ones' caste (*Jat Phalne*). It was quite unacceptable for the Brahmans to consume chicken delicacies, since the fowl used to be taken as a "filthy" and untouchable creature. These boys had gathered in the jungle hideout so that they could enjoy the chicken meal without the notice of the elders in their own village. After finishing their meal, they would dig a hole in the ground and hide all the feathers and remains of the chicken so that no one could have a slightest guess of what they might have cooked there. Eating chicken in a hideout, their *Jaat* was not shredded. They could still remain Brahmans.

That sounds like a joke now. All the traditional barriers and taboos regarding food have been broken. People have developed a liberal attitude in consuming otherwise "untouchable", filthy" or "unpermissible food". Even Brahmans, who are not supposed to consume chicken, have accepted chicken as a quite normal and common food. In fact, they prefer the so-called filthy foods such as chicken than anything else. They think it very backward not to consume chicken. Most Hindus still abstain from beef, for cow is still regarded as a sacred animal. Otherwise, food habit of the Nepalese people is changing considerably. Taboos and restrictions have been broken and new norms are being shaped.

Until a few decades ago, people had specific feeding habits and preferences. There were taboos and restrictions on what one could eat and what one was supposed to abstain. But these days people are exercising much liberal attitudes towards food. Even formerly pious Brahmans have increasingly accepted drinking alcohol and consuming "filthy food" (such as onions and tomatoes), which they were not supposed to traditionally.

People are increasingly attracted to new food styles. Increasing crowd at fast food places and ice-cream parlors justifies people's switching off traditional habits towards modern ones. For example, a fast-food place called *Wimpy* was welcomed by the youngsters in Kathmandu, who started to crowd the place within a few days it opened. Eating out is becoming common. This is becoming evident by increasing number of Nepalese people at restaurants and other food places, especially in the evenings. With several forms of traditional entertainment declining, eating and drinking has become a major form of entertainment..

Manners related to kitchen habits are also changing. For example, walking into the kitchen of a Brahmin household with clothes and shoes on could be an absurd manner some twenty years ago. Today, taking shoes off and clothes to enter a dining room can be a ridiculous behavior and people are not expected to do so. Eating small has also become a new manner associated with the lives of the people. Over eating habit, practiced by many Brahmins especially by the priests, has been a subject of ridicule. There are jokes about gluttony, which was appreciated sometime ago, and is now ridiculed and satired.

According to traditional practices, children used to be regarded as untouchable until they got approval by some kind of religious rites (eg.

V*ratabandha* or marriage). For most hard-line Hindu priestly families, their children were not allowed to cook or touch their food until they were married. In case of a male Brahman child, the access to *Chulo* (the sacred place in the kitchen) could be achieved only after performing of V*ratabandha*. Untouchability used to be a way of life and part of social customs among many Hindus in Nepal. There used to be outcasts and untouchables. Although such taboos still remain in some communities, Nepalese society at large has abandoned such practice. Definite cultural patterns against untouchability is emerging, especially in relation to food.

But where food does matter, these days, is among the upwardly mobile and emerging rich class, which is becoming more and more health conscious. Eating less has not only become a fashion, it has become compulsive habit for all the kinds of ailments that are being known. Ghee will increase your cholesterol. Red meat will hike the uric acid. Sweets would change your blood sugar and salty and food is not good for your "hypertension". What is left then.

One-time prime minister of Nepal, who was a very rich person with several hundred *bighahas* of land in the Terai, was on tour of his vast *khet*, his farms. He had to spend a night in the house of one of his tenants, who was a poor peasant with virtually nothing to offer to his famous guest. Before the poor peasant went into panic worried about what to offer the former Prime Minister reportedly told him that he would only eat a *roti* and some *Sag* (green vegetable). Bewildered by the kind of thing the guest has asked and relaxed by the easy nature of demand, the peasant replied jockingly, "those are the things we poor eat, why would you need so much of farmland to eat only those ordinary things". The problem is those who have it cannot eat, because of one kind of ailment or another. Those, who don't have, will eat less, because they cannot afford. Therefore, eating less has become a compulsive new fashion

THE SLIMMING SOCIETY

Anil, an architect, and Kishore, a computer professional, go regularly to a fitness club. They pull, push, bend, and stroll with several machines that are put there recently. In addition, they go for almost one-hour "run" every morning. Jaya, a bank cashier, skips her lunch and avoids fatty food. She attends an aerobic lesson every Friday. Laxmi, a 45-year wife of an army General plays badminton almost regularly with spouses of other army officials. Anil, Kishore, Jaya, and Laxmi are the people of a society, which lives under intense pressure to look and remain fit and slim.

Until some decades ago, statements like "you are getting fatter", and "your belly has become bigger" were used to complement the person being addressed. Becoming fat used to be considered as a sign of prosperity and even being more beautiful or more handsome. On the contrary, "you are thin" could be sometimes insulting. But with growing awareness of health, people dislike being addressed as "fat". Staying fit is emerging as a new concept. A large number of people have started regular jogging and exercises. Many have joined sports and physical fitness clubs. The urban Nepalese society seems to be readying towards slimming.

Increasingly large number of people have started to realize being fat is not being prosperous. People have started to recognize that obesity is a disease, not something to be admired. But it is the pressure to look smart and beautiful that allures people to squeezing, pulling, pushing, and doing anything to punish their body so that they could look smarter. Among the women, the pressure to look slimmer emanates from the flashy models and ads in the TV. For men, the consciousness is a bit slower, but emerging.

As obesity is becoming ubiquitous, upwardly mobile Nepalese people are trying out every weapon in their battle against the fat. Tummy trimmers, corset belts, runs, walks and diets have become the common vocabularies in the emerging lifestyles in Kathmandu. The increasing popularity of aerobics, swimming, gyms, and the health clubs speak of this trend of awareness of fitness. Several such clubs have sprang in Kathmandu, recently. More and more people are going to these fitness centers and clubs to look smarter and to remain healthier. Others just do the same as a fashion, to demonstrate the status making use of their disposable income. But interestingly, not many people have resorted to the traditional practices of Yoga, which has so many cures to many such problems.

Until some years ago, people used to share their health information. There used to be no secret regarding one's health. Most people still know a lot about medical things and feel comfortable to give advises about any ailment. Drink hot boiled water with turmeric if you have common cold, eat this for that, apply that for that. People offer advises, even if they are not asked to do so. This is seen as being smart and informative and not an invasion to one's privacy. People even ask what did you eat the other day, if they know you have some ailment. These types of personal questions are either asked to show intimacy or to express formality. In any case, they are not meant to be intrusive to one's privacy. The consciousness about health is increasing generally.

THE FASHION FRENZY

As increasing number of students started turning up in dresses showing off the latest fashion trends, the campus authorities of Mahendra Multiple Campus of Dharan, the eastern town more popularly known as couture capital of the country, was forced to introduce uniforms for the campus students to arrest "pollution" of the college environment, reported a weekly tabloid in November 1997. This signals a trend in the dress codes and fashion that is gripping the Nepalese youths, especially in the urban areas. But even the rural areas are not spared.

One is bewildered to observe the dresses of masses Kathmandu. People of all caste and creeds, rich and poor, affluent and miserable have one thing in common. They are almost dressed uniformly. It does not reflect from the dresses people are wearing that they are Nepalese people. People wearing beach hats outnumber those wearing Nepali caps, which used to be mandatory until a few decades ago. A feature article in a leading Nepali newspaper reported that Nepalese traditional business for making and selling caps is on the decline. Where as the population of Nepal is increasing, the decrease cap business leads one to conclude that there is a lack of interest in the Nepalese caps. Today, a cap is not a symbol of nationality as it used to be a couple of decades earlier. The headgear is a symbol of backwardness, ignorance and illiteracy. A Nepali man wearing a traditional cap is either diminished or ridiculed by the smart urban youngsters. Abandoning traditional dressing code and adopting modern clothing, people are trying to achieve status and smartness.

Traditional *Daura Suruwal* is now reduced to a formal outfit for some senior bureaucrats and nationalism savvy politicians who uphold public positions. Even in the government office, where *Daura Suruwal* used to be mandatory for officers, rarely a few senior officers put the traditional dress that too only during formal occasions. Though many women still put *Saris* and *Cholos,* most young women wear Indian, rather Punjabi *Kurta Suruwal.* But the traditional home-made Saris have now become very rare, except in some Newars in the suburbs of Kathmandu Valley. Nepalese women are increasingly allured to Jeans and T-shirts.

Some years ago, being fashionable for the Nepalese women meant wearing Kurta Suruwal. But the new fashion trend suggests that Nepalese women are being abreast with "trendy" fashion, the sleevelesses, the miniskirts, and all kinds of designer wear. Also trendy are the dark colored and mercury sun glasses. Young fashion fans do not hesitate to copy the latest fashion of the MTV VJs, models and film and pop stars. People have almost abandoned their traditional attires in the urban areas. But in the rural areas, there are a little bit a different scenes. Old men still prefer to put a cap, though the young people dislike dressing Nepalese. But youngsters opt for T-shirts and trousers.

Fifteen years ago, Tharus of Sunsari were different than they are now, especially in their dress codes. Recently, this author had an opportunity to visit a huge weekly bazaar, called Haat locally, in Duhubi, Sunsari district. People were swarming into the fair from all directions. Some fifteen years ago, Tharu women coming to such a fair used to wear traditional tribal attires with beautiful ornaments. Today, the attire has changed. People are getting dressed up like urban residents. Instead of traditional Tharu dresses, women are seen wearing *Kurta Salwar,* which is more urban and Indianized attire. Although many women still prefer to put on the traditional ornaments, Tharu women no more look unique and different from other people in terms of their dresses. This shift is becoming obvious in other areas of people's lifestyles.

As Bombay's "Bollywood" actors and pantheons of actresses change their costumes a dozen times in each song and a couple of hundred times in each feature film, Kathmandu's youngsters get a bizarre impression of the fashion. But they don't lag behind in copying anything starting from embroidered and silhouetted dresses to transparent and revealing costumes. "Fashion parades", and "gala" have become very common in Kathmandu and the number of models is increasing day by day. These fashion shows provide an opportunity to express one's aesthetics, creativity and imagination, says Srijan

Yonjan, a fashion designer.[1] But others blame the fashion shows to have brought distortion in the traditions and culture. Yet others voice against the "exploitation of women" in these shows. But this does not prevent the young women from entering the fashion frenzy. If it is not only "exhibitionism" that is alluring young Nepalese people to the fashion frenzy, it is the identity crisis which attracts the youngsters to do something different and something new. But many adopt the latest in the fashion because it looks good, or one can show one is abreast with the latest thing.

It is not uncommon in Kathmandu to see young women wearing revealing dresses, which expose almost everything from the naval to cleavage and breasts to bums. They are increasingly becoming prey to their own fantasy to becoming abreast with the fashion world. Even housewives are very adaptive to the changes in the fashion. They don't leave without trying anything that is new and on their notice. Their valued possessions have started become the designer dresses, not the expensive Sarees and the gold ornaments.

Khadi, the sacrosanct symbol of political soberness, is being abandoned except for the Congress politicians, who take the Gandhi style Khadi Kurta as the brand of their political status. What are becoming important are Levi's jeans and polo shirts. *Bhangra* (coarse-cloth made of fiber of a plant called *Lokta* in the mountains) or *khadi* (hand woven cotton cloth) are being forgotten forever

---

[1] *Himal,* 16-30 Kartik, 2057 BS (1-15 Novemer, 200)

The Rhythm Interrupted

It is supposed to be a party time. A couple settled in Kathmandu, is celebrating the "rice-feeding" of their son, the third child after two daughters. Like in the similar occasion of their two previous children, they would invite most of the relatives, friends and colleagues at the their workplaces. But they could not do this time because their budget was already unbalanced due to the educational expenses of the first two children and the recurring medical expenses of the new child. So they have invited only four guests, two of them the child's maternal grandparents. The baby boy, dressed in a yellow shirt, instead of traditional dress for the occasion, is fed with some preparations of rice. There is no ritual, nor the presence of an officiating priest. And the whole thing is finished in less than ten minutes.

Rice feeding, which is known as *Pasni* or *Annaprasanna*, used to be an important family ritual, in which the newborn child was fed with rice and other delicacies for the first time. Performed in the fifth or sixth month depending on the sex of the child as well as on the custom of different communities, this ritual used to be celebrated with much of festive activities and fanfare in most communities. The cultural significance of the ritual was to introduce the baby to the food he or she was supposed to be taking and introducing him or her to all the relatives.

These days, many nuclear families skip this ritual altogether. Those who can afford, do it in a very short-cut way and have modified this into a form of social gathering and entertainment. Big family feasts are organized and invitee may bring colorful presents to the new child. But the enthusiasm associated with this ritual is declining. And the ritual of *Pasni*, these days, is performed not for the cultural merit and significance associated with the ritual. Several people have abandoned this just because it is too expensive. Several others give importance to the feast, not to the actual ritual, which is often bypassed or even ignored.

Among Newars, there is a custom of repeating rice-feeding rituals at one's old age. Called as *Ashworatharohan* (the riding of a horse chariot) or *Budho Junko*, this ritual is performed like *Pasni*. This ritual may be performed on 77th, 88th or 99th birthdays. This is however getting less and less in the practice for the lack of interest as well as for the shorter life span of the people.

It is not just *Pasni or Budho Junko*. Most *Sanskaras*, as rituals of life are commonly known, are performed less regularly, less religiously and less enthusiastically as they used to be done earlier. People simply do not have enough time, resources and commitment to continue the same. Perhaps, people are reinterpreting the rituals in the rational sense and are not continuing them for the sake of continuing.

Among other things, the emerging nuclearity of the Nepalese families, growing pressure to divert the available income to consumer items such as plastic gadgets, and an attitude of labeling the rituals as backward and not abreast with modernity, are the major factors responsible for the declining interest in the rhythm of the rituals among the Nepalese people

Nepalese life style used to be rhythmic and cyclical. People used to celebrate cultural rites and practices again and again with same enthusiasm and cherishing. People used to give a lot of importance and priority to perform various rituals of life. The traditions and customs were continued at all costs. But the interest in such cultural activities in diminishing. Whatever rituals are continued, they are detached from the philosophical rationality and are merely copied and repeated without any reason whatsoever. Thus, the rhythm of life is being interrupted.

SANSKARAS SKIPPED

Nepalese people, especially Hindus, are supposed to undergo several rituals during their life. Such rituals of life, called *Sanskaras*, used to begin before birth and continued until after the death. *Garbhadhana* ritual was performed to start the insemination. People used to perform religious rites for being blessed for a son. *Putresthi Yagya* is often cited in religious texts and the history for initiation to get a male child. *Jata Karma* ritual used to be performed at the birth of a child. In this, the father used to touch and smell the child and utter some *Mantras* into the child's ears wishing a long life and intelligence. Then the child used to be fed with honey and butter and mother's breast for the first time and the umbilical cord used to be separated. These days, the rituals like *Garbhadhana, Jata Karma*, and *Putresthi* seem funny and most people don't even know the existence and importance of such rituals, let alone perform such rites. Even the better known rituals such as *Chhaithi, Nwaran, Pasni, Bratabandha* and *Shraddha* are getting less and less ritualized, short-cut and less customary.

A DIFFERENT FIRST ALPHABET

Hindu children are supposed to be given the first alphabet on a special rite called *Akshararambha*. This rite is usually performed on the occasion *of Basanta Panchami*, since this day is supposed to be the day of *Saraswoti*, the goddess of wisdom and knowledge, and is regarded as an auspicious day for starting new learning. This ritual is believed to enhance the child's ability to learn. A simplified version of this rite used to be teaching the first alphabet to a child by the child's father or male guardian or a priest. Some families used to organize rituals in presence of an officiating priest. People used to be seen on *Saraswoti* shrines teaching their children the first alphabet writing on the walls of the shrines with a chalk or a rock. Usually, the first letter taught was either *Ouhm* (sacred Hindu alphabet) or *Ka* (the first letter of Nepali *Devanagari* script). This ritual has been almost forgotten by the people. Very rarely people bother to perform this rite, let alone recognize the merit of learning the sacred Hindu letter *Ouhm* and initiate the learning on the day of *Saraswoti Puja*.

Instead, most Nepalese children today learn the English alphabet first instead of the Nepalese alphabet. In fact, the primary school curricula recognize Nepali teaching in Grade One, two years after kids spent time in schools, whereas they start learning English at the very first year in the Kindergarten.

On the sixth night after the birth, people used to observe *Chhaithi* ritual to celebrate the fortune-writing of the newborn. In this, a pen, a light, and a blank paper is kept beside the head of the baby during the sixth night and the door is kept open in the belief that *Bhawi* (the fortune goddess) or *Shashtika Devi* comes and writes the fortune of the baby. People have almost forgotten the practice of worshipping *Shashtika Devi* on the sixth night after birth for the "fortune writing of a child". Though several people still ironically possess the belief that everyone's fate is written and that whatever is written in unchangeable, the rituals attached with this belief is being forgotten. If people can abandon the rituals, it is strange why they cannot shed the belief associated with them?

UNHAPPY BIRTHDAY

While Nepalese people have abandoned many rituals and customs, they have started to adapt to new style of celebrating the important events in their lives.

Most Nepalese people's birthday used to go unnoticed and uncelebrated. Some people used to perform special birthday rites in presence of an officiating priest. Some people still perform the traditional cultural rites to celebrate the birthday. But parties and feasts, on such an occasion, used to be uncommon. But these days, celebrating one's birthday has almost become mandatory especially among the urban children. The celebration is not a *puja* in presence of an officiating priest. People throw a party and guests bring gifts like in a Western birthday party. Candle burning and cake cutting becomes ceremonial with singing the "happy birthday". Putting the candles off, which is inauspicious and ominous to Nepalese traditions, is being accepted in the Western style birthday celebration by many people, especially in the urban areas. An alien cultural practice is being socialized in the urban population in Nepal.

Nwaran or name-giving ritual is not performed as enthusiastically as it used to be performed earlier. Today, the ritual is reduced to a short cut formality, sometimes without an officiating priest. The name of the new born child used to be given after the first letters which corresponded to the particular constellation at the time of the birth of the child. This name, in some cases, used to be superseded by an actual given name in the later age of the child. But these days, people's names no more correspond with the constellation. Most kids are given abstract names instead of the names of the gods and the goddesses. People have also abandoned the practice of using the middle names For example, the Brahmins hardly use *Prasad, Nath, Ram, Raj,* etc. as their middle names. Likewise, one rarely sees the Chhetri middle names like *Bahadur* Newars middle names like *Lal, Man,* etc in the name list of the telephone directory. Increasing number of people have abandoned the middle names, not because they want to conceal their identity, but because, it has become fashionable to be seen in non-traditional names. That is also visible in the changing patterns of the names of the people, especially those of the urban areas. In the old days, most people's name used to be derived after gods and goddesses like *Vishnu, Laxmi, Shiva, Rama, Sita, Krishna, Radha, Parvati*. These days, in the urban areas and even in the villages, the given name is usually an abstract word meaning like *Bhawana* (feelings), *Rachana* (composition), *Tripti* (satisfaction), etc.

Hindus are supposed to clean shave their head on several occasions, on mourning and while performing ancestral rituals. For the first time, this has to be performed in a special rite called *Chudakarma* or *Chhewar*. This ritual is specific to a male child only and is usually performed on the third or the fifth year. The child is bathed and head-shaved amidst a ritual performed by an officiating priest. This ritual signifies the celebration of the child's introduction to the rules of bodily hygiene. Like most other rituals of life, head- shaving is disappearing. Instead of signifying the purity of the ritual, the clean-shaved head, these days, may be a subject of ridicule and may signify one's superstition towards the rituals.

THE THREAD NO MORE

In the traditional hierarchy, a triple-cord made of cotton and worn around the neck and right under-arm by the male Hindus used to be the most powerful symbol of distinction and superiority. People wearing it were known collectively as *Tagadhari* (the thread- wearing people). Known as *Janai*, the sacred thread used to give status, symbol and access to the *Vedic* and religious literature, and access to performing religious and cultural rites. The thread wearing people were supposed to be superior and of higher echelon of the society than *Matwali*, the alcohol-drinking people. The distinction of wearing the triple-cotton cord was given to a male child after the completion *Upanayana or Vratabandha* ceremony, usually performed at the age of eight. After the rites were performed, male Hindus used to obtain privileges to read Vedas, to perform the rituals (*Yagya*), to receive alms and to gift to the priests and teachers. The young men, especially among the Brahmins, Thakuris, Chhetris and some Newars, were also given a sacred prayer called *Gayatri Mantra*, a prayer of the Sun god, during the ritual. After getting this thread and *Mantra*, a Brahmin child used to be licensed to go to the upper sacred part of kitchen and to perform religious rites, to recite religious texts, and to officiate religious ceremonies. After this ritual, the child used to enter *Brahmacharya Ashram*, the first stage in the life. For this reason, a Brahmin was also called *Dwija* (twice born): first as a common person and second after wearing the sacred thread (spiritual birth). After getting the triple cord, a Brahmin boy used to be raised to noble rank of priesthood. The sacred-thread wearing Hindus were not allowed to eat "filthy food" such as chicken and drinking alcohol was strictly forbidden. They were supposed to invoke the prayer of *Gayatri Mantra* every morning holding their sacred thread. The thread was so much sacred that men wearing it were supposed to elevate the cord around the left ear while excreting themselves. They were not supposed to touch a number of things and humans included in the "untouchable" category.

For good or bad, this distinction is disappearing. Young Brahmans these days seldom wear the sacred thread and they have relaxed attitude towards drinking alcohol. Today, most young Brahmans think wearing a *Janai* signifies lack of modernization and they have simply abandoned wearing the sacred thread. Janai, which used to be a symbol of status, high caste, respect, superiority and sanctity, has been abandoned by many youths. These days, many people who wear it are interpreted as people too much rigid and unable to modernize. Ironically, the ritual of *Vratabandha* or *Upanayana*, which is performed to give the sacred *Mantra* and the sacred thread to a young male, is still performed. But the age of such performance, which used to be at the eighth year is now shifting to a later age. But the vivacity in which the ritual used to be performed has disappeared altogether and it is done to complete minimum formality required for the young males to get married. The concept of access to the kitchen (*Chulo*) has vanished, save in some very pious Hindu Brahmans. Elevating the *Janai* to left ear during relieving bodily calls and changing to Dhoti to get ready to go to kitchen to cook and have regular meals sound like big jokes.

MARRIAGES MINGLED

Marriage customs are also changing. Increasing demand for dowry (*daijo*), extravagant parties, pressure to show status even at the cost of borrowing, use of western music bands instead of traditional *Panchebaja*, short cuts in the actual rituals, occasions of non-traditional marriages (e.g. *Janabadi Bibaha* and court marriages) are imposing changes in the Nepalese marriage customs.

Today the institution of marriage is changing very much. Although some communities like Humli Tamang still continue polyandry and some village people still practice polygyny, most marriages are becoming monogamous.[1] There are economic compulsions and social pressures attached to the practice of monogamy. Divorce, which used to be rare, is becoming common. The strong marital bonds that used to tie people for life is gradually unfastening and nuptial relationships are getting shorter in duration. Though there is no data available, it can be safely said that rate of divorce and separation is one the rise.

Arranged marriages still continue, but a trend towards increasing number of "love marriages" is on the rise. Young people increasingly fantasize "love marriages". The Hindi cine version of love is what is considered a dream of the most of the Nepalese youngsters today. It is this fantasy in the cinema in which the young actor and actress dance wearing colorful dresses in beautiful scenery and their relationship ends up in marriages, which is dreamt by the most Nepalese youngsters. Inter-caste marriages, which used to be rare, are increasingly becoming common. Rigidity of caste structure in the choice of marriage partners has also lessened (Gurung in Rana & Dhungel, 1998, p.12). Inter-caste (inter-ethnic) marriages are more common in urban areas, where a more uniform culture is observed among the different castes and ethnic groups than in the rural areas (Karan & Ishii, 1996, p. 163). This kind of marital relationship is not only becoming common in "love marriages", this is also becoming

---

[1] Even among the Humli Tamangs, environmental degeneration and a growing tendency towards the fragmentation of land has shifted the practice of polyandry to monogamy (Gurung, 1994). Fraternal polyandry was practiced by Humli Tamangs because it helped keep joint families intact and avoid fragmentation of holdings, while enabling the joint family of brothers to earn income from various sources (brothers adopting different occupations: one as herdsman, another as trader and another staying at the house) and to pool their earnings (Gurung, 1994). But a shift in the occupation and the cultural practices has challenged the practice of polyandry. There have been instances where younger brothers have revolted against the practice and resorted to separate marriages. Such a shift is tantamount to changes in the traditional institutions of marriage in the various ethnic groups of people.

common in arranged marriages. And the marriages are becoming more and more a tryst of love of the young couples, though this has yet to take a visible shape in the culture.

Even the ritual of weddings and custom associated with this is getting a blow. Nepalese youths dance Nepali version of discos on cacophonic Hindi cine band music played by drummers (forget about playing traditional *Panchebaja*) during the marriage processions. The bridegroom weans modern Western suit with a neck-tie rather than a Nepali *labeda-suruwal.* Traditionally, Hindus regarded marriage as a ritual and formality essential for continuation of life and to herald the start the household life (*Grihasthashram*). Marital bonds used to be very strong and seldom broken. Among many pious people, the marriage used to be essential for liberation (*Moksha*). Marrying was regarded as a *Dharma* (religious act) in order to continue life.

Despite the ban imposed by the law, child marriage is still very much common in many rural communities. In Terai communities, the marrying age is usually between 10 and 16 years for a male child and 8 and 14 for a female child. But among the urban communities, the child marriage has almost disappeared. Marrying age is on the rise compared to earlier practices. Marriage by capture, which used to be common in some hill communities is gradually decreasing.

Although, the ritual of *Ihi* is still performed, the significance of wedding the girls with an wood apple is understood to have less importance than it used to have earlier by many Newar people,

A late comer in the social evils is the practice and custom of dowry. The menace this practice has created in society is the most shameful of all tradition Nepalese people have adopted from adjoining areas. Traditionally, Nepalese society *did* practice some degree of dowry in which the bride's parents used to offer some gifts to the bridegroom's family. But that was mostly voluntary or imposed by societal norms and status consciousness. But lately, this has taken the form of the price paid for the bridegroom. Dowry is becoming an institution of corrupt marriage. The amount of dowry demanded and paid is determined by the professional and economic status of the groom. Doctors, engineers and government officers apparently top the list in the market. In some cases, the dowry exceeds million rupees and accompanied with such material gifts as a modern house, and a car. Mundane items like the television, and refrigerators are offered even by the most ordinary middle class families. It is because of this practice of exorbitant dowry that people in certain families mourn the birth of a girl child. Many families could go indebted offering such dowry to the prospective grooms. It is not the dowry, which is so shameful. But the practice of harassing and torturing women for not being able to bring enough dowry is more disgraceful. In the extreme cases, the women who are unable to bring dowry are also beaten to death and burnt alive in some families of the Nepalese Terai. Lately, the menace of dowry has been gradually creeping from the Terai to the other parts of the country, mainly the urban areas.

Before three decades or so, the negotiated marriage used to start with the men's side asking and requesting for a female partner for marriage. The burden of seeking a partner rested solely on the male side. But this has reversed these days. In many communities, the men's side still has "to beg" the woman's hand. But in the most urban areas and among different neo-rich families, the girls' side has to take the initiatives. The woman's side has to offer dowry or to make other compromises and concessions to have their woman arranged for marriage with a man. The price to be paid for a well-to-do and educated man has started to become very difficult and expensive, often out of the reach and affordability to many people.

Yet another changing scenario in the matrimonial practice is the emergence of institutions for fixing marriages. Nepalese society did have the custom of the traditional match-makers called *Lami*, who used to fix the weddings of various couples. But these days, the match-making has started to commercialize. Though the Nepalese people have not started to advertise their matrimonial needs in the scale of adjacent India, some institutions for fixing the arranged marriages have taken commercial shapes. These emerging "marriage centers" have become quite popular in finding the suitable couples for the youngsters. Similarly, the priests, who perform the wedding and other rituals have also institutionalized themselves in such centres. They have the possibility of pushing aside the traditional customs, institutions and practices of marriages in Nepal.

THE FORGOTTEN ANCESTORS

In each Hindu Brahman family, an ancient family personage *is* respected as *Gotra*. People are supposed to identify themselves according to their *Gotra* and are strictly forbidden to marry within one's own *Gotra*, which represents a root where the clan originated from. They are the most sacred and most venerated personages and their names are held sacred and invoked by people while chanting mantras, performing rituals and even while introducing oneself. These are even represented in constellations and stars[2].

Today, many young people don't even know what their *Gotra* is, let alone pay homage to the family personage. *Gotra* is remembered only when performing rites and while arranging marriages, which are supposed to be inter-*Gotra*. Not only are the distant ancestors being forgotten, many Nepalese people have started to disremember their immediate ancestors. These days, people seldom perform the regular ancestral rites such as *Shraddha*. Among the urban residents, such a rite is becoming an additional and social burden, not an essential cultural practice. It is not only the economic compulsions, which may not support such expenses, performing this type of rites can also be seen as being backward.

Further, it is difficult to keep track of these things. How on the earth can one remember when is one's grandfather's *tithi*, the lunar calendar day on which he had deceased years ago? The lunar calendar is the not the most easiest thing to follow. The lunar days do not correspond to the solar calendar that is in the daily use. Further, one has to consult a local priest or astrologer to be sure even if one knows a little bit of the lunar system.

People have also abandoned the custom of wearing white clothes as mourning for a year on the demise of their parents. People, these days, hardly avoid wearing leather shoes while attending funerals or attending the mourners. Similarly abstaining "filthy food" during one-year mourning is also decreasing. Whatever ritual is performed in the name of the dead ancestors is not done for its cultural or religious merit, but the same is continued for the sake of saving the public criticism that one has forgotten one's ancestors altogether. In the callous rage to be catch up with the present and the future, people are generally abandoning their linkage with the past, including their bondage with their ancestors.

---

[2] For example, *Saptarishi* (The Great Bear) is a name given to seven stars representing seven Hindu sages (*Kasyapa, Atreya, Bhardwaj, Gautam, Vishwamitra, Janamdagni*, and *Vashishtha*), who had attained the heaven.

THE DECLINING RESPECT

Apart from the changes in the attitude and the changes in the affording capacity of the people, the *Sanskaras* are being a difficult to manage because of the scarcity of the priests, who officiate such rituals. In the first place, today there are a very few schools where the *Karma-Kanda*, the science of rituals, is taught. People no longer think this as a lucrative and attractive vocation, except in some urban areas where the demand of the priests is increasing because they are getting less in number and people still need to perform certain rites, especially marriages. Much of the ritual knowledge is disappearing and is becoming more and more rare. Even priests are forgetting the actual codes of procedures and the texts are rarely available at the market.

Priests used to occupy respected places in the Nepalese society. Scholarly pundits and gurus used to enjoy much of respect and fame. They were known for legendary power for rhetoric speeches. They lived in *Ashrams* and founded religious institutions of their followers. Today, such a respect for knowledge and spirituality is fast disappearing. The sacrosanct status enjoyed by the religious gurus is declining.

Hindu traditional students were taught to give utmost respect to their teachers. At *Gurukul*, students used to learn the merits of life. At the end, the teachers used to have the right to ask their pupils for *Guru Dakshina* (teacher's gift). It used to be regarded as the student's duty to fulfill their teachers' wishes. There are several stories based on the deeds of the students to satisfy their teacher's wish. But this tradition has almost vanished. Though some Hindus celebrate *Gurupuja* (the teacher's day) with paying homage and respect to their respective teachers, who gave them education and *Diksha* during *Vratabandha*, this practice is very much decreasing.

Today, the word *guru* is used by the youngsters to satire priests and people, who are religious-minded and unaware of modernity. People feel ashamed to be addressed as a "*guru*" if they are modern enough to study in an English school. Instead of being respected, the term can be insulting to many people. Today, this term is especially applied to Brahmins who are weak, feeble and who perform cultural rites. Today, the term "guru" itself is used to demean a Brahman person.

Brahmin priests used to enjoy the most respected place and status in the society. They used to be greeted with a bow down to their feet. Priests were usually fed with delicious sweetmeats and fruit. They were invited in almost all-important religious or cultural ceremonies. Their advice used to be mandatory in performing *Sanskaras* and rites. They had to be consulted before performing rites to find the auspicious dates. Priests knew sacred and secret *Mantras* they learned from various texts.

A priest used to be called to give a new name to a new born baby, to feed the baby with rice, to give the sacred thread, to perform a marriage ritual, or to perform the death ritual. Priests were also needed to purify a place, to start building a house, and to consecrate a temple. No worship was complete or conducted without their presence. People used to attach a lot of importance in *Purohits* because most people could not perform the rites on their own. *Purohits* only knew the *Mantras* and the prayers required for performing such rites. They only knew which books to recite. Each family usually had a designed priest, who had a fixed client-hood.

But these days, the priesthood is becoming a gradually a declining profession. The priesthood is hardly seen as a prestigious profession as it used to be. Except some Pundits (professional reciters of Vedas), most ordinary priests who perform the rites are addressed with derogatory terms like *Baje* and *Bahun*. They are seen as backward and less modern people.

There used to be a large number of people who used to make their living as priests. But the breed of people is becoming endangered. People don't pay the actual amount of respect the priests used to get some time ago. Priests are ridiculed as *Bahuns* and are satired as *Tapare*, one who collects the sweetmeats in the leave-sewn plates used in the rituals.

Traditionally, each community in Nepal used to have a respected person entitled as a priest. In many families, they had clan priests, who performed religious and cultural rites and officiated almost all the family religious ceremonies. They were given distinct names and in some cases identified with peculiar dresses. *Lama* of Sherpas or Tamangs, *Ghyabring* of Gurungs, *Bharra* of Tharus, and *Bijuwa* of Rai people were very much respected in their respective communities. With the emergence of new democratic structure and social framework, the traditional respect given to the tribal priests is also decreasing. The traditional authority of the priests and chieftains is being challenged in the new democratic framework, in which it is no more mandatory to keep the traditional loyalties intact. But it is the lack of interest in continuing rituals and practices, which is degrading the importance of the tribal priests in almost all communities.

Confused Dreams

A group of Nepalese youths have assembled in a evening hangout in Kathmandu. Most are drinking one of Nepal's several beers and munching *momo*, pizza or burgers. One of them is wearing a reversed baseball cap and a Chicago Bulls T-shirt. Other is putting a T-shirt, which has stars, and stripes. Most boys are dressed in Jean trousers. Some have put "accessory" rings on their ears and some have sported relatively longer hairs. Subject of their discussion ranges from the latest computer games, the season's cricket schedules, new "hot" sites in the Internet, the television serial *Baywatch*, and the latest MTV releases of the *Spice Girls, Britney Spears*, and the *Backstreet Boys*. Though their conversation is going in Nepali, they broadly mix English intermittently and it would not be difficult for English speaking persons to understand what they were talking about.

Today Nepalese youths, who are supposed to be the flag-bearers of the culture in the society, are dismayed and confused due to an increasing disillusionment. They are not only neglecting their own culture and tradition, they are exhibiting signals of violence and dissatisfaction. Modernism, which the Nepalese youths have been accepting with much of enthusiasm, has been disregarding the cultural, social and economic values. While the youths are loosing the Nepaleseness, the fabric of Nepalese society is becoming more confused.

According to a research carried out by some Nepalese youth,[1] the new generation, though having their own preferences and desires about the society, would prefer to live under the accepted norms of the present social environment. They would like to call themselves a "very future-conscious generation" that wants to see the society and its views change to accommodate their priorities. But not everybody agrees that all young people in Nepal have such a futuristic vision. Neither is there any strong evidence to suggest that the new

---

[1] *"Freedom as Defined by Youths"*, by the students of Kathmandu School of Management had said (*The Rising Nepal*, January 13, 1999)

generation Nepalese are not rejecting the traditional norms of the society.

Nepalese youths have become highly vulnerable to frustrations, revengeful activities, and introversion. While unlimited ambition has become a major challenge among many Nepalese youths, lack of vision and mission of life and confusion about the future is disorienting a large number of other Nepalese youths. Youngsters are seeking their identity with clothes, relationships, technology, and new careers. They are in the forefront of embracing unusual trends in their attire, their choice of music. Jeans, Coca-Cola, the Internet, fusion music, fast foods and anything from the West have become the ideals of the Nepalese youths.

The level of anxiety of many Nepalese youths is increasing due to complexities of modern life, inability to cope with dynamics in the society, difficulty to adjust with the high-cost economy, and inability to deal with cultural and social obligations and the like. Due to a declining awareness of shared culture and a shift towards the individual culture, the social patterns and behavior are changing.

A VIOLENT VOYAGE

A young motorcyclist is just hit by a taxi, while the motorcyclist wanted to cut a curve overtaking the cab from the wrong side. This is a minor accident and there is no injury. The young man leaves his motorcycle in the middle of the road and approaches the taxi diver, drags him out of the cab and blows a few fists in his jaw. Before several pedestrians and by-passers gather and intervene, the two drivers engage in a few more exchanges of blows.

This type of erratic and violent behavior is becoming common among the young people. Tolerance and respect is decreasing. Revenge is on the rise. And there is an increasing recourse to physical methods for taking revenge. People learn such revenges from the melodramatic Indian and western movies.

A lot of such anger and intolerance persists due to the frustration among young people about the state of affairs in general. But a major attitudinal dimension is that taking revengeful physical action is considered and believed to be a heroic deed and something of good moral order translating one's smartness into reality.

Not only is the fist fight becoming common phenomenon in social disputes, many young people are increasingly allured to sports which have some relationship with harming other physically. An increasing attraction towards the martial sports evidently justifies this notion. The rise in popularity of martial sports like Judo, Wushu, Taekwando, Boxing and Karate has very much to do with the attitude of playing physical smartness. Thanks to the increasing interest and aptitude in the martial sports, Nepal stood in 2nd place in the Eighth South Asian Federation Games (1999), ahead of Pakistan, Sri Lanka and Bangladesh. Though most of these sports do not support violence, but teach self-discipline and defense to the youngsters, the increasing liking of these sports could be an outcome of the attraction to the culture of violence as well.

This raises a question: are we heading towards a violent society? The discernible trend suggests that the answer is "yes". The rise in the violent crimes like murder, rape, assault, and robbery and increasing domestic and political violence explicitly sends signals of increasing violence in the Nepalese society.

If we start to think in terms the value system, some element of violence or recourse to physical punishment has been an important element of Nepalese society. The documentary history proves that some degree of violence was accepted, warranted, admired and even adored by the Nepalese people. In the history, Nepal's ruling court had been the common ground for hatching conspiracies, killings and coups. During Malla period, Kaji Bhim Malla was killed by his jealous opponents and his wife had cursed the posterity which is known popularly as *Satiko Shrap*. King Parthivendra Malla was poisoned to death by the conspiracy of the court officials. Similarly King Yog Narendra Malla was poisoned to death. King Rajya Prakash Malla was deprived of his eye-sight by the "notorious" Pradhans of Patan, while the former sat on the throne of Patan for some time. Even King Prithvi Narayan Shah's assault on Kathmandu during the unification of Nepal had seen "ruthless" violence such as that in the battle of Kirtipur.

While the Nepalese people have the intense desire for peace, their reputation for violence, especially during battles and wars is also well known. Nepalese war heroes had championed the patriotic cause of Nepal fighting famous battles against the British in India. Famous war hero Amar Singh Thapa fought in the battles of Malaun, Almoda and Ramgarh, during the British-Nepal War (1814-15). In Malaun, he defeated the troops of British India commanded by General Octorlony. He fought against the British East India company during British-Nepal War at the Battle of Almoda, which was a decisive battle and a truce was signed by the Nepali side (May 29, 1815). Another Nepali war-hero was Bala Bhadra Kunwar. During British-Nepal War, he fought bravery in the battle of Kalanga. In that battle (October to November 1814), Nepalese troops fought bravery against the troops headed by General Gilespi, who was killed in the battle. The British troops established a stone tablet in the honor of his bravery after his death in the battle.

Known for their valiant warring skills and bravery, the Gurkhas have demonstrated their courage and strength around the world. Nepalese Gurkhas have demonstrated their great fighting skills. Even today, a large number of Nepalese youths aspire to serve as mercenaries as Gurkhas in the British and Indian army.

In various historical episodes, several court officials and even Prime Ministers were slain on various occasions. In Kot Massacre (1846) alone, some four hundred court officials were slain by Jung Bahadur Rana, who then became the Prime Minister. In Bhandarkhal Parba, Jung Bahadur cleared his rest of court enemies. He outplotted (1847) king Rajendra Bikram Shah's plan to recapture power and arrested the King and killed his men in Alau, near Birgunj. The episode, which included a battle (July 28, 1847), is known as Alau parba in the history of Nepal. In Adatis Sal Parba more people were killed. Many court officials came to power killing their opponents and enemies. Bhimsen Thapa came to power killing Mukhtiar Damodar Pande. Bir Shamsher became the prime-minister killing his uncle Rannodip Singh when the later was the prime minister.

The popularity of the *Shakti* cult of sacrificing animals to pacify blood-thirsty goddesses, the episodes of mass slaughters in the royal courts, conspiracies and plots of murders, abrupt fighting between different small states were the facts of history. Yet the overall characteristics of the society was highly peaceful and tolerant. Though Nepalese history had absorbed traumas and shocks of such events, violence had not creeped into people's lives as a very common day to day thing.

In a note to the statement that Nepalese people stand for peace, Stiller has said:

"Visitors to Nepal sometimes interpret this to mean there is no violence in Nepal and are shocked to find that individual can be quite aggressive. As a nation, however, the Nepalese are peaceful, their respect for human life and values deep and abiding. There is violence in Nepal today, concentrated mostly in the cities or near them. Political instability has allowed young Nepalese people to vent their resentment against a social system that seems to exclude them from the benefits they see as their right and their frustration at the slow pace of development. It is worrying because the level of violence has escalated, over the last thirty years" (Stiller, 1993, p. 13).

Youngsters, who indulge in violence, are driven by the inability to fathom the consequences and by their youthful impulsiveness. Youths may be unable to comprehend the consequences. But it is the movie world, which makes crime a holy thing. The sanctification of the crime by the movie world is among the major sources of such youngster violence. In numerous Hindi and even upcoming Nepali movies, murder, killings, and violence is shown as something, which is unavoidable and even desirable to prove one's smartness. This is definitely sending a wrong signal to the youngsters.

Today, dissatisfaction has become the fact of life. Every sphere of life is full of discontent. Comments of dissension can be heard on in conversations, read in newspaper articles, and even in the contemporary literature. People's tone while talking about things is overtly negative. It is next to impossible to find someone who is expressly positive about the state of things in the social, cultural, economic and political life. Most Nepalese youths have been highly frustrated by the state of things in their nation. Their motivation often gets spoiled due to the "lack of adequate opportunities" to fulfill their dreams.

Their dreams are getting shattered and they are resort to means like drugs, crimes and violence in order to satisfy their increasing frustrations and desperations. The Nepalese youngsters are not only becoming increasingly jobless, they are also becoming missionless without any objective of their life except to make fun, chat, laugh, drink, play and enjoy. And they get frustrated if all of these are not available. While the youngsters are falling in the grind of the entertainment industry, the culture and the nation is witnessing a great despair and neglect.

Average Nepalese youth, with regards to society and the nation, has started to accumulate the belief that there is a lack of adequate individual capacity to change the whole system and continuation of the deteriorating trends. The youngsters response is that of rejection (I damn care it !) or abdicating responsibility (what can I do about it?) or indifference (It does not matter to me).

It is not that people accept things quietly. Youngsters holistically break the metal bars in Ratna Park and around Tundikhel during demonstrations. They proudly destroy telephone cabinets and set ablaze vehicles during strikes. They cheer and force cars to stop or else smash their windows. In the jungles of some 19 districts, many Nepalese youths carry guns and fight with police their "people's war" for their Maoist cause. Are we embarking in a new culture, in which the strength of the youth are measured by the degree of violence they can resort to when needed ? Or are we just heading towards a more violent disposition, in which might is the right?

JOURNEY TO FANTASY

Animesh, 19, has colored his hair with peroxide and dressed it with a gel to point upwards. He has several tattoos on his arms, puts an "accessory" ring in one of his ears, and wears a Heavy Metal band T-shirt and a pair of loose trousers and "Dingo" shoes with scores of zippers. Bipin, the only son of a moderate social worker from east Nepal, has shaven his head, wears a boxer outfit, put a huge poster of a "Rap star" in his room. Santhosh, 20-year old son of a teacher, puts a reversed baseball cap, keeps sideburn cuts, wears everything loose, listens to the "Scorpions" and the "Kiss" over his Walkman ignoring members of his family often dancing in the tune not heard by others. Animesh, Bipin and Santosh represent a whole brand of youngsters who prefer to be addressed as "Y" generation. They are increasingly identifying themselves with things alien to the Nepalese youths until a few decades earlier. They are in a constant search of fascination and new identities.

An increasingly visible number of young people in Kathmandu are seen keeping long hairs, wearing different rings and unique dresses. Police called "junkie cleaning". The move in 1995 was initiated to discourage the Nepalese youths wearing fashions "unacceptable to the society". The police said that more than ninety percent of such youths were involved in alcoholism, drug abuse, flirting young women, violence and "distorted sexes".

The youths think they have the "human right" to choose freely whatever they like to wear or put. But police thought the change was not acceptable and needed to be "cleaned". The long-haired youths have been signaling their choice, the search of unique identity. They were expressing their frustration and desperation with the existing state of affairs and willing to identify themselves with something exotic and unique. This trend sometimes suggests the expression of the unfulfilled desire.

The "aggressive outfit" is a distortion, a kind of negative or uncommon behavior, symbol of frustration and dissatisfaction and expression of disagreement to the society's norms and attraction to increasing Westernization, says a sociologist.

Drinking alcohol has become a kind of fashion among the urban youths. Beers have become in-thing and drinking has become an important way of socializing and making peers among the young people in Nepal. Search for fascination is an emerging problem among the Nepalese youths. Many Nepalese have been allured to the world of sports, music, cinema, fashion, and travels abroad. Many others have also resorted to drug abuse in such a quest. This problem has been menacing the social order of the younger generations. Young people are increasingly willing to escape from reality due to the soul-destroying pace of the competitive world, the disruption of the traditional standards and the elevation of the non-traditional materialistic and hedonistic drives.

Many youths have resorted to drugs to be able to confront with fears, obsessions, anxieties and feeling of inadequacy. These young people are in an urge to satisfy their excitement and fun of experimentation with drugs. Several people have taken drugs to pacify boredom due to leisure and apparent lack of meaningful activity, alienation, and disinterest in the state of affairs in the world. Further, young people are becoming highly vulnerable to persuasion of other young people and are under increasing pressure to conform to the norms of the peer groups.

The trend of drug abuse among the youths signifies that there is an increasing alienation of individuals from the groups and society, which has retarded the individual's motivation to conform to the social norms. That is why people are willing to experiment something new, like drugs. It is also the feeling of estrangement and separation not only from the societies and established values, but also from the subculture and from individuals' life goals and meanings.

It is not only the drugs, where Nepalese youth are in search of fun and fantasy. They are being attracted to whatever offers the same. "Let us have fun" has become the mantra of the Asian youths, says John Naisbitt (1996). Nepalese youth are no exceptions. Increasingly, Nepalese youths are being allured to the fun and fantasy offered by the Western pop music, dance and the culture. It is more so because of the increasing availability of disposable income at the hands of the Nepalese youth. Today, at fast food joints, at dance restaurants, and at FM fan clubs, it is the young Nepalese people, who are crowding the scenario in search of fun and fantasy.

The identity crisis does not stop at the individual level. Young people gang up together wearing similar jeans, putting stylish earrings, and listening to certain music. Several strange group names can be heard over the FM radio channels in Kathmandu. These youngsters like to identify themselves with such group names while dedicating songs and participating in numerous talk shown in the round-the-clock FM radio channels in Kathmandu. They are not just falling prey to the identity crisis, they are also becoming the victim of "snob values" which will lead them to nowhere but a mere aping of the alien values. Many are allured abroad in quest for these values. While a small number of Nepalese youths make their way through the visa offices and manage to go abroad, many are left behind, frustrated and desperate, unemployed and missionless. And all they are left with the insatiable desire to accumulate the junk of the alien culture.

NOTHING TO DO

A large number of Nepalese youths remain unemployed. A government statistics says there are 650,000 unemployed people in the country. This means fourteen in every hundred people in Nepal are jobless. Add to that a large number of people who are under-employed and are in disguised employment, mainly in rural agriculture. Many people, who are categorized as self-employed in the agriculture, are also only partially engaged in the occupation in the farming seasonal only. The 1991 census showed that only 65% of the economically active population in Nepal were employed, that also for eight months in a year.

In the rural areas, where agriculture is supposed to be providing employment to most of the people, there is an overwhelming evidence of under-employment. Majority of the people has only small pieces of land, not enough to generate work for the family throughout the year. Labor use per unit of land in the rural agriculture is very small. And the opportunities for non-farm employment are either non-existing or very limited.

In the urban areas, there is a burgeoning private sector focused on manufacturing, commerce and service. But that is not enough to absorb the increasing number of educated youths both from the cities and from the villages. These youths, in their perennial search of jobs and better opportunities, are left without anything to do. Many aspire to seek employment as manual and unskilled workers abroad. Others try to be recruited in the army, and police. Some *do* get chances. But others are left confused, dismayed, disillusioned and frustrated.

And the unemployment "appears to have gravely disturbing social fabric, a cherished asset of Nepali people", writes the Federation of Nepalese Chambers of Commerce and Industry (FNCCI) in an introduction to the Socio-Economic Summit (1999) for "Strategy for the New Millenium". The emerging work ethic that educated persons should stay away from their farms and should not be doing manual work is also contributing to the increase in youth unemployment. After finishing their schools, Nepalese youth can hardly return to their farms. They prefer to remain unemployed than to go back to the toils of farming

More than anything else, it is this unemployment, which adds to the confusion and frustration of the youngsters in Nepal. Without nothing to do and confused dreams, the Nepalese youth are plunged into a very uncertain and dark future, which alienates them from the mainstream society. They are further separated from the traditions and culture of the past. In utter confusion, Many such youths in the rural areas join the violent "people's war" groups.

In the colleges, the youngsters, who are the victims of the "snob values" and "mock culture" spend their idle times flirting the bypassing women. Their attraction to things like throwing water-filled balloons at passing women becomes an enthused affair than organizing any other extra-curricular activity. What you wear or ride is becoming much more important than how you stand in the studies. Even the attraction to the sports is getting far behind the attraction to the fashion, music and cinema. What you talk is almost invariably derived from either movie world, cyberspace, or the magic box the television.

This group of idle youth also falls prey to the politics, which has a breeding ground in the colleges. Student activists are given tickets to parliamentary seat and often win with the support of major parties. Student organizations are openly admitted and recognized as "sister organizations" by political parties. They are divided in a mirror like fashion according to the division in the political parties. Hooliganism, politics, lack of trust and faith in the capability of education to pay back becomes the major source of frustration and desperation for those who really want to accomplish something academically.

It may also been seen that some of the Nepalese youngsters are also becoming, innovative, daring, achievement-oriented, health-conscious and above all street-smart with an ambiance of what has been named as an "attitude" of the Generation Next. But it is the youngsters who are falling victim to the "global trap", courtesy the ongoing opportunities of globalization and liberalization of economy, which allows invasion of the market with consumer products of the "me generation".

As the youngsters are allured to the glitter and glaze of the new products, new life styles and craze for new things, they have to be adept in the making of the fast buck. When they fail to do so, they get frustrated and confused.

Today Nepalese youths have adopted an entirely new identity with denims, with fast beat pop, with English speaking ability, and with a casual attitude to their lives. A Nepalese youth today has nothing Nepalese, he or she is a world creature, an imitation of a youth of the Western world. Youths are being allured to a blind travesty being subservient to the pros and cons associated with it.

While the youngsters are being allured to the West, they are not attaining the positive values of the Western culture. Value systems like recognition of the women's social status, dignity of manual labor, absence of notion of caste hierarchy, value of the self and the individual freedom are yet to be fully copied.

Today's Nepalese youths, street-smart and aggressive, are interested in leading their lives aping the values alien to the Nepalese societies. Wearing unconventional designer dresses, rocking round the clock to the fast and frenzied music, aspiring fast and easy money and instant success, the Nepalese youths are preparing themselves to be abreast with the alien culture. And the pursuit of hedonism to a lifestyle loaded with pleasure, fun, entertainment, and accumulation of materials and gadgets, is pushing the youths in an irreversible cultural transformation.

For many street youngsters, their bravery and genius lies in their ability to tease and flirt young women. For example, seven days before *Holi*, the festival of colors, the youngsters throw water filed balloons to the women, especially girls of their age and above. They spend times fooling others and making fun out of people's mistakes and accidents which they stage. A young boy's hero is a friend, who is violent and can flirt women and can do silly things.

In the craze, what is ignored is the good things about the Nepalese culture: respect for the elders, camaraderie of living in a society, mutual support and belongingness in families, high morality in social life and generosity in general behavior with others.

WILL YOU BE MY VALENTINE?

On February 13, a large number of Nepalese youngsters send cards to their beloved ones. They publish messages of love in local tabloids. Some even send roses and chocolates to their love. Unknown to most Nepalese until a few decades ago, the Valentine's Day has become a festive occasion for the Nepalese youth, especially those going to the colleges and schools in urban centers. Hardly any youngster in the decade of seventies had heard things like "will you be my Valentine?" Today, youngsters not only send messages, flowers, chocolates, music tapes and cards to their "Valentines", they also celebrate the occasion with wild parties. "If you do not have a Valentine, you are nobody", says a Nepali young man buying gifts for his beloved.

With the changes in everything else, the relationship between the youngsters of the opposite sex is also changing visibly. In the old days, the romance used to be confined some stolen glances, long walks along the parks and hours in the library. Today, youths prefer coffee joints, momo parlors, and fun fairs as their favorite trysts. Lately gyms, dancing restaurants, cyber coffee joints, and discos have become available as the rendezvous points for new beginners as well.

The traditional love letters have been replaced by Valentine's Day messages and similar columns in one of several magazines. More than one page of Kantipur's *Saptahik*, which comes out every Friday, is packed with such messages sent by people who have adopted phony acronyms and titles.

The arrival of the FM has also contributed to such relationships. Most of the broadcasts in all of seven or so FM channels in Kathmandu almost round-the clock are programs related to love songs, debate about relationships, dedication of songs, and messages to loved ones. Send a message in your cryptic names, dedicate a favorite song to your BF or GF (Boyfriend or Girlfriend), or speak over the telephone to the host of the program to tell how much you miss so and so. This FM thing has given a boost to the business of love, says a music cassette seller in Kathmandu.

But it is the email thing, which has given the Valentine generation a respite from the usual hurdles of delivering a love letter, or difficulty of being listened in the phone or the FM by another member of the family. All you have to get is a private hotmail, which is free, if you have internet access in your computer. No way other people can read it, even if you are sharing a family computer. Plus you can "chat" endlessly with several others in several such sites on any matter you would like, from Monica Lewinsky to Madhuri Dixit, from Pam Anderson to Cindy Crawford, from Baywatch to Bollywood rumors, all embedded with messages and romances of the fantasy world.

When it comes to relationships between young men and women, many Nepalese are struggling between the tradition and modernity. There are traditional parents who think love before marriage is a sin. But they might have their children changing boy or girl friends and affairs, which last less than a season. And having a partner of opposite sex has started to become a status symbol in the colleges. Many college girls prefer to have their guys, who pay for their fun. Best are the guys who bring their cars and easy money from their rich parents. Those who can make their own money might do well. And those smart guys coming in motor cycles have a fair chance. Today, you don't meet your boyfriend. You date him. You do not go to Godavari with your girlfriend in that jammed minibus, you borrow a car or a motorcycle from your friend. Sorry to the poor guys who can only bring a bicycle and can hardly pay the movie and momo bills. Even the girls have their own mopeds, tiny motor scooter. " I have no idea how you date with such girls", says a college student. The parents of these youngsters would have no clue to the new types of relationships between young men and women.

This craze has even gripped the schools, as one teacher tended to suggest. "These days, children start learning love before they start learning algebra", the teacher complains. "My son keeps changing girl friends", said the father of a boy to prove how smart his son is.

THE CARD CULTURE

In the little corner of Maharajgunj, a posh area in Kathmandu, there is a shop sign, which reads *Archies*. It is a gift-shop that offers a range of items and significantly displays cards on varying themes. Youngsters come here to buy gifts and cards to express their greetings and feeling to their friends and relatives. This is only one of several such outfits, which sell various kinds of cards with messages to suit any occasion. There are cards available with messages with every conceivable human situation, greetings, love, sorrow, happiness, congratulations etc..

Until a few decades ago, a piece of chewing nut used to be sufficient for inviting people in occasions like weddings, religious ceremonies, and family occasions. These days, glossy printed cards are pervasively used to invite people in different occasions. Today, the card culture is not just confined to inviting and exchange of greetings. Most social occasions have become all card-oriented. In birthdays, anniversaries, new-years and lately in Valentines Days, people feverishly buy and exchange cards. People buy and give cards to their friends, relatives, clients, and colleagues to express their greetings, good wishes. Occasions like Dashain Christmas, New Year's Day have almost become the card season. But new phenomena of the cards are that these glossy forms of expression have invaded occasions like birthdays and anniversaries and even Pasnis (rice-feeding rituals). The card culture, alien to the Nepalese traditions, is invading the lives of the Nepalese people.

Many of today's lovers are brave enough to go around parks, restaurants, and public places in couples. Earlier, they used to go around in groups. And the love has started to be more direct. You curtail the "preliminaries", no going around the libraries, no coffee sessions, no meeting through groups. You can take off from the first sight and first meeting. You never know how long your love or "infatuation" will last. But what you wear is more important than who you are with. So bare midrffs, Jeans and T-shirts have taken place of the traditional dresses. Guys prefer the trendy hairstyles, ear studs and accessories, sunglasses and reversed hats. Girls like the silver backpacks and different shades of lipsticks. What matters in the "teen culture" is the image, you create around you with your physical attributes, your clothes, and your partners. All you have to do is look "cool".

Like in the old sixties and seventies, hardly any of the relationships last until marriages. Neither are the emotions so high while youngsters are in love. A young woman might consider getting married if the career is matching, if her guy can make enough money, and if he can buy physical amenities to her life. Preferred are the ones, who have their houses in Kathmandu, who have chances of going abroad taking you along. For a woman, if your father is a big shot, your chances are higher than any body else's. But if you are all to win the best boyfriend, you better be trendy in the fashion, glamour and lifestyles. Otherwise, don't complain, someone betrayed you.

Unlike few decades earlier, when the young unmarried couple in love were not easily accepted by their parents, young couples aspiring to be partners of life are accepted and socialized easily, especially among the upwardly mobile Nepalese society in the urban areas. People no more make rumors and gossips around such couples. They are not outlaws until they get married. So the trick is not to hide your relationship, as in the earlier days. You go public about your new partnerships. Despite that, the youngsters are continuously confused on how to fall in love, on how to maintain a love partner, on how to reveal their relationship to the society, and on how to take it up to their marriage, if they wish so. The business of relationships is adding to the confusion of the youngsters, who are already dismayed by so many things changing simultaneously.

Though there is very little research and information available, Nepalese youngsters have not been spared by the intrusion of alien values in sex, relationships and love, and attitudes regarding marriage and family. While extra-marital and pre-marital sex is openly rejected, but it is being absorbed into the society's fabric. Except in a few communities in the hilly areas, pre-marital sex used to be totally a taboo. Conventional wisdom suggested that youngsters should never learn anything about sex. Many people still believe the less their children learn about the sex, the better it is. But people's attitude and knowledge of sex is changing. Pre-nuptial chastity, which used to be supposed mandatory according to Hindu marital value systems, is not valued as importantly. Male chastity (*Brahmacharya*) and female chastity (*Koumarya*) used to be regarded as of equal importance. But these days, this value system has started to deteriorate and the chastity is hardly verified and discussed. Although, sex is still a taboo and people don't talk about it in public, awareness about the same is increasing. Increasing access to sex literature is evident. In Kathmandu's tabloid market, lot of "sex education materials" is sold although most of that is a kind of pornography.

In principle, the youngsters reject the increasing influx of pornographic magazines and materials in the Nepalese tabloid market. For example, some student activists, outraged by the presence of a series of porno magazines like *Samagam, Trishna, Aina, Abhisarika, Pyarki Pyas*[2], symbolically burned some of the magazines to protest their availability. But most youngsters quietly accept these things, mostly because their opposition does not count much and they feel powerless to make any difference. Further, they are confused as to whether these materials are worse than the bare legs and cleavages they get to see every time they turn their television on. This has infused a value system otherwise alien to the Nepal's youngsters.

---

[2] *Himalayan Times*, December 21, 1996

Changing Work Ethic

In the busy business area of Kathmandu, a young woman in her early thirties comes in a self-driven car wearing a smart silk skirt and suit. As she briskly enters the office, the guard in blue uniform attentively opens the door for her offering a salute. The woman, who is smart, bold and confident-looking, sits on a revolving chair facing a computer terminal behind the glass partition.

The entire room has four other cubicles like hers and is well lit and carpeted wall-to-wall. As business goes usual, she responds feverishly over the telephone, receives and sends email from and to her business clients and professional contacts. She dashes around for meetings and is sometimes too much performance-oriented and "less human" as her staff criticize her.

This is one of the several outlets, which have become the high-tech work places in today's Kathmandu. Air-conditioned rooms, elegant furniture, wall-to-wall carpeting, smart-looking and English-speaking secretaries and receptionists, smartly dressed professionals working on computer terminals, and busy executives hunting around for results, performance and profit have become the symbols of such high-tech workplaces.

Included in this category are several finance companies, joint venture banks, hotels, private airlines, travel agencies, departmental stores, and foreign private companies, who are desperately trying to win over the customers by presenting their smart look, showing efficiency in services and championing the businesslike environment to perform better in the emerging competitive market. And these are the places where the "dream jobs" of Kathmandu's young people are being generated.

The high-tech workplace has not only absorbed a substantive portion of the youngsters, who get their education from several English medium schools, and who, somehow, have not made their way though the visa offices of one of the foreign Embassies, it has also spurred the growth of several training institutions who focus on English language training, computer courses, and secretarial courses. A large portion of

Kathmandu's tabloid advertisement is covered by materials for competing individuals for various jobs in the high-tech workplace.

A whole new kind of work-place is emerging- different from the bundles tied up in white clothes and stacked over archaic almirah, distinct from the rusting and rattling typewriters around, and overcrowded workplaces in the government bureaucracies. This has infused a new work culture, which is based on the ideology of smartness, modernity, better pay, efficiency, competition and something of "today".

Nepalese work ethic is undergoing discernible changes. Due to changing employment patterns, shifting wealth ethic and economic compulsions, the traditional work ethic is being challenged and new pattern of work behavior is emerging. Among other things, the challenge of survival and the notion of accumulation of material wealth has reversed the work ethic of most Nepalese people.

Although the locus of control is shifting, at the same time, people are also searching an escape from work. There are shifts in the sycophancy patterns and work behavior in the workplace, typically the government bureaucracy, which are becoming increasingly prone to politicizing.

But the Nepalese society is yet to fully adopt performance and merit as the ladder to upward mobility which still depends much on corrupt money, power and the relation to those holding the high political and bureaucratic offices.

THE BESIEGED BUREAUCULTURE

If anything has contributed most to the development of the work ethic among the Nepalese people, it is the system of government bureaucracy. Traditionally, kings used to compensate their servicemen and army with pieces of land called *jagir*, which was not only a source of some economic returns, it was also the source of status and hierarchical differentiation in the society. In the apex was the king, who was assisted by several courtiers. As the state needed an unified administration, servicemen were recruited from various places. Preference was given to Brahmans, who had some access to education and to the Chhetris, who were skilled in the art of administration and statecraft. The Newars had the advantage of being in the close proximity of the power. Thus, Jagir was a privilege of a selected few.

Even today, the concept of Jagir shadows the Nepalese work ethic quite a lot. Despite so many new developments, including the culture of work and entrepreneurship, the job in government bureaucracy is called *Jagir Khane* (eat the job) instead of *Kam Garne* (do the job). That means, the position in the government offices is meant to be exploited and to be devoured.

The Nepalese society has inherited a lot of legacy of sycophancy and subordination from the government bureaucracy of the bygone era, mainly of the Rana and Panchayat period. During the Rana Period, these used be an annual review of appointments, transfer, terminations and promotions of the public servants. This system of *Pajani* had strengthened the culture of Chakari, in which the public servants had to please their masters in order to continue their jobs. Even today, many people still believe that a person in power, especially in the politics and the bureaucracy can give them jobs. It is with this belief that people congregate in the power centers to secure news jobs or better position in the existing jobs. There is a concept of "source-force", which means one can one's connections- family, kinship, regional or political and otherwise- to get things done. Apart from the conventional culture of bureaucracy, new forms of distortions are plaguing the work culture in Nepal. Avoidance of responsibility, generating and cultivating rumors, delay in making decisions, sycophancy in the language and behavior and new forms of *Chakari,* and the proliferation of corruption are some of them.

Further, Nepalese work culture continues to enjoy more free time and intervals at work place. People take several tea breaks and escape from office for personal businesses. Every time is tea-time. "Tea is a big menace to the work", observed a visitor from abroad. "Come tomorrow" disease has plagued all the government departments and ministries. The file clerk is on leave, the typist is out for paying the personal electricity bill, the dispatch person is gone out for tea.

The decline in the organization culture of the public institutions has become very disgusting. Government departments and projects are prone to corruption and misuse of funds and resources. Employees take public offices as recourse to making "extra gains". People are treated with apathy. High level of politicizing has divided employees as the working wings of the major political parties. In public enterprises, work stoppages and strikes have become common. There is a complete disregard to the quality of service and public servants take rules as iron gates to muscle their power.

In such a mess, people, who get a chance to run the public institutions have been alleged to have initiated a race of misuse of the public resources and funds. Influencing public institutions for personal gains and for illegally nursing one's constituency has become quite common. With this infamous image, public servants chat and spread rumor, talk politics at the workplace and elude form office for hours. Attendance is routinized just in order to secure salary.

Today, a typical Nepalese bureaucrat is one who is extremely dubious of other people and who always keeps things secret. He (rarely a woman) hides things from colleagues, and from the public as an art of efficient administration. He seeks to create his indispensability in office. In bureaucracy, files travel in coveted routes. Doors are locked for making even unimportant decisions and drafting clandestine letters. But a lot of back door input is still gathered by clandestine and esoteric process. Even with an increasing demand for accountability and transparency, this behavior is not changing very visibly.

People who command others are considered to be of higher status than those who actually work. High positions are taken as something to be enjoyed (called rent-seeking behavior), not something of responsibility and duty towards the society. In fact, work itself is considered something of low status. The dignity of human labor is very low and is considered to be the domain of low, menial and lesser mortals. This low dignity of labor also applies to the work ethic of people in the rural villages. After a little access to a school, one detests to work in the toil of the field and prefers to remain idle playing cards rather than to go back to the fields. Though the high profile politicians, bureaucrats, professionals and businessmen tend to demonstrate their business as a status symbol, they actually show that not by physically working hard, but by piling bundles of files on the desk, keeping clients and chakariwalas waiting outside, ad answering all sorts of telephone calls at all hours of the day and attending even trivial meetings to show how much they are preoccupied with things. Due to an attitude of thinking oneself as a master, not as a public servant, there is a widening gap between the people and the officials.

One of the major reasons for lack of positive changes in bureaucracy is lack of attitudinal changes among the civil servants. Without attitudinal change, all other changes have become futile. Attitudinal problem is not only creating hurdles in the bureaucracy. This disease plagues every other activity in the society, politics, business and social life included. People are seeking changes. They are focusing on institutions, procedures, methods, laws and economics, but the real problem of attitude remains to be addressed.

Pointing upwards is one of the most emerging work behavior among the Nepalese bureaucrats. Orders and instructions come from the top. Files go upwards and seldom return. Everything is either pending or hanging because there is indecision on the top level. There is no delegation of power and authority, since the Nepalese work behavior does not promote shared responsibilities. The bureaucrats have lost their ability to stand up and say this is right or that is wrong. They are increasingly becoming "yes men", who don't always take the most morally sound paths in the course of decision making. In public offices, only one person is seen working: the boss, who is always busy. Telephone rings continuously at the his (rarely a woman) office and at his house. People queue up to see him or her to get things done. Applications and files pile up on the boss's desk. He is the only person attending meetings. All the decisions are made by the boss. Everything emanates from the chief and ends there. Well-known Nepali poet Bhupi Sherchan coined the term "blind boss on a revolving chair". A typical Nepalese bureaucrat and administrator easily fits into this category, even toady.

On the contrary, all other employees in the office are under-worked. They are free and easy. There is no work, no responsibility. They gather at one place and chat, criticize, make rumors and discuss personal and political matters. It is generally taken that the meager salary is for securing the attendance at the offices and if there is the need to work, then some kind of incentive is required. That perhaps supports the idea of corruption. If the work has to be done, some should pay for it, whether it is the government or the clients, who need the service.

Another factor responsible for the deterioration of the work culture in the government bureaucracy is the increasing importance of rumors. Rumor occupies a very important aspect of bureaucratic life in Nepal. The first thing people talk about in the morning is about rumors. The rumor mechanism is a very strong informal communication channel in the administration. To know or create rumors is viewed as having access to power and information, which operates behind the curtain. People not only share much of the information through the grapevine and back-doors, they also feel enriched to know about rumors. Rumors are sometimes created by for gathering views and to assess how the public and employees view that. Nepalese generally give some importance to any kind of rumor. Rumors and decisions often tally. "The leaf does not move, if there is no wind", it is often said. Lack of confidence among each other, extreme secretiveness of the administration and lack of transparency are some of the factors contributing to the cropping of rumors.

Further, the Nepalese work behavior inherits much of the "cat-tying ritual". In old days, people used to tie a cat during the ancestral homage ritual (*shraddha*) so that the unholy and ominous feline would not cross and touch the holy rites and sacred offerings. After some generations, people started to think that cat tying was mandatory. They started to borrow a cat to tie during the ritual because they thought cat tying was an essential part of the ritual. This behavior at work place is very much evident. People do things because they were and supposed to be like that. No one seeks any rationale for any thing they do. Risk taking and innovation are usually dwarfed and people usually stick to things as they had been traditionally.

The bureaucratic culture is not confined to the government. Even in the private sector, non-government organizations and the academic institutes, this mentality has been occupying somewhat center-stage. Nepalese professionals and academics have been excelling in jobs and institutions abroad. But the same people cannot do better in their jobs back home. Somewhere, somehow, there is a problem either in the work environment or in the attitude towards the work in general.

CONTROLLING THE SWITCH

For most Nepalese people, the locus responsibility for success and failure used to be an external factor. There used to exist a staunch belief that the individual had no control over society and the things happening in the world. An external source, usually a supernatural power or fate, used to be believed to control. Horoscopes, which have regular appearance in newspapers and magazines, used to be very popular in predicting the events in their lives or at least for the reported period.

IS PERFORMANCE CONTAGIOUS?

There was a teacher in a college of Tribhuvan University in Kathmandu. He was not the most punctual and the best teacher. He used his notes from previous years and very rarely consulted new books, let alone look for journals or periodicals in his subject. Though he conducted extensive tutorials for the students who thought the study in the campus was not enough, his teaching in the college was not the most admired. Then, he got an offer for a teaching position in a private college opened by his Head of the Department. With a little extra money, he started to take his job in the new private campus more seriously. He started to become punctual and never missed any class. He started to consult the new textbooks, and reference materials from the old college, where he still retained his position as a side job.

With an opportunity to build on his contact with a visiting scholar to their private college, this young lecturer managed to get admitted to a college in the U. S. of A. After usual hurdles with money and visa, he eventually started a degree course there. It was entirely a new environment and was quite an adjustment in living and studies. Overwhelmed and overburdened by assignments, he almost thought of going back to his relaxed pace of life back home. As he did OK in the first term, and did a little more than mediocre in the next, he advanced to excel in the rest. After completing his M. S. and then Ph. D., he is now a professor in the same college. He is regarded as one of the best and sincerest teachers and one of the best academic staff.

What was wrong in the job back home? People blame environment. "Performance is contagious", it is said in management jargon. Perhaps, they are right. The organization culture back home in government bureaucracy, in universities, and in the public institutions are not that conducive for excellence and high performance. The work ethic is not shaped by merit, high performance and achievement orientation. Nepalese society has yet to adopt merit and performance as yardsticks for upward mobility. Therefore, despite the capacities to work better, Nepalese professionals are under performing back home.

The belief in "fatalism" had a "devastating effect on the work ethic and achievement motivation, and through these, on Nepalese response to development with consequences on sense of time and concept of planning, orientation to the future, sense of casualty, human dignity and punctuality", wrote Bista in his *Fatalism and Development in Nepal* (Bista, 1991). Most Nepalese people believed in Karma philosophy, according to which one is not responsible for one's status, rights, privileges and obligations in the society. Hindu philosophy of "intentless work" (*Niskam Karma*) had profound impact on Nepalese people's work ethic, which was guided by the thought that work and duty should be performed without expecting any returns. Since people believed in fate, very rarely did they try to intervene in the divine order. The conventional Nepalese work ethic admitted that the success and failure was determined by fate, not by one's competence. Traditionally, people believed in the external locus of control. They believed in an external fate, which controlled their lives. There was little room for achievement motivation.

The traditional interpretation that the Nepalese people believe on the external locus of control and on fatalism has started to be questioned and challenged. Increasingly large number of young people are seeking to establish relationship between their effort and performance. A discernible trend in the people's belief in the external locus of control has been seen in the rush to business and entrepreneurial activities, exodus abroad to seek jobs, and increasing competition. Though these achievement-oriented behaviors can be labeled as desire to copy instant success, not as inner motivation for innovation, there are evidences in favor of people's belief in internal control and achievement motivation. It seems that increasingly more and more Nepalese people have started to possess the switch that controls their lives. It is becoming increasingly evident that fatalism is a belief espoused by the poor and is increasingly not the main ethic of the powerful and rich people, especially the *noveaux riches*.

ESCAPE FROM WORK

While a large number of Nepalese people have started to become pressured with too much work and hectic lifestyles, there seems to be a perennial search for escape from work. There are too many holidays. Work is given low dignity. Absence from work is excused. And people push things to the last hour.

Nepalese work ethic favors a lot of rest and intermittent holidays and absence from work. In the festival like *Dashain*, the government offices are closed for up to nine consecutive days. There are several other festivals, which are celebrated as public holidays. In Kathmandu Valley, there are additional public holidays for occasions like the *Gaijatra* (cow festival), *Bhotojatra* (the exhibition of Lord *Machhendranath*'s vest) and *Indrajatra* (the festival to fete the rain God).[1] Besides, employees are given a number of leaves. People can earn festive leave, casual leave, annual leave and leave of absence. And, recently the government has introduced a five-day work week scheme. If that is not enough, the government employees simply sign the attendance register at the office and elude for the rest of the day for their private business. One good aspect of this is that importance is given to Nepal's numerous cultural festivals and occasions. But the government employees on such holidays spend less time on the cultural activities. They enjoy the most public holidays playing cards or doing personal errands.

Holidays and absence from work is not only common in the government offices. Even private enterprises and the competitive entities suffer from this disease. Though people hardly celebrate the festivals, observe family rites, and go to pilgrimage centers to take holy baths or attend ceremonies of the family members, the holidays attributed to such occasions are still practiced. Absence from work for such cultural activities are excused and accepted. Ironically, the customs and traditions are not observed despite people escape from work giving cultural excuses.

Nepalese education psychology is also highly detrimental to the work culture. Education is viewed as a recourse to doing away with the physical labor, which is considered of something of low order in the social hierarchy. The traditional Hindu caste system ha allotted the task of performing trade and agriculture to *Vaishyas* and services to *Shudras*, while the education remained in the domain of Brahmans. Whereas the relevance of such a tradition of classification has been fading, many Nepalese people still think and believe that education is for doing non-manual jobs. Labor is still considered a low profile and low status job in the society. There exists a belief that the physical

---

[1] Some of these holidays have been withdrawn recently, especially after the introduction of the five-day work week.

labor lies in the domain of the people of "lower hierarchy" in the caste structure. The dignity of labor has yet to be established in the Nepalese society. The concept is built around the traditional Hindu work ethic, which categorizes work according to one's caste. The *Vaishyas* wee supposed to undertake trade, industry and agriculture and *Shudras* the services. People of the "higher caste" (Brahman-Chhetris) were not supposed to do physical labor. It is still quite difficult to see a Brahman plowing or carrying a back-load of things for other people. Though the traditional value system has served as a barrier to the dignity of physical labor, the traditional concept of division of labor no more holds true and people have moved across occupations, despite their caste and traditional businesses.

Nepalese work ethic has been increasingly appreciating, promoting and warranting the eleventh hour efficiency. Things are not done until they approach the last hour. Increasing temporal disorientation, and limited sense of the importance of time has made people consider past, present, and future as a continuum and accept a sense of timelessness. Nepalese reward system increasingly appreciates management by crisis and the eleventh hour work ethic. People act slowly until the time runs out.

Though temporal orientation is shifting, most Nepalese accept, anticipate and plan late arrivals to meetings, seminars and appointments. There is a relaxed attitude towards a point of time and a short delay is usually justified and excused easily. The pace of life is very slow. Except for the hectic business persons, people seldom felt pressured by the time. Though, there is an increasing shift towards the fast lane and program orientation and people are becoming more punctual and conscious of time planning, the ridicule of "Nepali time", a substitute word for late starter still occupies the people's temporal psyche related to work.

SYCOPHANCY SHIFT

Literally it means to wait upon, to serve, to appease and to seek favor. *Chakari* was introduced during Rana Period in order to have the subordinates and the followers attend the power courts showing loyalty and dedication to their patrons. Certain hours of the day were set aside for the supporters, followers and subordinates to come attend and wait upon so as to let them express their loyalty and reliability. For the people who went on *Chakari*, it was something to achieve confidence, job security and expression loyalty to their patrons and chiefs.

It was a passive behavior aimed at demonstrating dependency, eliciting the favor of the person depended upon (Bista, 1991). Although *Chakari* has been abolished formally, its legacy is still an integral part of the social organization in Nepal, especially in the government bureaucracy. Poor people respect and appreciate the rich because the later have more access to power and wealth. People of "lower caste" wait upon those of the "higher caste" and economic status to get some benefits.

As an informal social organization, *Chakari* includes attending the living room of the benefactor to join the gaffe, bringing material gifts, offering services and favors, pleasing and flattering the host person. This is where rumors are spread, secrets are unraveled, back-door inputs to decisions at work place gathered, opponents criticized and leg-pulled and information for advancement and fulfillment of one's hidden objectives created, gathered and propagated. *Chakari* is also an institution for socialization of the bosses, who are amused and entertained by their followers, praised and given feed backs on what is happening and what is of their interest.

A typical *chakariwala* goes to the house of his patron early in the morning, before anyone has reached there. He (rarely a woman) waits upon in the boss's living room. He finds out if one has to go to buy vegetables or bring milk from a store nearby. He may also bring Ghee from dairy and convince that is the best ghee produced from his own cow's milk. He may buy fish from local market and tell the boss that this is the best quality fish from his own pond. Things like Soybeans, dried meat, pickle, fruits or anything may be brought as a toke of material gift. Many bring what is peculiar in the area they come from or they are assigned to. One assigned in Solukhumbu may bring woolen carpets. One working in a lucrative Terai office is pleased to offer Basmati rice and a Dashain goat. A sophisticated one does not bother on these petty things. He will find out if the patron's son is admitted to a school, if the patron needs to see a good doctor for his chronic illness or what happened to the patron's daughter-in-law's nomination for going abroad.

But the most advanced ones are those who simply resort to praising the boss, giving some unsolicited information, catching up rumors and new developments and writing their academic papers for trips abroad. The efficiency and competence of a person in a high position is usually propagated by the army of their supporters. Others simply amuse the boss with their Gaff, which is an active form of social interaction and is considered as highly acceptable. Sometimes the status of a high office is weighed in society and family in terms of how much *Chakari* one gets and one is entitled to.

These days, it has become fashionable to deplore the *Chakari* system. Many people openly criticize the traditional sycophancy. Many patrons and bosses openly reject any form of it. Despite social pressure from their families for not getting the "benefits" of the office, they actively avoid this channel of support, information and feedback. But they face social isolation. Though *Chakari* is actively rejected and criticized many young and idealistic people who have advanced to higher positions by education, especially through the training in the west, they are criticized as being "insensitive" to the Nepalese work environment and are openly ridiculed. People rejecting *Chakari* are also labeled as closed and introvert individuals and anti-social persons. They are seen to be blocking grievances and feedback. Hence new form of *Chakari* is invented. A different form of patron-client and give-and-take are emerging in the bureau-culture and society at large. Today, *Chakari* as a word is hated and criticized by every one, but practiced with a little bit different connotations like cooperation, friendship and understanding. It still exists as networking, power associations, and interest groups.

OF HUMAN BONDAGE

If anything has clogged the Nepalese work ethic most, it is the institution of the *Afno Manchhe*, one's own people. In his famous book *Fatalism and Development in Nepal*, Dor Bahadur Bista (1991) identified *Afno Manchhe* as formal social institution and an important group behavior, which was a significant cultural variable interfering with pace of socio-economic development in Nepal. It can be implied that it is this institution, which blocks the Nepalese society from adopting merit and performance as the criteria of upward mobility. Instead, the family, ethnic, cultural or geographical bondage is applied to seek and give favors at the workplace as well as in the overall inter-personal relationships in the country. It is the informal institution of people who have their own inner circle of their own people, usually close relatives, kin and friends and people of same ethnic groups and same geographical region. Maintained for social identity and mutual benefits, this is a cohesive group of people, who have similar objectives, interests and a great deal of interdependence. The institution of *Afno Manchhe* not only provides identity, status, belongingness and support among each other, it can also bring advancement, achievement and mutual respect in the society. It is this group or inner circle of people, who are available for help in times of need and to share the joy. Though the inclusion in the *Afno Manchhe* circle is usually defined by the clan relationship, proximity, and mutual interest, such a bondage may also be developed through the institution of by *Chakari*.

Asking favor for one's own people at the work place may be taken as politically incorrect, but it is socially warranted and mandatory in the Nepalese society. Though people criticize this norm in principle, they hardly can escape the practice of seeking and giving favor to or from one's own people. This is why the work place and the government mechanism acts as a "soft state" in which the powerful and privileged few including those in upper reaches of government bureaucracy, influential business, and higher level politics continue to get a treatment superior to their fellow compatriots who are week and powerless. The state serves as a "subsidized canteen" for the privileged few and neglects the interests of the poor and weak.

Interestingly, the circle of one's own people is a dynamic concept, especially in the middle class people. There are constant new addition and changes in the group as one advances in the social hierarchy. People try to find some acquaintance or one's own people to get things done at government offices and even at private enterprises. Referrals are mandatory in things like licenses, transfers, contracts, assignments etc. on the basis of one's relation to some influential personalities. If a person doesn't recommend (use "source" as it is said) in favor of his or her own people, he or she are highly anti-social and subject to a kind of boycott. `Source force' is used to save status. People prefer to go through acquaintance channel and wait for hours including the time spent on tea offered by the acquaintance rather than to go by person and to get things done in the minutes. What can be done without knowing anyone is not important, how it is done is very important and that really matters. That gives status and satisfaction. This has become an acceptable norm among the civil servants and the general public.

It should not be the outright conclusion that nepotism has gripped the entire Nepalese society and hence the work place. But the kinship is still playing important role in shaping the workplace behavior in Nepal. An uncle here and an in-law there will definitely increase the chances of getting things done in public offices. Waiting ascendancy up the career stairs, getting luscious postings, securing nominations for trips to every corner of the planet earth will definitely become easier with presence of even distant relatives than if one is the sole fry on one's own. If you have a nuptial knot tied up to an influential family, which has a boss here and master there, things will be easy. But it is not always necessary to have the relation bestowed upon you. You can nurture one as you know some one a distant relative is going ascend upwards in the power hierarchy. Your sister's friend's brother-in-law or your wife's friend's father-in-law can become "close relatives" and you could discover the route to reach them. If you are the client of a patron, then all rules can be bent. But when economic incentives are involved, one can even avoid the relatives saying you are unable to do a favor because it has become either too much political or the matter is under scrutiny of one of the several probe agencies.

With the rise of individualism and emergence of nuclear families, even the social institution of one's own people is shaking. People of "me generation" are increasingly disregarding this human bondage. People's bondage with other people is being increasingly guided by "give and take". People are becoming highly instantaneous in relation to others. Only if there are present gains that people reciprocate favors as one's own people. This new trend has threatened and challenged the traditional concept of one's own people, which is becoming more fluid and unstable.

THE WORK *POLITIC*

Like most other aspects of the Nepalese society, the work place is not free from politicizing. In the last three decades, the government bureaucracy has been target of politicization and subordination by politics. Professor Khanal puts it well: [2]

> In Nepal, politics has always restricted and has never been allowed to evolve through liberal political process into an autonomous responsible and responsive system capable of communicating with all elements of society and reconciling and resolving their varied interests. On the other hand, successive ill-tamperings have accentuated the autonomy and integrity of public administration not only to the loss of creative, as against servile, interaction but, what is not often realized, to the loss of the autonomy and integrity of the political process itself.

The Ranas used to appoint public officials in order to subordinate them to collect revenues and maintain law and order. There used to be an annual recruitment called *Pajani*. The appointments, transfers and promotions were held on the basis of loyalty, not performance. During Panchayat era, the state required the civil servants that they support the system and key appointments and transfers were based on the basis of commitment to the political ideology. Even with the advent of democracy, politicization of the bureaucracy has not abated. "Every successive government that has been formed after the restoration democracy has invariably wrought changes in the bureaucracy, .. appointing individuals with close affiliations with (the) party in power or its leaders", says Nepal Human Development Report (1998). People have blamed "*Congressization*" and *UMLization* of the public bureaucracy in different times. There have been instances of dismissals of several employees on the basis of their political alignment. Appointments, transfers and placements based on political affiliation is becoming the fact of bureaucratic life. There are allegations that people are frequently transferred on the basis of such alliances to political parties.

Such a politicizing and patronizing behavior has induced a lot of changes in the work ethic of the Nepalese civil servants. Association to a political party has started to become more important than performance and merit. The trend of politicizing has definitely put bureaucracy under the control of political authorities. But the

---

[2] Professor Y. N. Khanal in a paper (1995) entitled *"Politics and Administration in Nepal"*, presented at a seminar organized by the Public Administration Association of Nepal (PAAN)

bureaucracy has not ceased to become dysfunctional. Bureau-pathological symptoms are being strengthened. Corruption has been institutionalized and "rent-seeking behavior" is becoming common.

Unionism, a late comer in the Nepalese work environment, is posing a big menace to the work ethic. Though, the right to form associations has been regarded as the fundamental right of the workers guaranteed by the constitution and the law of the land, the practice of unionism in the government, public enterprises, and industries and in the service sector is greatly changing the work behavior of the Nepalese people. Strikes, lockout, picketing and "no-work" or "pen-down" moves have become increasingly common. Not only are the unions working as the wings of some political parties, there are greater political concerns than professional concerns in the activities of many public and private sector unions in the country. Membership of the associations has shielded many employees from being punished against the practices of corruption, under-work, and sometimes absence from the work. This, perhaps, has brought yet another decay in the work ethic.

Exit Of the Other Half

In 1983, Sonudevi Bonuin started pedaling a rickshaw between Birgunj and Raxaul, two border cities between Nepal and India. Raksha Rana became the first Nepalese woman to fly an aircraft as a pilot some years ago. In 1995, Usha Nepal became the first woman Chief District Officer and became the boss of the country's hot seat in Kathmandu district in 1997. Sumitra Dangal became the first woman to drive a commercial three-wheeler auto rickshaw in Kathmandu. Sahana Pradhan was the leader of United Left Front, which rallied with the Nepali Congress Party during the people's movement (1990) for establishing democracy and later became the President of her own party. In 1998, Shailaja Acharya became Nepal's first woman Deputy Prime Minister.

Sonudevi, Sumitra, Raksha, Usha, Sahana and Shailaja are not exceptions. Today, there are several women who are seen performing roles and jobs, which were traditionally under the domain of men. In a country where we continue to hear the stories of women being beaten to death for "not bringing enough dowry" or for supposedly practicing the secret art of the witchcraft, the exit of women from the traditional taboos and household has heralded an entirely a new culture shift.

Women have made a "spectacular entrance into the urban labor market" in Nepal, observed a researcher some years ago (Mercier, 1993). This notion was justified by the increasing number of working women in the service sector, especially in areas of teaching and health services. The proportion of women employed in professional and technical occupations almost tripled during the decade of 1981-1991 (Mercier, 1993). Today, the rise in the number of professional women is justified by their visible presence in various government jobs, professional associations and non-government organizations. Women in Science and Technology (WIST), one such association draws members from women in professions like teaching, government service, and private sector that have a direct involvement in science and technology. In the fields like forestry, engineering, topography, and wildlife management, where males had traditionally domain, women are making remarkable entry. In fields like biology, chemistry, environment science, laboratory techniques, and medicine, where women used to have some presence, their number is dramatically increasing. Similarly there are professions like banking, travel agencies, and hotels, in which women have constituted a significant proportion of the workforce. In Kathmandu's numerous carpet and garment factories, women constitute a significant proportion of the work force.

Among several indicators of the change, i.e. the entrance of women in non-traditional work force outside their homes, is the growing business of childcare. Even in families where women used to seek work outside their homes, there used to be some elder members of the family who used to spare some time to take care of the child. But with the breakdown of the extended family into nuclear units, there are hardly any people left at home to look after the young children until they start going schools. And the childcare and babysitting becomes a business.

Another indicator of the exit of the women from the domestic chores is the increasing number of women driving their own vehicles in Kathmandu. The number of women holding driving licenses is increasing. It is evident by increasing number of women applying for the permits. In Kathmandu's ring road, several young women are seen driving sedans with "L" sign posted at the vehicle. This proves that women are seeking exits from the domestic realm.

Entry of women into the work force has heralded several significant culture shifts, especially in the urban lifestyles of the people. There are traumas and stresses experienced by the family and children in particular. There are backlashes by male members of the family. In a time, where women are still being criminally assaulted and socially discriminated, the exit of females in economic and academic world outside the domestic boundaries is bound to exert several influences. Changing notion of discrimination against women, vociferous slogans for women's empowerment and their participation in development, and shifting concept of an ideal womanhood, are a few to name.

The exit of the "other halves" from the domestic domain to the mainstream society has not only changed the traditional status of women, it has also reversed the attitude of the society at large towards them. With the freedom of women from the domestic domain, most middle-class women, especially in Kathmandu, have been pressed with the need for creating "new public femininity", in which they continue to seek the "middle-class respectability" and preserve the "acceptable standards (usually double) of sexual propriety", concluded a researcher (Liechty, 1996).

With the changing party politics, emerging market economy, enlarging education opportunities, and fledgling consumer culture, the practices of Nepalese womanhood, which was in the form of a "domesticated femininity" has been recast in the new discourses of modernity, fashion, family and nation. It is especially so among the middle-class woman in Kathmandu, who are confronting the traditional social framework based on male domination or patriarchy (Lietchy, 1996).

At the same time, there is the increasing desire among the Nepalese men to search working mates, or women who are employed. This is not only associated with the benefit of the economic support of the working partner, it has also a lot to do with the emerging difference in the role of women in general in the Nepalese society. Today, a working woman enjoys more freedoms, and is respected in the family in the society at large than she was a few decades earlier.

The rhetoric of political freedom of women, especially after the democracy has not translated into the social freedom. The political dispensation has not liberated the social taboos against the women to a larger extent. Though women have started to celebrate their freedom in politics, in careers and in economy, they continue to struggle against the social taboos, that threatens them housebound and makes their exit a difficult endeavor. Women who have made exit from the domestic world into the public, have been exposed to continuous challenges and threats of sexual harassment and male backlashes.

Though the participation of women in the national development is still negligible, and a large number of female population in Nepal are still forced to follow the outdated, traditional chores (Shtri Shakti, 1995), women are no more confined to the domestic domains. In families, Women may still be continued to be kept aside from decision making, in which males only dominate. But efforts to bring women in the "mainstream" has begun to be a strong debate, not only in development slogans, but also in the political discourse.

Though Nepalese women continue to be marginalized in terms of literacy, education, job opportunities, legal rights and general control over their lives (Shtri Shakti, 1995), their voice has started to be heard. Recently in 1998, women in Kathmandu organized massive protests demanding equal rights in property and are trying to persuade bills that gives them equal property and representation rights as that of men. But at the same time, the "realities of expanded economic opportunities and a greater social mobility have resulted in greater social violence and the marginalization of women from the mainstream development benefits" (Shtri Shakti, 1995).

Even in the rural areas, women have "started to become more active and aware of their rights and are oriented towards self-reliance.", says Amrita Banskota[1]. "Their increasing activities in Forest Consumer Committees, anti-alcohol activities and participation in the livestock, agriculture, and skill development are on the rise. Women are increasingly getting more access to the money, to the power, and increasing role in the society". To a rural woman, the freedom may be liberation from the heavy labor, tyrannical mother-in-laws, control over their lives by male members, and freedom to interact openly with the males in the public. But to an urban woman establishing a public identity and being treated equal by men constitutes the "new public femininity" (Lietchy, 1996).

Today, the women have become the agents of cultural change in the Nepalese society. Though women are burdened by their exit from the domestic realm into the public life, they continue to be given the sole responsibility of maintaining the household things and giving continuity to the traditions. Women, who have achieved some degree of freedom from the domestic controls, have bee shouldering the responsibility of continuing the rituals and the traditions.

Access to education is considered yet another major freedom for women, both urban and rural, middle class and lower class. It is the education, which heralds entry into the public life and possibly a career outside home. Though the number of educated women has gradually increased in the past decade, even the economically secure highly educated women are still confined to conservatism and traditionalism (Shtri Shakti, 1995).

---

[1] Amrita Banskota in *Saptahik*, Kantipur Publications, January 16, 1998.

As new generation women start going to schools and colleges as a routine thing, not as a privilege enjoyed due to their family status or due to the generosity of their male guardians, they not only focus on traditional education. A host of other education and activities like music, sports, fashion and arts also become increasingly available to the Nepalese women.

But as they exit from the households to the public life via education, careers, labor, social service, Nepalese women continue to be haunted by the prestige of their femininity. Not that they are under pressure to be the quintessential Sati or Sita. But any deviation of the behavior in relation to the men, a small frankness, a more than introvert outspokenness, and a little outgoing nature becomes a gossip and women in public life constantly risk being ridiculed, joked and satired with questions on their integrity.

A DIFFERENT DISCRIMINATION

Discrimination against the Nepalese women[2] has been there for ages. There used to be taboos and restrictions against women. Women were so much dominated by the men that they were required to obey their husbands and male guardians in every aspect of their lives. Discrimination used to begin before birth. People often believed that a male child was mandatory in order to attain liberation from the ancestral obligation and life. Only after one had a male child to offer ancestral rites that one could take a breath of sigh. People used to keep trying for more children until there was a male child. Birth of a woman child used to be sometimes mourned whereas that of a male child celebrated.

A girl child was rarely sent to a formal institution for education.[3] At home, she used to be taught to be modest, polite, non-demanding

---

[2] I would like caution the readers that a generalization of the Nepalese women is not possible because of a huge diversity among them in view of the differences in their economic status and practices of various ethnic groups. Hence, the term Nepalese women should be taken in the relative context.

[3] By a strange irony, the Nepalese families, who worshipped a female goddess Saraswoti as the divinity of wisdom and learning, did not give adequate emphasis on the education of women and gave priority for the education of their male children.

and obeying men's and elder's orders. She was taught to learn the skills required to become a household woman. She was supposed to take care of her younger brothers and sisters and to help her mother and sisters. She was asked to bring water, get grass and fodder and look after the cattle. Her duties included sweeping floors, fetching water, cleaning household pots, cooking little things. Despite all the skills she might have learnt, a young woman in her parent's home was considered a liability. Investment in a woman child used not to be considered wise and was given far less importance than that for a male child.

The physical and strategic needs of the women were discouraged or ignored. Women were considered and accepted for their ability to work long hours. Works of little value and less importance were assigned to women, whereas men performed those with more value and importance. A woman's place used to be inside the house and in the interior or internal activities. Women were hardly and rarely involved in major decision making and were always outside the mainstream of the family decisions.

Though women were considered as one of the two wheels of a chariot of human life, they were represented as a weaker wheel. Except in some communities, women in Nepal had weaker positions in the society. They enjoyed lesser physical freedoms and less equal property rights. Women were subjects of amusement and commodity for men's pleasure. They were given decorative roles. They were supposed to be beautiful and they were brought in for making things more beautiful. Many macho men took pride in marrying as many women as they could. They could remarry or abandon women. In some communities, women used to be the mere machines for delivering a man's child.

Such a notion about women is gradually changing. Today, many parents in the urban areas have started to impart skills to their daughter that will make them confident and self-standing. Even in the rural areas, increasingly large number of people have started to send their girl child to schools treating their daughters not different from their sons. Increasingly a large number of people have started to realize that children are the same despite of the sex and parental obligations regarding them.

Although the gender roles are gradually changing, discrimination still persists. People have started to realize that there is a lot of discrimination against women. With the rise in the number of working women, change of traditional housekeeping roles of the women, and gradual changes in marriage and child rearing ethics, discrimination against women is gradually being attacked and deplored.

BEAUTIFYING BUSINESS

At work places, where there are only a few women, they are under constant pressure to look beautiful. Dark skin is still identified with the toil and sweat of hard labor in the fields, while fair skin is associated with a gentle upscale lifestyle and a sign of beauty. It is with this notion that the "fairness creams" and brands of skin whitening soaps, lotions, and powders are sold with a lot of enthusiasm. Culturally, the fair skin is related to the positive values of womanhood of the high class. Some people think it is difficult to marry off a dark complexioned daughter. The fair skin is so much associated with the concept of beauty in the Nepalese culture that people wish to describe their color of skin as "wheatish", even though many have relatively darker skins.

There has been a visible rise in the number of "beauty parlors" in Kathmandu valley. One can see a beauty parlor at every major street. This may sound opposite to women's liberation. But, the liberation from home does not totally signal liberation at work place. There is still a strong force of domination and discrimination against women at the work place. They are still under much pressure to be good looking. Furthermore, the working women have better access to extra money, which they can use to beautify themselves. Women's exit into the workforce has also influenced their dress codes. Though most working Nepalese women still prefer to wear traditional Saree, many women have been attracted to the silk coats and mini-skirts and other working women's attires from the West.

Today, discrimination continues in a different manner. At the first place, many Nepalese today, do not keep trying to get more children hoping to get a son, especially if they already have three or four daughters. The birth of a female child may not be celebrated as joyously as that of a male child. But it is not mourned either. Today, even in the rural areas, the parents send their daughters to the schools, though the enrollment ratio is lower and drop-out rate is higher for the girls than for the boys. There is an increasing awareness that girl child should also get access to education, though the priority may not the same as that given to the male child. The traditional notion of discrimination is changing at least at the attitudinal level. For example, a survey conducted by Media Service International in 1999 said 90% Nepalese people want the daughters to be given the equal rights as that of the sons and 64 % favored equal parental property rights between male and female children.

Women have come out of seclusion, though they have not found adequate decision-making roles in the society. The increasing number of women's groups such as mother's groups, credit groups etc., even in the rural villages, justify this.

In many urban work places, women may have found some employment. But they are mainly employed in service sectors, where "women's service" counts most. The service industry like travel trade and hotels still "require much the beauty of the woman than their competence". Therefore most of the Nepalese women employed outside their home are still confined to the so-called "pink-colored jobs", such as the receptionists, hostesses and clerks. Wherever they are employed or wherever they go, the women are continuously harassed by men. Young men tease young women in colleges, classrooms, cafeteria, public transports, and even in temples. Women find it difficult to go around single, especially at night. The women's exit to the outside world is still full of threats, hassles and struggles.

THE INFAMOUS EXODUS

Though the exit of women from the domain of the households may have heralded a new ear of consciousness and empowerment of mown, some of such exits have becoming derogatory to the Nepalese women, and is unsuitable to the Nepalese society altogether. Whether it is the fashion parades, dancing restaurants, massage parlors, or uncanny brothels at home and abroad, Nepalese women are being constantly exploited. In the fashion and glamour world, the exploitation may be subtle. But in the brothels and sex industry, the exploitation is not only derogatory and demeaning to the Nepalese women, it is also tearing the fabric of the society as a whole.

Though they call it "beauty pageant", some blame it as an "ugly game". There is a debate, whether there should be fashion parades, which continuously expose women. Though some young women are enthusiastic about it because the fashion parades give them an "opportunity to develop their personality", there are others who oppose "commercialization" and "exploitation" of women's physical attributes. While the so-called judges sit and watch the half-dressed young women of their photogenic capability, their etiquette, their physical and "mental" capabilities, the protesters carry banners outside only to be marauded by the police. Despite the protests, the programs go with a lot of fanfare, enthusiasm and campaigning. Some NGO workers and social activists protest against such pageants and fashion shows here and there. But the shows under the banners of like "Miss Nepal", "Miss World Nepal" etc continues. In weeks following the crowning of the "beauty queen", the local newspapers and television are flooded with advertisements congratulating the young woman and carrying advertisements with her pictures identifies with some commercial products.

Nepalese culture does not permit the idea of contesting the women in terms of their physical or even "mental beauty". Neither the Nepalese aesthetic values accept the commercialization of woman's physical attributes. But ironically, the imported concept of beauty pageant is liked by increasing number of young people in Kathmandu. It is justified by the fact that these beauty pageants and fashion parades are crowded with viewers and sponsors, who pay hefty charges for each show. Today, the commercialization of women is not just confined to fashion and beauty pageants. Several young girls are being allured to the world of music, modeling, and the show biz with all the glamour and glitter, which greatly ignore the Nepalese cultural values and norms. "Invaded by an open sky and inundated by regular fashion shows", the teenagers have been pushing towards a headlong plunge to become models. Women have been increasingly used as "tools" for commercial advertisements. Even the indigenous Nepalese movie industry exploits the Nepalese women's physical attributes and hardly promotes their talents. This type of "objectification" of women has turned into an ugly game.

"Provocative dress-ups, and practice of alien culture and styles including the music, dance and songs during the shows threaten the teenagers' vulnerability and ultimately the nation's culture and tradition" warns a feature article. [4]

These slimy women who wear the latest and pass the stage doing "catwalk" don't know how much negative signals they are sending to the youngsters in the Nepalese society. They hardly realize they are doing something, which is not best suited to their tradition and culture. And the frenzy continues. Looking at the beauty pageant, fashion shows, increasing body exposure of women in the Nepalese movies, and even in dance restaurants, it is becoming difficult to ascertain, whether it is the liberation or exploitation of the women, which is becoming common.

Yet another exit of Nepalese women from their traditional domain is more disgusting and demeaning their human values. On February 5, 1996, Bombay police, acting on the instructions of the Bombay High Court, raided city's several brothels and rounded up 456 sex workers, among them 218 Nepali women, and asked them to leave the city. Many of them obeyed the order.

They are not the only Nepalese women who are indulged in the undignified profession. Several young and innocent Nepalese women are brought to brothels in India's Bombay and other cities, by brokers who sell them to the owners of the brothels at hefty prices. Girls from district near Kathmandu are forcibly trafficked to various brothels.

Though there is a history of the communities like the *Deuki, Badi* and *Devadashi* from Western Nepal engaging in prostitution, the cross-border trafficking of girls from Nepal is a relatively new practice. Poverty, lack of employment opportunities, low social status of the girl child, a general lack of education and awareness, and open border with India, lax laws and weak law enforcement machinery are the major causes of this social menace, says Aburadha Koirala of *Maiti Nepal,* which runs a rehabilitation center for women freed from brothels (Koirala, 1998).

Though prostitution is usually a taboo and people in general have strongly negative attitude towards it except is in some localities, the exodus to the red light brothels is becoming a more than infamous. In Bombay's red-light district, many young women

---

[4] Khadka, *Spotlight*, Feb 13, 1997.

smuggled from the rural villages of Nepal are kept captive in the brothels so that their flesh can be sold to the woman-hungry men. The number is unknown. Hundreds are salvaged from their captors and brought back to Nepal by some activists. But many are forced to remain there.

THE ATTENDANTS OF GODS

They are supposed to remain celibate. They are supposed to spend their lives in the temples they are dedicated to. Known popularly as *Deuki*, they are women offered to religious shrines as attendants of gods and goddesses. Famous in far-western Nepal, the custom of offering women as devotees and attendants of gods and goddesses is said to have been introduced in about 14th century AD by a *Khas* king. Gradually, *Deukis* were accepted as prostitutes and their children were bought by people, who offered them to the religious shrines. Melauli, a rural village, in Baitadi district, far western Nepal, known as the home of several *Deukis*, who have settled there, used to be infamous for prostitution. But, these days, *Deukis* are spending normal lives there. There are projects for education of the children of *Deukis*. Commonly accepted and practiced in far western Nepal until a decade ago, today, this custom is on the decline. Yet, there have been reports of incidences, in which young women have been forcibly offered to the temples. In certain cases, it is kept secret and unreported, until the offered woman starts going to the temple. This custom of offering of young women (sometimes one's own children and sometimes bought from others) to the temples in order to pacify certain deities and to fulfill their wishes, especially to get an offspring, has been grossly rejected by law and customs. Though many *Deukis* remain unmarried, they have given birth to children. Several such children are a part of the social problem in the far western Nepal. Several *Deukis* are not getting married. In the temples, where *Deukis* offered (*Melauli, Tripura Sundari, Nigala Saini, Ugratara, Badala Saini, Popla Saini* etc), such a tradition still exits. But it has been started to be deplored and something not desirable in the society.

There are villages in Nuwakot and Sindhupalchok districts, hardly 150 km away from Kathmandu, where young women are being trafficked to brothels in Bombay and other places. Gangs of brokers involved in this trade are active in these regions. In some places, even the parents sell their daughters for a small amount of money, some newspapers have reported.

Poverty has been described as a strong factor driving women into sex trade. The other reasons like gender inequality, increased aspiration for living standards, and lack of education, absence of alternative employment opportunities cannot be ruled out.

Many such women who have returned from Bombay and other places have been found infested with AIDS and other sexually transmitted diseases. Some NGO groups have been active raising awareness. But these have been grossly ineffective in the light of the gravity of the problem. This social crime is not on the declining trend. And the infamous exit continues.

A DIFFERENT IDEAL WOMAN

Sarita and Manju go out for morning walk almost every day. They wear expensive jogging suits and sports shoes imported from abroad. Going for jogging wearing dresses not traditionally identified with Nepalese women, they are explicitly showing that they are liberated from domestic control of their male members in the family without any inhibition in the kind of dress they are wearing. They are also identifying themselves in male lifestyles.

They may not be representing the majority of the Nepalese women. But they represent the want-to-bes and are being seen as ideal womanhood, who are liberated from the domestic domain and exhibiting male lifestyles. The number of these women, who are not housebound, seems to be increasing in the overwhelming exit of the women from the traditional chores.

In Hindu religious thought, women were supposed to be like Sita, Sati and Savitri. This implied, they had to be devout to their husbands. Women were supposed to worship their husbands as *Patidev*, their god. In some traditional families, women were supposed to take a sip of water from the washed toes of their husbands. They had to bow down to their husbands' feet and obey their orders like anything.

This notion is being greatly challenged, especially in the urban areas and in most rural areas. Women are no more supposed to be worshipping their husbands. Although domination of women by men exists in one form or another, the concept of Patidev is gradually declining. Except for festive occasions like *Teej,* very rarely do Nepalese women think of worshipping their husbands. That too exists very much in a fashion, copied under social pressure, not as a value system.

The traditional notions of ideal womanhood such as that of Sita of the Ramayana era, who left the luxuries and accompanied her husband to the forest to adjust to the hardships, are still cited in conversations and in the write-ups. That ideal and sanctitious image of woman, totally devoted to her husband as a *Sati-Sabitri,*[5] is gradually abandoned as an ideal womanhood in Nepal.

In traditional concept, there were thirty-two characteristics (*Battis Lakshan*) required to be identified as an ideal woman. Though that was the men's definition and most of those characteristics were realted to physical attributes, which are derogatory to women, traditional Nepalese women were in constant pressure to be seen as an ideal one based on those traditional concept of thirty-two characteristics. Today, the significance of these characteristics has been forgotten. In fact, hardly anyone knows what these characteristics are. Today the ideal womanhood is not determined by these physical attributes, but by their characters. A ideal Nepalese woman today is the one who is mostly quiet, who works a lot, remains active in household jobs, is less outgoing, and accepts things imposed by men.

The ideal Nepalese woman is not a social goddess, who is the replica of the womanhood of the Ramayan era Sita. While the media and advertisements project Nepalese women as slim and beautiful creatures nicely dolled up in designer garments, and glittering ornaments, the average Nepali woman remains poverty-stricken, over-worked, illiterate, malnourished, and the least powerful person in the society and even in the family. Ironically, the image of womanhood that was carefully molded to meet the needs of men is

---

[5] In Hindu mythology, there were other ideal women like Ahilya, Draupadi, Tara and Mandodari. Though each of these women was identified with some blemish, their devotion to their husbands was not questionable. Ahilya was seduced by disguised Lord Indra. Tara was abducted by the Moon. Draupadi was married to five men. Even Sita was once abducted by her husband's enemy Ravana. But they were still regarded as great women for their devotion to their husbands.

not changing to a large extent. Those timid figures tangled in gold, wearing pinkish or red garments desired by every men continue to be the ideal woman despite the exit of the Nepalese woman from the households.

But the role model for many young Nepalese women are increasingly known to be the artists from the movie, fashion and music world, not from mythology and history. Today actresses in Hindi films, not Hindu goddesses of ideal womanhood, are considered ideal and aspired as role models. Though the ribbon of social approval still defines the Nepalese womanhood, young Nepalese women are increasingly allured in beautifying themselves focusing on their physical attributes. They are under constant pressure to balance the between society's demand to possess a good moral "character" (read sexual propriety) and need to look attractive and beautiful.

Today, the Nepalese woman still lives in the mercy of men, her husband, father or a male guardian. She learns the tenets of the ideal womanhood for her male benefactor. She socializes into the "dos" and "don'ts" defined by men. Do not go out at night. Always sit behind in the discussions. Eat your meal after the male members have finished and many more. Traditionally, women used to enjoy a lot of respect in the Nepalese society. The father and the brothers used to bow down to her legs. In every religious or cultural rite, the young woman used to be given Tika and a small amount of money as *Dakshina*. A woman was labeled as Laxmi (the Goddess of Wealth) and men often used to take pride saying their wives as *Griha Laxmi* (the goddess of wealth of the house). *Yatra Naryastu Pujyante, Ramante Tatra Devata'* (where a woman is worshipped, gods will be pleased) used to be a popular saying quoted from *Manusmriti*, which suggests women in the society were venerable and respected.

But as women became weak economically, socially, even politically, discriminatory rules and traditions appeared gradually. Most women were taught to accept their fate. *Chhoriko Janma Hareko Karma* (the life of a woman is a lost fate) was proverbial saying accepted by many women. Therefore, women hardly tried to break the rules and came out to fight for the inequalities and the injustice against them. Discrimination was rationalized by men and accepted by women. Today, such rationalization and acceptance is being reversed. Women have started to think of equality and liberation.

Women's organizations are emerging and are demanding their empowerment.

In the recent decade, with the vociferous slogan of "women in development", the participation of women into the mainstay of the society and "gender sensitization" have been common vocabulary. There are programs like women's credit, women's entrepreneurial training, and women's education. This has started to increase awareness at least among the urban and educated women and, to some extent, among the rural women. Concerns have been started to be raised against such discriminatory pieces of legislation and customs.

After the restoration of democracy in 1991, the new political dispensation has guaranteed equal rights to the women as it does to the women. At least, the words and the spirit of the constitution says so. The political change has also liberated the dormant energy of the Nepalese women and the women have started to be more active demanding more political freedoms. Women's rights activists have been able to attract a lot of public attention, debate and discussions. The greatest achievement "with regard to women's advancement has been in the area of conceitization" and a large number of women have become "alert to the issues of inequality, social injustice, and gender discrimination" (Tuladhar, 1996). There have been initiatives to amend the provisions in the New Civil Code and other legislation, which are discriminatory against the women. Women's rights and upliftment have started to become a political movement. Though the poor representation of women in positions of authority and inadequate control of women over property and resources have posed formidable challenge in eliminating various forms of gender discrimination prevailing in the society (Tuladhar, 1996), voices are being heard against such discriminations.

The government has started to commit itself to the cause of advancing the status of women in Nepal. Women's rights, concerns and activities are supposed to an integral part of the planning and policy framework. It has been pledged that all laws, which were infringing upon the equal rights of men and women, would be amended and provisions relating to violence against women would be enforced. It has also been pledged in the international conferences (HMGN, 1995) that all development programs would be implemented in gender perspectives.

Explicit plan and policy commitments have appeared in consecutive plan documents. Among other things, the ostensible Eighth Plan (1992-97) had pledged to enhance women's participation through training, employment opportunities and credit facilities, and to set up an organization structure to implement the women development related programs. Today, there are programs, which provide women production credit and micro-credits, teach, train and give them self-employment. A separate Ministry for Women's Development and Welfare has been set up. It is debatable whether the status of women has changed due to these. But it has reassigned the role to the Nepalese women in the social as well as economic perspectives. Voices of women, who remained marginalized in the society, have started to be heard.

Studies have shown that the Nepalese women have attained higher literacy, greater social mobility, and an increased awareness in the last decade (Shtri Shakti, 1995). But many are still confined to the traditional household roles, which gives them "lower status and subordination to men within the patriarchal socio-cultural, economic, legal and political frameworks". The demand for outlawing of the pieces of legislation that contradicted the property rights of women tells that women's importance is being ascertained. Issues like property rights, the rights to marriage and crimes related to sex are openly discussed. Although such concerns are limited to the conference rooms and some tabloids, it will take not too long before this has taken the shape of a political movement. Some women activists have started to organize demonstrations and rallies for their causes. The lost fate is being regained.

Women have become more assertive. Thanks to economic independence and education and political awareness. But their assertion of right and freedom has become source of conflict in the family. This has become a potential factor for de-destabilization of the traditional equilibrium in the family in one hand and source of social conflict at the other. As women have changed and men not, the latter are finding it difficult to cope with the emerging realities. In this battle, the Nepalese women are slowly shredding the chorus of tradition and culture. In their pursuit of equality and access to modernity, the Nepalese women are becoming the agents of the culture change in the society.

The Religious *Laissez Faire*

The robust image near *Pashupatinath*, the holiest Hindu shrine in Kathmandu, may not be emerging as it is supposed or believed to be by many Hindus. But the epoch of evil, which this half-submerged image of *Birupaksha* is signifying, seems to be coming out and reaching its peak Nepal. The present epoch, known by Hindus as *Kaliyuga*, is supposed to be marked with the rise of evil and victory of evil over the truth. *Kalki*, the tenth incarnation of Vishnu, is said to be heralding the growth of the epoch of evil. An increasing rate of crime and corruption, deteriorating moral fiber, growth of materialistic pursuit, and the neglect of the spiritual values of the past are in fact already signaling the epoch of evil has been approaching its peak. The staunch belief that the truth will eventually triumph over the evil has started to shake. And many people have started to accept the emergence of "*Kaliyuga*" as a fact of life. This has not only made easier for people to accept the increasing level of immorality in the society, it has also allowed people to rationalize crime and unethical things. Such a rationalization has creeping effect on people's belief in the religion and culture.

Most Nepalese people used to be very rigid in the religious codes of conduct. There used to be strict adherence, taboos and practices attached to religion. Religion used to guide the way of life of the most Nepalese people. People used to go on pilgrimages, perform regular worships and observe religious codes of conduct. But an increasing *laissez faire* attitude, in which religion is left to be shaped by the invisible hand of a callous populace, is bringing a great deal of dynamism in the culture of the Nepalese people. People's attitude towards religion in general is changing dramatically. Increasingly a large number of Nepalese people have accepted changes in the religious practices as a normal course. While religious merit is being forgotten due to increasing pressures of day-to-day problems, enthusiasm associated with the pilgrimage, worships, and festivities is decreasing. Though the religious faith is still there, the aim is to fulfil self-centered desires and absolve oneself from the sins of day to day lives, not the ultimate liberation from the worldly things, as it used to be earlier.

People's participation in institutions and practices established over centuries by religious usage has been declining. There seems to a dilemma over which traditional values should be continued and which rejected. Religious anarchy is on the rise and people have started to accept distortions in the religious practices in the name of modernization.

While the religion of the ethnic groups face distortion and decline, even the mainstream Hinduism is being seen in peril. Increasingly, people's desire for liberation is not being achieved through religions (e.g. *Moksha* or *Nirvana*), but through hedonistic and materialistic pursuits, while the religion is left to the domain of the old, conservative and orthodox few.

THE SMALLER GOD IS THE LOSER

If anything is becoming obvious in the culture shift era, especially in the domain of religion, it is the loss of tribal and ethnic religions. Whereas many of the ethnic minorities used to practice their religions such as *Bonpo*, animism, shamanism and nature worship, their religion has witnessed transformation mainly towards adoption of Hindu way of life and generally towards the abandoning religious faith altogether, which is being discerned all over the country.

There has been a very fast change of various indigenous and tribal people along the lines of Hindu way of life and religion. "The increasing incidence of *Hinduization* that are evident among the tribal and other non-Hindu groups have followed fast upon the improvements in transportation and communication facilities" (Baral & Baral in Toffin, 1993. p. 12). Hinduism being the mainstream religion and basis of culture for many people, several ethnic groups had opted for the religion in order to be assimilated into the mainstream society, thereby abandoning their own culture and sometimes their own religion over a long period of time. The indoctrination of non-Hindus along Hinduism is also manifested at political level. This is well evident as Hinduism has been adopted as the state religion of Nepal, despite the existence of many non-Hindu ethnic and religious groups of people in the country.

Sanskritization, i.e. a process of "assimilating 'low' Hindu castes and tribal groups into the traditions of 'higher caste' making them acquire some of the accepted norms of Hindu culture and religion", has initiated a "scope for social, political and economic mobility within the caste hierarchy" (Sharma, 1973, p. 73). It involves the observance of the basic Hindu rules and rituals relating to the birth, marriage and death and the acceptance of Brahmin priests and dietary restrictions. As a "dynamic cultural force", *Sanskritization* had been brought by medieval rulers of Nepal, who included immigrant Hindus afraid of Muslim invasions like in India in the 18th century. *Hinduization* has been speedy in communities where contacts are more frequent. For example, several *Magar* people have adopted Brahman priests and observe several Hindu festivals.

There have been instances of such upgrading to `higher castes'. Some Magars in Central Nepal (such *as Bhujel, Budhathoki, Thapa, Gharti* and *Rana*) and *Matwali Chhetris* in western Nepal may have been initiated into the `higher' culture of the upper caste. Such a preference to adopt "higher castes" has been observed among Thakalis, who put *Chan*, a Thakuri surname as suffix to their surnames (like *Shercahn, Gauchan, Hirachan, Bhattachan*). In the Terai, the `lower occupational castes' such as Teli (the oil crusher), Kalwars (liquor dealers) have adopted family titles of Shah, which is a Thakuri surname. Although *Sanskritization* "gradually paved the way for the unification of social, political and economic norms, and harmonized behavior and value-systems bringing rationalized interaction between various groups of people", people were pursued to adopt new cultures and abandon their original customs. It has put tremendous psychological pressure among people of the non-Sanskritized castes.

Influences have occurred from different ethnic and religious contacts. Gurung (1993) has identified the influence of Lamaistic Buddhism and Hinduism on traditional Gurung culture of Gandaki region. Several Gurungs in Gandaki region practice Lama priests. The traditional Gurung priests "adopted the idea of the five celestial Buddhas of *Vajrayana* in their religion and honored *Padma Sambhavas*, their spiritual teacher" (Gurung in Toffin, 1993, p. 135). Gurung further adds:

> "It was compulsory for them to follow the Hindu rules. So they adopted Hindu manners and customs to gain favor of the Hindu kings. These rulers also had their own interest to keep control over the Gurungs. They appointed to become *umara* and *talukdar* those Gurungs who adopted the Hindu rules. The *umara*, the chief of a fort, and *talukdar*, an authorized landholder of a jurisdiction, were the local

agents of the Hindu monarch. The *umara* and *talukdar* came into contact with Hindu priest who performed the state rituals like Dasain at the fort."

Decay and degeneration of religious authority is also seen among the Sherpas. Katia Buffertrile (in Toffin, 1993) spoke of degeneration of the power and status of the Lamas in a study on Sherpa village. "It was a time when Lamas were very powerful: they could speak with divinities, fly in the air and go underground. Nothing was impossible for those who had the appropriate powers. This time has passed. We are now in an era of degeneration. The power of practitioners is no more what it used to be." One may tend to suggest that if people with different religion and culture had met each other, there must have been influences upon each. Though there is also some evidence of "higher caste" adopting "lower caste" customs,[1] it is the smaller god, who is usually the looser. Though "*Sanskritization* is unlikely to exert influence in Nepal in the future and its place is likely to be taken by *Westernization* or modernization" (Sharma, 1977), the loss of ethnic religions, is all but likely to continue. "It is the small good who is the looser", says Ramble (1997) suggesting the ethnic culture and religions will loose their hold first.

Even Buddhism, which is observed by a sizeable population in Nepal, has seen deterioration in Nepal, the land of the birth of its founder Buddha. Though Buddhism is gaining prominence in other parts of the world as a more rational religion, it has not flourished in Nepal. Buddhism, "which has been acclaimed as the highest expression of Asiatic humanity, which spread throughout the countries of the south and far east Asia, refining art and literature, wiping out misunderstanding and prejudice, shattering the bond of caste and promising peace and redemption for all, the religion which led primitive society to the dawn of civilization, lost out completely in the land of its birth", writes Gnoli (quoted in Bista, 1991, p. 22).

Though there have been initiatives to develop Lumbini, the birth- place of Buddha, as an international pilgrimage centre for Buddhists, Kapilvastu, which was the center of Buddhist genesis, now remains in ruins. Very rarely people observing Buddhism live in

---

[1] Marie Lecomte (in Toffin, 1990) observed that Brahmins and Chhetris ("*Parbate*") of Gulmi district Central Nepal have adopted the *Magar Bhume* cult, i.e. the worship of the spirit of the land.

that area. Kapilvastu municipality (earlier Taulihawa) is mostly inhabited by Moslems and Guptas who have arrived from northern India. It is difficult to believe Kapilvastu was once the center of Buddhist Shakya rule.

Today Nepalese will have to go to Japan, Thailand or Sri Lanka to study the tenets of Buddhism. There is not even one Buddhist university in Nepal. In history, there were onslaughts against Buddhism. For example, the arrival of Hindu guru Shankaracharya was especially detrimental to the then flourishing Buddhism in Nepal. Today, the state support to Buddhism is no less different from that to Hinduism, except that the latter is recognized as a state religion. In fact, the institutions like the monarchy lends almost equal support to Hinduism and Buddhism. But despite all that, Buddhism is a yet another looser in the ensuing decay of all the religions, particularly that observed by the minority communities in the country.

HINDUISM IN PERIL

It may not sound quite convincing that Hinduism is in peril in Nepal, the world's only Hindu kingdom, whereas a resurgence of the religion is being witnessed in her relatively "secular" neighbor. But Hinduism in Nepal is seeing atrophy for a number of reasons. It is not only the influences of other religions, a callous attitude towards the religion in general is also causing the decline. Though some ethnic religions are being swallowed into the mainstream society of the Brahmans, Hinduism itself is in peril due to *laissiz faire* attitude of the people and degeneration of state patronage for the same. People can still be a Hindu without performing rituals and practicing the worship and religious conduct. Even if one does not worship Ram, Shiva and Vishnu, or does not recite a sacred text like Ramayana, Mahabharata, Upanishads and Vedas, does not consider cow as a sacred animal, does not wear a *chandan* or ash on his or her forehead, never wears a saffron robe, neither takes a dip in "holy waters" of Bagmati and the Ganges, and never goes to a pilgrimage center except occasionally and casually, one can still continue to be a Hindu. It is not the belief in "ouhm", or "rebirth" that makes a person Hindu. One's birth identifies one's religion. This kind of lax attitude in the practice of Hinduism, relaxation to conformity of the rituals, and flexibility of the codes of conduct has diverted people from the religion altogether and they are enjoying the freedom not only in the sense of religious freedom but also freedom from the religion, literally.

The Hindu civilization may not be declining as a whole. But the moral vigor and intellectual debate that is required for the sustenance of a religion is obviously lacking among the Nepalese Hindus. Neither is the political awakening of Hinduism, as in the case of adjoining India, taking a visible shape of a movement of sorts. As religion is not a strong political parameter in Nepal, people don't debate religious sentiments on "secular" or "communal" terms of politics. In other words, Nepal does not have to debate whether a state should be made secular.

The framers of new democratic constitution (1990) of Nepal had no intention to make Nepal a theocratic state. Therefore, a Hindu secular state, where Hinduism is the state religion with freedom to all religious practices and faiths, was adopted probably to preserve the cultural and religious identity of the country. Hinduism "so boldly inserted in the Constitution of Nepal (1990) is elusive at best for it is impossible to delineate the Hindu character of Nepal, aside from the fact that an overwhelming majority of the population happens to be 'Hindu' in the loose sense of the term", writers Sharma (1996). Though the consecutive constitutions have declared Nepal as a Hindu state, that has been adopted as a "window-dressing, retained for political reasons" (Sharma, 1996). Neither is the state governed in accordance with *Dharmashashtras,* nor is the most distinctive aspect of Hinduism, caste system, practised in the codes of laws. In fact, the New Civil Code (1963) has banned all the caste system. Hinduism in the state is retained by a "ban on cow slaughter, sponsored broadcasts of religious programs in the state radio and television, declaring a few Hindu festivals as national holidays and clamping down on proselytisation (Sharma, *ibid.,* p. 24). The state is not highly committal to the promotion of Hinduism as a religion. Even the constitutional status of the Hindu state seems to have been left untouched more for reasons of historical continuity than to make Nepal resemble, however remotely, a theocratic state (Acharya, 1993 in Sharma, 1997).

Hinduism as a philosophy and a way of life is fine, but its rituals and taboos are all to difficult to practice to the most Nepalese, especially the emerging rich and middle class, who are more than enthusiastic to break the rules of tradition to be abreast with the modernity. "If the philosophical aspects of Hinduism are bewildering, its day-to-day ritualistic practices are far more confusing with as many contradictory customs as one cares to ask for", writes Gyawali in *Himal* (May 1996). Such rituals are "crying for rationalization and re-interpretation", which is "felt more strongly by the urbanized Hindu middle class whose secular scientific exposure is the most effacious and ambit of interaction with the traditional "outside" is increasing day to day" (Gyawali, *ibid.*, 1996).

And above all, the education we impart to our children is conspicuously devoid of any philosophical, spiritual, moral and even factual element of Hinduism. Today, in most urban areas and small towns, Nepalese youths go to private boarding schools, which preach English as a sanctitious language and look down upon the Sanskrit language and prohibit students from speaking their own mother tongue Nepali. It is hardly convincing to suggest that they induce elements of the merits of traditional learning, let alone introduce curricula, which teaches their pupils the merits of Hinduism as a religion.

Dismayed by the lack of interpretation of rationality and bewildered by too many modern developments in their lives, many youngsters in urban Nepal today consider Hinduism "nothing more than family history and boring rituals", writes a Peace Corps Volunteer[2] from a short experience in Nepal. "Temples have become tourist attraction, the epics soap operas for television and religious festivals a time to stay home and watch television".

Further, Hinduism is a very liberal and accommodating religion. There is no strict adherence required for each Hindu person. There is no organized religious institution like a church. Gods are plural and plenty. No one paramount deity exists. There is no single most important religious text to adhere to. Neither there is an unified code of moral law or manual that could be prescribed. *Dahrma Shashtra*s are numerous and give rooms for various interpretations. Such a liberal *dharma* can only survive by inner motivation and commitment of the people, which is seems to be faltering, in any case.

---

[2] Eckerd, Stephan Truax (1996), Is it Enough to be Born Hindu? *Himal*, Vol. 9, No. 3, May 1996.

Perhaps, Hinduism is too big a way of life to be practiced. There are more than 330 million deities. Shines worship are numerous and aplenty adding to a confusion where to go for worship. Caste system, for example, could have been perfectly all right in the 1st century AD, when *Manusmriti* was encoded, but hardly relevant in the beginning of the twentieth century. In fact, the caste system is the single most important factor that gives Hinduism a bad name. This is not only responsible for creating fragmentation in the society, the practices such as untouchability, feelings of higher and lower hierarchy has become a cancer of the Hindu society, writes Ramesh Bikal[3].

Ramesh Bikal also blames the individualistic and self-centered interpretation of Hinduism as one of the factors for pushing Hindu society to a difficulty situation. For a religion, which advocates *basudhaiva kutumakam* (let there be goodwill and understanding in the whole earth and humanity), and which teaches *tamashoma jyotirgamaya* (let there be light in the darkness everywhere), the self-centered desire for performing rituals for achieving the divine blessings has been leading to a narrow interpretation.

In the history, there were resistance and efforts to escape from the Hindu rigidity. Perhaps Buddha, Mahavira and Nanak, who founded their own religions later recognized by Hindus as off-shots of Hinduism, represented such resistance or efforts to liberalize Hinduism. But the modern rational Nepalese, as most other Hindus, do not make genuine effort to liberalize the rules, they simply break it, *albeit* at personal and subtle level. Perhaps this is the strongest blow to Hinduism, as may be true with other religions as well.

There is an ongoing shift, even at the personal attitude level. There used to be an attitude *of "Swadharma Nidhanam Shreyam Paradharmo Bhayabaha"* (better die in one's own religion than face danger in other). But such an attitude has now a little bit relaxed. In fact, some modernists regard observance of the religious code of conduct as something of being backward and becoming unable to adjust with the changes demanded by time.

Another reason of the steady decline in Hinduism, as said by a noted Hindu speaker Khemraj Keshav Sharan, is that it has sealed off intakes with strict codes. Though, by definition, one could become Hindu believing in the power of *"ouhm"*, worshipping the

---

[3] *Gorkhapatra*, Saturday Kartik 19, 2057 BS (2000).

sacred cow, and believing in rebirth, lack of norms for people to enter into this religion through formal channels like conversion, is making new intakes sealed off.

Yet another factor responsible for the decline of Hinduism is increasing disinterest in its study. The study of Vedanta is considered something of the past. Sanskrit language, the repository of Hinduism, is hardly studied and taught, save in some government schools. Much of the Hindu corpus of literature is still confined to Sanskrit, which is highly incomprehensible to those who have no formal education in the language. Though the literature is now being made available in English, the coverage in Nepali and other native languages is almost lacking.

Though millions of Nepalese people watch each and every episode of cine version Hindu epic Ramayana and Mahabharata enthusiastically and crowd some temples in Kathmandu on holidays and some festivals, they don't focus on the merit of Hinduism. They simply enjoy the religious soap operas for their drama and glamour and go to the temples as pastime and to absolve their misdeeds.

Besides, like most other world religions, Hinduism is a divided house. There are several small sects faiths and cults. But Hinduism lacks a dominant cult or faith. Some observe Shaivism, worship of Lord Shiva, the famous destroyer God. There are several devotees of the Vaisnavism, veneration of Lord Vishnu and his famous ten incarnations. Yet another is the cult of Shakti, in which people propitiate, worship and offer animal sacrifices to the blood-thirsty goddesses under various names. Thus Hinduism in Nepal is a diffused religion with no central organization or structure that can accommodate all these sects into one.

Further, in a democracy, the dynamics of the interest groups and minorities often diffuse and erode the structures and institutions of a majority, which is being witnessed in the case of Hinduism in Nepal. Whereas, there are vociferous demands of the ethnic minorities, who tend to practice different religions, the voices in favor of Hinduism are relatively unheard of. Even if there is some activism, that may be labeled as domination over the minorities.

Apprehensions are also expressed about the rising influence of other religions, mainly Christianity and Islam. According to a report,[4] there are nearly 200 churches all over Nepal (there were hardly a few

[4] *The Kathmandu Post,* June 21, 1998

until a few decades ago) and some 200,000 Nepalese have been converted into Christianity, mostly under monetary, and material temptation, whereas the 1991 census showed there were only 31,000 Christians in Nepal. Various Western Christian missionaries are at work in Nepal, mostly in their coveted aim of converting Hindus or animist believers to Christianity. A cover story[5] lists 31 institutions working as Christian missionaries at various places of Nepal and says in some remote Tamang villages more churches have been built than there are primary schools. Bhim Rawal, one time Minister of Nepal, writes in an article: [6]

> Today, Hinduism is facing challenges of other religions. Many Hindus have converted their religion into Christianity and most of them belong to lower strata of our society. This because of the so-called untouchability, a system which incidentally started as a division for labor before it became the tradition. This is unfair and to change this. People do not need a catalyst in the form of Christian missionaries.

Though the law of the land forbids forced conversion, the constitution guarantees the freedom to observe any religion. The Christian Missionaries are said to be exploiting this openness and are entering the scene with coveted programs of development and social service. The main target groups of conversion have been the people of the lower rungs of economy and the traditional caste hierarchy. Motivated by the economic attraction and rejected by the dejected status in the caste system, many people in the rural areas have been attracted to the conversion propagated by the various Christian missionaries.

Scholars on Hinduism have expressed the view that the Western influence has "polluted the Hindu religion and nation".[7] There are concerns about the Western influence and changes being experienced in the religion and culture. In its conference on January 9, 1995, the World Hindu Federation expressed concern in a that Hinduism in Nepal "faces threats from Christian expansion".

---

[5] Nepal, fortnightly, 16-30 Mansir (2057 BS).

[6] Bhima Rawal, in article entitled "Missionaries at Work", in *The Kathmandu Post* (August 21, 1999)

[7] Swami Prapannacharya in a seminar, quoted in a newspaper.

Christian preaching is said to be expanding and "reaching to the poorest" and the so-called "lower castes" of Hindus. People are said to being "converted" into Christianity on the basis of "purely economic motivation". There is also a rise of Tibetan monastic influence in Kathmandu valley. Helffer (1993) has described the emergence of Buddhist monasteries around *Bouddhanath* as a "recent phenomenon" (in Toffin, 1993). The study revealed that "parallel to the urbanization of the area, more than a dozen monasteries have been built around the stupa of *Bouddhanath*". The monastic communities in the region have been increasing in the last three decades.

Even Islam, which has relatively small presence in Nepal, is supposed to be influencing the religious scenario in Nepal. Every Friday, thousands of Muslims gather around a mosque in the heart of Kathmandu for their weekly prayers. Some twenty years ago, the number used to be quite small and unnoticeable. These days, the crowd is getting bigger. This may be due to increased freedom to observe the Islam in Nepal. But an increasing migration of the Muslim people into the Kathmandu Valley cannot be ruled out. To quote J. N. Dixit, one time Foreign Secretary of India from his *My South Block Years* (1996), "A large number of Muslims from Jammu and Kashmir... have been gaining easy entry into Nepal (because Indian citizens do not need a visa to enter Nepal) They have made successfully into the tourist trade in Pokhara and even in Kathmandu". This is not without total credibility.

Professor Baral also observes a "phenomenal increase in the Moslem population in the Kathmandu Valley and outside". Its cause is seen in the "inflow of migratory peoples from across the Indo-Nepal border". "The size of Moslem congregation every Friday is taken as an indicator prompting some observers to believe that such uninterrupted flow of Muslim and other people into the capital may spark off religious conflicts in the future" (Baral, 1998).

Pressures against Hinduism not only emanate from the tendency of rejection of religion in general, the opposition to Hinduism by the activists of the ethnic minorities also pose challenges to it. *Janjati* activists not only reject the institutionalization of Hinduism opposing the adoption of Hindu state in the constitution, they have started to boycott traditions that they had absorbed over the years by process of *Hinduization* or *Sanskritization*. Increasingly, Hinduism is being seen as a religion of the Brahman-Chhetris, the so-called upper caste elite, who are supposed to opposing the integration of the various ethnic groups of people, who do not practice Hinduism. This narrow interpretation of Hinduism as a form of Bahunism may be motivated politically. But that has reduced the importance of Hindu society and culture, which is dwindling in its traditional significance.

A DIFFERENT LIBERATION

Dogmatic Hindu philosophy accepts theological assumption that life is a chain of links of births in the past and the future. Most religiously-conscious Hindus regard the human life as a stage of transition from the past births towards future births until the final liberation (*Moksha*) is achieved. Every birth or life is thus considered as an opportunity to free oneself from the chain of rebirths.

Hindus generally believe in the transmigration of the soul and in the rebirth. There is also a belief that one's good or bad deeds will determine the next incarnation or birth. The results of one's present life thus is supposed to be achieved in the next life. One's present status of rewards and punishment is explained in terms of the action in the past life. Actions in the present life will be responsible for results in the next life. This value system was a strong motivator for good deeds and for obtaining religious merit, which would assure a good next life. But since people are becoming materialistic they have started to interpret that the result of the bad deeds will be seen in the next life which no one knows and believes for sure. Therefore the state of morality and religious merit is on the gradual decline.

The Buddhist doctrine of religious achievement based on the concept of enlightenment (*Nirvana*) is also seen being diffused as a genuine moral in today's public life of economic and materialistic compulsions and realities. People hardly practice *Dharma* (religious code of conduct) and it is becoming increasingly difficult for people to remain in *Sangha* (religious organization) wearing saffron robes as monks. Achieving *Nirvana* (enlightenment) is hardly believed to be an ultimate goal achievable by practicing meditation and in-depth practice and study of the Buddhist religion.

Though "the tendency of Nepali religious traditions, both Hindu and Buddhist, to overemphasize the spiritual and magical concerns has not encouraged a rational confrontation of the worldly problems of time, space and matter" (Sharma, 1973, p. x), religion has started to conflict with rationality and has worked as a tremendous force for social inertia.

With the advent of modern consumerism and materialism, people are more tending to achieve materialistic comfort rather than spiritual liberation. In the traditional value system, liberation (*Moksha* in Hinduism and *Nirvana* in Buddhism) used to be the ultimate goal of people's lives. People used to abandon the material world in order to achieve religious merit and liberation from the worldly affairs. Or at least, they were taught like that. But today, people tend to accumulate wealth, achieve material success and disregard spiritual emancipation. People are seeking a different liberation, a materialistic one, instead of the spiritual one.

Ancient philosopher Charbak had suggested that everything must be consumed and enjoyed in this world. "Enjoy your material life until you are alive, even at the cost of borrowing from others", he had said, adding "how can the dead body come back again after being burnt into ashes, if you don't". This philosophy seems to be on the holding these days. Although, some people are still seeking to obtain religious merit for their "next lives", the average attitude is that of consuming this world, gaining access to the physical amenities. A feature article puts it well:

> "The sacred tinkling of bells in the auspicious hours of dawn, the year-round religious festivals and ceremonies, and the ubiquitous shrines devoted to a motley crowd of gods can deceive any one into concluding that Nepal is a unique nation of devotees. A nation where people single-mindedly pursue spiritual merits, and where materialism is unheard of. ..While it is true that Nepali devotees sincerely believe in the gods of their choice, their ethics curiously resembles that of materialistic hedonists... The number of people subscribing to this ethical ideal is growing in Nepal..." [8]

The Nepalese are gripped by the grounded ethics that of getting access to the physical amenities jettisoning the moral pursuits of their lives. Whatever religious observance is remaining is done so for the sake of fulfilling self-interest demanding a richer and more

---

[8] Limbu, Ram (1998), Materialism in Nepali life, *The Kathmandu Post* February 23, 1998

pleasant life. Visiting temples and worshipping deities, the Nepalese today may be actually seeking the blessing of the God to fulfill their materialistic desire, not the spiritual emancipation.

VANISHING VENERATION

Hinduism is the religion with the most number of gods and goddesses. Apart from Hindu trinity (*Brahma, Vishnu* and *Shiva*), there are some 330 million deities *(Tettis Koti Devata)*. They include the families and pantheon of the principal gods and goddesses. People in Nepal are supposed to take care and attend several such deities. Some deities are to be pacified, some to be devoted, some worshipped, some propitiated and some sanctified. There used to be numerous *jatras*, festivals, days and occasions for several different deities to celebrate these activities. People used to attend fairs, go on pilgrimages, offer animal sacrifices and pay homage to such numerous deities. People's lifestyles used to be inextricably linked with these numerous gods and goddesses and beliefs, legends, faiths and practices related to them.

But most of these gods and goddess are being forgotten. Hindu pantheon is now mostly restricted to the religious texts. There are however several religious shrines dedicated to several gods and goddesses. But the relative importance of these deities and their worship is gradually declining. Except for some Shaktiite shrines, some temples of Shiva and Vishnu, most other temples are very poorly attended by the people. Remembering several Hindu deities and worshipping them has become simply unfeasible and impracticable to most people.

People would smear vermilion powder and garland an idol with flower and festoons on the numerous gods and goddesses and their shrines and images in Nepal. In the old days of religious supremacy, every passerby bowed against the site and that constituted a shrine in Nepal. A rock, a tree bottom, a pond, a cave, an emanating methane gas flame, a mountain and even a river was represented one or another form of a deity and worshipped, feared, propitiated and attended by the people.

People regarded these sites as abodes of gods or ancient sages and saints. They were visited as pilgrimage sites. They used to take holy baths and pay homage to various deities on various occasions.

But such veneration is vanishing. People have started to attach less significance to such natural sites, which used to be pilgrimage centers. Deities, once worshipped with much fanfare, are being ignored and abandoned.

Visiting religious shrines used to be a routine activity of many pious and ordinary Nepalese people. Most people used to go one some kind of religious tours at least in the later years of their lives. People used to make a lot of efforts to visit *Char Dham*, the famous four religious shrines in India. People saved money to go to pilgrimage at some stage of their lives. Usually such a pilgrimage consisted of a group of men and women from a village. They used to go to the pilgrimage centers like *Badri, Kedar, Ramesworam, Hardwar, Jagannatham, Dwarka* etc. in India and places like *Muktinath, Varaah Ksehtra,* and *Pashupatinath* in Nepal to obtain religious merit. They walked for long days, fasted and stayed in night vigils to obtain the merit. But people in new generation have started lessening such religious tours. The decrease in pilgrimage has not only to do with the loss of economic affordability. It has also to do with the attitudinal dimension that people are finding less and less significance and merit in such visits to the religious sites.

There used to be perennial pilgrimage to religious shrines around Kathmandu. Visiting Pashupatinath used to be a routine activity of many people in Kathmandu. One can still see several people going to Pashupatinath early in the morning. Many do this for good health and physical fitness. But people visiting religious shrines for religious merit is decreasing. Young people these days use their free time especially on Saturday morning to go to Pashupatinath. They enjoy seeing the friends and acquaintances and sometimes flirting with women more than the *darshan* of the actual shrine. Even when they seek the *darshan*, they do so jumping the queue, without any offerings, and more for amusement than for religion.

A RENAISSANCE IN THE MAKING?

Though there is a decline in Hinduism in general, there seems to be a renaissance of Vainsavite Hinduism in Eastern, and Central Terai. Old people in almost every family have adopted *Vaisnavism*, a cult of worshipping Lord Vishnu. Though *Vaisnavism* is on of the oldest religious cults in Nepal practiced since the time of the Lichhavis introduced it, the resurgence of *Vaisnavism* is a relatively new phenomenon. Old men and women get sacred mantras from omnipotent Gurus. They start putting long *Chandan* mark on the forehead and start cooking (*Swayampaki*) their own food. They are completely vegetarian and spend most time devoting to Lord Vishnu.

This represents a religious movement to the return of the religious practice to the good old days of Lichhavi rule, when the worship of Vishnu and His incarnations was the main religious cult. In an age so much obsessed with bad deeds, evils, crime and corruption, the renaissance of the cult of Vishnu is viewed as a strange shift in the culture.

The Vaisnav culture was introduced in Nepal in around the 4th century by the Licchavis. They installed famous four Narayanas in the four corners of Kathmandu Valley namely *Changu Narayan, Shesh Narayan, Ichangu Narayan, Bisankhu Narayan*. They were among the patron deities of the Lichhavis and were adored and venerated for centuries with much of devotion and compassion. Vaisnavism was kind of abandoned with flourishing of Shaiviite, Tantric and Shaktiite cults. But the reappearance of the Vaisnavite culture in the some parts of Nepal is like revival of *Satya Yuga*, the epoch of the truth. But the adherents of the religious cult are especially old people, who have resorted to the cult to "absolve their sins".

Yet another renaissance seems to be on the making on the convergence of various sects and faiths in Hinduism. Hindus used to concentrate their devotion on a certain divinity considering others as minor gods and goddesses. There used to be cults of Shiva, Vishnu and female goddesses.[9] But in most Hindu families, these days, there is no strict adherence to a particular cult, sect or school. Elderly people may be practicing Vaisnavism worshipping Lord Vishnu. Youngsters may be celebrating the Shaktiite festival of Dashain enthusiastically offering animal sacrifices and enjoying the new clothes. Others worship Lord Shiva as a routine religious activity. They pay homage to the holy phallic emblem (*Shivalinga*) of the ascetic deity with equal devotion. Many other gods and goddesses are worshipped, visited and paid homage on different festive occasions.

---

[9] The cult of Brahma was not observed in Nepal, though the deity is among the three main gods according to Hindu pantheon.

Further, the same people may be seen visiting different temples and shrines on different occasions. People are Vaisnavites on *Ekadashis*, especially *Haribodhini* and *Harishayani*. They fast and pay home to Vishnu and Narayan shrines on this occasion. During *Shivaratri, Teej, Akshyaya Tritiya* and *Balachaturdashi*, people become Shaiviites. But in *Dakshinkali*, looking at the slain goats, chicken and other animals, it looks like most people are Shaktiites. Thus, there is a convergence in the cult of Vaisnavism, Shaivism and Shaktiism.

Similar convergence is also seen in the Hindu social organization of *Varnashram*. Hindus, especially Brahmans are supposed to progress in their lives through four stages: *Brahmacharya* (the stage of obtaining sacred thread and education remaining celibate), *Grihastha* (the stage after marriage and settling in the house), *Vanaprastha* (the stage of inhabitation of the wilderness after being satiated from the world), and *Sanyas* (the stage of remaining in solitude, begging alms and abandoning worldly things). But this distinction is disappearing. The four stages of life are converging into one. People are continuing the practices that lead to consuming and enjoying, and abandoning those which are meant for obtaining education, meditation and ethical merits.

THE DOMAIN OF THE OLD

Religion is increasingly being pushed to the domain of the old people and the people of the previous generation. Young people are being distracted away form the religious practices and beliefs. In religious activities and ceremonies like *Saptaha Shrawan, a* recital of sacred texts explaining and describing the significance of the Puranic stories held for seven days to purify the soul of the deceased and to obtain religious merit, the listeners to the recital are usually people mostly sixty years and older. People of the economically active working age dislike attending religious ceremonies. Visiting pilgrimage centers, and observing the religious conduct is left to the domain of the old people. And young people are actively screening out themselves from religious and cultural activities.

The concept that religious performance can earn merit in the lives of people is getting its value lost in the general public save people of the old age. Youngsters not only find it irrelevant to indulge into the religion, they are actively separated and denied opportunity to learn their own religion. A few Sanskrit schools focus on a very small number of Brahmans. School curricula do not even educate the basic tenets of religion, let alone develop the spiritual values and religious faith. There is no such institution, which teaches Hinduism in totality. The Karmakandi schools focus on the ritual side rather than the philosophical side of the religion. And that too is weakening day by day.

But the youth today are not ready to abandon the religion completely. At least, some think so:

> "Contrary to the common feeling that the present new generation do not give religion and culture their due respect, we can conclusively say that this is not rue. They do not reflect total ignorance towards culture and religion, as believed, but are more selective. The selective behavior reflected by people saying that they do give important ceremonies and religious functions the respect they deserve and enthusiastically participate in them".[10]

One may agree that youngsters still flock to the religious shrines on the festive activities and participate in the family rituals quite regularly. But the motive may not be the religious merit, but the need to have fun and flirting with the peers. Otherwise, the core aspect of details of the rituals and their merit and significance is left at the hands of the elderly in the family or in the society. Even the moral aspect of religious activities and principles is being left to the old people, as the youngsters gradually deny responsibility in the same.

MAY LORD PASHUPATINATH PROTECT ALL OF US !

The increasing callous attitude towards the religions in general may have brought about by the scientific interpretation of the worldly things and by the increasing knowledge of the cause and effect. But most Nepalese people still hold a strong faith that the divine power can prevent the worst and protect them from any mishap. People invoke the name of their most favorite deity, while they are in danger

---

[10] Quoted from a research entitled "Freedom as Defined by Youths" (*The Rising Nepal*, January 13, 1999), carried out Nepalese students of Kathmandu School of Management:

or while they are doing something important. The name of Pashupatinath, the lord of animals and people alike, is invoked during several occasions. Earlier, people believed that they were naturally protected by Lord Pashupatinath. But even that unshakable belief seems to have started to erode. Today, people use such an invocation as a subject of social ridicule and satire. Even if things are wrong, they are right because all of us have been protected by Lord Pashupatinath. Perhaps, such a satire is also diminishing the religious merit and importance of religion as a whole. May Lord Pashupatinath protect all of us! This saying is sometimes used to satire the existing anomalies in the society inferring only Lord Pashupatinath can protect us. But, I mean it.

Epilogue

While discussing the idea of this book, someone said, "this sounds like projecting million mistakes of your own culture". Another respondent asked, do you intend to suggest that people should remain tied up with traditions, which are full of superstitions and ignorance? Can you turn against the tide of the changes sweeping the world over? Hence this epilogue.

It is quite natural that people sometimes feel powerless in this cultural battle, which they seem to be loosing. We think that we can hardly do anything in the wake of the sweeping changes engulfing our culture. And we kind of quietly accept us being overwhelmed in the process, loosing our identities and culture. It is better to light one candle than to curse the darkness, it is said. Even small and incremental steps carried by individuals can be very strong and positive step to preserve one's culture. Even a journey of miles long starts with one step, says a Chinese proverb. And small drops to make an ocean, goes a Nepalese saying. There are things that can be put into right track with a little more conscious policy choice and planning by the state, social institutions, families, and individuals.

Culture is a dynamic but important variable for shaping the destiny of a nation and its people. If the culture is articulated to release the dormant energy of the various communities binding them together and giving them a sense of identity, it can lead to not only peace and harmony but also to pride and prosperity. If provoked, it can lead to the destruction of a civilization and may lead to conflict in the society. We in Nepal should choose the first path, that of peace and harmony, that of pride and dignity. There should be a conscious and deliberate articulation of the pluralistic concerns of various ethnic groups and castes to make them feel and behave like a collective whole. Politicizing of culture should be avoided to do away with any cultural conflicts. But it does not mean that culture should be out of political agenda of the country.

Ways of maintaining a consciously led cultural identity should be in the political debate, not the provocation of differences of perception among different ethnic groups of people. In the new pluralistic and democratic framework, the consciousness of various ethnic groups has been liberated. But the need for harmony has increased. Fair and secular policies should be reflected in the state's treatment to various ethnic groups of people, in recognizing their political demands, in allocating the resources, social, moral and economic, to all the communities equitably. A value system based on a shared consciousness and an appreciation of pluralism and diversity and an understanding of the importance of other's cultural aspiration is very crucial to a healthy preservation and promotion of the people's culture. The genuine demands and aspirations of different communities or groups of people should be addressed. A mere reiteration of the rich cultural heritage or diversity will not serve the purpose.

Nepalese culture is and should be allowed to glitter like a crafted piece of jewelry in which each precious stone retains its distinctiveness but combines with the others to produces an identity of its own. We need not retain the 24-carat pure culture. Neither we can even if we wish. But can we retain the gold's identity so that it does not look lime an amalgam of various metals with a small portion of gold in it. The identities of the ethnic minorities should remain distinct and the Nepalese identity should not be portrayed as an amalgam or homogenization of the cultural identities of the ethnic groups of people. But it should be projected as a collective sum total of all the ethnic and caste cultures.

Differences and difficulties in the Nepalese culture is not a "zero-sum" game. We can definitely arrive at "win-win" situation, in which both the ethnic identity and collective culture is retained in its purest possible form, contributing to the diversity and pluralism, which is the major characteristics of the Nepalese culture. South African Leader Nelson Mandela calls it a "rainbow nation", in which the cultures with different currents mingle forever to produce a "rainbow river". We can also follow similar model in preserving our cultural diversity.

The momentum of fresh cultural arousal in the country, as the awakening for the revival of their ethnic identity and culture among the ethic minorities, and for revival of the traditions and culture among the caste people, should be sustained without any conflict and clash of interests. The two should not be viewed as opposite to each other. In fact, they should compliment each other.

Imposing language, national symbols, and particular religion and other means of "integration" will not help for the cause of culture of certain ethnic groups. Neither the vociferous opposition to a particular religion and the attitudes of the caste system will yield direct fruits. All ethnic languages, religions, and practices and culture should be preserved to reflect the diversity of the Nepalese culture. The compartmentalized notion of the Nepalese culture into ethnic groups as Newars, Gurungs, Magars etc. will not represent the real and dynamic picture of the Nepalese culture. There might be a "need to devise polycentric nationalism" that fosters feeling of belongingness and promotes national integration" (Gurung, 1997). "Nepal's major concern today is to continue its past traditions without having to give rise to the trends of intense ethnic conflict as is observed in other countries and regions", writes Professor Lok Raj Baral (Baral, 1998).

The state can play an important role in preserving these cultural traditions. Removing the myopic vision of a fragmented culture, we could start promoting the food, dresses, dances and artifacts of various ethnic groups as the national symbols. There is no reason why the Nepal Sambat cannot be adopted as a national calendar era, instead of the Bikram Sambat, which is an imported one bearing the label of an Indian King. Simliarly, the dress, food, festivals and shrines of various ethnic groups should be promoted to represent the national culture in totality.

As recommended by the the World Culture Report (UNESCO, 2000), the government policy should define cultural recognition as a basic right of human beings and that the cultural justice should be promoted as part of efforts to achieve economic, political and social justice. To maintain cultural pluralism, the various cultural groups should be granted the right to diversity in the public sphere and there should some degree of political self-government for all such groups (UNESCO, 2000). We can follow that path.

The preservation of the Nepalese culture requires a lot of energy, resources and motivation. This can only be retained by a willing population, which has active linkages with the traditions and the cultural heritage of the past. We should come out of the thought that culture is something of the past and a sentiment of the bygone era only to be protected by some traditional dances, musicians, priests and religious leaders. Preservation of culture is everyone's responsibility, for now and for future. It is not necessary that every one should wear a saffron robe and chant *"Om Namo Shibaya"* smear white *chandan* on forehead and put *Janai* around the body. Neither that every rituals and customs of the diverse ethnic minorities should be performed to the exact original details. In fact, it is possible to retain one's culture while being abreast with the sweeping changes in the science and technology. For example, the Japanese people have the reputation of preserving their culture, despite the massive modernization. There is a need to create a vision on how we could embrace development and modernity and globalization, without being succumbed to the power of "universalization" and "homogenization". We need not abandon our culture and tradition in order to be abreast with modernity. It is not the dogmatic conservatism that will avert the destructive forces against the culture. Neither the intellectual concern alone to forge an identity seeking balance between tradition and modernity will be enough to redress the onslaught of the Culture Shift era.

We can retain our religion and culture being a little more considerate, giving a little more attention, and maintaining interest in the past. In most cases, the preservation would be sufficient. In others, there may even be the need to revive the culture. It may be a time to reassess the system of injecting the values to our people, right from the childhood. The inherent design of our education may need to be reversed. It should be made clear that people can continue to enjoy modernity without loosing traditions. There may be a need for Levis instead of Labeda. There might be stronger attraction to a Disco than picnicking at Dakshinkali. But one needs not to abandon Rodi to sing a Rap. Nepalese youths can wear Lacoste shirt, Wrangler jeans, Nike shoes and Ray-ban sunglasses. But values like touching down the feet of the parents and grandparents in respect, taking off shoes while entering kitchen, and smiling generously when meeting a stranger needs not be abandoned.

We can continue to enjoy the products and services available due to the influx of science and technology. But we can name the products in Nepali instead of the English and Western names. A television produced in Nepal will still be a television no matter whether you name it *Gaurishankar,* instead of *Goldstar.* Don't we have ways of expressing things in our own methods without resorting to the phony acronyms in English? Can we teach our youngsters that adopting Nepali things is not being backward?

Sometimes it reflects our hypocrisy. While we venerate things from the West, in science and technology and in values like liberalism and democracy, why should we be opposing their culture, fashion, music and food? asked a professor during discussions with this author.

But we must start to understand that the development in science and technology and ideology of liberalism and democracy does not represent a culture or civilization and does not pose threat to yet another culture, but the latter (food, language, clothes, cinema, and attitudes) does.

"Neither total isolation a cultural cocoon nor absolute global homogenization" should be acceptable to any sensible Nepalese citizen, says Bhattachan (1998). "There should be something in between. But the degree of indigenousness of one's own society and culture should never be compromised with globalization" (Bhattachan, 1998). Nepalese people should take an informed choice on what to take from alien society and what to preserve from their own tradition, Bhattachan concludes.

Someone asked, are you suggesting that we need to install a "culture police", which could prevent the deterioration of the glorious past, both at the physical and at the attitudinal level? In Singapore, they have "manners police". You cannot sell or take chewing gums. There is fine for every little mistake related to mannerisms, including for littering. In Nepal, this may not be a strong debate today. But it will certainly become a strong debate tomorrow. The role of state as a culture police can only be an unwise prescription. But some sanctions against those who violate the cultural norms can be introduced.

Norms should be developed for the preservation of the cultural heritage and legislation should be enacted to prevent the violation of such norms. The existing legislation should be implemented effectively. For example, the indiscriminate expansion of the slum housing in Kathmandu Valley could be checked with stringent zoning laws, allocating spacing for residential and commercial purposes, preventing encroachment of the heritage sites and introducing some mandatory Nepalese architecture in the private constructions, the booklet says. All of that requires role of culture police by the state, or the municipality in this case. Expansion of the green belt, more stringent sanitation standards (compulsory safety tanks), tax incentives to vernacular architecture, restriction to modern constructions in traditional heritage areas, cleaning of the rivers, relocating the industries, and banning graffiti and posters that deface the city could be some of the examples of state's role in protecting the heritage. Without such policing, preservation of heritage and culture becomes difficult.

It cannot be inferred that Nepalese things have ceased to attract the Nepalese people. Though there is an increasing craze for things from abroad, Nepalese people have not abandoned things back home completely. If there is the craze for *Baywatch*, there is also an equal amount of enthusiasm in Santosh Pant's uniquely Nepali *Hijo Aajaka Kura*. It is not only Fast Food places becoming popular, youngsters continue to queue in Kathmandu's numerous momo stalls. If Bryan Adams and Madonna have become popular, Nepalese have not forgotten Narayan Gopal and Aruna Lama. If there is a craze to go to a fashion show, the enthusiasm to go to Manakamana has not faded. In fact, the number of people going to the hill shrine has increased, though the fun may be the major motive than the religious merit for many youngsters. If people are crowding in the pubs and the discos, the queue in Pashupatinath and Dakshinkali have not declined. The crowd of women on red Sarees on Teej festival in Kathmandu and the red Tika on every forehead on Bijaya Dashami suggests that the culture is alive and the cultural ethos celebrated with a lot of enthusiasm. Nepalese culture continues to bind people together in the traditional rhythm. We should rather focus on these strengths of our culture than the weaknesses.

There are mutually contradictory views regarding the cultural traditions in the country. Many people advocate social change in the practice of superstitious customs in the name of social reform. Whereas there are people who give a cry against the deteriorating cultural change and therefore stick to preserving the old culture. People who advocate changes in the superstitious rules are not escaping from the traps of traditional thinking like untouchability, and caste structure. There are people who have abandoned the practices and institutions of their ancestors and forefathers. There are people who undermine the foundations of their own cultural heritage and traditions and who ignore the spiritual quality of life in their religion. And there are people who are fanatics who oppose reforms. The latter category thinks accepting *Westernization* is accepting inferiority. They try to insist and advocate the spiritual superiority of the Eastern culture and religion and decry and defame the materialistic outlook of the west. Neither is serving the cause of culture in the country.

Nepalese culture has always been innovative to adopt positive aspects and selective to abandon bad sides in culture. People have abandoned age-old superstitions and mystic beliefs that were detrimental to human values and health. Customs and practices that were inhuman were abandoned. The abolishing *Sati Pratha*, the practice of forced cremating of the women with their deceased husbands, outlawing the custom of slavery are some such examples. Even in the modern times, the abolition of legal recognition of the caste system by introducing the New Civil Code and lately the recognition by the constitution (1990) of the multi-lingual and multi-ethnic status and pluralism of the Nepalese society are yet other examples. For example, people are discussing how to reform the rigid and discriminatory life rituals taking into account the changes in the lifestyles. There is the talk of simplifying the rituals of life, of which only six out of sixteen such rituals are in use, in a rational manner. Even the World Hindu Federation has initiated such reforms in the Sanskaras based on caste system, untouchability, and discriminatory practices.

If we were to take stock of the nation's cultural balance sheet, our gains could be awareness, modernity, freedom, liberalism, exposure to the world etc. Our losses, none-the-less, are much more worrisome: loss of traditions, Nepaleseness, and identity. Though the exposure to the rest of the world is not without cultural implications, we cannot contain the process of such exposure, let alone go against the tide of the sweeping changes. Today, any isolationist stand will not be able to preserve the culture. In fact, we have to start teaching the rest of the world the values and merits of our culture so that the good aspects of the same could be replicated even outside. Though we are in the receiving end of culture, a reverse globalization of culture can be possible if we can promote our culture in a sustained campaign.

In fact, we have to adopt to learn to preserve our culture in the existing and anticipated nature of changes that may be unleashing wrath against our culture. The question then arises as to if it is possible to absorb elements of modernization and Westernization without loosing our culture. As there have been differing responses to modernization, it becomes obvious to ask if Nepal's response to modernization will be unique? Though it is said that modernization and Westernization are not the same and that it is possible to modernize without being Westernized, it can be questioned if Nepal's culture can take this course of modernization without falling prey to Westernization and globalization? If unique characteristics of the Nepalese people like generosity, friendliness, ever smiling response, simplicity, non-confronting, god-fearing, entertainment-loving desires, and festive, and relaxed attitude are to be retained, we must focus on our strengths, not weaknesses.

What shall we do with the satellite television, which is supposed to be polluting the culture? Shall we ban the satellite antennae and force people to watch Bhajans and classical dances in the Nepal Television. We should neither wish nor afford to do this. But the cable broadcasters could be made to broadcast certain minimum number of hours of programs, which are locally produced or at least compatible to the local cultural standards. Censorship may not be the answer. But incentives certainly are. One could also give incentives like tax cuts for programs locally produced and aired instead of the products of little relevance. Simlilarly, we can use these channels to inculcate the values of heritage preservation and culture among the viewers.

Even the responsibility of the business community could be of high value. People could give their products Nepali names, spell them correctly, give sponsorships to the activities related to the preservation of culture. Their ad campaigns could be sensitive to the use of cultural practices. They could encourage creativity and traditional aesthetic values. Though the private business firms are mainly motivated by profit, they can fulfil several social responsibilities. They cannot only exercise restraint making profit at the expense of the society and culture, they can also play a very instrumental role in preserving the traditions and the cultural heritage. Private firms can prevent the imitation and commercialization of the cultural symbols and can refrain from misleading advertisements. They can also refrain from polluting the heritage sites and pilgrimage centers with their advertising materials. They can also reduce the social cost of preservation by reducing the polluting.

Heritage will only be effectively conserved if people value their heritage sufficiently to keep it. Unless the motivation for conservation comes from within the community itself, long-term conservation will be difficult, if not impossible. But the society must collectively be able to afford the conservation process and people must see that in some way it will benefit their lives. This may be cultural but it may also be purely economic. In addition, an appropriate institutional framework needs to be in place to facilitate the process. (HMG/IUCN, 1992)

Individuals should give up the self-interest and short-term obsessions and should contribute to the enduring progress and preservation of culture. At institutional level, inculcating the sense of social sensibility in the society could be a major starting step. The cultural industry such as the film industry and entertainment business should also be given some role to play to preserve the national culture. They can continue to give some elements of the national culture, instead of just injecting the alien cultural values to the people.

Nepalese people living abroad may be finding the world as a global village. But how can they contribute to the enrichment or continuation of the Nepalese culture, while they live abroad. While the Nepalese community abroad may have greater impulse to identify themselves with the Nepalese culture, their capacity to do so is limited because of their dispersed nature and small populations anywhere. Even though, they can build alliances, continue to network among themselves and compatriots back home, donate whatever they can to preserve the heritage back home and observe whatever festivals they can under the circumstances they live in. The Nepalese living abroad can also launch a sustained campaign for raising funds and awareness for the preservation of the heritage and for bringing back the stolen images from the temples of Nepal.

Even the Internet, which has been a kind of accelerator of the culture shift, as discussed earlier, can be used for the benefit of the preservation of the cultural heritage. This medium can be used to document the stolen images, heritage sites needing conservation and the efforts made by various agencies. Nepalese cultural values and symbols can be widely circulated through the net. Moreover, the web can be used for an effective networking of the individuals and institutions working for heritage preservation.

Culture cannot be preserved by the sole control by the market forces. Culture, if left to the market forces, will be driven by market consideration and commercial interests. It requires state's conscious guidance in order to be protected from being derailed. The state and the civil society will have a definite role to play. The national institutions, which endeavor to promote national culture, should be promoted and preserved. At the state level some conscious policy choice should be adopted.

For example, tourism should be promoted as a cultural industry taking into account of the environment, heritage and sustainability so that it does not intrude in the heritage. In fact, a properly managed tourism can help revitalize the local culture, especially the traditional art and craft, generating resources for preserving the heritage. The success in renovation and maintenance of Bhaktapur Durbar square with the help of a small fee levied to the tourists can be replicated elsewhere.

If the values and culture has to be preserved, new role models will have be developed, new value system will have to be inculcated. Perhaps the most important method to induce preservation is to introduce curricula on importance and management of preservation of the cultural heritage. Inequalities in economic and social strata, differences in gender, and grievances of the "underclass" will have to be addressed. But all of these need not be a one-time reform. Small beginning and one-by-one small step changes will have to be introduced. Reforms will have to be introduced in the society in pragmatic terms. Any suggestion, which is not practical in the sense of today's technological and economic imperatives, will not be palatable to the people. People can take bath in their bathrooms instead of polluted "sacred rivers" while mourning their deceased. What is important is that the basic values behind the customs and rituals, not the details of them.

There might also be need for legislation to preserve some aspects of our culture. Legal measures could be instrumental in preventing mass reproduction of artistic and cultural objects. Stringent legal and administrative measures preventing the loss of images from the heritage shrines could be introduced. The overhead wiring and transformers within the heritage sites should be put underground paying due regard to archaeological cultural levels and the introduction and repair of water supply and sewage services should respect the historic fabric.

The detailed inventories should be compiled to identify national monuments, the status of which should exclude demolition. Special attention will have to be directed towards monuments in private ownership. Since these inventories will take a number of years to complete, preliminary lists should be prepared and gazzetted annually. It would also be worthwhile to classify the cultural monuments according to their cultural importance and the need to preserve them.

Efforts at private initiative can contribute a lot. For example, Music Nepal, a private music recording company, has formed a *Sanskriti Samrakshyan Parishad*, which will collect, and preserve old Nepali songs and music recorded many years ago. This will preserve the "old and gold aura from vanishing in the age of musical invasion all over the world", says Music Nepal's homepage. Efforts like these should be encouraged.

What is needed is the "cultural renaissance". We may not need the self-styled gatekeepers of the Nepalese culture, nor the advocators of the fictionalized past. Even the "morality cops" fearing everything alien as amoral is detrimental to the preservation of the cultural sanctity. Too much mesmerizing of the glorious past and an effort to introduce fundamentalism in the culture may be like driving a car looking only at the rear view mirror, which could lead to a disaster ahead. Reforms in the culture should be futuristic and forward-looking. When there was no bridge in the river, one would cross it on foot, taking the shoes off, pulling the trousers up. But once there is a bridge in place, no one should mockingly try to go into cross the water barefoot instead of crossing the river over the bridge.

The objective of any religion or culture is to give the moral and spiritual dimension to the life. Plus the same also gives people a sense of identity and dignity. If that can be achieved in a better and rational way, it is not necessary to stick to the old superstitious methods and practices. Traditions, which are rationally justifiable, should be preserved and superstitions can be abandoned. But any such rationalization should not be a sole pretext to allowing the alien culture to be absorbed at the cost of the local culture.

References

Acharya, Madhu R. ed. (1994), *Nepal Encyclopedia*, Nepal Encyclopedia Foundation, Kathmandu.

Agrawal, Govind Ram (1990), *Mobilization of Foreign Resources for Nepal's Development*, CEDA and Asian Development Bank, Manila

Ahmed, Ishtiq (1996), *State, Nation and Ethnicity in Contemporary South Asia*, Pointer, London, New York

Allen, N. J. (1997), Hinduization: The Experience of Thulung Rai, in Gellner et. al (1997) ed., *Nationalism and Ethnicity in a Hindu Kingdom*, Harwood Academic Publishers, The Netherlands.

Amatya, Saphalya (1991), *Art and Culture of Nepal*, Nirala Series-12, Nirala Publications, New Delhi

Amatya, Soorya Lal (1996), The Ethnic Minorities of Nepal, *Annual Journal of the Nepal Council of World Affairs*, Kathmandu, Nepal Council of World Affairs

Aryal, D., R. Regmi, and N. Rimal (eds.) (1982), *Nepal District Profile* - A district wise socio-techno-economic profile of Nepal, National Research Associates, Kathmandu, Nepal.

Bangdel, Laina Singh (1982), *Prachin Nepali Murtikaloko Itihash*, Royal Nepal Academy, Kathmandu.

Bangdel, Laina Singh (1982), *The Early Scriptures of Nepal*, Vikas Publishing House, New Delhi.

Bangdel, Laina Singh, *The Stolen Images of Nepal*, Kathmandu.

Baral, Lok Raj (1977), *Oppositional Politics in Nepal*, Abhinav Publications, New Delhi.

Baral, Lok Raj (1993), *Nepal: Problems of Governance*, Konark Publishers, New Delhi.

Baral, Lok Raj (1994), The return of party politics in Nepal, *Journal of Democracy*, pp. 121-133,. - Vol. 5, no 1

Baral, Lok Raj (1998), "Ethnicity and Constitutional Reforms in Nepal", *Ethnicity and Constitutional Reforms in South Asia*, ed. Iftekharuzzaman, University Press Limited, Dhaka, pp. 84-107.

Bell, Daniel (1976), *The Cultural Contradiction of Capitalism*, Basic Books, New York.

Berreman, Gerald (1972), *Hindus of the Himalayas: Ethnography and Change*, University of California Press, Berkeley.

Bhattachan, Krishna B. (1998), Globalization and its impacts on Nepalese Society and Culture, in Dahal, Madan ed. (1998), *Impact of Globalization in Nepal*, Nepal Foundation for Advanced Studies, Kathmandu.

Bista, Dor Bahadur (1967), *People of Nepal*, Ratna Pustak Bhandar, Kathmandu.

Bista, Dor Bahadur (1987), "The Process of Nepalization", *Anthropological and Linguistic Studies of the Gandaki Area in Nepal*, Tokyo

Bista, Dor Bahadur (1991), *Fatalism and Development; Nepal's Struggle for Modernization*, Orient Longman Limited, Calcutta.

Burghart, Richard (1996), The Category Hindu in the Political Discourse in Nepal. *The Conditions of Listening: Essays on Religion, History and Politics in South Asia*, C. J. Fuller and Jonathen Spencer eds. Oxford University Press, New Delhi.

Burkert, Claire (1997), Defining Maithali Identity: Who is in Charge, in Gellner et. al. (1997), *Nationalism and Ethnicity in a Hindu Kingdom*, Harwood Academic Publishers, The Netherlands.

Caplan, L. (1975), *Administration and politics in a Nepalese Town, the Study of a District Capital and its Environs*, Oxford University Press, London.

Caplan, Lionel (1970), *Land and Social Change in East Nepal*, A study of Hindu-Tribal Relations, London, University of California Press.

Chitrakar, Ramesh Chandra (1994), *Foreign Investment and Technology Transfer in Developing Countries*: Motivating Factors and Financial and Economic Performance in Nepal. Aldershot, Eng.: Avery.

Chomsky, Noam (1996), *Powers and Prospects*, Reflections on human Nature and the Social Order, Madhyam Books, Delhi

CNAS (1987), Seminar on Nepali Emigrants in India, *CNAS Current Issues Series* no. 4, Tribhuvan University, Kathmandu.

Cox, Thomas (1989), Langtang Tibetans and Hindu Norms as Political Language: A Critical Perspective on Sanskritization Theory, *Contributions to Nepalese Studies*, vol. 16, no. 1, January 1989, Centre for Nepal and Asian Studies, Kathmandu.

Dahal, D. R. (1985) *An Ethnographic Study of Social Change among the Athpahariya Rai of Dhankuta*, CNAS, Kathmandu

Dahal, D. R. (1995): Ethnic Couldron, Demography and Minority Politics: The Case of Nepal, in Kumar, D. ed., *State Leadership and Politics in Nepal*, CNAS, Tribhuvan University, Kathmandu.

Dahal, Madan K. (1997), "Globalization and the Future of Nepalese Economy: Economic Nationalism Revisited", *The Political Economy of Small States*, Nepal Foundation for Advanced Studies (NEFAS) and Fredrich Ebert Strifftung (FES), Kathmandu

Des Chene, Mary (1996), "In the Name of Bikas", *Studies in Nepali History and Society*, vol. 1, no. 2, December 1996, Mandala Books, Kathmandu

Des Chene, Mary (1996), Ethnography in the Janajati-yug: Lessons from Reading Rodhi and other Tamu writings, *Studies in Nepalese History and Society*, June 1996, Mandala Book Point, Kathmandu.

Dixit, J. N. (1996), *My South Block Years*, Memoirs of a Foreign Secretary, UBS Publishers' Distributors Ltd., New Delhi.

Dixit, K. (1998): "Highlanders on the Move", *Himal* 1(1): 3-5.

Dixit, Kanak Mani (1999), "Gods in Exile", *Himal* Vol. 12 No. 10 (October 1999), Kathmandu.

Dumont, Louis (1970), *Homo Hierarchicus, The Caste System and Its Implications*, University of Chicago Press, Chicago.

Fisher, J. F. (1978), *Homo Hierarchicus Nepalensis:* A Cultural Subspecies, in J F. Fisher ed., *Himalayan Anthropology: The Indo-Tibetan Interface*, The Hague and Paris, Mouton.

Fisher, J. F. (1986), "Tourists and Sherpas", *Contributions to Nepalese Studies*, 14(1) 37-62, Research Center for Nepal and Asian Studies, Kathmandu

Fisher, J. F. (1990): *Sherpas: Reflections in Change in Himalayan Nepal*, Oxford University Press, New Delhi

Fisher, William (1993), Nationalism and the Janjati, *Himal*, 6(2): 11-14.

Fukuyama, Francis (1992), *The End of History and the Last Man*, Penguin Books

Furer-Hiamendorf, Christopher von (1989): *The Sherpas Transformed*, Sterling, New Delhi.

Gaenszle, M. (1993) Interactions of an Oral Tradition: Changes in the *muddum* of the Mewahang Rai of east Nepal, in Toffin G. ed. *Nepal, Past and Present*, CNRS, Paris,

Gaige, F. (1975), *Regionalism and National Unity in Nepal*, University of California Press, Berkeley.

Gajurel and Vaidya (1984), *The Traditional Technology of Nepal*, Ratna Pustak Bhandar, Kathmandu.

Gellner, D. N. (1986) Language, Caste, Religion and Territory: Newar Identity, Ancient and Modern, *European Journal of Sociology*, 27: 102-148.

Gellner, David N, et. al. (1997*), Nationalism and Ethnicity in a Hindu Kingdom*, The Politics of Culture in Contemporary Nepal, Harwood Academic Publishers, The Netherlands.

Gellner, David N. and Declan Quigley, eds. (1995), *Contested Hierarchies: A Collaborative Ethnography of Caste in the Kathmandu Valley, Nepal.* Oxford, Calrendon Press.

Gilbert, Kate (1992), Women and Family Law in Modern Nepal: Statutory Rights and Social Implications. *New York University Journal of International and Politics*, 24:729-758 (Winter 1992).

Glover, Warren W (1965), Gurung Phonemic Summary, Summer Institute of Linguistics/ Tribhuvan University, Kathmandu.

Gurung Harka (1968), "Geographical Foundations of Nepal", *The Himalayan Review*, 1(1): 1-9.

Gurung, Ganesh M. (1988): "The Process of Identification and Sanskritization: The Duras of West Nepal", *Kailash*, 12. pp. 41-61.

Gurung, Ganesh M. (1994), *Indigenous People: Mobilization and Change*, Kathmandu

Gurung, H. (1998), Nepal: *Social Demography and Expressions*, Kathmandu

Gurung, Harka (1997), *Flying Geese and Sitting Ducks*, Patterns of Economic Growth in Asia, United Nations Association of Nepal, Kathmandu

Gurung, Harka Bahadur (1989), *Dimensions of Development*, Kathmandu.

Gurung, Harka, B. (1997), State and Society in Nepal, in Gellner, et. al. eds. (1997), *Nationalism and Ethnicity in a Hindu Kingdom*, Harwood Academic Publishers, The Netherlands.

Gutschow, N., and Kolver, B. (1975), *Concepts and Functions in a Town of Nepal*, Kommissionsverlg Franz Steiner Gmbh, Wiesbaden

Gyawali, Deepak (1996), Hinduism: Challenged by the Future, Shackled by the Past, *Himal*, Vol. 9, No. 3, May 1996.

Hagen, Toni (1961), *Nepal, the Kingdom in the Himalayas*, Berne, Kummerly and Frey.

Hamilton, Francis (1819), *An Account of the Kingdom of Nepal*, Edinburgh, (Reprinted Biliotheca Himalaica, vol. 10, series -1, 1971)

Hancock, Graham (1989), *Word of Poverty*, Reading, Berkshire: Cox & Wyman Ltd.

Hitchock, J. T.(1966), *The Magars of Banyan Hill*, New York, Holt; Rinehart, Winston.

HMGN (1995) *Country Report to the UN World Conference on Women in Beijing* (September 4-15, 1995), National Planning Commission, Kathmandu

HMGN (1997), Statistical Yearbook of Nepal 1997, Central Bureau of Statistics, Kathmandu.

Hoschschild, Adam (1998), Globalization and Culture, *Economic and Political Weekly*, May 23, 1998.

Huntington, Samuel P. (1996): *The Clash of Civilizations and the Remaking of the World Order*, Simon and Schuster.

Huntington, Samuel P. (1998) : Clash of Civilizations? The Many Faces of the Future, *Span*, May/June 1998.

Hutt, Michael (1997), Being Nepali Without Nepal: Reflections on a South Asian Diaspora, in Gellner et. al, ed., *Nationalism and Ethnicity in a Hindu Kingdom*, Harwood Academic Publishers, The Netherlands.

Hutt, Michael, "Diversity and Change in the Languages of Highland Nepal", *Contribution to Nepalese Studies*, Vol. 14, No.1, Dec. 1986, pp. 1-24.

IDS (1983), *Foreign Aid and Development in Nepal*, IDS, Kathmandu

Iijima, Shigeru (1963), "Hinduization of a Himalayan Tribe in Nepal, *Kroeber Anthropology Papers*, No. 29

Iijima, Shigeru (1977), "Ecology, Economy and Cultural Change among the Thakalis in the Himalayas of Central Nepal", *Changing Aspects of Modern Nepal*, Shigeru Iijima (ed.), Tokyo, Institute for the Study of Languages and Cultures of Asia and Africa (pp. 69-92).

IUCN/HMGN (1992), *The Conservation of National Heritage in Nepal*, National Planning Commission, in Collaboration with Nepal Heritage Society and IUCN- The World Conservation Union

Johnson, R. J. & Watts, M. J. ed. (1995), *Geographies of Global Change*, Blackwell.

Jones, Rex (1976), "Sanskritization in Eastern Nepal", *Ethnology*, 15, I. pp. 63-75

Josephson (1988), *Nepal Manadala*, abridged.

K.C., Bal Kumar, (1992), Migration and urbanization in Nepal, in K.C. Bal Kumar (ed.), *Population and development in Nepal*, Tribhuvan University, Kathmandu, 129-158.

Karan, Pradyumna P. & Ishii, Hiroshi (1996), *Nepal: A Himalayan Kingdom in Transition*, United Nations University press, Tokyo, New York, Paris, Bookwell, New Delhi

Keiter, Robert B (1995), Preserving Nepal's National Parks: Law and Conservation in the Developing World. *Ecology Law Quarterly*, 22:591-675.

Kennedy, Paul, *Preparing for the Twenty-First Century*, Fontana Press, London (1994)

Khadga, Narayan (1991), *Foreign Aid, Poverty and Stagnation in Nepal*, Vikas, New Delhi.

Khanal, Prof. Y N (1996), *Nepal after Democratic Restoration*, Ratna Pustak Bandar, Kathmandu.

King, Anthony D., d. (1991), *Culture, Globalism and the World*, contemporary conditions for the representation of identity, State University of New York at Brighamton.

Knox, P. ed. (1995), *World Cities in a World System*, Cambridge University press.

Koirala, Anuradha (1998) "Trafficking in Girl-Children and Women, A Nepalese Perspective", *Maiti*, newsletter of Maiti Nepal, November-December 1998.

Kumar, Krishna, *Brahmin and The King*, Logic of State Sullenness, The Time of India (September 14, 1996), New Delhi

Levi, Sylvian, *Historical Study of the Hindu Kingdom*, vol. III, Kathmandu.

Levy, R. I. (1990), *Mesocosm: Hinduism and the Organization of a Traditional Newar City*, Berkeley, University of California Press, Berkeley.

Liechty, Mark (1994) *Fashioning Modernity in Kathmandu: Mass media, Consumer Culture and the Middle Class in Kathmandu*, Ph. D. Dissertation, University of Pennsylvania.

Liechty, Mark (1997), *Consumer Culture in Kathmandu*, Internet Website http://iias.leidenuniv.nl /iiasn6/south/liechty.html.

Lietchy, Mark (1996) Paying for Modernity: Women and the Discourse of Freedom in Kathmandu, *Studies in Nepalese History and Society* (June 1996), vol. 1, no. 1, Mandala Book Point.

Macfarlane, Alan (1997): Identity and Change among the Gurungs (Tamu-mai) of Central Nepal, In Gellner et. al. ed. (1997), *Nationalism and Ethnicity in a Hindu Kingdom*, Harwood Academic Publishers, The Netherlands.

Malla, K. P. (1992): "Bahunbada's Myth and Reality", *Himal, 5 (3): 22-24.*

Malla, Kamal Prakash (1973), "The Intellectual in Nepalese Society" in Rana and Malla eds., *Nepal in Perspective*, Kathmandu, CEDA

Malla, Kamal Prakash (1989), *Nepal: Perspectives in Continuity and Change*, Centre for Nepal and Asian Studies, Tribhuvan University, Nepal

Maskay, Bishwa K. (1997), Social Development in Nepal, United Nations Association of Nepal, Kathmandu.

McDonaugh, Christian (1997), "Losing Ground, Gaining Ground: Land and Change in a Tharu Community ion Dang, West Nepal", in Gellner, David N, et. al. (1997), *Nationalism and Ethnicity in a Hindu Kingdom*, Harwood Academic Publishers, The Netherlands.

Mercier, Nadia (1993) "Socio-Economic Determinants of Women's Work in the Services Sector", *The Anthropology of Nepal: From Tradition to Modernity*, Gerard Toffin (ed.), French Cultural Centre, Kathmandu

Messeschmidt (1982) The Thakali of Nepal: Continuity and Socio-cultural Change, *Ethnography*, 29 (4): 265-80.

Naisbitt, John (1996), *Megatrends Asia*, The Eight Asian Megatrends That are Changing the World, Nicholas Brealey Publishing, London.

NESAC (1998), *Nepal: Human Development Report*, Nepal South Asia Center, Kathmandu

Norbu, Dawa (1992), *Culture and Politics of the Third World Nationalism*, London.

OECD (1987) *Aid Coordination: Nepal Case Study*, Development Assistance Committee, Paris.

O'Neill, Tom, "People and Polity: Ethnography, Ethnicity and Identity in Nepal", *Contributions to Nepalese Studies*, CNAS, vol. 21, No. 1, January 1994, pp. 45-72

Onta, Lazima (1995), *Situation Analysis of Street Children in Nepal*, report submitted to Child Welfare Society for UNICEF-Nepal, quoted in Onta-Bhatta, L. (1996).

Onta, Pratyoush (1996): Creating a Brave Nepali Nation in British India: The Rhetoric of Jati improvement, rediscovery of Bhanubhakta and the writing of Bir history, in Onta, P. et. al. eds. *Studies in Nepali History and Society*, No. 1 Vol. a (June 1996), Mandala Book Point, Kathmandu.

Onta-Bhatta, Lazima (1996), Street Children: Contested Identities and Universalizing Categories, *Studies in Nepali History and Society*, Mandala Book Point (June 1996).

Pandey, Devendra Raj (1999), *Nepal's Failed Development*, Reflections on the mission and the maladies, Nepal South Asia Center, Kathmandu.

Pfaff-Czarnecka, Joanna (1997): "Vestiges and Visions: Cultural Change in the Process of Nation Building in Nepal" in Gellner et. al. eds. (1997), *Nationalism and Ethnicity in a Hindu Kingdom*, Harwood Academic Publishers, The Netherlands.

Piper, J. (1975), "Three Cities of Nepal, in Oliver, P. ed. *Shelter, Sign and Symbol*, Barrie and Jenkins, London, pp. 52-69.

Pradhan, K. (1991), *The Gorkha Conquests: The Process and Consequences of the Unification of Nepal with special reference to Eastern Nepal*, Calcutta: Oxford University Press.

Quigley, D. (1987), Ethnicity with Nationalism: The Newars of Nepal, *European Journal of Sociology*, 28: 152-170.

Ramble, Charles (1997), "Tibetan Pride and Place: Or Why, Nepal's Bhotiyas are not an Ethnic Group", in Gellner et. al. eds. (1997), *Nationalism and Ethnicity in a Hindu Kingdom*, Harwood Academic Publishers, The Netherlands.

Rana, Jagadish (1995), *Nepal: A Concise History of Cultural Scenario in the Himalayan Kingdom*, Nirala Publications, New Delhi

Rana. P. SJB. & Dhungel, D. N., eds. (1998), *Contemporary Nepal*, Vikas, New Delhi.

Regmi, Mahesh C. (1965): *Land Tenure and Taxation in Nepal*, Institute of International Studies, Berkeley.

Regmi, Rhishikeshab (1999) *Nepali Society and Culture*, SANN Research Centre, Kathmandu.

Rose, Leo E. (1971), *Nepal: Strategy for Survival*, Oxford University Press, Bombay, Calcutta, Madras.

Rose, Leo E. (1974): "The Secularization of a Hindu Polity: the case of Nepal", in Smith, D. E. ed. *Religion and Political Modernization*, New Haven Yale University.

Rosser, Colin (1966), "Social Mobility in the Newar Caste System", in Hiamendorf, *Caste and Kin in Nepal, India and Ceylon*, Delhi

Sharma, K.R. (1993), *The evaluation of the 1991 Census of Population: Nepal*, paper presented at the 15th Population Census Conference, Seoul, 17-20 August, 1993.

Sharma, Kul Sekhar (1998), Good Governance in Nepal: Issues and Remedies, *The Spotlight*, May 29, 1998, Kathmandu.

Sharma, P. R. (1977): "Caste Social Mobility and Sanskritization: a study of Nepal's old legal code", *Kailash*, 10.

Sharma, P. R. (1997), Nation-Building, Multi-ethnicity and the Hindu State, in Gellner et. at. eds. *Nationalism and Ethnicity in a Hindu Kingdom*, Harwood Academic Publishers, The Netherlands.

Sharma, P. R. (1997): "How to Tend this Garden", *Himal*, 5 (3): 7-9.

Sharma, Prayag Raj (1986), "Ethnicity and National Integration in Nepal: A statement of the Problem", *Contributions to Nepalese Studies*, CNAS, TU, Vol. 18, No. 2, April 1986, pp. 129-136

Sharma, Prayag Raj ed. (1973), *Social Science in Nepal*, A report on the seminar on social science held in the Institute of Nepal and the Asian Studies, Tribhuvan University (October, 1973).

Sharma, Sudhindra (1996), How Hindu is the Other Hindustan? *Himal*, Vol. 9, No. 3, May 1996.

Shrestha, C.B. (1985), Trends in the redistribution of population in Nepal, in L.A. Kosinski and K.M. Elahi (ed.), *Population Redistribution and Development in South Asia*, Reidel, Dordrecht, 123-138.

Shrestha, N.R. (1990), Landlessness and Migration in Nepal, Westview Press, Boulder.

Shrestha, Nanda R. (1996), *In the name of Development: A Reflection on Nepal*. University Press Inc. Lanham, Maryland, USA.

Shrivastav, N. N. (1952), *Religion and Society Among the Coorgs in South Asia*, Clarendon Press, London.

Shtri Shakti (1995), *Women, Development, Democracy*, A study of the socio-economic changes in the status of women in Nepal (1981-93), Kathmandu

Singh, B. P. (1998), *India's Culture, the State, the Arts and Beyond*, Oxford University Press.

Singh, Nagendra K. (1997), *Nepal: Refugee to Ruler: A Militant Race of Nepal*, APH Publishing Corporation, New Delhi.

Stiller, Ludwig, F. S. J. (1993), *Nepal: Growth of a Nation*, Human Resources Development Center, Kathmandu.

Subedi, Abhi (1996), Literary Response to Panchayat Utopia in Onta, P. et. al. eds. *Studies in Nepali History and Society*, No. 1 Vol. a (June 1996), Mandala Book Point, Kathmandu.

Thapa, Prem Jung (1997), "Water-led Development in Nepal: Myths, Limitations and National Concerns", *Water Nepal*, Vol. 6, No. 1, 1997, pp. 35-57, Nepal Water Conservation Foundation, Kathmandu

Toffin, Gerard (1990), *Nepal: Past and Present*: Proceedings of the Franco-German Conference of Arc-er-Senans, June 1990, Sterling Publishers Pvt. Ltd.

Toffin, Gerard, ed. (1993), *The Anthropology of Nepal: From Tradition to Modernity*, Proceedings of the Franco-Nepalese Seminar held in the French Cultural Center, Kathmandu, 18-20 March 1992, French Cultural Center, French Embassy, Kathmandu.

Tuladhar, Jyoti (1996), "Social Development in Nepal: Gender Perspective", in Maskey, ed. (1996), *Social Development in Nepal*, UN Association of Nepal, Kathmandu.

UNESCO (2000), *World Culture Report*

UNFPA (1993), Contraceptive requirements and logistics management needs in Nepal, United Nations Population Fund, New York.

Unicef (1987), *Children and Women of Nepal:* A situation Analysis, Kathmandu

Uprety, Ram R. (1996), Cultural Component of Nepal-India Relations, in Baral, L. R. ed. *Looking to the Future,* Indo-Nepal Relations in Perspective, Animol Publications Pvt. Ltd., New Delhi.

URISD (1995), *States of Disarry, The Social Effects of Globalization,* report for the World Summit for Social Development, United Nations Research Institute for Socail Development.

Varma, Pavan K. (1998), *The Great Indian Middle Class,* Viking, India.

Varya, Tank Vilas (n. d.), *Nepal, The Seat of Cultural Heritage,* Educational Enterprises, Kathmandu

Whelpton, John (1997): Political Identity in Nepal: State, Nation and Community, in Gellner et. al eds. (1997) *Nationalism and Ethnicity in a Hindu Kingdom,* Harwood Academic Publishers, The Netherlands.

Index